VOLUME I

———

JOHANN WOLFGANG VON GOETHE

GOETHE AT WEIMAR

GOETHE AT WEIMAR

From the Painting by Wilhelm von Kaulbach

THE GERMAN CLASSICS

Masterpieces of German Literature

TRANSLATED INTO ENGLISH

𝕻atrons' 𝔈dition

IN TWENTY VOLUMES

ILLUSTRATED

THE GERMAN PUBLICATION SOCIETY
NEW YORK

Copyright 1913

by

THE GERMAN PUBLICATION SOCIETY

EDITORIAL ORGANIZATION

Editor-in-Chief

KUNO FRANCKE, Ph.D., LL.D., Litt.D.

Professor of the History of German Culture and Curator of the Germanic
Museum, Harvard University

Assistant Editor-in-Chief

WILLIAM GUILD HOWARD, A.M.

Assistant Professor of German, Harvard University

Literary Editor

WILLIAM TENNEY BREWSTER, A.M.

Professor of English, Columbia University

Editor, and Chief of the Board of Translators

ISIDORE SINGER, Ph.D.

Author of *Die beiden Elektren; Humanistische Bildung und der Klassische
Unterricht;* translator of Foucher de Careil's *Hegel et Schopenhauer*

Managing Editor

GEORGE EDWIN RINES

Editor of the *Encyclopedia Americana, The South in the Building of the
Nation, The Foundation Library,* etc.

CONSULTING EXECUTIVE BOARD

CONTRIBUTORS AND TRANSLATORS

VOLUME I

Special Writers

RICHARD M. MEYER, Ph.D., Professor of German Literature, University of Berlin:
General Introduction.

CALVIN THOMAS, LL.D., Professor of Germanic Languages and Literatures, Columbia University:
The Life of Goethe; Introduction to Faust.

KUNO FRANCKE, LL.D., Ph.D., Litt.D., Professor of the History of German Culture, Harvard University:
Editor's Preface; The Faust Legend from Marlowe to Goethe.

ARTHUR H. PALMER, A.M., LL.D., Professor of the German Language and Literature, Yale University:
Introduction to Hermann and Dorothea; Introduction to Iphigenia in Tauris.

Translators

CHARLES WHARTON STORK, Ph.D., Instructor in English, University of Pennsylvania:
Greeting and Departure.

A. I. DU P. COLEMAN, A.M., Professor of English Literature, College of the City of New York:
Hatem; Reunion; The One and the All; A Legacy; Nature and Art, etc.

E. A. BOWRING:
Mahomet's Song; Prometheus; The Sea-Voyage; To the Moon; The Fisherman, etc.

W. E. AYTOUN and THEODORE MARTIN:
Shepherd's Lament; Comfort in Tears; Epilog to " Schiller's Song of the Bell," etc.

ANNA SWANWICK:
Iphigenia in Tauris; Faust.

ELLEN FROTHINGHAM:
Hermann and Dorothea.

CONTENTS OF VOLUME I

ILLUSTRATIONS — VOLUME I

EDITOR'S PREFACE

IT is surprising how little the English-speaking world knows of German literature of the nineteenth century. Goethe and Schiller found their herald in Carlyle; Fichte's idealistic philosophy helped to mold Emerson's view of life; Amadeus Hoffmann influenced Poe; Uhland and Heine reverberate in Longfellow; Sudermann and Hauptmann appear in the repertory of London and New York theatres — these brief statements include nearly all the names which to the cultivated Englishman and American of today stand for German literature.

THE GERMAN CLASSICS OF THE NINETEENTH AND TWENTIETH CENTURIES has been planned to correct this narrow and inadequate view. Here for the first time English readers will find a panorama of the whole of German literature from Goethe to the present day; here for the first time they will find the most representative writers of each period brought together and exhibited by their most representative works; here for the first time an opportunity will be offered to form a just conception of the truly remarkable literary achievements of Germany during the last hundred years.

For it is a grave mistake to assume, as has been assumed only too often, that, after the great epoch of Classicism and Romanticism in the early decades of the nineteenth century, Germany produced but little of universal significance, or that, after Goethe and Heine, there were but few Germans worthy to be mentioned side by side with the great writers of other European countries. True, there is no German Tolstoy, no German Ibsen, no German Zola — but then, is there a Russian Nietzsche, or a Norwegian Wagner, or a French Bismarck? Men like these, men of revolutionary genius, men who start new movements and mark new epochs, are necessarily rare and stand isolated in any people and at all times. The three names mentioned indicate that Germany, during the last fifty years, has contributed a goodly share even of such men. Quite apart, however, from such men of overshadowing genius and all-controlling power, can it be truly said that Germany, since Goethe's time, has been lacking in writers of high aim and notable attainment?

It can be stated without reservation that, taken as a whole, the German drama of the nineteenth century has maintained a level of excellence superior to that reached by the drama of almost any other nation during the same period. Schiller's *Wallenstein* and *Tell,* Goethe's *Iphigenie* and *Faust,* Kleist's *Prinz Friedrich von Homburg,* Grillparzer's *Medea,* Hebbel's *Maria Magdalene* and *Die Nibelungen,* Otto Ludwig's *Der Erbförster,* Freytag's *Die Journalisten,* Anzengruber's *Der Meineidbauer,* Wilbrandt's *Der Meister von Palmyra,* Wildenbruch's *König Heinrich,* Sudermann's *Heimat,* Hauptmann's *Die Weber* and *Der arme Heinrich,* Hofmannsthal's *Elektra,* and, in addition to all these, the great musical dramas of Richard Wagner — this is a century's record of dramatic achievement of which any nation might be proud. I doubt whether either the French or the Russian or the Scandinavian stage of the nineteenth century, as a whole, comes up to this standard. Certainly, the English stage has nothing which could in any way be compared with it.

That German lyric verse of the last hundred years should have been distinguished by beauty of structure, depth of feeling, and wealth of melody, is not to be wondered at if we remember that this was the century of the revival of folk-song, and that it produced such song-composers as Schubert and Schumann and Robert Franz and Hugo Wolf and Richard Strauss. But it seems strange that, apart from Heine, even the greatest of German lyric poets, such as Platen, Lenau, Mörike, Annette von Droste, Geibel, Liliencron, Dehmel, Münchhausen, Rilke, should be so little known beyond the borders of the Fatherland.

The German novel of the past century was, for a long time, unquestionably inferior to both the English and the French novel of the same epoch. But in the midst of much that is tiresome and involved and artificial, there stand out, even in the middle of the century, such masterpieces of characterization as Otto Ludwig's *Zwischen Himmel und Erde* or Wilhelm Raabe's *Der Hungerpastor*, such delightful revelations of genuine humor as Fritz Reuter's *Ut mine Stromtid*, such penetrating studies of social conditions as Gustav Freytag's *Soll und Haben*. And during the last third of the century there has clearly developed a new, forcible, original style of German novel writing. Seldom has the short story been handled more skilfully and felicitously than by such men as Paul Heyse, Gottfried Keller, C. F. Meyer, Theodor Storm. Seldom has the novel of tragic import and passion been treated with greater refinement and delicacy than in such works as Fontane's *Effi Briest*, Ricarda Huch's *Ludolf Ursleu*, Wilhelm von Polenz's *Der Büttnerbauer*, or Ludwig Thoma's *Andreas Vöst*. And it may be doubted whether, at the present moment, there is any country where the novel is represented by so many gifted writers or exhibits such exuberant vitality, such sturdy truthfulness, such seriousness of purpose, or such a wide range of imagination as in contemporary Germany.

All these dramatists, lyric poets, and novelists, and with them not a few essayists, philosophers, orators, and publicists,* of the nineteenth and twentieth centuries will speak in the following volumes to America and other countries of the English language. They have been arranged, in the main, chronologically. The first three volumes have been given to the mature work of Goethe and Schiller—time-tested and securely niched. Volumes IV and V contain the principal Romanticists, including Fichte and Schelling; Volume VI brings Heine, Grillparzer, and Beethoven to view;

---

* For lack of space, scientists and historians have been excluded.

Volume VII, Hegel and Young Germany; Volume VIII,
Auerbach, Gotthelf, and Fritz Reuter; Volume IX, Hebbel and Ludwig; Volume X, Bismarck, Moltke, Lassalle.
Of the second half of the collection there might be
singled out: Volume XIV (Gottfried Keller and C. F.
Meyer); Volume XV (Schopenhauer, Wagner, Nietzsche,
Emperor William II.); Volume XVIII (Gerhart Hauptmann, Detlev von Liliencron, Richard Dehmel). The last
two volumes will be devoted to the most recent of contemporary authors.

The editors have been fortunate in associating with them-
selves a notable number of distinguished contributors from
many universities and colleges in this country and abroad.
A general introduction to the whole series has been written
by Professor Richard M. Meyer of the University of Berlin.
The last two volumes will be in charge of Professor Julius
Petersen of the University of Basel. The introductions to
Goethe and Schiller have been prepared by Professor Calvin Thomas, of Columbia University; that to the Romantic
Philosophers by Professor Frank Thilly, of Cornell University; that to Richard Wagner by Professor W. R. Spald-
ing, of Harvard University. And, similarly, every important author in this collection will be introduced by some
authoritative and well known specialist.

The crux of the whole undertaking lies in the correctness
and adequacy of the translations. How difficult, if not
impossible, a really satisfactory translation is, especially
in lyric poetry, no one realizes more clearly than the editors.
Their only comfort is that they have succeeded in obtaining
the assistance of many well trained and thoroughly equipped
scholars, among them such names of poets as Hermann
Hagedorn, Percy MacKaye, George Sylvester Viereck, and
Martin Schütze.

KUNO FRANCKE.

PUBLISHERS' FOREWORD

THE GERMAN CLASSICS is the first work issued by The German Publication Society in pursuance of a comprehensive plan to open to the English-speaking people of the world the treasures of German thought and achievement in Literature, Art and Science.

In the production of this monumental work the thanks and appreciation of the Publishers are especially due to Hugo Reisinger, Esq., whose loyal support and constant encouragement have made possible its publication.

Acknowledgment is also gratefully made to the work of Dr. Isidore Singer, who conceived the idea of The German Classics; to the editors and translators for their painstaking care; to the advisory committees and the Committee of Patrons for their cordial coöperation and support; and to authors and publishers for their courtesy in granting the use of special copyright material.

THE PUBLISHERS.

GENERAL INTRODUCTION

By Richard M. Meyer, Ph.D.

Professor of German Literature, University of Berlin

WEN formerly pictured the origin and development of a literature as an orderless play of incalculable forces; out of a seething chaos forms more or less definite arose, and then, one day, behold! the literary earth was there, with sun and moon, water and mountains, animals and men. This conception was intimately connected with that of the origin of individual literary compositions. These likewise — since the new " theory of genius," spreading from England, had gained recognition throughout the whole of Europe, especially in those countries speaking the Germanic languages — were imagined to be a mere succession of inspirations and even of improvisations. This view of the subject can no longer be held either wholly or in part, though in the origin and growth of literature, as in every other origin and development, much manifestly remains that is still incomprehensible and incalculable. But even as regards the individual literary work, writers themselves — as latterly Richard Dehmel — have laid almost too strong an emphasis on the element of conscious deliberation. And concerning the whole literary product of an individual, which seems to offer the most instructive analogies to the literary achievement of a people, we received a short time ago a remarkable opinion from Carl Spitteler. He asserts that he is guided in his choice of definite styles and definite forms by an absolutely clear purpose; that he has, for example, essayed every kind of metre which could possibly be suited to his " cosmic " epic, or that he has written a novelette solely in order to have once written a novelette.

Although in these confessions, as well as in Edgar Allen Poe's celebrated *Poet's Art,* self-delusion and pleasure in the paradoxical may very likely be mingled, it still remains true that such dicta as these point to certain peculiarities in the development of literatures. Experiments with all kinds of forms, imitation of certain literary *genres* without intrinsic necessity, and deliberate selection of new species, play a larger part in the history of modern German literature than people for a long time wished to admit. It is true, however, that all this experimenting, imitating, and speculating, in the end serves a higher necessity, as well in the poet of genius as in a great literature.

Three kinds of forces virtually determine the general trend of all artistic development as, indeed, of all other forms of evolution — forces which constitute the sum total of those that we comprehend under the joint name of *tradition,* a sum total of progressive tendencies which we will designate as *esthetic ideals,* and, mediating between the two, the *typical development of the individuals themselves* — above all, naturally, individuals of genius who really create literature.

These powers are present everywhere, but in very different proportion. Characteristic of Romance literatures and also of the English, is the great predominance of the conservative elements. Thus not only is the literature of the constitutional mother-country democratic, but also the literature of France, otherwise so decidedly aristocratic: a majority dictates its laws to the distinguished individual and is inclined to ostracize him, if too headstrong, and exile him from the " Republic of Letters." This, for instance, is what happened to Lord Byron among the British. On the other hand, German literature, like Germanic literatures in general, is disposed to concede, at least at times, a dictatorial leadership to the individual, even at the cost of tradition — as, for example, to a Klopstock, a Goethe, or a Richard Wagner. But, in exchange, the leader is often forced to uphold his power, no matter how much it may

have been due to his achievements, by coercive measures
— as, again for example, by means of a prætorian guard
of partisans, such as Klopstock first created for himself
in the Göttinger " Hain," but which was most effectively
organized by Wagner, and such as Victor Hugo, imitating
the German model, possessed in the Young Guard which
applauded *Hernani*. Another method of enforcing his
mastery is the organization of a systematic reign of
terror, consisting of bitter satires, such as Schiller and
Goethe (after the model of Pope) founded in the *Xenien*,
and the Romanticists established in many different forms
— satires much more personal and much better aimed than
was the general sort of mockery which the Romance or
Romanized imitators of Horace flung at Bavius and
Mævius. In saying all this, however, we have at the same
time made it clear that the power and influence of the
individual of genius receives much more positive expression in German literature than in those which produced
men like Corneille, Calderon, yes, even Dante and Shakespeare. German literary history is, more than any other,
occupied with the *Individual*.

If we now try rapidly to comprehend to what extent each
one of the already enumerated literary forces has partici-
pated in the development of modern German literature, we
must, first of all, emphasize the fact that here the question
is, intrinsically, one of construction — of a really new
creation.

German literature since 1700 is not simply the continuation of former literature with the addition of radical innovations, as is the case with the literature of the same period
in England, but was systematically constructed on new
theories — if it may be said that nature and history systematically " construct." A destruction, a suspension of tradition, had taken place, such as no other civilized nation
has ever experienced in a like degree — in which connection
the lately much-disputed question as to whether the com-

plete decay dates from the time of the Thirty Years' War
or the latter merely marks the climax of a long period of
decadence may be left to take care of itself. In any event,
about the year 1700 the literature of Germany stood lower
than that of any other nation, once in possession of a great
civilization and literature, has ever stood in recent times.
Everything, literally everything, had to be created *de
novo;* and it is natural that a nation which had to struggle
for its very existence, for which life itself had become a
daily questioning of fate, could at first think of renovation
only through its conservative forces. Any violent commotion in the religious or political, in the economic or social,
sphere, as well as in the esthetic, might prove fatal, or at
least appear to be so.

The strongest conservative factor of a literature is the
language. Upon its relative immutability depends, in general, the possibility of literary compositions becoming the
common possession of many generations — depends absolutely all transmission. Especially is poetic language wont
to bear the stamp of constancy; convenient formulas,
obvious rhymes, established epithets, favorite metaphors,
do not, in periods of exhaustion, afford much choice in the
matter of phraseology. On the other hand, however, a new
tenor of thought, often enough a new tenor of feeling, is
continually pressing forward to demand a medium of expression. This battle between the established linguistic
form and the new content gives rise to charming, but at
the same time alarming, conflicts. In the seventeenth century it was felt strongly how much the store of linguistic
expression had diminished, partly on account of a violent
and careless "working of the mine," which made prodigal
use of the existing medium, as was the case in the prose of
Luther and, above all, of Johann Fischart and his con-
temporaries; partly on account of a narrow confinement to
a small number of ideas and words, as in the church hymns.

This impoverishment of the language the century of
the great war tried to remedy in two opposite ways. For

the majority the easiest solution was to borrow from their richer neighbors, and thus originated that affectation of all things foreign, which, in speaking, led to the most variegated use and misuse of foreign words. Patriotically-minded men, on the contrary, endeavored to cultivate the purity of their mother tongue the while they enriched it; this, above all, was the ambition of the various " Linguistic Societies." Their activity, though soon deprived of a wide usefulness by pedantry and a clannish spirit, prepared the way for great feats of linguistic reorganization. Through Christian Wolff a philosophic terminology was systematically created; from Pietism were received new mediums of expression for intimate conditions of the soul; neither must we quite overlook the fact that to some extent a new system of German titles and official designations was associated with the new institutions of the modern state. More important, however, than these details — which might have been accomplished by men like Johann Gottfried Herder, Immanuel Kant and Goethe; like the statesman, Heinrich Freiherr von Stein; and the warrior, General von Scharn- . horst — was this fact that, in general, an esthetic interest had been again awakened in the language, which too long had served as a mere tool. Also the slowly developing study of language was of some help; even the falsest etymology taught people to look upon words as organisms; even the most superficial grammar, to observe broad relationships and parallel formations. So, then, the eighteenth century could, in the treatment of the mother tongue, enter upon a goodly heritage, of which for a long time Johann Christoph Gottsched might not unjustly be counted the guardian. It was a thoroughly conservative linguistic stewardship, which received gigantic expression in Adelung's Dictionary — with all its deficiencies, the most important German dictionary that had been compiled up to that time. Clearness, intelligibleness, exactitude were insisted upon. It was demanded that there should be a distinct difference between the language of the writer and that in everyday use, and again a difference between poetic language and prose; on the other hand, great care had to be taken that the difference should never become too great, so that common intelligibility should not suffer. Thus the new poetic language of Klopstock, precisely on account of its power and richness, was obliged to submit to the bitterest mockery and the most injudicious abuse from the partisans of Gottsched. As the common ideal of the pedagogues of language, who were by no means merely narrow-minded pedants, one may specify that which had long ago been accomplished for France — namely, a uniform choice of a stock of words best suited to the needs of a clear and luminous literature for the cultivated class, and the stylistic application of the same. Two things, above all, were neglected: they failed to realize (as did France also) the continual development of a healthy language, though the ancients had glimpses of this; and they failed (this in contrast to France) to comprehend the radical differences between the various forms of literary composition. Therefore the pre-classical period still left enough to be done by the classical.

It was Klopstock who accomplished the most; he created a new, a lofty poetic language, which was to be recognized, not by the use of conventional metaphors and swelling hyperboles, but by the direct expression of a highly exalted mood. However, the danger of a forced overstraining of the language was combatted by Christoph Martin Wieland, who formed a new and elegant narrative prose on Greek, French, and English models, and also introduced the same style into poetic narrative, herein abetted by Friedrich von Hagedorn as his predecessor and co-worker. Right on the threshold, then, of the great new German literature another mixture of styles sprang up, and we see, for example, Klopstock strangely transplanting his pathos into the field of theoretical researches on grammar and metrics, and Wieland not always keeping his irony aloof from the most solemn subjects. But beside them stood Gotthold Ephraim

Lessing who proved himself to be the most thoughtful of the reformers of poetry, in that he emphasized the divisions — especially necessary for the stylistic development of German poetry — of literary categories and the arts. The most far-reaching influence, however, was exercised by Herder, when he preached that the actual foundation of all poetic treatment of language was the individual style, and exemplified the real nature of original style, i. e., inwardly-appropriate modes of expression, by referring, on the one hand, to the poetry of the people and, on the other, to Shakespeare or the Bible, the latter considered as a higher type of popular poetry.

So the weapons lay ready to the hand of the dramatist Lessing, the lyric poet Goethe, and the preacher Herder, who had helped to forge them for their own use; for drama, lyrics, and oratory separate themselves quite naturally from ordinary language, and yet in their subject matter, in the anticipation of an expectant audience, in the unavoidable connection with popular forms of speech, in singing, and the very nature of public assemblies, they have a basis that prevents them from becoming conventional. But not quite so favorable was the condition of the different varieties of narrative composition. Here a peculiarly specific style, such as the French novel especially possesses, never reached complete perfection. The style of Wieland would necessarily appear too light as soon as the subject matter of the novel became more intimate and personal; that of the imitators of Homer necessarily too heavy. Perhaps here also Lessing's sense of style might have furnished a model of permanent worth, in the same way that he furnished one for the comedy and the didactic drama, for the polemic treatise and the work of scientific research. For is not the tale of the three rings, which forms the kernel of *Nathan the Wise,* numbered among the great standard pieces of German elocution, in spite of all the contradictions and obscurities which have of late been pointed out in it, but which only the eye of the microscopist can perceive?

In general it is the "popular philosophers" who have, more than any one else, produced a fixed prose style; as a reader of good but not exclusively classical education once acknowledged to me that the German of J. J. Engel was more comprehensible to him and seemed more "modern" than that of Goethe. As a matter of fact, the narrator Goethe, in the enchanting youthful composition of *Werther,* did venture very close to the lyrical, but in his later novels his style at times dangerously approached a dry statement of facts, or a rhetorically inflated declamation; and even in *The Elective Affinities,* which stands stylistically higher than any of his other novels, he has not always avoided a certain stiltedness that forms a painful contrast to the warmth of his sympathy for the characters. On the other hand, in scientific compositions he succeeded in accomplishing what had hitherto been unattainable — just because, in this case, the new language had first to be created by him.

Seldom are even the great writers of the following period quite free from the danger of a lack-lustre style in their treatment of the language, above all in narrative composition. It is only in the present day that Thomas Mann, Jacob Wassermann, and Ricarda Huch are trying along different lines, but with equal zeal, to form a fixed individual style for the German prose-epic. The great exceptions of the middle period, the writers of prose-epics Jeremias Gotthelf and Gottfried Keller, the novelists Paul Heyse and Marie von Ebner-Eschenbach, the narrator of anecdotes Ludwig Anzengruber, with his greater predecessor Johann Peter Hebel, and his lesser contemporary Peter Rosegger, the portrayer of still-life Adalbert Stifter and a few others, have, more by a happy instinct than anything else, hit upon the style proper to their form of composition, lack of which prevents us from enjoying an endless number of prose works of the nineteenth century, which, as far as their subject matter goes, are not unimportant. In this connection I will only mention Karl Gutzkow's novels describing his own period, or, from an earlier time, Clemens Brentano's fairy tales, Friedrich Hebbel's humoresques, or even the rhetorically emotional historical compositions of Heinrich von Treitschke, found in certain parts of his work. But this lack of a fixed specific style spread likewise to other forms of composition; Schiller's drama became too rhetorical; Friedrich Rückert's lyric poetry too prosaically didactic; that of Annette von Droste-Hülshoff often too obscure and sketchy.

If, therefore, the struggle with the language was fought out successfully by modern German literature only on the battleground of the lyric (and even there, as we have seen, not without exceptions), on the other hand a second conservative force was placed at the service of the literary development with more uniform success, namely *Metrics*. To be sure, here again this applies only to verse, for the corresponding art of prose rhythm has been as good as lost to the Germans, in contrast to the French, and almost more so to the English. In prose also a conscious and systematic attempt to make an artistic division into paragraphs, chapters, and books, has only been made in recent times, above all in and since the writings of Nietzsche. For as far as the treatment of language in itself is concerned, German literature has hardly yet fully developed an artistic form; writers still continue to treat it far too much as a mere tool. But verse is felt to be an object for artistic molding, although here too the naturalistic dogmas of the Storm and Stress writers, of the Romanticists, Young Germans and Ultra-Moderns, have often shaken the theories upon which the artistic perfection of our poetry is based.

In this regard, likewise, there was, in the seventeenth century, a great difficulty to be overcome. Changes in language, the effect of French and Italian style, the influence of music, had weakened the foundations of the German art of verse, which were already partly broken down by mechanical wear and tear. The comparatively simple regulation contrived by an ordinary, though clever, poet,

Martin Opitz, proved capable of enduring for centuries; a
connection was established between the accent of verse and
natural accent, which at the same time, by means of more
stringent rules, created barriers against variable accent.
It was merely a question of arranging the words in
such fashion that, without forming too great a contradiction to the common-place order of words, the way in
which the accents were placed upon them should result in
a regularly alternating rise and fall. On the whole, this
principle was found to be sufficient until the enthusiasm
of the new poetic generation demanded a closer connection
between the poetic form and the variable conditions of the
soul; they found a way out of the difficulty by carrying a
rhythmical mood through a variety of metrical divisions,
and thus came upon the "free rhythms." From whatever
source these were derived, either from the misunderstood
poems of Pindar, from the language of the Bible or of the
enthusiastic mystics, or from the poetic half-prose of the
pastoral poet Salomon Gessner, they were, in any case,
something new and peculiar, and their nature has not been
grasped in the least degree by the French in their "vers
libres," or at any rate only since the half-Germanic Fleming Verhaeren. They received an interesting development through Goethe and Heinrich Heine, while most of
the other poets who made use of them, even the greatest
one, Novalis, often deteriorated either into a regular, if
rhymeless, versification, or into a pathetic, formless prose.

Another method of procuring new metrical mediums of
expression for the new wealth of emotions was to borrow.
Klopstock naturalized antique metres, or rather made them
familiar to the school and to cultivated poets, while on the
other hand Heine's derision of August von Platen's set
form of verse was welcomed in many circles, and even the
elevated poems of Friedrich Hölderlin, which approached
the antique form, remained foreign to the people, like the
experiments of Leconte de Lisle in France; in Italy it
fared otherwise with Carducci's *Odi barbare*. Only one

antique metre became German, in the same sense that
Shakespeare had become a German poet; this was the
hexameter, alone or in connection with the pentameter; for
the ratio of its parts to one another, on which everything
depends in higher metrics, corresponded, to some extent,
to that of the German couplets. For the same reason the
sonnet — not, however, without a long and really bitter
fight — was able to win a secure place in German reflective
lyric poetry; indeed it had already been once temporarily
in our possession during the seventeenth century. Thus
two important metres had been added to German poetry's
treasure house of forms: first, the hexameter for a
continuous narrative of a somewhat epic character, even
though without high solemnity — which Goethe alone once
aspired to in his *Achilleis* — and also for shorter epigram-
matic or didactic observations in the finished manner of
the distich; second, the sonnet for short mood-pictures and
meditations. The era of the German hexameter seems,
however, to be over at present, while, on the contrary, the
sonnet, brought to still higher perfection by Platen, Moritz
von Strachwitz and Paul Heyse, still exercises its old power
of attraction, especially over poets with a tendency toward
Romance art. However, both hexameter or distich and
sonnet have become, in Germany, pure literary forms of
composition. While in Italy the sonnet is still sung, we
are filled with astonishment that Brahms should have set
to music a distich — *Anacreon*. Numerous other forms,
taken up principally by the Romantic school and the
closely related "Exotic School," have remained mere literary playthings. For a certain length of time the ghasel
seemed likely to be adopted as a shell to contain scattered
thoughts, wittily arranged, or (almost exclusively by
Platen) also for mood-pictures; but without doubt the un-
deservedly great success of Friedrich von Bodenstedt's
Mirza Schaffy has cast permanent discredit on this form.
The favorite stanza of Schiller is only one of the numerous
strophe forms of our narrative or reflective lyric; it has

never attained an " ethos " peculiar to itself. Incidentally, the French alexandrines were the fashion for a short time after Victor Hugo's revival of them was revivified by Ferdinand Freiligrath, and were recently used with variations by Carl Spitteler (which, however, he denies) as a foundation for his epic poems. So, too, the " Old German rhymed verse " after the manner of Hans Sachs, enjoyed a short popularity; and one saw virtuosos playing with the canzone or the makame. On the whole, however, German lyric poetry is rather made up of simple formations in the style of the folk-song, especially since the important rhythmic transformation of this material by Heine created new possibilities for accommodating the inner form to new subject matter without conspicuously changing the outer form. For two great simplifying factors have, since Goethe, been predominant in protecting our lyric poetry from unfruitful artificiality; the influence of the folk-song and the connection with music have kept it more full of vital energy than the too literary lyric poetry of the French, and richer in variety than the too cultivated lyric of the English. Whoever shut the door on the influences spoken of, as did Franz Grillparzer or Hebbel, and, in a different way, Annette von Droste-Hülshoff or Heinrich Leuthold, at the same time nullified a good part of his efficiency.

The drama almost exclusively assumed a foreign, though kindred, form as a garb for the more elevated styles of composition: namely, the blank verse of the English stage, which Lessing's *Nathan the Wise* had popularized and A. W. Schlegel's Shakespeare had rendered omnipotent, and which Schiller forced upon his successors. The Romanticists, by playing unsuccessfully with different forms, as in Ludwig Tieck's *Octavianus*, or Immerman's *Alexis*, or by adopting pure antique or Spanish metres, attempted in vain to free themselves from the restraint of form, the great danger of which consisted in its similarity to commonplace sentence construction, so that the verse ran the risk either of becoming prosaic, or else, in trying forcibly to avoid this, of growing bombastic. An escape was provided by inserting, in moments of emotion, a metre of a more lyrical quality into the uniform structure of the usual vehicle of dramatic dialogue, particularly when partaking of the nature of a monologue; as Goethe did, for example, in the " Song of the Fates " in *Iphigenia,* that most metrically perfect of all German dramatic poems, and as Schiller continued to do with increased boldness in the songs introduced into *Mary Stuart.* Perhaps the greatest perfection in such use of the principle of the " free rhythm " as applied to the drama, was reached by Franz Grillparzer in the *Golden Fleece,* on the model of certain fragments by Goethe, such as the *Prometheus.* On the other hand, the interesting experiments in the *Bride of Messina* are of more importance for the development of the opera into a work of art complete in itself, than for that of the drama. In general, however, it is to be remarked as a peculiarity of modern German drama, that it seeks to escape from monotony, which the French classical theatre hardly ever succeeded in avoiding, by calling in the aid of the other arts. Plastic art is often employed for scenic arrangement, and music to produce effects on and behind the stage. Both were made use of by Schiller; and it was under his influence that they were tried by Goethe in his later period — though we find a remarkable sporadic appearance of them even as early as *Götz* and *Klavigo.* The mastery which Grillparzer also attained in this respect has been striven after by his fellow countrymen with some degree of success: as, for example, by Ferdinand Raimund, by Ludwig Anzengruber, and also by Friedrich Halm and Hugo von Hofmannsthal.

Besides blank verse, the only other garb in vogue for the serious drama was prose: this was not only used for realistic pictures of conditions of a decidedly cheerful type (since Lessing had introduced the *bourgeois* dramas of Diderot into Germany), but also for pathetic tragedies, the vital power of which the lack of stylistic disguising of

language was supposed to increase. This was the form
employed in the Storm and Stress drama, and therefore
in the prison scene of *Faust,* as also in Schiller's youthful
dramas, and again we find it adopted by Hebbel and the
Young Germans, and by the naturalistic school under the
leadership of Ibsen. The Old German rhymed verse found
only a temporary place between these two forms. It was
glorified and made almost sacrosanct by having been used
for the greatest of our dramas, Goethe's *Faust;* Wildenbruch in particular tried to gain new effects with it.
Other attempts also went hand in hand with deeper-
reaching efforts to reconstruct the inner form of the drama;
thus the tendency to a veiled polyphony of language in the
folk-scenes of Christian Dietrich Grabbe and in all the
plays of Heinrich von Kleist; this in Hofmannsthal's
Œdipus led to regular choruses, of quite a different type,
however, from those of the *Bride of Messina.* Gerhart
Hauptmann's *Weavers* and *Florian Geyer* may be considered the culminating points of this movement, in spite
of their apparently entirely prosaic form.

Modern German drama, which in its peculiar style is still
largely unappreciated because it has always been measured
by its real or supposed models, is, together with the free-
rhythm lyric, the greatest gift bestowed upon the treasure
of forms of the world-literature by the literature of Germany which has so often played the part of recipient.

On the other hand, when speaking of the development of
narrative prose, we should remember what we have already
accomplished in that line. The " Novelle " alone has attained a fixed form, as a not too voluminous account of a
remarkable occurrence. It is formally regulated in advance
by the absolute domination of a decisive incident — as, for
example, the outbreak of a concealed love in Heyse, or the
moment of farewell in Theodor Storm. All previous incidents are required to assist in working up to this climax;
all later ones are introduced merely to allow its echo to
die away. In this austerity of concentration the German

" Novelle," the one rigidly artistic form of German prose, is related to the " Short Story " which has been so eagerly heralded in recent times, especially by America. The " Novelle " differs, however, from this form of literary composition, which Maupassant cultivated with the most masterly and unrivaled success, by its subordination to a climax; whereas the Short Story, in reality, is usually a condensed novel, that is to say, the history of a development concentrated in a few incidents. Our literature also possesses such short " sketches," but the love of psychological detail in the development of the plot nearly always results in the greater diffuseness of the novel. The real " Novelle " is, however, at least as typical of the Germans as the Short Story is of the Americans, and in no other form of literary composition has Germany produced so many masters as in this — and in the lyric. For the latter is closely related to the German " Novelle " because it loves to invest the way to and from the culminating point with the charm produced by a certain mood, as the half-German Bret Harte loves to do in similar artistic studies, but the Russian Tschechow never indulges himself in, and the Frenchman Maupassant but seldom. On this account our best writers of " Novellen " have also been, almost without exception, eminent lyric poets; such were Goethe, Tieck, Eichendorff, Mörike, Keller, Heyse, Theodor Storm and C. F. Meyer; whereas, in the case of Marie von Ebner-Eschenbach, who otherwise would form an exception, even what appears to be a " Novelle " is in reality a " small novel."

The novel, on the contrary, still enjoys in Germany the dangerous privilege of formlessness. In its language it varies from the vague lyric of romantic composition to the bureaucratic sobriety of mechanically-compiled studies of real life. In its outline, in the rhythm of its construction, in the division of its parts and the way in which they are brought into relief, it has, in spite of masterly individual performances, never attained a specific literary form, such as has long been possessed by the English and the French novels. Likewise the inclination, sanctioned by Goethe and the Romantic school, to interpolate specimens of the least formed half-literary *genres* — namely, letters and diaries — worked against the adoption of a fixed form, notwithstanding that this expedient augmented the great — often indeed too great — inner richness of the German novel. Thus the German novel, as well as the so justly favorite form of letters and diaries, is of infinitely more importance as a human or contemporary " document " than as a direct work of art. We have, however, already drawn attention to the fact that the never-failing efforts to clothe the novel in a more esthetically pure form have, in our own day, happily increased.

The traditional *material* of literary compositions is, however, also a conservative power, just as are language and form. The stock of dominating motives naturally undergoes just as many transformations as language or metrics; but, in both cases, what already exists has a determining influence on everything new, often going so far as to suppress the latter entirely. Customary themes preferably claim the interest of the reader; as, for example, in the age of religious pictures it would have been exceedingly hard to procure an order for a purely worldly painting. The artists themselves unconsciously glide into the usual path, and what was intended to be a world-poem flows off into the convenient worn channel of the love-story. But the vivifying and deepening power of the Germanic spirit has here, more than in any other domain, destroyed the opposing force of inertia.

The oldest poetry is confined to such subjects as are of universal interest — one could also say of universal importance. War and the harvest, the festivals of the gods and the destinies of the tribe, are the subjects of song. These things retain their traditional interest even where a healthy communal life no longer exists. Epochs which are absolutely wanting in political understanding still cultivate the glory of Brutus in an epic or dramatic form; or those ages which can scarcely lay claim to a living religious interest still join in choruses in honor of Apollo or in honor of the Christian religion. Every literature carries with it a large and respectable ballast of sensations that are no longer felt, of objects that are no longer seen, culminating in the spring-songs of poets confined to their room, and the wine-songs of the water-drinkers. A stagnating literature, as that of the seventeenth century was essentially, always has an especially large amount of such rubbish. Poems composed for certain occasions, in the worst sense — that is to say, poems of congratulation and condolence written for money, trivial reflections and mechanical devotion, occupy an alarmingly large space in the lyric of this period. Drama is entirely confined, and the novel for the greater part, to the dressing up in adopted forms of didactic subject matter of the most general type. Men of individuality are, however, not altogether lacking: such were lyric poets like Andreas Gryphius and Paul Fleming, gnomologists like Johann Scheffler, and narrators like J. J. Christoffel von Grimmelshausen; but even with them the personal note does not dare to sound openly. The first to give free expression again to intimate sensations is Christian Günther, and he arouses thereby contradiction, together with admiration. The court poets about the year 1700 work more in a negative way, i. e., by that which they did not express in their verses. The great merit of the pre-classical writers is to have created space, on the one hand, for personal sensations, and, on the other, for the great new thoughts of the age. Hagedorn, with the elegant frivolity of the man of the world, continued the necessary sifting of antiquated material; Albrecht von Haller, with the deep seriousness of the great student of nature, once more squarely faced the eternal problems. But the entire wealth of inner experience, in its most exclusively individual sense, was first revealed, not only to the literature of Germany but to modern literature in general, by Klop-

stock. Along this path Goethe pressed forward gloriously,
his whole poetic work presenting, according to his own
testimony, a single great confession. From Haller, on the
contrary, proceeds the effort to develop a poetical style
that would enable individuals to share in the great thoughts
of the age. Lessing strides onward from *Minna von Barnhelm* — the first drama of contemporary history since the
Persians of Æschylus — to *Nathan the Wise,* herein following the lead of the " literature with a distinct purpose "
(*Tendenz-Dichtung*) of France, and especially of Voltaire,
otherwise antipathetic to Lessing. Lessing's great dramatic heir is Schiller, whose tradition is in turn carried on
by Kleist, the latter allowing his personality to penetrate the subject matter far more even than either of his
predecessors.

But the utmost was done by Goethe, when in *Werther*
and *Götz*, in *Prometheus* or *Satyros*, but above all event-
ually in *Faust*, he lived through in advance — or, as he
himself said, he " anticipated " (*vorfühlte*) — the peculiar
experience of the age with such intensity that, in the work
which resulted, the individual experience became the direct
experience of the whole generation.

Out of the " reverence for nature " (*Naturfrömmigkeit*)
with which he contemplated all created things — from " the
Cedar of Lebanon to the hyssop which grows on the wall,"
from the mighty movement of the stream in *Mahomet* to
the bit of cheese that is weighed by the old woman in *Die
Geschwister* — out of all comes a widening of the poetic
horizon, the like of which had never before been seen in
any age. The Romanticists in reality only made a watchword out of this practice of Goethe's when they demanded
" progressive universal poetry," by which they meant that
the poet should live through the whole experience of creation in his own person. In demanding this, they — as the
aging Goethe had himself done — formed too narrow a
conception of the personal, and rejected too absolutely the
problems of politics and of science, so that once more a

narrowing process ensued. But even in their own ranks this tendency was offset by the exigency of the times; after the wars of liberation, political and in general, poetry written with a purpose was actually in the ascendency. The poetry of the mood, like that of a Mörike, remained for a long time almost unknown on account of its strictly intimate character. In the success of Ernst von Wildenbruch we see provisionally the last victory of this sort of literature — which directly proclaims what is worth striving for — at least in its loftier form. For the contemporary novel constantly takes for its subject the emancipation of woman, or the fight for culture, the protection of the Ost-Mark, or the fight against alcohol.

On the other hand the Romantic school has also broadened the realm of poetic material in a very important manner, by adding to it the provinces of the phantastic, the visionary, the fairy-like, and by giving to the symbolical an undreamed-of expansion.

On the whole, modern German literature has probably a richer field from which to choose her material than any other literature can boast of. In fact it is perhaps too variegated, and thus, because of the richness and originality of its subject matter, allows too much latitude to genius. One field only in poetry, considered from the viewpoint of real art, is almost uncultivated. All the efforts and all the attempts on the part of both Catholics and Protestants have not succeeded in producing religious poems of any degree of importance since Annette von Droste-Hülshoff ceased to sing; whereas, on the other hand, poetry that is hostile to the church has brought to maturity some great productions, not only in Anzengruber or Karl Schoenherr, in Friedrich Theodor Vischer, in Storm, and Keller, but, above all, in Nietzsche. A turn in the tide that seems just now to be taking place is exemplified in the important epic poems of Enrica von Handel-Mazzetti.

Finally, as the last and, in a certain sense, the strongest, pillar of permanency we will name the public. It is just as much a product as a contributing factor of literature; in both respects, however, preëminently important as a conservative force. The predominant and enduring tendencies, forms, and subjects are naturally chiefly conducive to the formation of a circle of " fixed subscribers " among the crowd of possible patrons. These subscribers, on their part, of course insist upon the preservation of those tendencies, forms, and subjects by which they are attracted. In the same way that, in general, a large " reading world," or a regular public for a theatre, or a solid community of devotees for each of the different species of song (as for example, the religious song, the folk-song, the student's song) is organized, so do important personalities call into being a special following of admirers, such as the partisans of Hebbel, the Wagnerians, and the adherents of Stefan George. But these narrow circles are often much more intolerant of every effort on the part of the master to depart from the program he has sworn to, than are outsiders. The history of the German public, unlike that of the English or French, is less a church-history than a sect-history. Schiller alone succeeded in becoming the national poet of his people — and he had his merits as well as his weaknesses to thank for it. Lessing is the one who comes next to him, whereas Goethe really reached the masses in only a few of his compositions. On the other hand, he made a stronger impression upon, and gave more happiness to, the intellectual classes than any of our poets since Klopstock. After him, only poets of a decidedly esoteric character, such as Stefan George or Friedrich Nietzsche, have had such a profound effect or one so capable of stirring the remoter depths of the soul. Even with Jean Paul the impression produced was more superficial. Latterly, however, periodicals, lecture-courses and clubs have replaced the " *caucus* "— which was formerly held by the most influential readers and hearers of the literary fraternities. This change has gone so far that the intimacy of the relations between a poet and his admirers, which was still possible in the early days of Hauptmann, Hofmannsthal, George, and Dehmel, now actually exists only for those poets who have not attained any special renown, such as Alfred Mombert, or, perhaps, we might also include Spitteler. An amalgamation of the different groups, which in Germany are wont to prove their love for their patron by combatting his supposed or real opponents rather than by actively fostering his artistic tendencies, might have produced a strong and effective reading public. But sooner can a stenographer of the Stolze school agree with one of the Gabelsberger system than can a votary of Dehmel dare to recognize the greatness in George, an admirer of Schnitzler see the importance of Herbert Eulenberg, or a friend of Gustav Frenssen acknowledge the power of Ricarda Huch. Our public, by its separatist taste and the unduly emphasized obstinacy of its antipathies, will continue for a long time still to hinder that unity, which, rising above even a just recognition of differences, is the only element which makes a great literature possible. Of course the critics are to be reckoned among the public, whether we consider criticism by professional reviewers or the more discriminating criticism of theatre directors, composers, etc.

In all the foregoing discussion of the prevailingly conservative forces in the development of literature we have seen that none of these forces has a completely restraining effect. Language always undergoes a certain change, even in the most benumbed periods, since it is obliged to suit itself to the new demands of trade, of society, even of literature itself. We also saw that form and material were not an inert mass, but were in continual, though often slow, movement. Finally, though the public itself always demands essentially the same thing, it has, nevertheless, new variations which are forced upon it by its avidity for new subjects; it also demands, when it has enjoyed a higher artistic education (as in the days of the Classical and Romantic writers), perfection of technique and increase in specifically artistic values.

Between the abiding and the progressive, between the conservative and revolutionary tendencies, *the typical development of the individual himself* takes its place as a natural intermediary factor. No literary "generation" is composed of men actually of the same age. Beside the quite young who are merely panting to express themselves, stand the mature who exercise an esthetic discernment, even as regards their own peculiar experience; finally, there are also the older men who have already said their say. In the same way every public is made up of people of all ages. These make different demands of their poets; youth wishes to conquer, manhood to fortify, old age merely not to lose. It is self-evident that points of conformity are to be found between the most widely differing fields: as, for example, conservative tendencies are present in the camp of the destroyers, revolutionary tendencies in that of the conservatives. In other words, in every community of men, no matter of what description, who are united by any kind of higher interest, new ideals grow up out of this very community of interest. Men who happen to be thrown together mutually cause one another's demands to increase; those who work in common try to outdo one another. Out of their midst personalities arise, who, brought up with the loftiest ideals, or often spurred on by the supineness of the public, with passionate earnestness make what merely filled up the leisure hours of others the sole purpose of their lives. Thus, in Germany above all, the new ideal has been born again and again, constituting the strongest motive power which exists, besides the personality of genius itself.

Of the greatest importance, to begin with, is the *ideal of a national literature itself*. Gottsched was the first in Germany, if not to apprehend it, at least to ponder it and to advocate it with persistent zeal. The literature of antiquity and the literature of France offered types of fixed national units. The affinity between the two as national units had been pointed out in France and England by means of the celebrated " Combat of the ancients and moderns," which also first gave living writers sufficient courage to think of comparing modern art with ancient.

Gottsched presented a program which he systematically strove to carry out, and in which one of the most important places is given to the building up of an artistic theatre, after the model of the great civilized nations. He surely had as much right to show some intolerance toward the harlequin and the popular stage as Lessing (who supplanted him while continuing his work) had to indulge in a like prejudice against the classical theatre of the French. Lessing, however, as we have already seen, goes at the same time more deeply into the matter by proposing not only a systematic but also an organic construction of the separate *genres*, and Herder took the last step when he demanded an autochthonous growth — that is to say, a development of art out of the inner necessity of personalities on the one hand, and of nationalities on the other. To be sure, the great poets who now appeared were not included in the program, and Gottsched did not appreciate Haller, nor did Lessing form a correct estimate of Goethe, or Herder of Schiller. There is, however, a mysterious connection between the aspirations of the nation and the appearance of genius.

Klopstock probably felt most directly what was wanting in the literature of his people, as he was also the most burning patriot of all our classical writers; and at the same time, as is proved by the *Republic of Letters*, his strange treatise on the art of poetry, he was the one among them who bore the most resemblance to the literary pedant of the old days. He is, therefore, continually occupied with the comparison between German and foreign art, language, and literature, which endeavor was continued later on and with other methods by A. W. Schlegel. But Herder also, in his comparison of the native art of Germany with the art of antiquity, of the Orient and of England, produced effective results; no less did Lessing, although the latter seeks to learn from the faults of his neighbors rather than from their excellencies. Goethe's criticism is dominated to such a degree by his absorption in the antique, and also in French and English general literature, that he has no understanding of national peculiarities when they do not conform to typical literary phenomena, as Uhland's lyric and Kleist's drama — two literary phenomena which we, nowadays, consider eminently national. The Romantic school was the first to try to place the conception of national literature as a whole on an autochthonous basis, and the scientific speculation to which Romanticism gave rise, has, since the Brothers Grimm, also resulted in serviceable rules gained from the increasingly thorough knowledge of language, of national development, and of social conditions. This new point of view reaches its climax in the attempts of Karl Müllenhoff and Wilhelm Scherer to trace the native literary development directly back to the nature and destiny of the German nation. But even as that proved scientifically unsuccessful, so likewise it was not feasible practically to establish a poetry confined to native materials, forms, and opinions. In vain did Tieck try to play off the youthful Goethe, as the only national one, against the Goethe of the Weimar period, which attempt many after him have repeated; or again, it was proposed to strike Heine out of the history of our literature as un-German — the last two literary events of European significance in Germany, according to Nietzsche. On the contrary, a comparison of German literature with those of foreign nations was not only necessary but also fruitful, as a certain exhaustion had set in, which lent an aftermath character to the leaders of the German "intellectual poetry" (*Bildungs-Poesie*) of that time. It was necessary once again to compare our technique, our relationship between the poet and the people, our participation in all the various literary *genres* and problems, with the corresponding phenomena in the countries of Zola, Björnson, Tolstoy, Ibsen, and Strindberg.

This, now, leads up to another question, to that concerning *poetic ideals*, and not only poetry in itself; the poet also becomes the object of interest and expectation. Every age embodies a different ideal, by which in all instances the already existing type and the loftier hopes of youth are welded into one — if we may be allowed so to express it. Antiquity asked that the poet should fill the heart with gladness; the Middle Ages desired edification with a spiritual or a worldly coloring; the first centuries of modern times applied to him for instruction. This last ideal was still in vogue at the beginning of modern German literature. But gradually the conception of "instruction" altered. The poet of the Germanic nations had now to be one who could interpret the heart. He should no longer be the medium for conveying those matters which the didactic novel and the edifying lyric had treated — things valuable where knowledge of the world and human nature, intercourse and felicity are concerned — but he must become a seer again, an announcer of mysterious wisdom. "Whatever, unknown or unminded by others, wanders by night through the labyrinth of the heart"— that he must transmit to the hearer; he must allow the listener to share with him the gift of "being able to give expression to his suffering." Thus the chief task of the modern poet became "the reproduction of the objective world through the subjective," consequently "experience." Real events, objects, manifestations must pass through a human soul in order to gain poetic significance, and upon the significance of the receiving soul, not upon the "poetic" or "unpoetic" nature of the subject itself, depends the poetic significance.

With this new conception, however, new dangers are connected. Near at hand lies the fear of a too open declaration of the most intimate feelings. In many old-style poets of modern times, in Hölderlin, in Kleist, Grillparzer, and Annette von Droste-Hülshoff this fear assumes the character of ethical aversion to baring their feelings in public.

But near, too, lies the hunt after interesting experiences —
the need to " experience something " at any price — which
marred the life of a romantic poet of Brentano's talents,
and also affected the conduct of the realist Grabbe.   A new
responsibility was placed upon the shoulders of the German poet, which rested heavily on men like Otto Ludwig,
and on account of which writers like Hebbel or Richard
Wagner thought themselves justified in claiming the royal
privileges of the favorites of the gods.

An entirely new method of poetic study began, which
perhaps originated with Heinrich von Kleist: a passionate
endeavor to place the whole of life at the service of observa-
tion or to spend it in the study of technique.   The consequence was not seldom a nervous derangement of the whole
apparatus of the soul, just at the moment when it should
have been ready for its greatest performances, as in the
case of Nikolaus Lenau; however, it also frequently resulted in an endlessly increased receptivity for every
experience, as in the case of Bettina von Arnim, Heine, or
Annette von Droste, and the most recent writers.

The infinitely difficult task of the modern poet is made
still harder by the fact that, in spite of all his efforts, he,
happily, seldom succeeds in transforming himself into, one
would like to say, an artistically working apparatus, such
as Ibsen very nearly became; not, however, without deplor-
ing the fact at the close of his life.   The German poet in
particular has too strong a lyrical inheritance not to reëcho
the impressions *directly* received by his heart.   The struggle between the demands of a purely artistic presentation
of reality, i. e., one governed exclusively by esthetic rules,
and its sympathetic rendering, constitutes the poetic
tragedy of most of our " naturalistic writers," and
especially of the most important one among them, Gerhart
Hauptmann.   But from this general ideal of the poet, who
only through his own experience will give to reality a true
existence and the possibility of permanence, there follows
a straining after technical requirements such as was for-

merly almost unknown. This results in an effort in Germany all the more strenuous in proportion to the former slackness regarding questions of artistic form. The peculiarities of the different literary *genres* are heeded with a severity such as has been practised before only in antiquity or perhaps by the French. Poets like Detlev von Liliencron, who formerly had appeared as advocates of poetical frivolity, now chafed over banal aids for rhyming, as once Alfred de Musset had done. Friedrich Spielhagen, the brothers Heinrich and Thomas Mann, and Jacob Wassermann are seen to busy themselves with the technical questions pertaining to the prose-epic, no longer in a merely esthetical and easy-going fashion, but as though they were working out questions vital to existence; and truly it is bitter earnest with them where their art is concerned. Often, as in painting, technique becomes the principal object, and the young naturalism of Arno Holz and Johannes Schlaf has in all seriousness raised technique to a dogma, without, however, in the long run being able to get the upper hand of the German need of establishing intimate relations with the subject of the art.

We must, however, at this point again remind ourselves that the question is not one of abstract " poets " but one of a large number of living *men* who, happily, differ widely from one another. Above all, when considering them we must think of the typical development of the generations. Those for whom patriotic interests, at least in a direct sense, seemed to have little meaning, were always followed by generations patriotically inspired. The Germany of today hides, under the self-deluding appearance of a confinement to purely esthetic problems, a predominating and lively joy in the growth of the Fatherland, and naturally also in its mental broadening. To have given the strongest expression to this joy constitutes the historical significance of Gustav Frenssen, just as solicitude for its future inspired the muse of Wilhelm von Polenz.

The preference shown to individual literary *genres*

changes in an almost regular order of sequence — the Swiss
Bovet has even tried recently to lay down a regular law
of alternation.   Especially is the theatre from time to time
abused for being a destructive negation of art, in just as
lively a fashion as it is declared at other times to be the
sole realization of the artistic ideal.   As to prevailing tem-
peraments, a preferably pathetic tone — as, for example,
in the epoch of Freytag, Geibel, Treitschke — alternates
with a sceptically satiric one — as in Fontane who (like
so many writers, in Germany especially) did not belong to
his own generation nor even to the immediately succeeding
one, but to the next after that!   With these are associated preferences for verse or prose; for idealism or
realism and naturalism; a falling away from philosophy
or an inclination to introduce it into poetry; and numerous
other disguises for those antagonistic principles, to which
Kuno Francke in a general survey of our literature has
sought to trace back its different phases.

We have now said about all that, in our opinion, seems
necessary for a general introduction to modern German
literature.   For the rest, it is of course quite obvious that
it is German — and that it is a literature.   That it is German, is precisely why it is not exclusively German:
for in every epoch has it not been proclaimed in accents
of praise or of blame, until we are almost tired of hearing
it, that the inclination to take up and appropriate foreign
possessions is peculiar to the German nation — and to the
Germanic spirit in general?   Thus we possess special
presentations of German literature considered from the
standpoint of its antique elements, and also from that of
its Christian elements, and we could in the same way
present theses which would show its development from the
standpoint of the Romance or of the English influence.
And yet latterly an exactly contrary attempt has been
made — in a spirited, if somewhat arbitrary book by Nad-
ler, which consists in trying to build up the history of
German literature entirely upon the peculiarities of the

different tribes and provinces. For the essence of the German, nay, even of the Swabian, or Bavarian, or North German, or Austrian individuality, is in the long run nourished rather than extinguished by all foreign influences. In spite of this, it is of course important in the consideration of the eighteenth and nineteenth centuries, to observe how the French pattern that is at first followed almost with the unquestioned obedience accorded to a fixed ethical model, is confronted by the English, which brings about the celebrated — and probably overrated — struggle between Gottsched and the Swiss School. We should also notice precisely how the tendency of British literature toward originality — in which the insular peculiarities were strongly emphasized — served to increase the self-reliance of German literature; how a new movement in the style of the antique was cultivated by the classical writers; and how the Romantic School favored medieval-Christian tendencies — much to Goethe's annoyance. It is of importance likewise to note the way in which Young Germany learned how to gain political-literary effects from the new French models; and finally, how the Northern realism of presentation, amalgamated with Tolstoy's, Björnson's, Strindberg's and also Ibsen's ethical subjectivity, educated the naturalism of the Germans. It is precisely those poets that are especially characterized by German peculiarities who have also trained themselves in the use of foreign subjects and forms: thus did Uhland, Mörike, Hebbel, and all the Romanticists. We have already had occasion many times to call attention in detail to the educational effect of foreign countries.

German literature is, in short, one that possesses the typical moments of development which mark all literatures, and which Wilhelm Scherer was the first to call to our notice: that is to say, it is a complicated organism in which the most varied tendencies cross one another, the most dissimilar generations of writers meet together, and the most remarkable events occur in the most unforeseen manner.

If we should now try to get a closer view of the last and by far the most important factor of literature, namely, the individual writers themselves, this difficulty in obtaining a general view of the whole, this working of the different parts against one another, this pulling away from one another, presents itself more clearly to us here than anywhere else. The attempt to classify the development of our literature into distinct groups according to the personalities which compose them has been frequently made, since I, in spite of all the difficulties and dangers of such a hazardous enterprise, first undertook, in my *German Literature of the Nineteenth Century,* to give an historical and complete presentation of a literature which had as yet scarcely become historic. I can here merely refer in passing to my own efforts and to those of Bartels, Biese, Riemann, and Soergel — to name only these; for in compliance with the purpose of this introduction we must confine ourselves to giving a general comprehensive outline — although it would be easy to improve upon it if one went more into detail.

It seems to me under these conditions that the groundlines of the development of our literature from 1700–1900 would be best impressed upon us by comparing the order of its evolution with that of the most "normal" poetic genius who ever lived — namely, with that of Goethe; and thereby we should prove its development to be an essentially normal one.

Like all "natural geniuses" Goethe begins as an imitator, dependent upon others; for the poet also must first learn to speak and to walk. The earliest literary effort of his which we possess is the poem *On Christ's Descent into Hell,* which naturally seemed strange enough to Goethe when this long forgotten first printed specimen of his literary productiveness was laid before him again after he had grown old. In this poem traditional phrases are repeated without the addition of anything new and original; conventional feelings are expressed, usual methods are employed; all this, however, not without a certain moderation of expression constituting a first sign of the otherwise still completely concealed poetic individuality.

Such is the character that the world of virtuosos also bears about the year 1700. The poems of Rudolf von Canitz and Johann von Besser are, though in entirely different spheres, just the same kind of first attempts of an imperfect art anxiously following foreign models as Goethe's first Christian poem — though truly with the tremendous difference that they represented the utmost that Frenchified courtly art could ever attain to; while Goethe's poem, on the contrary, was the immature sprig cut away before its time from the stem of a tree soon to stand in the full glory of its bloom.

When now in the Leipzig period the young student discovers the poet within him, he first does so in the customary way: he recognizes the ability on his part to handle the language of the contemporary poets, and also perhaps to imbue it with his own personal feelings. His poems inserted in letters, which make a show of the elegant pretence of improvisation, but in reality already display a great dexterity in rhyming and in the use of imagery, may be compared to Hagedorn's poetry; but at the same time Goethe is trying to attain the serious tone of the " Pindarian " odes, just as Haller's stilted scholarly poetry conquered a place beside Hagedorn's Epicurean philosophy of life. The *Book of Annette* (1767) as a whole, however, presents the first attempt on the part of Goethe to reach a certain completeness in his treatment of the poetic theme. In all his subsequent collections of poems the same attempt is made, it is true with increasingly rigid interpretation of the idea of " completeness," and in so far one is reminded in this connection of the theoretic intentions and performances of Gottsched.

The " New Songs " (*Neue Lieder*) of 1770 give a lopsided exhibition of the style which Leipzig and the times suggested to the young poet: namely the Anacreontic. This kind of poetry, learned from France and actually very far removed from the serious poetic manner of the Germans, so that one is almost as astonished at its rapid success as at that of the *Minnesang*, is certainly nearly related to Hagedorn's joy of living: what is new about it is that which divides the revolutionary poetry of a Georg Herwegh from the political poetry of Chamisso or Hoffmann von Fallersleben. The older generation are satisfied to announce their theory of life with comfortable diffuseness, or with sarcastic sharpness, but still with them it is always a private affair — though of course the addition of moral applications is never lacking at the opportune moment. The younger, on the contrary, are agitators; they seem, as it were, to enact the proper line of conduct in pantomime before the people, and rouse them by means of effectual refrains to practical imitation. Thus these Anacreontic poets, Johann Peter Uz, J. W. L. Gleim, even Lessing himself with his *Kleinigkeiten*, and the most elegant of the group, J. G. Jacobi, began, at least in appearance, to tear down the paper-made wall of division between poetry and life. It is indeed only in appearance, though; for to almost all of them the antithesis of Heine's mocking verse would apply: in public they sang of wine and in secret they drank water! But in still another sense the "New Songs" (*Neue Lieder*) of Goethe have the same significance for Goethe's career, as the poems of the Anacreontic poets have for the development of German poetry. They realized a new intimacy between the lyric and music, a step in the separation of the poem to be sung from the book to be read.

But now for Strassburg in 1770–1771! There Goethe received a double stimulation of the greatest importance: in Herder he learned to know for the first time a real living genius, and at the same time a man before whose energy and acumen he had to bow — and no one has ever become great who has not once been forced to admire a great man.

And then above all in Strassburg the first genuine love
seized him, the love for Frederika. Added to these were
other things which were connected with both: the discovery
of the varied nature of the landscapes peculiar to different
parts of the country, of art intimately connected with history — the rediscovery of Shakespeare. In Alsace the
young Goethe first became a poet in the broadest sense of
the word — it was there that he wrote the *Sesenheim
Songs* and important dramatic fragments — combining at
the same time the qualities of Lenz and Grabbe: though
once more, indeed, that which for the lyric poet Lenz and
the dramatic poet Grabbe was the final maximum, for him
was to be merely a transition stage! This is the epoch in
Goethe's life in which for the first time his poetry gains
an "intrinsic value," such as German literature gained
through the patriotic-political poetry, through Gleim's
Grenadier-Lieder, through the whole poetic work of the
excellent Ewald von Kleist, and through Lessing's *Minna
von Barnhelm.*

Frankfurt, Darmstadt, Wetzlar — the whole time of
ripening and waiting which Fate had decreed for him to
pass through before the Weimar period — are characterized by the after-effects of Herder's influence, or rather let
us say by the sprouting of all those seeds which had long
been planted in Goethe, but which now germinated and
were nourished through the influence of the great peda-
gogue. We can especially remark two apparently contra-
dictory tendencies: the trend in the direction of the antique
on the one hand, and the "emerging Germanity" on the
other. But in both cases his grasp of a strong original
autochthonous art is the essential point, in contrast to the
easy appropriation of adopted forms in Frankfurt and
Leipzig. Thus both tendencies also came together in
Klopstock who up to the time of the mature period of
Goethe's lyric had, in spite of the number of imitators,
remained a solitary phenomenon. Goethe's literary activity
up to this time, however, is more like music between the

acts. Two great acts follow: in 1773 comes *Götz;* in 1774, *Werther.* And with *Götz* the great "subjects of humanity" seize possession of Goethe's poetry, as they had taken possession of the poetry of Germany with Lessing — as shown by his whole work up to *Nathan:* for Lessing, the strongest adversary of mere "estheticism," really accomplished what those Anacreontic poets had merely wished to do — or seemed to wish — and brought literature into close touch with life. *The Sorrows of Werther* lays hold of the subjective problems of the age just as the drama of liberty lays hold of the objective; in them a typical character of the times is analyzed not without zealously making use of models — both innovations of Wieland! But now indeed comes the most important of all, that which in its greatness represents something completely new, although in detail Goethe had here all his teachers to teach him — Lessing who had written *Faust*-scenes, and Wieland who was so fond of placing the two souls of man side by side, and Herder who had an absolutely Faust-like nature; so that people have tried, with the exaggeration of the theorist, to hold up before us the whole *Faust* as a kind of dramatized portrayal of Herder! And with *Faust* Goethe in German literature has reached his own time — "For his century bears his name!"

But in the period which followed the predominating position of the classical writers we once more find the same parallelism of development. Again with Goethe's dilettante beginnings we compare a school of weak imitators, which unhappily was protected by Goethe himself (and also by Schiller in his literary organs); again with the Strassburg period and its Storm and Stress we compare Romanticism, which is characterized by its German nationalism and its antique tendencies, which is sentimental and philosophical, critical and programmatical like the time of *Götz,* which latter surely must have had a strong effect on men like Tieck and Arnim. And out of the sentiment for his country, which, in Goethe's whole literary career, is peculiar only to the poetry of the Strassburg period, tendencies develop like those which manifest themselves in the literature of the Wars of Liberation, of the Swabian School, in the older poetry of political conflict — in short, like all those tendencies which we connect with Ludwig Uhland's name.

Goethe's literary satires and poems for special occasions are a prelude to the purely literary existence and the belligerent spirit of men like Platen and Immermann, who both, as it were by accident, found their way into the open of national poesy. The self-absorption in *Werther,* the delving after new poetical experiences and mediums of expression; the method of expression hovering between form and illusory improvisation — all this we find again in the strongest individualists, in Heine, in Annette von Droste, in Lenau. The Weimar period, however, when the poet by means of a great and severe self-discipline trains himself to the point of rigidity in order to become the instrument of his art — that period is, with *Tasso,* paving the way for the school of Grillparzer, while that infinite deepening of the poetic calling is a preparation for Otto Ludwig, Richard Wagner, and Friedrich Hebbel. The contemporary novel in the style of *Wilhelm Meister* is revived by the Young Germans, above all by Gutzkow, in the same way that tendencies found in *Nathan* and in *Götz* are brought out again in Gutzkow's and in Heinrich Laube's dramas, so rich in allusions. The national spirit of which *Egmont* is full also fills the novels of Willibald Alexis and Berthold Auerbach. Finally those works, besides *Tasso,* which we are wont to consider the crowning achievements of the Weimar period, above all, *Iphigenia,* have permanently served as models of the new, and in their way classical, " antiques " — for the Munich School, for the Geibels and the Heyses. But we must also remember Mörike and Stifter, and their absorption in the fullness of the inner life, which none of them could attain to without somewhat stunting the growth of life's realities — Hebbel perceived this clearly enough not only in Stifter but in Goethe himself. Above all, however, this whole epoch of the " intellectual poets " may, in a certain sense, be called the *Italian Journey* of German literature. Like Goethe in the years 1787–1788, the German muse in this period only feels entirely at home in Italy, or at least in the South; in her own country she feels misnamed.

Now let us consider Goethe after he had settled down in Weimar for the second time. Scientific work seems for a while to have entirely replaced poetic activity, as for a moment the scientific prose of Ranke and Helmholtz came near to being of more consequence for the German language than most of what was produced at the same time by so-called poetry. Then the *Campaign in Champagne* (1792), and the new employment of his time with political problems, constitutes for Goethe a temporary phase that may be compared with that recapturing of history by political-historical writers like Freytag and Treitschke, in the same way that *Hermann and Dorothea* (1796), in which an old historical anecdote of the time of the expulsion of the Protestants from Salzburg is transplanted to the time of the French Revolution, may be compared with the historical " Novellen " of Riehl, Scheffel, and C. F. Meyer. Goethe's ballads (1797–1798) maintain the tradition that was to be given new life by Fontane, Strachwitz, and C. F. Meyer. Goethe's later novels with their didactic tendencies, and the inclination to interpolate " Novellen " and diaries, lead up to Gottfried Keller, Wilhelm Raabe and again to Fontane. The table-songs and other convivial poetry of Goethe's old age are taken up again by Scheffel; Goethe's " Novellen " themselves were continued by all those eminent writers whom we have already named. The *Divan*, with its bent toward immutable relations, prepares the way for the new lyric, until finally, with the second part of *Faust*, mythical world-poetry and symbolism complete the circle, just as the cycle of German literature finishes with Nietzsche, Stefan George, Spitteler and Hofmannsthal. At the same time new forces are starting to form the new cycle, or, to speak like Goethe, the newest spiral: Hauptmann, Frenssen, Ricarda Huch, Enrica von Handel, to name only these. And how many others have we not previously left unnamed!

But all this has not been merely to exercise our ingenuity. By drawing this parallel, which is naturally only to be taken approximately, we have intended to make clear the comforting probability that, in spite of all the exaggerating, narrowing down, and forcing to which it has been obliged to submit, our modern and most recent German literature is essentially a healthy literature. That, in spite of all deviation caused by influential theorists — of the Storm and Stress, of the Romantic School, of the period of Goethe's old age, of the epigonean or naturalistic criticism, or by the dazzling phenomena of foreign countries,— nevertheless in the essentials it obeys its own inner laws. That in spite of all which in the present stage of our literature may create a painful or confusing impression, *we have no cause to doubt that a new and powerful upward development will take place, and no cause either to underrate the literature of our own day!* It is richer in great, and what is perhaps more important, in serious talents than any other contemporary literature. No other can show such wealth of material, no other such abundance of interesting and, in part, entirely new productions. We do not say this in order to disparage others who in some ways were, only a short time ago, so far superior to us — as were the French in surety of form, the Scandinavians in greatness of talents, the Russians in originality, the English in cultivation of the general public; but we are inspired to utter it by the hopeful joy which every one must feel who, in the contemplation of our modern lyric poetry, our novels, dramas, epic and didactic poetry, does not allow himself to be blinded by prejudice or offended vanity. A great literature such as we possessed about 1800 we of a certainty do not have today. A more hopeful chaos or one more rich in fertile seeds we have not possessed since the days of Romanticism. It is surely worth while to study this literature, and in all its twists and turns to admire the heliotropism of the German ideal and the importance which our German literature has won as a mediator, an experimenter, and a model for that world-literature, the outline of which the prophetic eye of the greatest German poet was the first to discern, and his hand, equally expert in scientific and poetic creation, the first to describe.

THE LIFE OF GOETHE

By Calvin Thomas, LL.D.

Professor of Germanic Languages and Literatures, Columbia University

OETHE, the illustrious poet-sage whom Matthew Arnold called the "clearest, largest, and most helpful thinker of modern times," was born August 28, 1749, at Frankfurt on the Main.* He was christened Johann Wolfgang. In his early years his familiar name was Wolfgang, or simply Wolf, never Johann. His family was of the middle class, the aristocratic *von* which sometimes appears in his name, in accordance with German custom, having come to him with a patent of nobility which he received in the year 1782.

Johann Caspar Goethe, the poet's father, was the son of a prosperous tailor, who was also a tailor's son. Having abundant means and being of an ambitious turn, Johann Caspar prepared himself for the profession of law, spent some time in Italy, and then settled in Frankfurt in the hope of rising to distinction in the public service. Disappointed in this hope, he procured the imperial title of Councilor, which gave him a dignified social status but nothing in particular to do. He thus became virtually a gentleman of leisure, since his law practise was quite insignificant. In 1748 he married Katharina Elisabeth Textor,

---

* The chief original sources for the life of Goethe are his own autobiographic writings, his letters, his diaries, and his conversations. Of the autobiographic writings the most important are (1) *Poetry and Truth from my Life*, which ends with the year 1775; (2) *Italian Journey*, covering the period from September, 1786, to June, 1788; (3) *Campaign in France* and *Siege of Antwerp*, dealing with episodes of the years 1792 and 1793; (4) *Annals* (*Tag- und Jahreshefte*), which are useful for his later years down to 1823. His letters, forty-nine volumes in all, and his diaries, thirteen volumes, are included in the great Weimar edition of Goethe's works. His conversations, so far as they were recorded, have been well edited by W. von Biedermann, ten volumes, Leipzig, 1889–1896.

whose father, Johann Wolfgang Textor, was the town's chief magistrate and most eminent citizen. She was eighteen years old at the time of her marriage — twenty years younger than her husband — and well fitted to become a poet's mother. The gift on which she especially prided herself was her story-telling. Wolfgang was the first child of these parents.

The paternal strain in Goethe's blood made for level-headedness, precise and methodical ways, a serious view of life, and a desire to make the most of it. By his mother he was a poet who liked nothing else so well as to invent dream-worlds and commune with the spirits of his imagination. He also ascribes to his mother his *Frohnatur,* his joyous nature. And certain it is that his temperament was on the whole sunny. As he grew to manhood men and women alike were charmed by him. He became a virtuoso in love and had a genius for friendship. But he was not always cheerful. In his youth, particularly, he was often moody and given to brooding over indefinable woes. He suffered acutely at times from what is now called the melancholia of adolescence. This was a phase of that emotional sensitiveness and nervous instability which are nearly always a part of the poet's dower.

Wolfgang grew up in a wholesome atmosphere of comfort and refinement. He never knew the tonic bitterness of poverty. On the other hand, he was never spoiled by his advantages; to his dying day he disliked luxury. At home under private tutors the boy studied Latin, French, and English, and picked up a little Italian by overhearing his sister's lessons. In 1758 Frankfurt was occupied by a French army, and a French playhouse was set going for the diversion of the officers. In the interest of his French Wolfgang was allowed to go to the theatre, and he made such rapid progress that he was soon studying the dramatic unities as expounded by Corneille and actually trying to write a French play. Withal he was left much to himself, so that he had time to explore Frankfurt to his heart's

JOHANN WOLFGANG VON GOETHE

From the Painting by C. Jäger

content. He was much in contact with people of the humbler sort and learned to like their racy dialect. He penetrated into the ghetto and learned the jargon of the Jews. He even attacked biblical Hebrew, being led thereto by his great love of the Old Testament.

It was his boyish ambition to become a great poet. His favorite amusement was a puppet-show, for which he invented elaborate plays. From his tenth year on he wrote a great deal of verse, early acquiring technical facility and local renown and coming to regard himself as a " thunderer." He attempted a polyglot novel, also a biblical tale on the subject of Joseph, which he destroyed on observing that the hero did nothing but pray and weep. When he was ready for the university he wished to go to Göttingen to study the old humanities, but his father was bent on making a lawyer of him. So it came about that some ten years of his early life were devoted, first as a student and then as a practitioner, to a reluctant and half-hearted grapple with the intricacies of Holy Roman law.

At the age of sixteen Goethe entered the University of Leipzig, where he remained about three years. The law lectures bored him and he soon ceased to attend them. The other studies that he took up, especially logic and philosophy, seemed to him arid and unprofitable — mere conventional verbiage without any bed-rock of real knowledge. So he presently fell into that mood of disgust with academic learning which was afterwards to form the keynote of *Faust*. Outside the university he found congenial work in Oeser's drawing-school. Oeser was an artist of no great power with the brush, but a genial man, a friend of Winckelmann, and an enthusiast for Greek art. Goethe learned to admire and love him, and from this time on, for some twenty years, his constant need of artistic expression found hardly less satisfaction in drawing from nature than in poetry.

His poetic ambition received little encouragement in university circles. Those to whom he read his ambitious

verses made light of them. The venerated Gellert, himself
a poet of repute, advised the lad to cultivate a good prose
style and look to his handwriting. No wonder that he
despaired of his talent, concluded that he could never be
a poet, and burnt his effusions. A maddening love-affair
with his landlady's daughter, Anna Katharina Schönkopf,
revived the dying lyric flame, and he began to write verses
in the gallant erotic vein then and there fashionable —
verses that tell of love-lorn shepherds and shepherdesses,
give sage advice to girls about keeping their innocence,
and moralize on the ways of this wicked world. They show
no signs of lyric genius. His short-lived passion for
Annette, as he called her, whom he tormented with his
jealousy until she lost patience and broke off the intimacy,
was also responsible for his first play, *Die Laune des
Verliebten,* or *The Lover's Wayward Humor.* It is a pretty
one-act pastoral in alexandrine verse, the theme being the
punishment of an over-jealous lover. What is mainly significant in these Leipzig poetizings is the fact that they
grew out of genuine experience. Goethe had resolved to
drop his ambitious projects, such as *Belshazzar,* and coin
his own real thoughts and feelings into verse. Thus early
he was led into the way of poetic " confession."

In the summer of 1768 he was suddenly prostrated by a
grave illness — an internal hemorrhage which was at first
thought to portend consumption. Pale and languid he returned to his father's house, and for several months it
was uncertain whether he was to live or die. During this
period of seclusion he became deeply interested in magic,
alchemy, astrology, cabalism, and all that sort of thing.
He even set up a kind of alchemist's laboratory to search
experimentally for the panacea. Out of these abstruse
studies grew Faust's wonderful dream of an ecstatic spirit-
life to be attained by natural magic. Of course the menace
of impending death drew his thoughts in the direction of
religion. Among the intimate friends of the family was
the devout Susanna von Klettenberg, one of the leading

spirits in a local conventicle of the Moravian Brethren.
This lady — afterwards immortalized as the " beautiful
soul " of *Wilhelm Meister* — tried to have the sick youth
make his peace with God in her way, that is, by accepting
Christ as an ever-present personal saviour. While he never
would admit a conviction of sin he envied the calm of the
saintly maiden and was so far converted that he attended
the meetings of the Brethren, took part in their communion service, and for a while spoke the language of a
devout pietist.

This religious experience of his youth bit deep into
Goethe's character. He soon drifted away from the pietists
and their ways, he came to have a poor opinion of priests
and priestcraft, and in time men called him a heathen.
Nevertheless his nature had been so deeply stirred in his
youth by religion's mystic appeal that he never afterwards
lost his reverence for genuine religious feeling. To the end
of his days the aspiration of the human soul for communion with God found in him a delicate and sympathetic
interpreter.

During his convalescence Goethe retouched a score of
his Leipzig songs and published them anonymously, with
music by his friend Breitkopf, under the title of *New Songs*.
He regarded them at the time as trifles that had come into
being without art or effort. " Young, in love, and full of
feeling," he had sung them so, while " playing the old
game of youth." Today they seem to convey little fore-
warning of the matchless lyric gift that was soon to awaken,
being a shade too intellectual and sententious. One hears
more of the critic's comment than of the poet's cry. It
was at this time also that he rewrote an earlier Leipzig
play, expanding it from one act to three and giving it the
title *Die Mitschuldigen,* or *The Fellow-culprits*. It is a
sort of rogue's comedy in middle-class life, written in the
alexandrine verse, which was soon to be discarded along
with other French fashions. We have a quartet consisting
of an inquisitive inn-keeper, his mismated sentimental

daughter, her worthless husband, and her former lover. They tangle themselves up in a series of low intrigues and are finally unmasked as one and all poor miserable sinners. Technically it is a good play — lively, diverting, well put together. But one can not call it very edifying.

In the spring of 1770 Goethe entered the University of Strassburg, which was at that time in French territory. It was a part of his general purpose to better his French, but the actual effect of his sojourn in Alsatia was to put him out of humor with all French standards, especially with the classic French drama, and to excite in him a fervid enthusiasm for the things of the fatherland. This was due partly to the influence of Herder, with whom he now came into close personal relations. From Herder, who was six years his senior and already known by his *Fragments* and *Critical Forests* as a trenchant and original critic, he heard the gospel of a literary revolution. Rules and conventions were to be thrown overboard; the new watchwords were nature, power, originality, genius, fulness of expression. He conceived a boundless admiration for Homer, Ossian, and Shakspere, in each of whom he saw the mirror of an epoch and a national life. He became an enthusiastic collector of Alsatian folksongs and was fascinated by the Strassburg minster — at a time when " Gothic " was generally regarded as a synonym of barbarous. Withal his gift for song-making came to a new stage of perfection under the inspiration of his love for the village maid Friederike Brion. From this time forth he was the prince of German lyrists.

In the summer of 1771 he returned to Frankfurt once more, this time with the title of licentiate in law, and began to practise in a perfunctory way, with his heart in his literary projects. By the end of the year he had written out the first draft of a play which he afterwards revised and published anonymously (in 1773) under the title of *Götz von Berlichingen*. By its exuberant fulness of life, its bluff German heartiness, and the freshness and variety

JOHANN WOLFGANG VON GOETHE

JOHANN WOLFGANG VON GOETHE

From the Painting by J. Stieler

of its scenes, it took the public by storm, notwithstanding
its disregard of the approved rules of play-writing. The
next year he published *The Sufferings of Young Werther*,
a tragic tale of a weak-willed sentimental youth of hyper-
esthetic tendencies, who commits suicide because of dis-
appointment in love. The story was the greatest literary
triumph that Germany had ever known, and in point of
sheer artistic power it remains to this day the best of novels
in the tragic-sentimental vein. These two works carried
the name of Goethe far and wide and made him the accepted
leader of the literary revolution which long afterwards
came to be known, from the title of a play by Klinger, as
the Storm and Stress.

The years 1773–1775 were for Goethe a time of high
emotional tension, from which he sought relief in rapid,
desultory, and multifarious writing. Exquisite songs,
musical comedies of a sentimental tinge, humorous and
satiric skits in dramatic form, prose tragedy of passionate
error, and poetic tragedy of titanic revolt — all these and
more welled up from a sub-conscious spring of feeling,
taking little counsel of the sober intellect. Several minor
productions were left unfinished and were afterwards
published in fragmentary form. Such is the case with
Prometheus, a splendid fragment, in which we get a glimpse
of the Titan battling, as the friend of man, against the
ever-living gods. Of the works completed and published
at this time, aside from *Götz* and *Werther*, the most notable
were *Clavigo* and *Stella*, prose tragedies in which a fickle
lover meets with condign punishment. Another prose
tragedy, *Egmont*, with its hero conceived as a '' demonic ''
nature borne on to his doom by his own buoyancy of spirit,
was nearly finished. Most important of all, a considerable
portion of *Faust*, which was to be its author's great life-
work, was '' stormed out '' during these early years at
Frankfurt.

The legendary Faust is presented as a bad man who
sells his soul to the devil for twenty-four years of power

and pleasure, gets what he bargained for, and in the end goes to perdition. Young Goethe conceived his hero differently: not as a bad man on the way to hell, and not — at first — as a good man on the way to heaven. He thought of him rather as a towering personality passionately athirst for transcendental knowledge and universal experience; as a man whose nature contained the very largest possibilities both for good and for evil. It is probable that, when he began to write, Goethe did not intend to anticipate the judgment of God upon Faust's career. The essence of his dramatic plan was to carry his hero through a lifetime of varied experience, letting him sin and suffer grandly, and at last to give him something to do which would seem worth having lived for. After the going down of the curtain, in all probability, he was to be left in the hands of the Eternal Pardoner. Later in life, as we shall see, Goethe decided not only to save his hero, but to make his salvation a part of the dramatic action.

The close of the year 1775 brought a momentous change in Goethe's life and prospects. On the invitation of the young duke Karl August, who had met him and taken a liking to him, he went to visit the Weimar court, not expecting to stay more than a few weeks. But the duke was so pleased with his gifted and now famous guest that he presently decided to keep him in Weimar, if possible, by making him a member of the Council of State. Goethe was the more willing to remain, since he detested his law practise, and his income from authorship was pitifully small. Moreover, he saw in the boyish, impulsive, sport-loving prince a sterling nature that might be led in the ways of wise rulership. For the nonce this was mission enough. He took his seat in the Council in June, 1776, with the title of Councilor of Legation. At first there was not very much for him to do except to familiarize himself with the physical and economic conditions of the little duchy. This he did with a will. He set about studying mineralogy, geology, botany, and was soon observing the homologies

1. GOETHE'S GARDEN HOUSE IN WEIMAR
2. GOETHE'S HOUSE IN WEIMAR

of the vertebrate skeleton.   Withal he was very attentive
to routine business.   One after another important depart-
ments of administration were turned over to him, until
he became, in 1782, the President of the Chambers and
hence the leading statesman of the duchy.

All this produced a sobering and clarifying effect.   The
inner storm and stress gradually subsided, and the new
Goethe — statesman, scientific investigator, man of the
world, courtier, friend of princes — came to see that after
all feeling was not everything, and that its untrammeled
expression was not the whole of art.   Form and decorum
counted for more than he had supposed, and revolution
was not the word of wisdom.   Self-control was the only
basis of character, and limitation lay at the foundation of
all art.   To work to make things better, even in a humble
sphere, was better than to fret over the badness of the
world.   Nature's method was that of bit-by-bit progress,
and to puzzle out her ways was a noble and fascinating
employment.   In this general way of thinking he was confirmed by the study of Spinoza's *Ethics*, a book which, as
he said long afterwards, quieted his passions and gave him
a large and free outlook over the world.   In this process
of quieting the passions some influence must be ascribed
to Charlotte von Stein, a woman in whom, for some twelve
years of his life, he found his muse and his madonna.
His letters often address her in terms of idolatrous endear-
ment.   She was a wife and a mother, but Weimar society
regarded her relation to Goethe as a platonic attachment
not to be condemned.

The artistic expression of the new life in Weimar is
found in various short poems, notably *Wanderer's Night-
song, Ilmenau, The Divine,* and *The Mysteries;* also in a
number of plays which were written for the amateur stage
of the court circle.   The Weimarians were very fond of
play-acting, and Goethe became their purveyor of dramatic
supplies.   It was to meet this demand that he wrote
Brother and Sister (*Die Geschwister*), *The Triumph of*

Sentimentalism, The Fisher-maid, The Birds, and other pieces. Much more important than any of these bagatelles, which were often hastily composed for a birthday celebration or some other festive occasion, are the two fine poetic dramas, *Iphigenie* and *Tasso*. The former was first written rather rapidly in stately rythmic prose and played by the amateurs, with Goethe himself in the rôle of Orestes, in the spring of 1779. Eight years later, the author being then in Italy, it was recast with great care in mellifluous blank verse. *Iphigenie* is essentially a drama of the soul, there being little in it of what is commonly called action. A youth who is the prey of morbid illusions, so that his life has become a burden, is cured by finding a noble-minded sister, whose whole being radiates peace and self-possession. The entire power of Goethe's chastened art is here lavished on the figure of his heroine who, by her goodness, her candor, her sweet reasonableness, not only heals her soul-sick brother, but so works on the barbarian king Thoas, who would fain have her for his wife, that he wins a notable victory over himself.

By the end of his first decade in Weimar Goethe began to feel that he needed and had earned a vacation. His conduct of the public business had been highly successful, but he had starved his esthetic nature; for after all Weimar was only a good-sized village that could offer little to the lover of art. Overwork had so told upon him that he was unable to hold himself long to any literary project. He had begun half a dozen important works, but had completed none of them, and the public was beginning to suspect that the author of *Götz* and *Werther* was lost to literature. The effect of the whole situation — that inner conflict between the poetic dreamer and the man of affairs which is the theme of *Tasso* — was to produce a feeling of depression, as of a bird caught in a net. So acute did the trouble become that he afterwards spoke of it as a terrible disease. In the summer of 1786 he contracted with the Leipzig publisher Göschen for a new edition of his works in eight

GOETHE IN THE CAMPAGNA

volumes; and to gain time for this enterprise he resolved to take a trip to the land upon which he had already twice looked down with longing — once in 1775 and again in 1779 — from the summit of the Gotthard. On the 3d of September, at three o'clock in the morning, he stole away from Karlsbad, where he had been taking the waters, and hurried southward, alone and incognito, over the Alps.

In Italy, where he remained nearly two years, Goethe's mind and art underwent another notable change. He himself called it a spiritual rebirth. Freed from all oppressive engagements, he gave himself to the study of ancient sculpture and architecture, reveled in the splendors of Renaissance painting, and pursued his botanical studies in the enticing plant-world of the Italian gardens. Venice, Naples, Vesuvius, Sicily, the sea, fascinated him in their several ways and gave him the sense of being richer for the rest of his life. Sharing in the care-free existence of the German artist-colony in Rome made him very happy. It not only disciplined his judgment in matters of art and opened a vast new world of ideas and impressions, but it restored the lost balance between the intellectual and duty-bound man on the one hand and the esthetic and sensual man on the other. He resolved never again to put on the harness of an administrative drudge, but to claim the freedom of a poet, an artist, a man of science. To this desire the Duke of Weimar generously assented.

On his return to Weimar, in June, 1788, Goethe made it his first task to finish the remaining works that were called for by his contract with Göschen. *Egmont* and *Tasso* were soon disposed of, but *Faust* proved intractable. While in Rome he had taken out the old manuscript and written a scene or two, and had then somehow lost touch with the subject. So he decided to revise what he had on hand and to publish a part of the scenes as a fragment. This fragmentary *Faust* came out in 1790. It attracted little attention, nor was any other of the new works received with much warmth by the public of that day. They expected

something like *Götz* and *Werther*, and did not understand
the new Goethe, who showed in many ways that his heart
was still in Italy and that he found Weimar a little dull
and provincial. Thus the greatest of German poets had
for the time being lost touch with the German public; he
saw that he must wait for the growth of the taste by which
he was to be understood and enjoyed. Matters were hardly
made better by his taking Christiane Vulpius into his house
as his unwedded wife. This step, which shocked Weimar
society — except the duke and Herder — had the effect of
ending his unwholesome relation to Frau von Stein, who
was getting old and peevish. The character of Christiane
has often been pictured too harshly. She was certainly
not her husband's intellectual peer — he would have looked
long for a wife of that grade — and she became a little too
fond of wine. On the other hand, she was affectionate,
devoted, true, and by no means lacking in mental gifts.
She and Goethe were happy together and faithful to each
other.

For several years after his return from Italy Goethe
wrote nothing that is of much importance in the history
of his literary life. He devoted himself largely to scientific
studies in plant and animal morphology and the theory of
color. His discovery of the intermaxillary bone in the
human skull, and his theory that the lateral organs of a
plant are but successive phases of the leaf, have given him
an assured if modest place in the history of the development hypothesis. On the other hand, his long and labori-
ous effort to refute Newton's theory of the composition of
white light is now generally regarded as a misdirection
of energy. In his *Roman Elegies* (1790) he struck a note
of pagan sensuality. The pensive distichs, telling of the
wanton doings of Amor amid the grandeur that was Rome,
were a little shocking in their frank portraiture of the
emancipated flesh. The outbreak of violence in France
seemed to him nothing but madness and folly, since he did
not see the real Revolution, but only the Paris Terror.

He wrote two or three very ordinary plays to satirize
various phases of the revolutionary excitement — phases
that now seem as insignificant as the plays themselves.
In 1792 he accompanied the Duke of Weimar on the inglo-
rious Austro-Prussian invasion of France, heard the can-
nonade at Valmy, and was an interested observer as the
allies tumbled back over the Rhine. Perhaps the best
literary achievement of these years is the fine hexameter
version of the medieval *Reynard the Fox*.

The year 1794 marks the beginning of more intimate
relations between Goethe and Schiller. Their memorable
friendship lasted until Schiller's death, in 1805 — the
richest decade in the whole history of German letters.
The two men became in a sense allies and stood together
in the championship of good taste and humane idealism.
Goethe's literary occupations during this period were very
multifarious; a list of his writings in the various fields of
poetry, drama, prose fiction, criticism, biography, art and
art-history, literary scholarship, and half a dozen sciences,
would show a many-sidedness to which there is no modern
parallel. Of all this mass of writing only a few works
of major importance can even be mentioned here.

In 1796 appeared *Wilhelm Meister's Apprenticeship*, a
novel which captivated the literary class, if not the general
public, and was destined to exert great influence on German
fiction for a generation to come. It had been some twenty
years in the making. In its earlier form it was called
*Wilhelm Meister's Theatrical Mission.** This tells the
story of a Werther-like youth who is to be saved from
Werther's fate by finding a work to do. His "mission,"
apparently, is to become a good actor and to promote high
ideals of the histrionic art. Incidentally he is ambitious to
be a dramatic poet, and his childhood is simply that of
Wolfgang Goethe. For reasons intimately connected with

---

* This earlier version was long supposed to be lost, but in 1910 a copy of
the original manuscript was discovered at Zürich and published. Its six
books correspond very nearly to the first four of the final version.

his own development Goethe finally decided to change his plan and his title, and to present Wilhelm's variegated experiences as an apprenticeship in the school of life. In the final version Wilhelm comes to the conclusion that the theatre is *not* his mission — all that was a mistaken ambition. Just what use he *will* make of his well-disciplined energy does not clearly appear at the end of the story, since Goethe bundles him off to Italy. He was already planning a continuation of the story under the title of *Wilhelm Meister's Journeymanship*. In this second part the hero becomes interested in questions of social uplift and thinks of becoming a surgeon. Taken as a whole *Wilhelm Meister* moves with a slowness which is quite out of tune with later ideals of prose fiction. It also lacks concentration and artistic finality. But it is replete with Goethe's ripe and mellow wisdom, and it contains more of his intimate self than any other work of his except *Faust*.

During this high noon of his life Goethe again took up his long neglected *Faust,* decided to make two parts of it, completed the First Part, and thought out much that was to go into the Second Part. By this time he had become somewhat alienated from the spirit of his youth, when he had envisaged life in a mist of vague and stormy emotionalism. His present passion was for clearness. So he boldly decided to convert the old tragedy of sin and suffering into a drama of mental clearing-up. The early Faust — the pessimist, murderer, seducer — was to be presented as temporarily wandering in the dark; as a man who had gone grievously wrong in passionate error, but was essentially " good " by virtue of his aspiring nature, and hence, in the Lord's fulness of time, was to be led out into the light and saved. The First Part, ending with the heart-rending death of Margaret in her prison-cell, and leaving Faust in an agony of remorse, was published in 1808. Faust's redemption, by enlarged experience of life and especially by his symbolic union with the Greek Queen of Beauty, was reserved for the Second Part.

MONUMENT TO GOETHE

(Berlin 1880)

Sculptor, Fritz Schaper

The other more notable works of this period are *Hermann and Dorothea*, a delightful poem in dactylic hexameters, picturing a bit of German still life against the sinister background of the French Revolution, and the *Natural Daughter*, which was planned to body forth, in the form of a dramatic trilogy in blank verse, certain phases of Goethe's thinking about the upheaval in France. In the former he appears once more as a poet of the plain people, with an eye and a heart for their ways and their outlook upon life. Everybody likes *Hermann and Dorothea*. On the other hand, the *Natural Daughter* is disappointing, and not merely because it is a fragment. (Only the first part of the intended trilogy was written.) Goethe had now convinced himself that the function of art is to present the typical. Accordingly the characters appear as types of humanity divested of all that is accidental or peculiar to the individual. The most of them have not even a name. The consequence is that, notwithstanding the splendid verse and the abounding wisdom of the speeches, the personages do not seem to be made of genuine human stuff. As a great thinker's comment on the Revolution the *Natural Daughter* is almost negligible.

The decade that followed the death of Schiller was for Germany a time of terrible trial, during which Goethe pursued the even tenor of his way as a poet and man of science. He had little sympathy with the national uprising against Napoleon, whom he looked on as the invincible subduer of the hated Revolution. From the point of view of our modern nationalism, which was just then entering on its world-transforming career, his conduct was unpatriotic. But let him at least be rightly understood. It was not that he lacked sympathy for the German people, but he misjudged and underestimated the new forces that were coming into play. As the son of an earlier age he could only conceive a people's welfare as the gift of a wise ruler. He thought of politics as the affair of the great. He hated war and all eruptive violence, being convinced that good would come, not by such means, but by enlightenment, self-control and attending to one's work in one's sphere. To the historian Luden he said in 1813:

" Do not believe that I am indifferent to the great ideas of freedom, people, fatherland. No! These ideas are in us, they are a part of our being, and no one can cast them from him. I too have a warm heart for Germany. I have often felt bitter pain in thinking of the German people, so worthy of respect in some ways, so miserable on the whole. A comparison of the German people with other peoples arouses painful emotions which I try in every way to surmount; and in science and art I have found the wings whereby I rise above them. * * * But the comfort which these afford is after all a poor comfort that does not compensate for the proud consciousness of belonging to a great and strong people that is honored and feared.''

In 1808 he published *The Elective Affinities*, a novel in which the tragic effects of lawless passion invading the marriage relation were set forth with telling art. Soon after this he began to write a memoir of his life. He was now a European celebrity, the dream of his youth had come true, and he purposed to show in detail how everything had happened; that is, how his literary personality had evolved amid the environing conditions. He conceived himself as a phenomenon to be explained. That he called his memoir *Poetry and Truth* was perhaps an error of judgment, since the title has been widely misunderstood. For Goethe poetry was not the antithesis of truth, but a higher species of truth — the actuality as seen by the selecting, combining, and harmonizing imagination. In themselves, he would have said, the facts of a man's life are meaningless, chaotic, discordant: it is the poet's office to put them into the crucible of his spirit and give them forth as a significant and harmonious whole. The '' poetry '' of Goethe's autobiography — by far the best of autobiographies in the German language — must not be taken to imply concealment, perversion, substitution, or

GOETHE'S MONUMENT IN ROME

(SCULPTOR, EBERLEIN)

Presented to the City of Rome by the German Emperor

(From Seidel's *Der Kaiser und die Kunst*)

anything of that gross kind. It lies in the very style of
the book and is a part of its author's method of self-revela-
tion. That he devotes so much space to the seemingly
transient and unimportant love-affairs of his youth is only
his way of recognizing that the poet-soul is born of love
and nourished by love. He felt that these fleeting amorosi-
ties were a part of the natural history of his inner being.

And even in the serene afternoon of his life lovely woman
often disturbed his soul, just as in the days of his youth.
But the poetic expression of his feeling gradually became
less simple and direct: he liked to embroider it with musing
reflections and exotic fancies gathered from everywhere.
Just as he endeavored with indefatigable eagerness of mind
to keep abreast of scientific research, so he tried to assim-
ilate the poetry of all nations. The Greeks and Romans
no longer sufficed his omnivorous appetite and his " pano-
ramic ability.'' When Hammer-Purgstall's German version of the *Dīwān* of Hāfīz came into his hands he at once
set about making himself at home in the mental world of
the Persian and Arabic poets. Thus arose his *Divan*
(1819), in which he imitated the oriental costume, but not
the form. His aim was to reproduce in German verse the
peculiar savor of the Orientals, with their unique blend of
sensuality, wit, and mystic philosophy. But the feeling —
the inner experience — was all his own. The best book
of the *Divan*, the one called *Suleika*, was inspired by a
very real liking for Marianne Willemer, a talented lady
who played the love-game with him and actually wrote
some of the poems long ascribed to Goethe himself.

At last, in 1824, when he was seventy-five years old, he
came back once more to his *Faust*, the completion of which
had long floated before his mind as a duty that he owed
to himself and to the world. There was no longer any doubt
as to what his great life-work was to be. With admirable
energy and with perfect clarity of vision he addressed
himself to the gigantic task, the general plan of which and
many of the details had been thought out long before.

It was finished in the summer of 1831.   About sixty years after he had penned the first words of Faust, the disgruntled pessimist at war with life, he took leave of him as a purified soul mounting upward among the saints toward the Ineffable Light, under the mystic guidance of the Eternal-Womanly.

Goethe died March 18, 1832.   The story that his last words were " more light " is probably nothing more than a happy invention.

Admirers of the great German see more in him than the author of the various works which have been all too briefly characterized in the preceding sketch.   His is a case where, in very truth, the whole is more than the sum of the parts. Goethe is the representative of an epoch.   He stands for certain ideals which are not those of the present hour, but which it was of inestimable value to the modern man to have thus nobly worked out and exemplified in practice. Behind and beneath his writings, informing them and giving them their value for posterity, is a wonderful personality which it is a delight and an education to study in the whole process of its evolution.   By way of struggle, pain and error, like his own Faust, he arrived at a view of life, in which he found inspiration and inner peace.   It is outlined in the verses which he placed before his short poems as a sort of motto:

> Wide horizon, eager life,
> Busy years of honest strife,
> Ever seeking, ever founding,
> Never ending, ever rounding,
> Guarding tenderly the old,
> Taking of the new glad hold,
> Pure in purpose, light of heart,
> Thus we gain — at least a start.

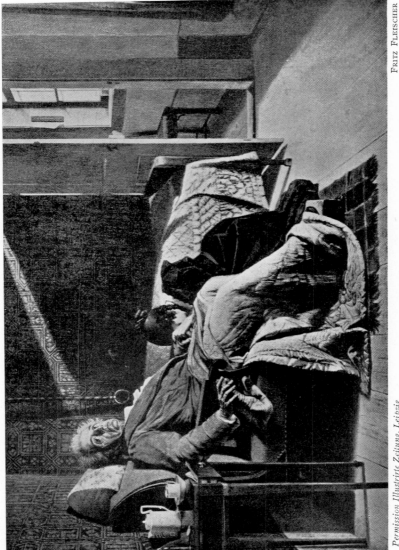

THE DEATH OF GOETHE

Fritz Fleischer

POEMS

GREETING AND DEPARTURE * (1771)

Y heart throbbed high: to horse, away then!
   Swift as a hero to the fight!
Earth in the arms of evening lay then,
   And o'er the mountains hung the night,
   Now could I see like some huge giant
     The haze-enveloped oak-tree rise,
While from the thicket stared defiant
   The darkness with its hundred eyes.

The cloud-throned moon from his dominion
   Peered drowsily through veils of mist.
The wind with gently-wafting pinion
   Gave forth a rustling strange and whist.
With shapes of fear the night was thronging
   But all the more my courage glowed;
My soul flamed up in passionate longing
   And hot my heart with rapture flowed.

I saw thee; melting rays of pleasure
   Streamed o'er me from thy tender glance,
My heart beat only to thy measure,
   I drew my breath as in a trance.
The radiant hue of spring caressing
   Lay rosy on thy upturned face,
And love — ye gods, how rich the blessing!
   I dared not hope to win such grace.

To part — alas what grief in this is! —
   In every look thy heart spoke plain.
What ecstasy was in thy kisses!
   What changing thrill of joy and pain!
I went. One solace yet to capture,
   Thine eyes pursued in sweet distress.
But to be loved, what holy rapture!
   To love, ah gods, what happiness!

* Translator: Charles Wharton Stork.

K. KOGLER

THE HEATHROSE

THE HEATHROSE* (1771)

Once a boy a Rosebud spied,
  Heathrose fair and tender,
All array'd in youthful pride,—
Quickly to the spot he hied,
  Ravished by her splendor.
Rosebud, rosebud, rosebud red,
  Heathrose fair and tender!

Said the boy, " I'll now pick thee
  Heathrose fair and tender! "
Rosebud cried "And I'll prick thee,
So thou shalt remember me,
  Ne'er will I surrender! "
Rosebud, rosebud, rosebud red,
  Heathrose fair and tender!

But the wanton plucked the rose,
  Heathrose fair and tender;
Thorns the cruel theft oppose,
Brief the struggle and vain the woes,
  She must needs surrender.
Rosebud, rosebud, rosebud red,
  Heathrose fair and tender!

MAHOMET'S SONG † (1773)

[This song was intended to be introduced in a dramatic poem entitled *Mahomet*, the plan of which was not carried out by Goethe. He mentions that it was to have been sung by Ali toward the end of the piece, in honor of his master, Mahomet, shortly before his death, and when at the height of his glory, of which it is typical.]

See the rock-born stream!
Like the gleam
Of a star so bright!
Kindly spirits
High above the clouds
Nourished him while youthful
In the copse between the cliffs.

*Adapted from E. A. Bowring.

† Translator: E. A. Bowring. (All poems in this section translated by E. A. Bowring, W. E. Aytoun and Theodore Martin appear by permission of Thomas Y. Crowell & Co.)

Young and fresh,
From the clouds he danceth
Down upon the marble rocks;
Then tow'rd heaven
Leaps exulting.

Through the mountain-passes
Chaseth he the color'd pebbles,
And, advancing like a chief,
Draws his brother streamlets with him
In his course.

In the vale below
'Neath his footsteps spring the flowers,
And the meadow
In his breath finds life.

Yet no shady vale can stay him,
Nor can flowers,
Round his knees all softly twining
With their loving eyes detain him;
To the plain his course he taketh,
Serpent-winding.

Eager streamlets
Join his waters.   And now moves he
O'er the plain in silv'ry glory,
And the plain in him exults,
And the rivers from the plain,
And the streamlets from the mountain,
Shout with joy, exclaiming: "Brother,
Brother, take thy brethren with thee.
With thee to thine agèd father,
To the everlasting ocean,
Who, with arms outstretching far,
Waiteth for us;
Ah, in vain those arms lie open
To embrace his yearning children;
For the thirsty sand consumes us

In the desert waste; the sunbeams
Drink our life-blood; hills around us
Into lakes would dam us!   Brother,
Take thy brethren of the plain,
Take thy brethren of the mountain
With thee, to thy father's arms!''—

Let all come, then!—
And now swells he
Lordlier still; yea, e'en a people
Bears his regal flood on high!
And in triumph onward rolling,
Names to countries gives he,—cities
Spring to light beneath his foot.

Ever, ever, on he rushes,
Leaves the towers' flame-tipp'd summits,
Marble palaces, the offspring
Of his fulness, far behind.

Cedar-houses bears the Atlas
On his giant shoulders; flutt'ring
In the breeze far, far above him
Thousand flags are gaily floating,
Bearing witness to his might.

And so beareth he his brethren,
All his treasures, all his children,
Wildly shouting, to the bosom
Of his long-expectant sire.

PROMETHEUS* (1774)

COVER thy spacious heavens, Zeus,
With clouds of mist,
And, like the boy who lops
The thistles' heads,
Disport with oaks and mountain-peaks;
Yet thou must leave

* Translator: E. A. Bowring.

My earth still standing;
My cottage too, which was not raised by thee,
Leave me my hearth,
Whose kindly glow
By thee is envied.

I know nought poorer
Under the sun, than ye gods!
Ye nourish painfully,
With sacrifices
And votive prayers,
Your majesty;
Ye would e'en starve,
If children and beggars
Were not trusting fools.
While yet a child,
And ignorant of life,
I turned my wandering gaze
Up tow'rd the sun, as if with him
There were an ear to hear my wailing,
A heart, like mine
To feel compassion for distress.

Who help'd me
Against the Titans' insolence?
Who rescued me from certain death,
From slavery?
Didst thou not do all this thyself,
My sacred glowing heart?
And glowedst, young and good,
Deceived with grateful thanks
To yonder slumbering one?

I honor thee! and why?
Hast thou e'er lighten'd the sorrows
Of the heavy laden?
Hast thou e'er dried up the tears

TITIAN

PROMETHEUS

Of the anguish-stricken?
Was I not fashion'd to be a man
By omnipotent Time,
And by eternal Fate,
Masters of me and thee?

Didst thou e'er fancy
That life I should learn to hate,
And fly to deserts,
Because not all
My blossoming dreams grew ripe?

Here sit I, forming mortals
After my image;
A race resembling me,
To suffer, to weep,
To enjoy, to be glad,
And thee to scorn,
As I!

THE WANDERER'S NIGHT-SONG * (1776)

Thou who comest from on high,
   Who all woes and sorrows stillest,
Who, for twofold misery,
   Hearts with twofold balsam fillest,
Would this constant strife would cease!
   What avails the joy and pain?
Blissful Peace,
   To my bosom come again!

THE SEA-VOYAGE † (1776)

Many a day and night my bark stood ready laden;
Waiting fav'ring winds, I sat with true friends round me,
Pledging me to patience and to courage,
In the haven.

And they spoke thus with impatience twofold:
" Gladly pray we for thy rapid passage,

* Adapted from E. A. Bowring.
† Translator: E. A. Bowring.

Gladly for thy happy voyage; fortune
In the distant world is waiting for thee,
In our arms thou'lt find thy prize, and love too,
When returning."

And when morning came, arose an uproar
And the sailors' joyous shouts awoke us;
All was stirring, all was living, moving,
Bent on sailing with the first kind zephyr.

And the sails soon in the breeze are swelling,
And the sun with fiery love invites us;
Fill'd the sails are, clouds on high are floating,
On the shore each friend exulting raises
Songs of hope, in giddy joy expecting
Joy the voyage through, as on the morn of sailing,
And the earliest starry nights so radiant.

But by God-sent changing winds ere long he's driven
Sideways from the course he had intended,
And he feigns as though he would surrender,
While he gently striveth to outwit them,
To his goal, e'en when thus press'd, still faithful.

But from out the damp gray distance rising,
Softly now the storm proclaims its advent,
Presseth down each bird upon the waters,
Presseth down the throbbing hearts of mortals.
And it cometh. At its stubborn fury,
Wisely ev'ry sail the seaman striketh;
With the anguish-laden ball are sporting
Wind and water.

And on yonder shore are gather'd standing,
Friends and lovers, trembling for the bold one:
" Why, alas, remain'd he here not with us!
Ah, the tempest! Cast away by fortune!
Must the good one perish in this fashion?
Might not he perchance * * *. Ye great immortals!"

Yet he, like a man, stands by his rudder;
With the bark are sporting wind and water,
Wind and water sport not with his bosom:
On the fierce deep looks he, as a master,—
In his gods, or shipwreck'd, or safe landed,
Trusting ever.

TO THE MOON * (1778)

BUSH and vale thou fill'st again
    With thy misty ray,
And my spirit's heavy chain
    Casteth far away.

Thou dost o'er my fields extend
    Thy sweet soothing eye,
Watching like a gentle friend,
    O'er my destiny.

Vanish'd days of bliss and woe
    Haunt me with their tone,
Joy and grief in turns I know,
    As I stray alone.

Stream beloved, flow on! flow on!
    Ne'er can I be gay!
Thus have sport and kisses gone,
    Truth thus pass'd away.

Once I seem'd the lord to be
    Of that prize so fair!
Now, to our deep sorrow, we
    Can forget it ne'er.

Murmur, stream, the vale along,
    Never cease thy sighs;
Murmur, whisper to my song
    Answering melodies!

* Translator: E. A. Bowring.

When thou in the winter's night
    Overflow'st in wrath,
Or in spring-time sparklest bright,
    As the buds shoot forth.

He who from the world retires,
    Void of hate, is blest;
Who a friend's true love inspires,
    Leaning on his breast!

That which heedless man ne'er knew,
    Or ne'er thought aright,
Roams the bosom's labyrinth through,
    Boldly into night.

THE FISHERMAN* (1778)

THE waters rush'd, the waters rose,
    A fisherman sat by,
While on his line in calm repose
    He cast his patient eye.
And as he sat, and hearken'd there,
    The flood was cleft in twain,
And, lo! a dripping mermaid fair
    Sprang from the troubled main.

She sang to him, and spake the while:
    "Why lurest thou my brood,
With human wit and human guile
    From out their native flood?
Oh, couldst thou know how gladly dart
    The fish across the sea,
Thou wouldst descend, e'en as thou art,
    And truly happy be!

Do not the sun and moon with grace
    Their forms in ocean lave?
Shines not with twofold charms their face,
    When rising from the wave?

---

* Translator: E. A. Bowring.

Georg Papperitz

THE FISHERMAN AND THE MERMAID

The deep, deep heavens, then lure thee not,—
　　The moist yet radiant blue,—
Not thine own form,—to tempt thy lot
　　'Midst this eternal dew?''

The waters rush'd, the waters rose,
　　Wetting his naked feet;
As if his true love's words were those,
　　His heart with longing beat.
She sang to him, to him spake she,
　　His doom was fix'd, I ween;
Half drew she him, and half sank he,
　　And ne'er again was seen.

THE WANDERER'S NIGHT-SONG * (1780)

[Written at night on the Kickelhahn, a hill in the forest of Ilmenau, on the walls of a little hermitage where Goethe composed the last act of his *Iphigenie*.]

　　　　Hush'd on the hill
　　　　　Is the breeze;
　　　　Scarce by the zephyr
　　　　　The trees
　　　　Softly are press'd;
　　The woodbird's asleep on the bough.
　　　　Wait, then, and thou
　　　　　Soon wilt find rest.

THE ERL-KING * (1782)

Who rides there so late through the night dark and drear?
The father it is, with his infant so dear;
He holdeth the boy tightly clasp'd in his arm,
He holdeth him safely, he keepeth him warm.

"My son, wherefore seek's thou thy face thus to hide?''
"Look, father, the Erl-King is close by our side!
　Dost see not the Erl-King, with crown and with train?''
"My son, 'tis the mist rising over the plain.''

---

* Translator: E. A. Bowring.

"Oh come, thou dear infant! oh come thou with me!
Full many a game I will play there with thee;
On my strand, lovely flowers their blossoms unfold,
My mother shall grace thee with garments of gold."

"My father, my father, and dost thou not hear
The words that the Erl-King now breathes in mine ear?"
"Be calm, dearest child, 'tis thy fancy deceives;
'Tis the sad wind that sighs through the withering
leaves."

"Wilt go, then, dear infant, wilt go with me there?
My daughters shall tend thee with sisterly care;
My daughters by night their glad festival keep,
They'll dance thee, and rock thee, and sing thee to sleep."

"My father, my father, and dost thou not see,
How the Erl-King his daughters has brought here for
me?"
"My darling, my darling, I see it aright,
'Tis the agèd gray willows deceiving thy sight."

"I love thee, I'm charm'd by thy beauty, dear boy!
And if thou'rt unwilling, then force I'll employ."
"My father, my father, he seizes me fast,
Full sorely the Erl-King has hurt me at last."

The father now gallops, with terror half wild,
He grasps in his arms the poor shuddering child;
He reaches his courtyard with toil and with dread,—
The child in his arms finds he motionless, dead.

THE GODLIKE * (1783)

Noble be man,
Helpful and good!
For that alone
Distinguisheth him
From all the beings
Unto us known.

* Translator: E. A. Bowring.

Hail to the beings,
Unknown and glorious,
Whom we forebode!
From *his* example
Learn we to know them!

For unfeeling
Nature is ever:
On bad and on good
The sun alike shineth;
And on the wicked,
As on the best,
The moon and stars gleam.

Tempest and torrent,
Thunder and hail,
Roar on their path,
Seizing the while,
As they haste onward,
One after another.

Even so, fortune
Gropes 'mid the throng —
Innocent boyhood's
Curly head seizing,—
Seizing the hoary
Head of the sinner.

After laws mighty,
Brazen, eternal,
Must all we mortals
Finish the circuit
Of our existence.

Man, and man only
Can do the impossible
He 'tis distinguisheth,
Chooseth and judgeth;
He to the moment
Endurance can lend.

He and he only
The good can reward,
The bad can he punish,
Can heal and can save;
All that wanders and strays
Can usefully blend.

And we pay homage
To the immortals
As though they were men,
And did in the great,
What the best, in the small,
Does or might do.

Be the man that is noble,
Both helpful and good,
Unweariedly forming
The right and the useful,
A type of those beings
Our mind hath foreshadow'd!

MIGNON * (1785)

[This universally known poem is also to be found in *Wilhelm Meister*.]

KNOW'ST thou the land where the fair citron blows,
Where the bright orange midst the foliage glows,
Where soft winds greet us from the azure skies,
Where silent myrtles, stately laurels rise,
Know'st thou it well?
                'Tis there, 'tis there,
That I with thee, beloved one, would repair.

Know'st thou the house? On columns rests its pile,
Its halls are gleaming, and its chambers smile,
And marble statues stand and gaze on me:
" Poor child! what sorrow hath befallen thee?"
Know'st thou it well?
                'Tis there, 'tis there,
That I with thee, protector, would repair!

* Translator: E. A. Bowring.

Know'st thou the mountain, and its cloudy bridge?
The mule can scarcely find the misty ridge;
In caverns dwells the dragon's olden brood,
The frowning crag obstructs the raging flood.
Know'st thou it well?
                                    'Tis there, 'tis there,
Our path lies — Father — thither, oh repair!

PROXIMITY OF THE BELOVED ONE * (1795)

I THINK of thee, whene'er the sun his beams
    O'er ocean flings;
I think of thee, whene'er the moonlight gleams
    In silv'ry springs.

I see thee, when upon the distant ridge
    The dust awakes;
At midnight's hour, when on the fragile bridge
    The wanderer quakes.

I hear thee, when yon billows rise on high,
    With murmur deep.
To tread the silent grove oft wander I,
    When all's asleep.

I'm near thee, though thou far away mayst be —
    Thou, too, art near!
The sun then sets, the stars soon lighten me,
    Would thou wert here!

THE SHEPHERD'S LAMENT † (1802)

UP yonder on the mountain,
    I dwelt for days together;
Looked down into the valley,
    This pleasant summer weather.

My sheep go feeding onward,
    My dog sits watching by;
I've wandered to the valley,
    And yet I know not why.

* Translator: E. A. Bowring.
† Translator: W. E. Aytoun and Theodore Martin.

The meadow, it is pretty,
  With flowers so fair to see;
I gather them, but no one
  Will take the flowers from me.

The good tree gives me shadow,
  And shelter from the rain;
But yonder door is silent,
  It will not ope again!

I see the rainbow bending,
  Above her old abode,
But she is there no longer;
  They've taken my love abroad.

They took her o'er the mountains,
  They took her o'er the sea;
Move on, move on, my bonny sheep,
  There is no rest for me!

NATURE AND ART* (1802)

NATURE and art asunder seem to fly,
  Yet sooner than we think find common ground;
  In place of strife, harmonious songs resound,
And both, at one, to my abode draw nigh.
In sooth but one endeavor I descry:
  Then only, when in ordered moments' round
  Wisdom and toil our lives to Art have bound,
Dare we rejoice in Nature's liberty.
Thus is achievement fashioned everywhere:
  Not by ungovernable, hasty zeal
    Shalt thou the height of perfect form attain.
Husband thy strength, if great emprize thou dare;
  In self-restraint thy masterhood reveal,
    And under law thy perfect freedom gain.

---

* Translator: A. I. du P. Coleman.

COMFORT IN TEARS * (1803)

How is it that thou art so sad
 When others are so gay?
Thou hast been weeping — nay, thou hast!
 Thine eyes the truth betray.

"And if I may not choose but weep
 Is not my grief mine own?
No heart was heavier yet for tears —
 O leave me, friend, alone!"

Come join this once the merry band,
 They call aloud for thee,
And mourn no more for what is lost,
 But let the past go free.

" O, little know ye in your mirth,
 What wrings my heart so deep!
I have not lost the idol yet,
 For which I sigh and weep."

Then rouse thee and take heart! thy blood
 Is young and full of fire;
Youth should have hope and might to win,
 And wear its best desire.

" O, never may I hope to gain
 What dwells from me so far;
It stands as high, it looks as bright,
 As yonder burning star."

Why, who would seek to woo the stars
 Down from their glorious sphere?
Enough it is to worship them,
 When nights are calm and clear.

" Oh, I look up and worship too —
 My star it shines by day —
Then let me weep the livelong night
 The while it is away."

---

* Translators: W. E. Aytoun and Theodore Martin.

EPILOGUE TO SCHILLER'S "SONG OF THE BELL" *

[This fine piece, written originally in 1805, on Schiller's death, was altered and recast by Goethe in 1815, on the occasion of the performance on the stage of the *Song of the Bell*. Hence the allusion in the last verse.]

> To this city joy reveal it!
> Peace as its first signal peal it!
> (*Song of the Bell* — concluding lines).

AND so it proved! The nation felt, ere long,
   That peaceful signal, and, with blessings fraught,
A new-born joy appeared; in gladsome song
   To hail the youthful princely pair we sought;
While in the living, ever-swelling throng
   Mingled the crowds from every region brought,
And on the stage, in festal pomp arrayed,
The HOMAGE OF THE ARTS† we saw displayed.

When, lo! a fearful midnight sound I hear,
   That with a dull and mournful echo rings.
And can it be that of our friend so dear
   It tells, to whom each wish so fondly clings?
Shall death o'ercome a life that all revere?
   How such a loss to all confusion brings!
How such a parting we must ever rue!
The world is weeping — shall not we weep, too?

He was our own! How social, yet how great
   Seemed in the light of day his noble mind!
How was his nature, pleasing yet sedate,
   Now for glad converse joyously inclined,
Then swiftly changing, spirit-fraught elate,
   Life's plan with deep-felt meaning it designed,
Fruitful alike in counsel and in deed!
This have we proved, this tested, in our need.

---

* Translators: W. E. Aytoun and Theodore Martin.

† The title of a lyric piece composed by Schiller in honor of the marriage of the hereditary prince of Weimar to the Princess Maria of Russia, and performed in 1804.

He was our own! O may that thought so blest
  O'ercome the voice of wailing and of woe!
He might have sought the Lasting, safe at rest
  In harbor, when the tempest ceased to blow.
Meanwhile his mighty spirit onward pressed
  Where goodness, beauty, truth, forever grow;
And in his rear, in shadowy outline, lay
The vulgar, which we all, alas, obey!

Now doth he deck the garden-turret fair
  Where the stars' language first illumed his soul,
As secretly yet clearly through the air
  On the eterne, the living sense it stole;
And to his own, and our great profit, there
  Exchangeth to the seasons as they roll;
Thus nobly doth he vanquish, with renown,
The twilight and the night that weigh us down.

Brighter now glowed his cheek, and still more bright,
  With that unchanging, ever-youthful glow,—
That courage which o'ercomes, in hard-fought fight,
  Sooner or later, every earthly foe,—
That faith which, soaring to the realms of light,
  Now boldly presseth on, now bendeth low,
So that the good may work, wax, thrive amain,
So that the day the noble may attain.

Yet, though so skilled, of such transcendent worth,
  This boarded scaffold doth he not despise;
The fate that on its axis turns the earth
  From day to night, here shows he to our eyes,
Raising, through many a work of glorious birth,
  Art and the artist's fame up toward the skies.
He fills with blossoms of the noblest strife,
With life itself, this effigy of life.

His giant-step, as ye full surely know,
   Measured the circle of the will and deed,
Each country's changing thoughts and morals, too,
   The darksome book with clearness could he read;
Yet how he, breathless 'midst his friends so true,
   Despaired in sorrow, scarce from pain was freed,—
All this have we, in sadly happy years,
For he was ours, bewailed with feeling tears.

When from the agonizing weight of grief
   He raised his eyes upon the world again,
We showed him how his thoughts might find relief
   From the uncertain present's heavy chain,
Gave his fresh-kindled mind a respite brief,
   With kindly skill beguiling every pain,
And e'en at eve when setting was his sun,
From his wan cheeks a gentle smile we won.

Full early had he read the stern decree,
   Sorrow and death to him, alas, were known;
Ofttimes recovering, now departed he,—
   Dread tidings, that our hearts had feared to own!
Yet his transfigured being now can see
   Itself, e'en here on earth, transfigured grown.
What his own age reproved, and deemed a crime,
Hath been ennobled now by death and time.

And many a soul that with him strove in fight,
   And his great merit grudged to recognize,
Now feels the impress of his wondrous might,
   And in his magic fetters gladly lies;
E'en to the highest hath he winged his flight,
   In close communion linked with all we prize.
Extol him then! What mortals while they live
But half receive, posterity shall give.

Thus is he left us, who so long ago,—
    Ten years, alas, already!—turned from earth;
We all, to our great joy, his precepts know,
    Oh, may the world confess their priceless worth!
In swelling tide toward every region flow
    The thoughts that were his own peculiar birth;
He gleams like some departing meteor bright,
Combining, with his own, eternal light.

ERGO BIBAMUS!* (1810)

FOR a praiseworthy object we're now gathered here,
    So, brethren, sing: ERGO BIBAMUS!
Tho' talk may be hushed, yet the glasses ring clear,
    Remember then, ERGO BIBAMUS!
In truth 'tis an old, 'tis an excellent word,
With its sound befitting each bosom is stirred,
And an echo the festal hall filling is heard,
    A glorious ERGO BIBAMUS!

I saw mine own love in her beauty so rare,
    And bethought me of: ERGO BIBAMUS;
So I gently approached, and she let me stand there,
    While I helped myself, thinking: BIBAMUS!
And when she's appeared, and will clasp you and kiss,
Or when those embraces and kisses ye miss,
Take refuge, till found is some worthier bliss,
    In the comforting ERGO BIBAMUS!

I am called by my fate far away from each friend;
    Ye loved ones, then: ERGO BIBAMUS!
With wallet light-laden from hence I must wend,
    So double our ERGO BIBAMUS!
Whate'er to his treasure the niggard may add,
Yet regard for the joyous will ever be had,
For gladness lends ever its charms to the glad,
    So, brethren, sing: ERGO BIBAMUS!

* Translator: E. A. Bowring.

And what shall we say of to-day as it flies?
  I thought but of: ERGO BIBAMUS!
'Tis one of those truly that seldom arise,
  So again and again sing: BIBAMUS!
For joy through a wide-open portal it guides,
Bright glitter the clouds as the curtain divides,
And a form, a divine one, to greet us in glides,
  While we thunder our: ERGO BIBAMUS.

THE WALKING BELL * (1813)

A CHILD refused to go betimes
  To church like other people;
He roamed abroad, when rang the chimes
  On Sundays from the steeple.

His mother said: "Loud rings the bell,
  Its voice ne'er think of scorning;
Unless thou wilt behave thee well,
  'Twill fetch thee without warning."

The child then thought: "High over head
  The bell is safe suspended — "
So to the fields he straightway sped
  As if 'twas school-time ended.

The bell now ceased as bell to ring,
  Roused by the mother's twaddle;
But soon ensued a dreadful thing! —
  The bell begins to waddle.

It waddles fast, though strange it seem;
  The child, with trembling wonder,
Runs off, and flies, as in a dream;
  The bell would draw him under.

He finds the proper time at last,
  And straightway nimbly rushes
To church, to chapel, hastening fast
  Through pastures, plains, and bushes.

---

* Translation: E. A. Bowring.

Each Sunday and each feast as well,
  His late disaster heeds he;
The moment that he hears the bell,
  No other summons needs he.

FOUND * (1813)

ONCE through the forest
  Alone I went;
To seek for nothing
  My thoughts were bent.

I saw i' the shadow
  A flower stand there;
As stars it glisten'd,
  As eyes 'twas fair.

I sought to pluck it,—
  It gently said:
" Shall I be gather'd
  Only to fade?"

With all its roots
  I dug it with care,
And took it home
  To my garden fair.

In silent corner
  Soon it was set;
There grows it ever,
  There blooms it yet.

HATEM † (1815)

Locks of brown, still bind your captive
  In the circle of her face!
I, beloved sinuous tresses,
  Naught possess that's worth your grace—

* Translator: E. A. Bowring.
† Translator: A. I. du P. Coleman.

But a heart whose love enduring
  Swells in youthful fervor yet:
Snow and mists envelop Etna,
  Making men the fire forget.

Yonder mountain's pride so stately
  Thou dost shame like dawn's red glow;
And its spell once more bids Hatem
  Thrill of spring and summer know.

Once more fill the glass, the flagon!
  Let me drink to my desire.
If she find a heap of ashes,
  Say, "He perished in her fire!"

REUNION * (1815)

CAN it be, O star transcendent,
  That I fold thee to my breast?
Now I know what depths of anguish
  May in parting be expressed.
Yes, 'tis thou, of all my blisses
  Lovely, loving partner — thou!
Mindful of my bygone sorrows,
  E'en the present awes me now.

When the world in first conception
  Lay in God's eternal mind,
In creative power delighting
  He the primal hour designed.
When he gave command for being,
  Then was heard a mighty sigh
Full of pain, as all creation
  Broke into reality.

---

* Translator: A. I. du P. Coleman.

Up then sprang the light; and darkness
  Doubtful stood apart to gaze;
All the elements, dividing
  Swiftly, took their several ways.
In confused, disordered dreaming
  Strove they all for freedom's range —
Each for self, no fellow-feeling;
  Single each, and cold and strange.

Lo, a marvel — God was lonely!
  All was still and cold and dumb.
So he framed dawn's rosy blushes
  Whence should consolation come —
To refresh the troubled spirit
  Harmonies of color sweet:
What had erst been forced asunder
  Now at last could love and meet.

Then, ah then, of life unbounded
  Sight and feeling passed the gates;
Then, ah then, with eager striving
  Kindred atoms sought their mates.
Gently, roughly they may seize them,
  So they catch and hold them fast:
" We," they cry, " are now creators —
  Allah now may rest at last!"

So with rosy wings of morning
  Towards thy lips my being moves;
Sets the starry night a thousand
  Glowing seals upon our loves.
We are as we should be — parted
  Ne'er on earth in joy or pain;
And no second word creative
  E'er can sunder us again!

PROŒMION * (1816)

In His blest name, who was His own creation,
Who from all time makes *making* His vocation;
The name of Him who makes our faith so bright,
Love, confidence, activity, and might;
In that One's name, who, named though oft He be,
Unknown is ever in Reality:
As far as ear can reach, or eyesight dim,
Thou findest but the known resembling Him;
How high soe'er thy fiery spirit hovers,
Its simile and type it straight discovers;
Onward thou'rt drawn, with feelings light and gay,
Where e'er thou goest, smiling is the way;
No more thou numberest, reckonest no time,
Each step is infinite, each step sublime.

What God would *outwardly* alone control,
And on His finger whirl the mighty Whole?
He loves the *inner* world to move, to view
Nature in Him, Himself in Nature, too,
So that what in Him works, and is, and lives,
The measure of His strength, His spirit gives.

Within us all a universe doth dwell;
And hence each people's usage laudable,
That every one the Best that meets his eyes
As God, yea, e'en *his* God, doth recognize;
To Him both earth and heaven surrenders he,
Fears Him, and loves Him, too, if that may be.

THE ONE AND THE ALL † (1821)

Called to a new employ in boundless space,
The lonely monad quits its 'customed place
  And from life's weary round contented flees.
No more of passionate striving, will perverse
And hampering obligations, long a curse:
  Free self-abandonment at last gives peace.

---

* Translator: E. A. Bowring.
† Translator: A. I. du P. Coleman.

Soul of the world, come pierce our being through!
Across the drift of things our way to hew
   Is our appointed task, our noblest war.
Good spirits by our destined pathway still
Lead gently on, best masters of our will,
   Toward that which made and makes all things that are.
To shape for further ends what now has breath,
Let nothing harden into ice and death,
   Works endless living action everywhere.
What has not yet existed strives for birth —
Toward purer suns, more glorious-colored earth:
   To rest in idle stillness naught may dare.
All must move onward, help transform the mass,
Assume a form, to yet another pass;
   'Tis but in seeming aught is fixed or still.
In all things moves the eternal restless Thought;
For all, when comes the hour, must fall to naught
   If to persist in being is its will.

LINES ON SEEING SCHILLER'S SKULL * (1826)

[This curious imitation of the ternary metre of Dante was written at the
age of seventy-seven.]

   WITHIN a gloomy charnel-house one day
      I viewed the countless skulls, so strangely mated,
   And of old times I thought that now were gray.
      Close packed they stand that once so fiercely hated,
   And hardy bones that to the death contended,
      Are lying crossed,— to lie forever, fated.
   What held those crooked shoulder-blades suspended?
      No one now asks; and limbs with vigor fired,
   The hand, the foot — their use in life is ended.
      Vainly ye sought the tomb for rest when tired;
   Peace in the grave may not be yours; ye're driven
      Back into daylight by a force inspired;
   But none can love the withered husk, though even
      A glorious noble kernel it containèd.

* Translator: E. A. Bowring.

To me, an adept, was the writing given
   Which not to all its holy sense explainèd.
When 'mid the crowd, their icy shadows flinging,
   I saw a form that glorious still remainèd,
And even there, where mould and damp were clinging,
   Gave me a blest, a rapture-fraught emotion,
As though from death a living fount were springing.
   What mystic joy I felt! What rapt devotion!
That form, how pregnant with a godlike trace!
   A look, how did it whirl me toward that ocean
Whose rolling billows mightier shapes embrace!
   Mysterious vessel! Oracle how dear!
Even to grasp thee is my hand too base,
   Except to steal thee from thy prison here
With pious purpose, and devoutly go
   Back to the air, free thoughts, and sunlight clear.
What greater gain in life can man e'er know
   Than when God-Nature will to him explain
How into Spirit steadfastness may flow,
   How steadfast, too, the Spirit-Born remain.

A LEGACY * (1829)

No living atom comes at last to naught!
Active in each is still the eternal Thought:
   Hold fast to Being if thou wouldst be blest.
Being is without end; for changeless laws
Bind that from which the All its glory draws
   Of living treasures endlessly possessed.

Unto the wise of old this truth was known,
Such wisdom knit their noble souls in one;
   Then hold thou still the lore of ancient days!
To that high power thou ow'st it, son of man,
By whose decree the earth its circuit ran
   And all the planets went their various ways.
Then inward turn at once thy searching eyes;

* Translator: A. I. du P. Coleman.

Thence shalt thou see the central truth arise
From which no lofty soul goes e'er astray;
There shalt thou miss no needful guiding sign —
For conscience lives, and still its light divine
Shall be the sun of all thy moral day.
Next shalt thou trust thy senses' evidence,
And fear from them no treacherous offence
While the mind's watchful eye thy road commands:
With lively pleasure contemplate the scene
And roam securely, teachable, serene,
At will throughout a world of fruitful lands.
Enjoy in moderation all life gives:
Where it rejoices in each thing that lives
Let reason be thy guide and make thee see.
Then shall the distant past be present still,
The future, ere it comes, thy vision fill —
Each single moment touch eternity.
Then at the last shalt thou achieve thy quest,
And in one final, firm conviction rest:
What bears for thee true fruit alone is true.
Prove all things, watch the movement of the world
As down the various ways its tribes are whirled;
Take thou thy stand among the chosen few.
Thus hath it been of old; in solitude
The artist shaped what thing to him seemed good,
The wise man hearkened to his own soul's voice.
Thus also shalt thou find thy greatest bliss;
To lead where the elect shall follow — this
And this alone is worth a hero's choice.

INTRODUCTION TO HERMANN AND DOROTHEA

By Arthur H. Palmer, A.M., LL.D.

Professor of German Language and Literature, Yale University

 ERMANN AND DOROTHEA is universally known and prized in Germany as no other work of the classical period of German literature except Goethe's *Faust* and Schiller's *Wilhelm Tell,* and, although distinctively German in subject and spirit, it early became and is still a precious possession of all the modern world. It marks the culmination of the renaissance in the literary art of Germany and perhaps of Europe.

Schiller hailed it as the pinnacle of Goethe's and of all modern art. A. W. Schlegel in 1797 judged it to be a finished work of art in the grand style, and at the same time intelligible, sympathetic, patriotic, popular, a book full of golden teachings of wisdom and virtue. Two generations later one of the leading historians of German literature declared that there is no other poem that comes so near to the father of all poetry (Homer) as this, none in which Greek form and German content are so intimately blended, and that this is perhaps the only poem which without explanation and without embarrassment all the modern centuries could offer to an ancient Greek to enjoy. In the view of the end of the nineteenth century, expressed by a distinguished philosopher-critic, this work is a unique amalgam of the artistic spirit, objectivity, and contemplative clearness of Homer with the soul-life of the present, the heart-beat of the German people, the characteristic traits which mark the German nature.

As Longfellow's *Evangeline,* treating in the same verse-form of the dactylic hexameter and in a way partly epic and partly idyllic a story of love and domestic interests in a contrasting setting of war and exile, was modeled on *Hermann and Dorothea,* so the latter poem was suggested by J. H. Voss' idyl *Luise,* published first in parts in 1783 and 1784 and as a whole revised in 1795. Of his delight in *Luise* Goethe wrote to Schiller in February, 1798: " This proved to be much to my advantage, for this joy finally became productive in me, it drew me into this form (the epic), begot my *Hermann,* and who knows what may yet come of it." But *Luise* is not really epic; it is without action, without unity, without any large historical outlook,— a series of minutely pictured, pleasing idyllic scenes.

In contrast herewith Goethe's purpose was in his own words, " in an epic crucible to free from its dross the purely human existence of a small German town, and at the same time mirror in a small glass the great movements and changes of the world's stage." This purpose he achieved in the writing of *Hermann and Dorothea* at intervals from September, 1796, through the summer of 1797, in the autumn of which year the poem was published.

The main sources from which the poet drew his material are four. In the first place the theme was invented by him out of an anecdote of the flight of Protestant refugees from the Archbishopric of Salzburg in 1731–1732. On the basis of this anecdote he drew the original outlines of the meeting and union of the lovers. Secondly, as a consequence of the French Revolution, Germans were forced to flee from German territory west of the Rhine. Goethe was present with Prussian troops in France in 1792, and observed the siege of Mainz in 1793. Hence his knowledge of war and exile, with their attendant cruelties and sufferings. Thirdly, the personal experiences of his own life could not but contribute to his description of the then German present. Features of Frankfurt and Ilmenau reappear. The characters show traits of Goethe's parents, and possibly something of his wife is in Dorothea. Hermann's mother bears the name of the poet's and reveals many of her qualities. But some of these are given to the landlord-father, while the elder Goethe's pedantry and petty weaknesses are shown in the apothecary. The poet's experiences in the field are realistically reproduced in many particulars of character and incident, as are doubtless also his mother's vivid reports of events in Frankfurt during July and August, 1796. We may feel sure too that it was the occurrences of this summer that led Goethe to transform the short, pure idyl of his first intention into a longer epic of his own present. The fourth source is literary tradition, which we may trace back through the verse idyl of Voss to the prose idyl of Gessner, thence through the unnatural Arcadian pastorals of the seventeenth and earlier centuries to the great Greek creators,— Theocritus, of the idyl, and Homer, of the epic.

From whatever source derived, the materials were transmuted and combined by Goethe's genius into a broad, full picture of German life, with characters typical of the truly human and of profound ethical importance, interpreting to the attentive reader the significance of life for the individual, the family, the nation.

HERMANN AND DOROTHEA (1797)*

TRANSLATED BY ELLEN FROTHINGHAM

CALLIOPE

FATE AND SYMPATHY

RULY, I never have seen the market and street
    so deserted!
How as if it were swept looks the town, or
    had perished! Not fifty
Are there, methinks, of all our inhabitants in
  it remaining.
What will not curiosity do! here is every one running,
Hurrying to gaze on the sad procession of pitiful exiles.
Fully a league it must be to the causeway they have to pass
    over,
Yet all are hurrying down in the dusty heat of the noonday.
I, in good sooth, would not stir from my place to witness
    the sorrows
Borne by good, fugitive people, who now, with their rescued
    possessions,
Driven, alas! from beyond the Rhine, their beautiful
    country,
Over to us are coming, and through the prosperous corner
Roam of this our luxuriant valley, and traverse its
    windings.
Well hast thou done, good wife, our son in thus kindly
    dispatching,
Laden with something to eat and to drink, and with store
    of old linen,
'Mongst the poor folk to distribute; for giving belongs to
    the wealthy.
How the youth drives, to be sure! What control he has
    over the horses!

Makes not our carriage a handsome appearance,— the new
    one? With comfort,
Four could be seated within, with a place on the box for
    the coachman.
This time, he drove by himself. How lightly it rolled round
    the corner!"
Thus, as he sat at his ease in the porch of his house on the
    market,
Unto his wife was speaking mine host of the Golden Lion.

Thereupon answered and said the prudent, intelligent
    housewife:
" Father, I am not inclined to be giving away my old linen:
Since it serves many a purpose; and cannot be purchased
    for money,
When we may want it. Today, however, I gave, and with
    pleasure,
Many a piece that was better, indeed, in shirts and in bed-
    clothes;
For I was told of the aged and children who had to go
    naked.
But wilt thou pardon me, father? thy wardrobe has also
    been plundered.
And, in especial, the wrapper that has the East-Indian
    flowers,
Made of the finest of chintz, and lined with delicate flannel,
Gave I away: it was thin and old, and quite out of the
    fashion."

Thereupon answered and said, with a smile, the excellent
    landlord:
" Faith! I am sorry to lose it, my good old calico wrapper,
Real East-Indian stuff: I never shall get such another.
Well, I had given up wearing it: nowadays, custom compels
    us
Always to go in surtout, and never appear but in jacket;
Always to have on our boots; forbidden are night-cap and
    slippers."

HERMANN'S PARENTS IN THE DOORWAY OF THE TAVERN

" See!" interrupted the wife; " even now some are yonder returning,
Who have beheld the procession: it must, then, already be over.
Look at the dust on their shoes! and see how their faces are glowing!
Every one carries his kerchief, and with it is wiping the sweat off.
Not for a sight like that would I run so far and so suffer,
Through such a heat; in sooth, enough shall I have in the telling."

Thereupon answered and said, with emphasis, thus, the good father:
" Rarely does weather like this attend such a harvest as this is.
We shall be bringing our grain in dry, as the hay was before it.
Not the least cloud to be seen, so perfectly clear is the heaven;
And, with delicious coolness, the wind blows in from the eastward.
That is the weather to last! over-ripe are the cornfields already;
We shall begin on the morrow to gather our copious harvest."

Constantly, while he thus spoke, the crowds of men and of women
Grew, who their homeward way were over the market-place wending;
And, with the rest, there also returned, his daughters beside him,
Back to his modernized house on the opposite side of the market,
Foremost merchant of all the town, their opulent neighbor,

Rapidly driving his open barouche,— it was builded in
Landau.
Lively now grew the streets, for the city was handsomely
peopled.
Many a trade was therein carried on, and large manu-
factures.
Under their doorway thus the affectionate couple were
sitting,
Pleasing themselves with many remarks on the wandering
people.
Finally broke in, however, the worthy housewife, exclaim-
ing:
"Yonder our pastor, see! is hitherward coming, and with
him
Comes our neighbor the doctor, so they shall every thing
tell us;
All they have witnessed abroad, and which 'tis a sorrow to
look on."

Cordially then the two men drew nigh, and saluted the
couple;
Sat themselves down on the benches of wood that were
placed in the doorway,
Shaking the dust from their feet, and fanning themselves
with their kerchiefs.
Then was the doctor, as soon as exchanged were the mutual
greetings,
First to begin, and said, almost in a tone of vexation:
"Such is mankind, forsooth! and one man is just like
another,
Liking to gape and to stare when ill-luck has befallen his
neighbor.
Every one hurries to look at the flames, as they soar in
destruction;
Runs to behold the poor culprit, to execution conducted:
Now all are sallying forth to gaze on the need of these
exiles,

Nor is there one who considers that he, by a similar fortune,
May, in the future, if not indeed next, be likewise o'ertaken.
Levity not to be pardoned, I deem; yet it lies in man's
  nature."

  Thereupon answered and said the noble, intelligent pastor;
Ornament he of the town, still young, in the prime of his
  manhood.
He was acquainted with life,— with the needs of his hearers
  acquainted;
Deeply imbued he was with the Holy Scriptures' im-
  portance,
As they reveal man's destiny to us, and man's disposition;
Thoroughly versed, besides, in best of secular writings.
" I should be loath," he replied, " to censure an innocent
  instinct,
Which to mankind by good mother Nature has always been
  given.
What understanding and reason may sometimes fail to
  accomplish,
Oft will such fortunate impulse, that bears us resistlessly
  with it.
Did curiosity draw not man with its potent attraction,
Say, would he ever have learned how harmoniously fitted
  together
Worldly experiences are? For first what is novel he covets;
Then with unwearying industry follows he after the useful;
Finally longs for the good by which he is raised and
  ennobled.
While he is young, such lightness of mind is a joyous com-
  panion,
Traces of pain-giving evil effacing as soon as 'tis over.
He is indeed to be praised, who, out of this gladness of
  temper,
Has in his ripening years a sound understanding developed;
Who, in good fortune or ill, with zeal and activity labors:
Such an one bringeth to pass what is good, and repaireth
  the evil."

Then broke familiarly in the housewife impatient, exclaiming:
" Tell us of what ye have seen; for that I am longing to
hear of!"

" Hardly," with emphasis then the village doctor made
answer,
" Can I find spirits so soon after all the scenes I have
witnessed.
Oh, the manifold miseries! who shall be able to tell them?
E'en before crossing the meadows, and while we were yet
at a distance,
Saw we the dust; but still from hill to hill the procession
Passed away out of our sight, and we could distinguish but
little.
But when at last we were come to the street that crosses
the valley,
Great was the crowd and confusion of persons on foot and
of wagons.
There, alas! saw we enough of these poor unfortunates
passing,
And could from some of them learn how bitter the sorrow-
ful flight was,
Yet how joyful the feeling of life thus hastily rescued.
Mournful it was to behold the most miscellaneous chattels,—
All those things which are housed in every well-furnished
dwelling,
All by the house-keeper's care set up in their suitable
places,
Always ready for use; for useful is each and important.—
Now these things to behold, piled up on all manner of
wagons,
One on the top of another, as hurriedly they had been
rescued.
Over the chest of drawers were the sieve and wool coverlet
lying;
Thrown in the kneading-trough lay the bed, and the sheets
on the mirror.

Danger, alas! as we learned ourselves in our great con-
flagration
Twenty years since, will take from a man all power of
reflection,
So that he grasps things worthless and leaves what is
precious behind him.
Here, too, with unconsidering care they were carrying with
them
Pitiful trash, that only encumbered the horses and oxen;
Such as old barrels and boards, the pen for the goose, and
the bird-cage.
Women and children, too, went toiling along with their
bundles,
Panting 'neath baskets and tubs, full of things of no man-
ner of value:
So unwilling is man to relinquish his meanest possession.
Thus on the dusty road the crowded procession moved
forward,
All confused and disordered. The one whose beasts were
the weaker,
Wanted more slowly to drive, while faster would hurry
another.
Presently went up a scream from the closely squeezed
women and children,
And with the yelping of dogs was mingled the lowing of
cattle,
Cries of distress from the aged and sick, who aloft on the
wagon,
Heavy and thus overpacked, upon beds were sitting and
swaying.
Pressed at last from the rut and out to the edge of the
highway,
Slipped the creaking wheel; the cart lost its balance, and
over
Fell in the ditch. In the swing the people were flung to
a distance,

Far off into the field, with horrible screams; by good
    fortune
Later the boxes were thrown and fell more near to the
    wagon.
Verily all who had witnessed the fall, expected to see them
Crushed into pieces beneath the weight of trunks and of
    presses.
So lay the cart all broken to fragments, and helpless the
    people.
Keeping their onward way, the others drove hastily by
    them,
Each thinking only of self, and carried away by the current.
Then we ran to the spot, and found the sick and the aged,—
Those who at home and in bed could before their lingering
    ailments
Scarcely endure,— lying bruised on the ground, complain-
    ing and groaning,
Choked by the billowing dust and scorched by the heat of
    the noonday.''

Thereupon answered and said the kind-hearted landlord,
    with feeling:
'' Would that our Hermann might meet them and give them
    refreshment and clothing!
Loath should I be to behold them: the looking on suffering
    pains me.
Touched by the earliest tidings of their so cruel afflictions,
Hastily sent we a mite from out of our super-abundance,
Only that some might be strengthened, and we might our-
    selves be made easy.
But let us now no longer renew these sorrowful pictures
Knowing how readily fear steals into the heart of us
    mortals,
And anxiety, worse to me than the actual evil.
Come with me into the room behind, our cool little parlor,
Where no sunbeam e'er shines, and no sultry breath ever
    enters

Through its thickness of wall. There mother will bring us
    a flagon
Of our old eighty-three, with which we may banish our
    fancies.
Here 'tis not cosey to drink: the flies so buzz round the
    glasses.''
Thither adjourned they then, and all rejoiced in the
    coolness.

  Carefully brought forth the mother the clear and glorious
    vintage,
Cased in a well-polished flask, on a waiter of glittering
    pewter,
Set round with large green glasses, the drinking cups meet
    for the Rhine wine.
So sat the three together about the highly waxed table,
Gleaming and round and brown, that on mighty feet was
    supported.
Joyously rang at once the glasses of landlord and pastor,
But his motionless held the third, and sat lost in reflection,
Until with words of good-humor the landlord challenged
    him, saying,—
'' Come, sir neighbor, empty your glass, for God in His
    mercy
Thus far has kept us from evil, and so in the future will
    keep us.
For who acknowledges not, that since our dread con-
    flagration,
When He so hardly chastised us, He now is continually
    blessing,
Constantly shielding, as man the apple of His eye watches
    over,
Holding it precious and dear above all the rest of His
    members?
Shall He in time to come not defend us and furnish us
    succor?

Only when danger is nigh do we see how great is His power.
Shall He this blooming town which He once by industrious
    burghers
Built up afresh from its ashes, and afterward blessed with
    abundance,
Now demolish again, and bring all the labor to nothing? ''

Cheerfully said in reply the excellent pastor, and kindly:
'' Keep thyself firm in the faith, and firm abide in this
    temper;
For it makes steadfast and wise when fortune is fair, and
    when evil,
Furnishes sweet consolation and animates hopes the
    sublimest.''

Then made answer the landlord, with thoughts judicious
    and manly:
'' Often the Rhine's broad stream have I with astonishment
    greeted,
As I have neared it again, after travelling abroad upon
    business.
Always majestic it seemed, and my mind and spirit exalted.
But I could never imagine its beautiful banks would so
    shortly
Be to a rampart transformed, to keep from our borders
    the Frenchman,
And its wide-spreading bed be a moat all passage to hinder.
See! thus nature protects, the stout-hearted Germans pro-
    tect us,
And thus protects us the Lord, who then will be weakly
    despondent?
Weary already the combatants, all indications are peaceful.
Would it might be that when that festival, ardently longed
    for,
Shall in our church be observed, when the sacred *Te Deum*
    is rising,

Swelled by the pealing of organ and bells, and the blaring
    of trumpets,—
Would it might be that that day should behold my Her-
    mann, sir pastor,
Standing, his choice now made, with his bride before thee
    at the altar,
Making that festal day, that through every land shall be
    honored,
My anniversary, too, henceforth of domestic rejoicing!
But I observe with regret, that the youth so efficient and
    active
Ever in household affairs, when abroad is timid and back-
    ward.
Little enjoyment he finds in going about among others;
Nay, he will even avoid young ladies' society wholly;
Shuns the enlivening dance which all young persons
    delight in.''

  Thus he spoke and listened; for now was heard in the
    distance
Clattering of horses' hoofs drawing near, and the roll of
    the wagon,
Which, with furious haste, came thundering under the
    gateway.

TERPSICHORE

HERMANN

  Now when of comely mien the son came into the chamber,
Turned with a searching look the eyes of the preacher
    upon him,
And, with the gaze of the student, who easily fathoms
    expression,
Scrutinized well his face and form and his general bearing.
Then with a smile he spoke, and said in words of affection:
'' Truly a different being thou comest! I never have seen
    thee
Cheerful as now, nor ever beheld I thy glances so beaming.

Joyous thou comest, and happy: 'tis plain that among the
    poor people
Thou hast been sharing thy gifts, and receiving their bless-
    ings upon thee.''

    Quietly then, and with serious words, the son made him
    answer:
'' If I have acted as ye will commend, I know not; but I
    followed
That which my heart bade me do, as I shall exactly relate
    you.
Thou wert, mother, so long in rummaging 'mong thy old
    pieces,
Picking and choosing, that not until late was thy bundle
    together;
Then, too, the wine and the beer took care and time in the
    packing.
When I came forth through the gateway at last, and out
    on the high-road,
Backward the crowd of citizens streamed with women and
    children,
Coming to meet me; for far was already the band of the
    exiles.
Quicker I kept on my way, and drove with speed to the
    village,
Where they were meaning to rest, as I heard, and tarry
    till morning.
Thitherward up the new street as I hasted, a stout-tim-
    bered wagon,
Drawn by two oxen, I saw, of that region the largest and
    strongest;
While, with vigorous steps, a maiden was walking beside
    them,
And, a long staff in her hand, the two powerful creatures
    was guiding,
Urging them now, now holding them back; with skill did
    she drive them.

HERMANN HANDS TO DOROTHEA THE LINEN FOR THE EMIGRANTS

Soon as the maiden perceived me, she calmly drew near
　　to the horses,
And in these words she addressed me: 'Not thus deplor-
　　able always
Has our condition been, as today on this journey thou seest.
I am not yet grown used to asking gifts of a stranger,
Which he will often unwillingly give, to be rid of the beggar.
But necessity drives me to speak; for here, on the straw, lies
Newly delivered of child, a rich land-owner's wife, whom
　　I scarcely
Have in her pregnancy, safe brought off with the oxen and
　　wagon.
Naked, now in her arms the new-born infant is lying,
And but little the help our friends will be able to furnish,
If in the neighboring village, indeed, where today we would
　　rest us,
Still we shall find them; though much do I fear they
　　already have passed it.
Shouldst thou have linen to spare of any description,
　　provided
Thou of this neighborhood art, to the poor in charity
　　give it.'

　　" Thus she spoke, and the pale-faced mother raised her-
　　self feebly
Up from the straw, and toward me looked. Then said
　　I in answer:
'Surely unto the good, a spirit from heaven oft speaketh,
Making them feel the distress that threatens a suffering
　　brother.
For thou must know that my mother, already presaging
　　thy sorrows,
Gave me a bundle to use it straightway for the need of
　　the naked.'
Then I untied the knots of the string, and the wrapper of
　　father's
Unto her gave, and gave her as well the shirts and the linen.

And she thanked me with joy, and cried: ' The happy
    believe not
Miracles yet can be wrought: for only in need we ac-
    knowledge
God's own hand and finger, that leads the good to show
    goodness.
What unto us He has done through thee, may He do to
    thee also!'
And I beheld with what pleasure the sick woman handled
    the linens,
But with especial delight the dressing-gown's delicate
    flannel.
' Let us make haste,' the maid to her said, ' and come to
    the village,
Where our people will halt for the night and already are
    resting.
There these clothes for the children I, one and all, straight-
    way will portion.'
Then she saluted again, her thanks most warmly ex-
    pressing,
Started the oxen; the wagon went on; but there I still
    lingered,
Still held the horses in check; for now my heart was
    divided
Whether to drive with speed to the village, and there the
    provisions
Share 'mong the rest of the people, or whether I here to
    the maiden
All should deliver at once, for her discreetly to portion.
And in an instant my heart had decided, and quietly
    driving
After the maiden, I soon overtook her, and said to her
    quickly:
' Hearken, good maiden; — my mother packed up not linen-
    stuffs only
Into the carriage, that I should have clothes to furnish the
    naked;

Wine and beer she added besides, and supply of provisions:

Plenty of all these things I have in the box of the carriage.

But now I feel myself moved to deliver these offerings also

Into thy hand; for so shall I best fulfil my commission.

Thou wilt divide them with judgment, while I must by chance be directed.'

Thereupon answered the maiden: ' I will with faithfulness portion

These thy gifts, that all shall bring comfort to those who are needy.'

Thus she spoke, and quickly the box of the carriage I opened,

Brought forth thence the substantial hams, and brought out the breadstuffs,

Bottles of wine and beer, and one and all gave to the maiden.

Willingly would I have given her more, but the carriage was empty.

All she packed at the sick woman's feet, and went on her journey.

I, with my horses and carriage, drove rapidly back to the city."

Instantly now, when Hermann had ceased, the talkative neighbor

Took up the word, and cried: " Oh happy, in days like the present,

Days of flight and confusion, who lives by himself in his dwelling,

Having no wife nor child to be clinging about him in terror!

Happy I feel myself now, and would not for much be called father;

Would not have wife and children today, for whom to be anxious.

Oft have I thought of this flight before; and have packed up together

All my best things already, the chains and old pieces of
    money
That were my sainted mother's, of which not one has been
    sold yet.
Much would be left behind, it is true, not easily gotten.
Even the roots and the herbs, that were with such industry
    gathered,
I should be sorry to lose, though the worth of the goods
    is but trifling.
If my purveyor remained, I could go from my dwelling
    contented.
When my cash I have brought away safe, and have rescued
    my person,
All is safe: none find it so easy to fly as the single.''

    '' Neighbor,'' unto his words young Hermann with em-
    phasis answered:
'' I can in no wise agree with thee here, and censure thy
    language.
Is he indeed a man to be prized, who, in good and in evil,
Takes no thought but for self, and gladness and sorrow
    with others
Knows not how to divide, nor feels his heart so impel him?
Rather than ever today would I make up my mind to be
    married:
Many a worthy maiden is needing a husband's protection,
And the man needs an inspiriting wife when ill is im-
    pending.''

    Thereupon smiling the father replied: '' Thus love I to
    hear thee!
That is a sensible word such as rarely I've known thee
    to utter.''
Straightway, however, the mother broke in with quickness,
    exclaiming:
'' Son, to be sure, thou art right! we parents have set the
    example;

Seeing that not in our season of joy did we choose one
 another;
Rather the saddest of hours it was that bound us together.
Monday morning — I mind it well; for the day that pre-
 ceded
Came that terrible fire by which our city was ravaged —
Twenty years will have gone. The day was a Sunday
 as this is;
Hot and dry was the season; the water was almost ex-
 hausted.
All the people were strolling abroad in their holiday
 dresses,
'Mong the villages partly, and part in the mills and the
 taverns.
And at the end of the city the flames began, and went
 coursing
Quickly along the streets, creating a draught in their
 passage.
Burned were the barns where the copious harvest already
 was garnered;
Burned were the streets as far as the market; the house of
 my father,
Neighbor to this, was destroyed, and this one also fell
 with it.
Little we managed to save. I sat, that sorrowful night
 through,
Outside the town on the common, to guard the beds and
 the boxes.
Sleep overtook me at last, and when I again was awakened,
Feeling the chill of the morning that always descends
 before sunrise,
There were the smoke and the glare, and the walls and
 chimneys in ruins.
Then fell a weight on my heart; but more majestic than
 ever
Came up the sun again, inspiring my bosom with courage.
Then I rose hastily up, with a yearning the place to revisit

Whereon our dwelling had stood, and to see if the hens
  had been rescued,
Which I especially loved, for I still was a child in my
  feelings.
Thus as I over the still-smoking timbers of house and of
  court-yard
Picked my way, and beheld the dwelling so ruined and
  wasted,
Thou camest up to examine the place, from the other
  direction.
Under the ruins thy horse in his stall had been buried;
  the rubbish
Lay on the spot and the glimmering beams; of the horse
  we saw nothing.
Thoughtful and grieving we stood there thus, each facing
  the other,
Now that the wall was fallen that once had divided our
  court-yards.
Thereupon thou by the hand didst take me, and speak to
  me, saying,—
'Lisa, how camest thou hither? Go back! thy soles must
  be burning;
Hot the rubbish is here: it scorches my boots, which are
  stronger.'
And thou didst lift me up, and carry me out through thy
  court-yard.
There was the door of the house left standing yet with its
  archway,
Just as 'tis standing now, the one thing only remaining.
Then thou didst set me down and kiss me; to that I
  objected;
But thou didst answer and say with kindly significant
  language:
'See! my house lies in ruins: remain here and help me
  rebuild it;
So shall my help in return be given to building thy
  father's.'

Yet did I not comprehend thee until thou sentest thy
mother

Unto my father, and quick were the happy espousals accomplished.

E'en to this day I remember with joy those half-consumed
timbers,

And I can see once more the sun coming up in such
splendor;

For 'twas the day that gave me my husband; and, ere the
first season

Passed of that wild desolation, a son to my youth had been
given.

Therefore I praise thee, Hermann, that thou, with an
honest assurance,

Shouldst, in these sorrowful days, be thinking thyself of
a maiden,

And amid ruins and war shouldst thus have the courage
to woo her.''

Straightway, then, and with warmth, the father replied
to her, saying:

''Worthy of praise is the feeling, and truthful also the
story,

Mother, that thou hast related; for so indeed every thing
happened.

Better, however, is better. It is not the business of all
men

Thus their life and estate to begin from the very foundation:

Every one needs not to worry himself as we and the
rest did.

Oh, how happy is he whose father and mother shall give
him,

Furnished and ready, a house which he can adorn with
his increase.

Every beginning is hard; but most the beginning a household.

Many are human wants, and every thing daily grows
    dearer,
So that a man must consider the means of increasing his
    earnings.
This I hope therefore of thee, my Hermann, that into our
    dwelling
Thou wilt be bringing ere long a bride who is handsomely
    dowered;
For it is meet that a gallant young man have an opulent
    maiden.
Great is the comfort of home whene'er, with the woman
    elected,
Enter the useful presents, besides, in box and in basket.
Not for this many a year in vain has the mother been busy
Making her daughter's linens of strong and delicate
    texture;
God-parents have not in vain been giving their vessels of
    silver,
And the father laid by in his desk the rare pieces of money;
For there a day will come when she, with her gifts and
    possessions,
Shall that youth rejoice who has chosen her out of all
    others.
Well do I know how good in a house is a woman's position,
Who her own furniture round her knows, in kitchen and
    chamber;
Who herself the bed and herself the table has covered.
Only a well-dowered bride should I like to receive to my
    dwelling.
She who is poor is sure, in the end, to be scorned by her
    husband;
And will as servant be held, who as servant came in with
    her bundle.
Men will remain unjust when the season of love is gone
    over.
Yes, my Hermann, thy father's old age thou greatly canst
    gladden,

If thou a daughter-in-law will speedily bring to my dwelling,
Out of the neighborhood here,—from the house over yonder, the green one.
Rich is the man, I can tell thee. His manufactures and
traffic
Daily are making him richer; for whence draws the merchant not profit?
Three daughters only he has, to divide his fortune among
them.
True that the eldest already is taken; but there is the
second
Still to be had, as well as the third; and not long so, it
may be.
I would never have lingered till now, had I been in thy
place;
But had fetched one of the maidens, as once I bore off thy
dear mother.''

Modestly then did the son to the urgent father make
answer:
'' Truly 'twas my wish too, as well as thine own, to have
chosen
One of our neighbor's daughters, for we had been brought
up together;
Played, in the early days, about the market-place fountain;
And, from the other boys' rudeness, I often have been
their defender.
That, though, is long since past: the girls, as they grew
to be older,
Properly stayed in the house, and shunned the more boister-
ous pastimes.
Well brought up are they, surely! I used sometimes to go
over,
Partly to gratify thee, and because of our former acquaint-
ance:
But no pleasure I ever could take in being among them;
For I was always obliged to endure their censures upon me.

Quite too long was my coat, the cloth too coarse, and the
   color
Quite too common; my hair was not cropped, as it should
   be, and frizzled.
I was resolved, at last, that I, also, would dress myself
   finely,
Just as those office-boys do who always are seen there on
   Sundays,
Wearing in summer their half-silken flaps, that dangle
   about them;
But I discovered, betimes, they made ever a laughing-stock
   of me.
And I was vexed when I saw it,—it wounded my pride;
   but more deeply
Felt I aggrieved that they the good-will should so far mis-
   interpret
That in my heart I bore them,—especially Minna the
   youngest.
It was on Easter-day that last I went over to see them;
Wearing my best new coat, that is now hanging up in the
   closet,
And having frizzled my hair, like that of the other young
   fellows.
Soon as I entered, they tittered; but that not at me, as I
   fancied.
Minna before the piano was seated; the father was present,
Hearing his daughters sing, and full of delight and good-
   humor.
Much I could not understand of all that was said in the
   singing;
But of Pamina I often heard, and oft of Tamino:
And I, besides, could not stay there dumb; so, as soon as
   she ended,
Something about the words I asked, and about the two
   persons.
Thereupon all were silent and smiled; but the father made
   answer:

'Thou knowest no one, my friend, I believe, but Adam
and Eve?'
No one restrained himself longer, but loud laughed out
then the maidens,
Loud laughed out the boys, the old man held his sides for
his laughing.
I, in embarrassment, dropped my hat, and the giggling
continued,
On and on and on, for all they kept playing and singing.
Back to the house here I hurried, o'ercome with shame
and vexation,
Hung up my coat in the closet, and pulled out the curls
with my fingers,
Swearing that never again my foot should cross over that
threshold.
And I was perfectly right; for vain are the maidens, and
heartless.
E'en to this day, as I hear, I am called by them ever
'Tamino.'"

Thereupon answered the mother, and said: "Thou
shouldest not, Hermann,
Be so long vexed with the children: indeed, they are all
of them children.
Minna, believe me, is good, and was always disposed to
thee kindly.
'Twas not long since she was asking about thee. Let her
be thy chosen!"

Thoughtfully answered the son: "I know not. That
mortification
Stamped itself in me so deeply, I never could bear to
behold her
Seated before the piano or listen again to her singing."

Forth broke the father then, and in words of anger made
answer:

"Little of joy will my life have in thee! I said it would
    be so
When I perceived that thy pleasure was solely in horses
    and farming:
Work which a servant, indeed, performs for an opulent
    master,
That thou doest; the father meanwhile must his son be
    deprived of,
Who should appear as his pride, in the sight of the rest
    of the townsmen.
Early with empty hopes thy mother was wont to deceive me,
When in the school thy studies, thy reading and writing,
    would never
As with the others succeed, but thy seat would be always
    the lowest.
That comes about, forsooth, when a youth has no feeling
    of honor
Dwelling within his breast, nor the wish to raise himself
    higher.
Had but my father so cared for me as thou hast been
    cared for;
If he had sent me to school, and provided me thus with
    instructors,
I should be other, I trow, than host of the Golden Lion!"

Then the son rose from his seat and noiselessly moved
    to the doorway,
Slowly, and speaking no word. The father, however, in
    passion
After him called, "Yes, go, thou obstinate fellow! I know
    thee!
Go and look after the business henceforth, that I have not
    to chide thee;
But do thou nowise imagine that ever a peasant-born
    maiden
Thou for a daughter-in-law shalt bring into my dwelling,
    the hussy!

Long have I lived in the world, and know how mankind
    should be dealt with;
Know how to entertain ladies and gentlemen so that con-
    tented
They shall depart from my house, and strangers agreeably
    can flatter.
Yet I'm resolved that some day I one will have for a
    daughter,
Who shall requite me in kind and sweeten my manifold
    labors;
Who the piano shall play to me, too; so that there shall
    with pleasure
All the handsomest people in town and the finest assemble,
As they on Sundays do now in the house of our neighbor."
    Here Hermann
Softly pressed on the latch, and so went out from the
    chamber.

THALIA

THE CITIZENS

Thus did the modest son slip away from the angry up-
    braiding;
But in the tone he had taken at first, the father continued:
" That comes not out of a man which he has not in him;
    and hardly
Shall the joy ever be mine of seeing my dearest wish
    granted:
That my son may not as his father be, but a better.
What would become of the house, and what of the city if
    each one
Were not with pleasure and always intent on maintaining,
    renewing,
Yea, and improving, too, as time and the foreigner teach us!
Man is not meant, forsooth, to grow from the ground like
    a mushroom,

Quickly to perish away on the spot of ground that begot him,
Leaving no trace behind of himself and his animate action!
As by the house we straightway can tell the mind of the
    master,
So, when we walk through a city, we judge of the persons
    who rule it.
For where the towers and walls are falling to ruin; where
    offal
Lies in heaps in the gutters, and alleys with offal are
    littered;
Where from its place has started the stone, and no one
    resets it;
Where the timbers are rotting away, and the house is
    awaiting
Vainly its new supports,— that place we may know is ill
    governed.
Since if not from above work order and cleanliness down-
    ward,
Easily grows the citizen used to untidy postponement;
Just as the beggar grows likewise used to his ragged
    apparel.
Therefore I wished that our Hermann might early set out
    on some travels;
That he at least might behold the cities of Strasburg and
    Frankfort,
Friendly Mannheim, too, that is cheerful and evenly
    builded.
He that has once beheld cities so cleanly and large, never
    after
Ceases his own native city, though small it may be, to
    embellish.
Do not the strangers who come here commend the repairs
    in our gateway,
Notice our whitewashed tower, and the church we have
    newly rebuilded?
Are not all praising our pavement? the covered canals full
    of water,

Laid with a wise distribution, which furnish us profit and
    safety,
So that no sooner does fire break out than 'tis promptly
    arrested?
Has not all this come to pass since the time of our great
    conflagration?
Builder I six times was named by the council, and won the
    approval,
Won moreover the heartfelt thanks of all the good
    burghers,
Actively carrying out what I planned, and also fulfilling
What had by upright men been designed, and left uncom-
    pleted.
Finally grew the same zeal in every one of the council;
All now labor together, and firmly decided already
Stands it to build the new causeway that shall with the
    highroad connect us.
But I am sorely afraid that will not be the way with our
    children.
Some think only of pleasure and perishable apparel;
Others will cower at home, and behind the stove will sit
    brooding.
One of this kind, as I fear, we shall find to the last in our
    Hermann.''

Straightway answered and said the good and intelligent
    mother:
'' Why wilt thou always, father, be doing our son such
    injustice?
That least of all is the way to bring thy wish to ful-
    filment.
We have no power to fashion our children as suiteth our
    fancy;
As they are given by God, we so must have them and love
    them;
Teach them as best we can, and let each of them follow
    his nature.

One will have talents of one sort, and different talents
  another.
Every one uses his own; in his own individual fashion,
Each must be happy and good.   I will not have my Hermann found fault with;
For he is worthy, I know, of the goods he shall one day
  inherit;
Will be an excellent landlord, a pattern to burghers and
  builders;
Neither in council, as I can foresee, will he be the most
  backward.
But thou keepest shut up in his breast all the poor fellow's
  spirit,
Finding such fault with him daily, and censuring as thou
  but now hast."
And on the instant she quitted the room, and after him
  hurried,
Hoping she somewhere might find him, and might with her
  words of affection
Cheer him again, her excellent son, for well he deserved it.

Thereupon when she was gone, the father thus smiling
  continued:
"What a strange folk, to be sure, are these women; and
  just like the children;
Both of them bent upon living according as suiteth their
  pleasure,
While we others must never do aught but flatter and praise
  them.
Once for all time holds good the ancients' trustworthy
  proverb:
'Whoever goes not forward comes backward.'   So must
  it be always."

Thereupon answered and said, in a tone of reflection,
  the doctor:
"That, sir neighbor, I willingly grant; for myself I am
  always

THE MOTHER DEFENDING HERMANN

Casting about for improvement,— things new, so they be
    not too costly.
But what profits a man, who has not abundance of money,
Being thus active and stirring, and bettering inside and
    outside?
Only too much is the citizen cramped: the good, though he
    know it,
Has he no means to acquire because too slender his
    purse is,
While his needs are too great; and thus is he constantly
    hampered.
Many things I had done; but then the cost of such changes
Who does not fear, especially now in this season of danger?
Long since my house was smiling upon me in modish
    apparel!
Long since great panes of glass were gleaming in all of the
    windows!
But who can do as the merchant does, who, with his
    resources,
Knows the methods as well by which the best is arrived at?
Look at that house over yonder,— the new one; behold with
    what splendor
'Gainst the background of green stand out the white spirals
    of stucco!
Great are the panes in the windows; and how the glass
    sparkles and glitters,
Casting quite into the shade the rest of the market-place
    houses!
Yet just after the fire were our two houses the finest,
This of the Golden Lion, and mine of the sign of the Angel.
So was my garden, too, throughout the whole neighborhood
    famous:
Every traveller stopped and gazed through the red pali-
    sadoes,
Caught by the beggars there carved in stone and the dwarfs
    of bright colors.
Then whosoever had coffee served in the beautiful grotto,—

Standing there now all covered with dust and partly in
    ruins,—
Used to be mightily pleased with the glimmering light of
    the mussels
Spread out in beautiful order; and even the eye of the
    critic
Used by the sight of my corals and potter's ore to be
    dazzled.
So in my parlor, too, they would always admire the
    painting,
Where in a garden are gaily dressed ladies and gentlemen
    walking,
And with their taper fingers are plucking and holding the
    flowers.
But who would look at it now! In sooth, so great my
    vexation
Scarcely I venture abroad. All now must be other and
    tasteful,
So they call it; and white are the laths and benches of
    woodwork;
Everything simple and smooth; no carving longer or
    gilding
Can be endured, and the woods from abroad are of all the
    most costly.
Well, I, too, should be glad could I get for myself some-
    thing novel;
Glad to keep up with the times, and be changing my fur-
    niture often;
Yet must we all be afraid of touching the veriest trifle.
For who among us has means for paying the work-people's
    wages?
Lately I had an idea of giving the Archangel Michael,
Making the sign of my shop, another fresh coating of
    gilding,
And to the terrible dragon about his feet that is winding;
But I e'en let him stay browned as he is: I dreaded the
    charges.''

EUTERPE
Mother and Son

Thus entertaining themselves, the men sat talking. The
  mother

Went meanwhile to look for her son in front of the
  dwelling,

First on the settle of stone, whereon 'twas his wont to be
  seated.

When she perceived him not there, she went farther to
  look in the stable,

If he were caring perhaps for his noble horses, the
  stallions,

Which he as colts had bought, and whose care he intrusted
  to no one.

And by the servant she there was told: He is gone to the
  garden.

Then with a nimble step she traversed the long, double
  court-yards,

Leaving the stables behind, and the well-builded barns, too,
  behind her;

Entered the garden, that far as the walls of the city
  extended;

Walked through its length, rejoiced as she went in every
  thing growing;

Set upright the supports on which were resting the
  branches

Heavily laden with apples, and burdening boughs of the
  pear-tree.

Next some caterpillars removed from a stout, swelling
  cabbage;

For an industrious woman allows no step to be wasted.

Thus was she come at last to the end of the far-reaching
  garden,

Where stood the arbor embowered in woodbine; nor there
  did she find him,

More than she had hitherto in all her search through the
  garden.

But the wicket was standing ajar, which out of the arbor,
Once by particular favor, had been through the walls of
    the city
Cut by a grandsire of hers, the worshipful burgomaster.
So the now dried-up moat she next crossed over with
    comfort,
Where, by the side of the road, direct the well-fenced vine-
    yard,
Rose with a steep ascent, its slope exposed to the sunshine.
Up this also she went, and with pleasure as she was
    ascending
Marked the wealth of the clusters, that scarce by their
    leafage were hidden.
Shady and covered the way through the lofty middlemost
    alley,
Which upon steps that were made of unhewn blocks you
    ascended.
There were the Muscatel, and there were the Chasselas
    hanging
Side by side, of unusual size and colored with purple,
All set out with the purpose of decking the visitor's table;
While with single vine-stocks the rest of the hillside was
    covered,
Bearing inferior clusters, from which the delicate wine
    comes.
Thus up the slopes she went, enjoying already the vintage,
And that festive day on which the whole country, rejoicing,
Picks and tramples the grapes, and gathers the must into
    vessels:
Fireworks, when it is evening, from every direction and
    corner
Crackle and blaze, and so the fairest of harvests is honored.
But more uneasy she went, her son after twice or thrice
    calling,
And no answer receiving, except from the talkative echo,
That with many repeats rang back from the towers of the
    city.

Strange it was for her to seek him; he never had gone to
　　a distance
That he told her not first, to spare his affectionate mother
Every anxious thought, and fear that aught ill had befallen.
Still did she constantly hope that, if further she went, she
　　should find him;
For the two doors of the vineyard, the lower as well as
　　the upper,
Both were alike standing open. So now she entered the
　　corn-field,
That with its broad expanse the ridge of the hill covered over.
Still was the ground that she walked on her own; and the
　　crops she rejoiced in,—
All of them still were hers, and hers was the proud-waving
　　grain, too,
Over the whole broad field in golden strength that was
　　stirring.
Keeping the ridgeway, the footpath, between the fields she
　　went onward,
Having the lofty pear-tree in view, which stood on the
　　summit,
And was the boundary-mark of the fields that belonged to
　　her dwelling.
Who might have planted it, none could know, but visible
　　was it
Far and wide through the country; the fruit of the pear-
　　tree was famous.
'Neath it the reapers were wont to enjoy their meal at the
　　noon-day,
And the shepherds were used to tend their flocks in its
　　shadow.
Benches of unhewn stones and of turf they found set
　　about it.
And she had not been mistaken, for there sat her Hermann,
　　and rested,—
Sat with his head on his hand, and seemed to be viewing
　　the landscape

That to the mountains lay: his back was turned to his
    mother.
Toward him softly she crept, and lightly touched on the
    shoulder;
Quick he turned himself round; there were tears in his
    eyes as he met her.

  "Mother, how hast thou surprised me!" he said in con-
    fusion; and quickly
Wiped the high-spirited youth his tears away. But the
    mother,
"What! do I find thee weeping, my son?" exclaimed in
    amazement.
"Nay, that is not like thyself: I never before have so seen
    thee!
Tell me, what burdens thy heart? what drives thee here,
    to be sitting
Under the pear-tree alone? These tears in thine eyes, what
    has brought them?"

  Then, collecting himself, the excellent youth made her
    answer:
"Truly no heart can that man have in his bosom of iron,
Who is insensible now to the needs of this emigrant people;
He has no brains in his head, who not for his personal
    safety,
Not for his fatherland's weal, in days like the present is
    anxious.
Deeply my heart had been touched by the sights and sounds
    of the morning;
Then I went forth and beheld the broad and glorious land-
    scape
Spreading its fertile slopes in every direction about us,
Saw the golden grain inclining itself to the reapers,
And the promise of well-filled barns from the plentiful har-
    vest.
But, alas, how near is the foe! The Rhine with its waters

LUDWIG RICHTER

MOTHER AND SON

Guards us, indeed; but, ah, what now are rivers and moun-
    tains
'Gainst that terrible people that onward bears like a
    tempest!
For they summon their youths from every quarter together,
Call up their old men too, and press with violence forward.
Death cannot frighten the crowd: one multitude follows
    another.
And shall a German dare to linger behind in his homestead?
Hopes he perhaps to escape the everywhere threatened
    evil?
Nay, dear mother, I tell thee, today has made me regretful
That I was lately exempt, when out of our townsmen were
    chosen
Those who should serve in the army.   An only son I am truly,
Also our business is great, and the charge of our household
    is weighty.
Yet were it better, I deem, in the front to offer resistance
There on the border, than here to await disaster and
    bondage.
So has my spirit declared, and deep in my innermost bosom
Courage and longing have now been aroused to live for my
    country,
Yea, and to die, presenting to others a worthy example.
If but the strength of Germany's youth were banded to-
    gether
There on the frontier, resolved that it never would yield to
    the stranger,
Ah, he should not on our glorious soil be setting his foot-
    steps,
Neither consuming before our eyes the fruit of our labor,
Ruling our men, and making his prey of our wives and our
    daughters.
Hark to me, mother: for I in the depths of my heart am
    determined
Quickly to do, and at once, what appears to me right and
    in reason;

For he chooses not always the best who longest considers.
Hearken, I shall not again return to the house; but directly
Go from this spot to the city, and there present to the
 soldiers
This right arm and this heart, to be spent in the father-
 land's service.
Then let my father say if there be no feeling of honor
Dwelling within my breast, nor a wish to raise myself
 higher.''

Then with significant words spoke the good and intelli-
 gent mother,
While from her eyes the quick-starting tears were silently
 falling:
'' Son, what change has come o'er thee today, and over thy
 temper,
That thou speakest no more, as thou yesterday didst, and
 hast always,
Open and free, to thy mother, and tellest exactly thy wishes?
Any one else, had he heard thee thus speak, would in sooth
 have commended,
And this decision of thine would have highly approved as
 most noble,
Being misled by thy tone and by thy significant language.
Yet have I nothing but censure to speak; for better I know
 thee.
Thou concealest thy heart, and thy thoughts are not such
 as thou tellest.
Well do I know that it is not the drum, not the trumpet
 that calls thee:
Neither in uniform wouldst thou figure in sight of the
 maidens;
Since, for all thou art honest and brave, it is thy vocation
Here in quiet to care for the farm and provide for the
 household.
Tell me honestly, therefore, what goads thee to such a
 decision?''

Earnestly answered the son: " Nay, thou art mistaken, dear mother:
One day is not like another. The youth matures into manhood:
Better in stillness oft ripening to deeds than when in the tumult
Wildering and wild of existence, that many a youth has corrupted.
And, for as still as I am and was always, there yet in my bosom
Has such a heart been shaped as abhors all wrong and injustice;
And I have learned aright between worldly things to distinguish.
Arm and foot, besides, have been mightily strengthened by labor.
All this, I feel, is true: I dare with boldness maintain it.
Yet dost thou blame me with reason, O mother! for thou hast surprised me
Using a language half truthful and half that of dissimulation.
For, let me honestly own,—it is not the near danger that calls me
Forth from my father's house; nor is it the lofty ambition
Helpful to be to my country, and terrible unto the foeman.
They were but words that I spoke: they only were meant for concealing
Those emotions from thee with which my heart is distracted;
And so leave me, O mother! for, since the wishes are fruitless
Which in my bosom I cherish, my life must go fruitlessly over.
For, as I know, he injures himself who is singly devoted,
When for the common cause the whole are not working together."

"Hesitate not," replied thereupon the intelligent
    mother,
"Every thing to relate me, the smallest as well as the
    greatest.
Men will always be hasty, their thoughts to extremes ever
    running:
Easily out of their course the hasty are turned by a hin-
    drance.
Whereas a woman is clever in thinking of means, and will
    venture
E'en on a roundabout way, adroitly to compass her object.
Let me know every thing, then; say wherefore so greatly
    excited
As I ne'er saw thee before, why thy blood is coursing so
    hotly,
Wherefore, against thy will, tears are filling thine eyes to
    o'erflowing."

Then he abandoned himself, the poor boy, to his sorrow,
    and weeping,
Weeping aloud on his kind mother's breast, he brokenly
    answered:
"Truly my father's words today have wounded me
    sorely,—
Words which I have not deserved; not today, nor at any
    time have I:
For it was early my greatest delight to honor my parents.
No one knew more, so I deemed, or was wiser than those
    who begot me,
And had with strictness ruled throughout the dark season
    of childhood.
Many the things, in truth, I with patience endured from
    my playmates,
When the good-will that I bore them they often requited
    with malice.
Often I suffered their flings and their blows to pass un-
    resented;

But if they ventured to ridicule father, when he of a Sunday
Home from Church would come, with his solemn and dignified bearing;
If they made fun of his cap-string, or laughed at the flowers of the wrapper
He with such stateliness wore, which was given away but this morning —
Threateningly doubled my fist in an instant; with furious passion
Fell I upon them, and struck out and hit, assailing them blindly,
Seeing not where. They howled as the blood gushed out from their noses:
Scarcely they made their escape from my passionate kicking and beating.
Then, as I older grew, I had much to endure from my father;
Violent words he oft vented on me, instead of on others,
When, at the board's last session, the council had roused his displeasure,
And I was made to atone for the quarrels and wiles of his colleagues.
Thou has pitied me often thyself; for much did I suffer,
Ever remembering with cordial respect the kindness of parents,
Solely intent on increasing for us their goods and possessions,
Much denying themselves in order to save for their children.
But, alas! saving alone, for the sake of a tardy enjoyment,—
That is not happiness: pile upon pile, and acre on acre,
Make us not happy, no matter how fair our estates may be rounded.
For the father grows old, and with him will grow old the children,
Losing the joy of the day, and bearing the care of tomorrow.

Look thou below, and see how before us in glory are lying,
Fair and abundant, the corn-fields; beneath them, the vine-
    yard and garden;
Yonder the stables and barns; our beautiful line of pos-
    sessions.
But when I look at the dwelling behind, where up in the
    gable
We can distinguish the window that marks my room in the
    attic;
When I look back, and remember how many a night from
    that window
I for the moon have watched; for the sun, how many a
    morning!
When the healthful sleep of a few short hours sufficed me,—
Ah, so lonely they seem to me then, the chamber and court-
    yard,
Garden and glorious field, away o'er the hill that is
    stretching;
All so desert before me lie: 'tis the wife that is wanting.''

Thereupon spoke the good mother, and thus with intelli-
    gence answered:
'' Son, not greater thy wish to bring thee a bride to thy
    chamber,
That thou mayst find thy nights a beautiful part of ex-
    istence,
And that the work of the day may gain independence and
    freedom,
Than is thy father's wish too, and thy mother's. We
    always have counselled,—
Yea, we have even insisted,— that thou shouldst elect thee
    a maiden.
But I was ever aware, and now my heart gives me assurance,
That till the hour appointed is come, and the maiden ap-
    pointed
Shall with the hour appear, the choice will be left for the
    future,

While more strong than all else will be fear of grasping the
    wrong one.
If I may say it, my son, I believe thou already hast chosen;
For thy heart has been touched, and been made more than
    wontedly tender.
Speak it out honestly, then; for my soul has told me before-
    hand:
That same maiden it is, the exile, whom thou hast elected.''

    '' Thou hast said, mother!'' the son thereupon with
    eagerness answered.
'' Yes, it is she; and if I today as my bride do not bring
    her
Home to our dwelling, she from me will go, perhaps vanish
    for ever,
Lost in the war's confusion and sad movings hither and
    thither.
Mother, forever in vain would then our abundant pos-
    sessions
Prosper before me, and seasons to come be in vain to me
    fruitful.
Yea, I should hold in aversion the wonted house and the
    garden:
Even my mother's love, alas! would not comfort my
    sorrow.
Every tie, so I feel in my heart, by love is unloosened
Soon as she fastens her own; and not the maid is it only
Leaves behind father and mother, to follow the man she
    has chosen.
He too, the youth, no longer knows aught of mother and
    father,
When he the maiden, his only beloved, sees vanishing from
    him.
Suffer me, then, to go hence wherever despair shall impel
    me:
Since by my father himself the decisive words have been
    spoken;

Since his house can no longer be mine if he shut out the
  maiden,
Her whom alone as my bride I desire to bring to our
  dwelling.''

Thereupon quickly made answer the good and intelligent
  mother:
'' How like to rocks, forsooth, two men will stand facing
  each other!
Proud and not to be moved, will neither draw near to his
  fellow;
Neither will stir his tongue to utter the first word of kind-
  ness.
Therefore I tell thee, my son, a hope yet lives in my bosom,
So she be honest and good, thy father will let thee espouse
  her,
Even though poor, and against a poor girl so decisive his
  sentence.
Many a thing he is wont to speak out in his violent fashion
Which he yet never performs; and so what he denies will
  consent to.
Yet he requires a kindly word, and is right to require it:
He is the father! Besides, we know that his wrath after
  dinner,—
When he most hastily speaks, and questions all others'
  opinions,—
Signifies naught; the full force of his violent will is excited
Then by the wine, which lets him not heed the language
  of others;
None but himself does he see and feel. But now is come
  evening,
Talk upon various subjects has passed between him and
  his neighbors.
Gentle, he is; I am sure, now his little excitement is over,
And he can feel how unjust his passion has made him to
  others.
Come, let us venture at once: success is alone to the valiant!

Further we need the friends, still sitting together there
  with him;
And in especial the worthy pastor will give us assistance.''

Thus she hastily spoke, and up from the stone then
  arising,
Drew from his seat her son, who willingly followed. In
  silence
Both descended the hill, their important purpose revolving.

POLYHYMNIA

THE CITIZEN OF THE WORLD

There the three men, however, still sat conversing
  together,
With mine host of the Lion, the village doctor, and pastor;
And their talk was still on the same unvarying subject,
Turning it this way and that, and viewing from every
  direction.
But with his sober judgment the excellent pastor made
  answer:
'' Here will I not contradict you. I know that man should
  be always
Striving for that which is better; indeed, as we see, he is
  reaching
Always after the higher, at least some novelty craving.
But be careful ye go not too far, for with this disposition
Nature has given us pleasure in holding to what is familiar;
Taught us in that to delight to which we have long been
  accustomed.
Every condition is good that is founded on reason and
  nature.
Many are man's desires, yet little it is that he needeth;
Seeing the days are short and mortal destiny bounded.
Ne'er would I censure the man whom a restless activity
  urges,

Bold and industrious, over all pathways of land and of
  ocean,
Ever untiring to roam; who takes delight in the riches,
Heaping in generous abundance about himself and his
  children.
Yet not unprized by me is the quiet citizen also,
Making the noiseless round of his own inherited acres,
Tilling the ground as the ever-returning seasons command
  him.
Not with every year is the soil transfigured about him;
Not in haste does the tree stretch forth, as soon as 'tis
  planted,
Full-grown arms toward heaven and decked with plente-
  ous blossoms.
No: man has need of patience, and needful to him are also
Calmness and clearness of mind, and a pure and right
  understanding.
Few are the seeds he intrusts to earth's all-nourishing
  bosom;
Few are the creatures he knows how to raise and bring to
  perfection.
Centred are all his thoughts alone on that which is useful.
Happy to whom by nature a mind of such temper is given,
For he supports us all! And hail, to the man whose
  abode is
Where in a town the country pursuits with the city are
  blended.
On him lies not the pressure that painfully hampers the
  farmer,
Nor is he carried away by the greedy ambition of cities;
Where they of scanty possessions too often are given to
  aping,
Wives and daughters especially, those who are higher and
  richer.
Blessed be therefore thy son in his life of quiet employment;
Blessed the wife, of like mind with himself, whom he one
  day shall choose him.''

Thus he spoke; and scarce had he ended when entered
the mother,
Holding her son by the hand, and so led him up to her
husband.
" Father," she said, " how oft when we two have been
chatting together,
Have we rejoiced in the thought of Hermann's future
espousal,
When he should bring his bride to be the light of our
dwelling!
Over and over again the matter we pondered: this maiden
Fixing upon for him first, and then that, with the gossip
of parents.
But that day is now come; and Heaven at last has the
maiden
Brought to him hither, and shown him; and now his heart
has decided.
Said we not always then he should have his own choice in
the matter?
Was it not just now thy wish that he might with lively
affection
Feel himself drawn to some maiden? The hour is come
that we hoped for.
Yes; he has felt and has chosen and come to a manly
decision.
That same maiden it is that met him this morning, the
stranger:
Say he may have her, or else, as he swears, his life shall
be single."

" Give her me, father," so added the son: " my heart has
elected
Clear and sure; she will be to you both the noblest of
daughters."

But the father was silent. Then hastily rose the good
pastor,

Took up the word and said: "The moment alone is
    decisive;
Fixes the life of man, and his future destiny settles.
After long taking of counsel, yet only the work of a moment
Every decision must be; and the wise alone seizes the right
    one.
Dangerous always it is comparing the one with the other
When we are making our choice, and so confusing our
    feelings.
Hermann is pure. From childhood up I have known him,
    and never
E'en as a boy was he wont to be reaching for this and the
    other:
What he desired was best for him too, and he held to it firmly.
Be not surprised and alarmed that now has appeared of a
    sudden,
What thou hast wished for so long. It is true that the
    present appearance
Bears not the form of the wish, exactly as thou hadst con-
    ceived it:
For our wishes oft hide from ourselves the object we wish
    for;
Gifts come down from above in the shapes appointed by
    Heaven.
Therefore misjudge not the maiden who now of thy dearly
    beloved,
Good and intelligent son has been first to touch the affec-
    tions:
Happy to whom at once his first love's hand shall be given,
And in whose heart no tenderest wish must secretly
    languish.
Yes: his whole bearing assures me that now his fate is
    decided.
Genuine love matures in a moment the youth into manhood;
He is not easily moved; and I fear that if this be refused him,
Sadly his years will go by, those years that should be the
    fairest.''

Straightway then in a thoughtful tone the doctor made
answer,
On whose tongue for a long time past the words had been
trembling:
" Pray let us here as before pursue the safe middle course
only.
Make haste slowly: that was Augustus the emperor's motto.
Willingly I myself place at my well-beloved neighbor's
disposal,
Ready to do him what service I can with my poor under-
standing.
Youth most especially stands in need of some one to guide it.
Let me therefore go forth that I may examine the maiden,
And may question the people among whom she lives and
who know her.
Me 'tis not easy to cheat: I know how words should be
valued."

Straightway the son broke in, and with wingèd words
made he answer:
" Do so, neighbor, and go and make thine inquiries; but
with thee
I should be glad if our minister here were joined in the
errand:
Two such excellent men would be irreproachable judges.
O my father! believe me, she's none of those wandering
maidens,
Not one of those who stroll through the land in search
of adventure,
And who seek to ensnare inexperienced youth in their
meshes.
No: the hard fortunes of war, that universal destroyer,
Which is convulsing the earth and has hurled from its deep
foundations
Many a structure already, have sent the poor girl into exile.
Are not now men of high birth, the most noble, in misery
roaming?

Princes fly in disguise and kings are in banishment living.
So alas! also is she, the best among all of her sisters,
Driven an exile from home; yet, her personal sorrows
    forgetting,
She is devoted to others; herself without help, she is
    helpful.
Great is the want and the suffering over the earth that are
    spreading:
Shall not some happiness, too, be begotten of all this
    affliction,
And shall not I in the arms of my wife, my trusted com-
    panion,
Look back with joy to the war, as do ye to the great con-
    flagration?''

  Outspoke the father then in a tone of decision, and
    answered:
'' Strangely thy tongue has been loosened, my son, which
    many a year past
Seemed to have stuck in thy mouth, and only to move on
    compulsion!
I must experience today, it would seem, what threatens all
    fathers,
That the son's headstrong will the mother with readiness
    favors,
Showing too easy indulgence; and every neighbor sides
    with them
When there is aught to be carried against the father and
    husband.
But I will not oppose you, thus banded together: how could
    I?
For I already perceive here tears and defiance before-
    hand.
Go ye therefore, inquire, in God's name, bring me the
    daughter.
But if not so, then the boy is to think no more of the
    maiden.''

Thus the father. The son cried out with joyful demeanor,
" Ere it is evening the noblest of daughters shall hither be
    brought you,
Such as no man with sound sense in his breast can fail to
    be pleased with.
Happy, I venture to hope, will be also the excellent maiden.
Yes; she will ever be grateful for having had father and
    mother
Given once more in you, and such as a child most delights in.
Now I will tarry no longer, but straightway harness the
    horses,
Drive forth our friends at once on the footsteps of my
    beloved,
Leaving them then to act for themselves, as their wisdom
    shall dictate,
Guide myself wholly, I promise, according to what they
    determine,
And, until I may call her my own, ne'er look on the
    maiden.''
Thus he went forth: the others meanwhile remained in
    discussion,
Rapid and earnest, considering deeply their great under-
    taking.

Hermann hasted straightway to the stable, where quietly
    standing
Found he the spirited stallions, the clean oats quickly de-
    vouring,
And the well-dried hay that was cut from the richest of
    meadows.
On them without delay the shining bits he adjusted,
Hastily drew the straps through the buckles of beautiful
    plating,
Firmly fastened then the long broad reins, and the horses
Led without to the court-yard, whither the willing assistant
Had with ease, by the pole, already drawn forward the
    carriage.

Next to the whipple-tree they with care by the neatly kept
traces
Joined the impetuous strength of the freely travelling
horses.
Whip in hand took Hermann his seat and drove under the
doorway.
Soon as the friends straightway their commodious places
had taken,
Quickly the carriage rolled off, and left the pavement behind it,
Left behind it the walls of the' town and the fresh-whitened
towers.
Thus drove Hermann on till he came to the well-known
causeway.
Rapidly, loitering nowhere, but hastening up hill and down
hill.
But as he now before him perceived the spire of the
village,
And no longer remote the garden-girt houses were lying,
Then in himself he thought that here he would rein up the
horses.

Under the solemn shade of lofty linden-trees lying,
Which for centuries past upon this spot had been rooted,
Spread in front of the village a broad and grass-covered
common,
Favorite place of resort for the peasants and neighboring
townsfolk.
Here, at the foot of the trees, sunk deep in the ground was
a well-spring;
When you descended the steps, stone benches you found at
the bottom,
Stationed about the spring, whose pure, living waters were
bubbling
Ceaselessly forth, hemmed in by low walls for convenience
of drawing.

Hermann resolved that here he would halt, with his horses
    and carriage,
Under the shade of the trees. He did so, and said to the
    others:
" Here alight, my friends, and go your ways to discover
Whether the maiden in truth be worthy the hand that I offer.
That she is so, I believe; naught new or strange will ye
    tell me.
Had I to act for myself, I should go with speed to the
    village,
Where a few words from the maiden's own lips should
    determine my fortune.
Ye will with readiness single her out from all of the others,
For there can scarcely be one that to her may be likened
    in bearing.
But I will give you, besides, her modest attire for a token:
Mark, then, the stomacher's scarlet, that sets off the arch
    of her bosom,
Prettily laced, and the bodice of black fitting close to her
    figure;
Neatly the edge of her kerchief is plaited into a ruffle,
Which with a simple grace her chin's rounded outline
    encircles;
Freely and lightly rises above it the head's dainty oval;
And her luxuriant hair over silver bodkins is braided;
Down from under her bodice, the full, blue petticoat falling,
Wraps itself, when she is walking, about her neatly shaped
    ankles.
Yet one thing will I say, and would make it my earnest
    petition,—
Speak not yourselves with the maiden, nor let your intent
    be discovered;
Rather inquire of others, and hearken to what they may tell
    you.
When ye have tidings enough to satisfy father and mother,
Then return to me here, and we will consider what further.
So did I plan it all out in my mind while driving you hither."

Thus he spoke. The friends thereupon went their way
    to the village,
Where, in the houses and gardens and barns, the people
    were swarming;
Wagons on wagons stood crowded together along the broad
    highway.
Men for the harnessed horses and lowing cattle were
    caring,
While the women were busy in drying their clothes on the
    hedges,
And in the running brook the children were merrily splash-
    ing.
Making their way through the pressure of wagons, of people
    and cattle,
Went the commissioned spies, and to right and to left looked
    about them,
If they a figure might see that answered the maiden's
    description;
But not one of them all appeared the beautiful damsel.
Denser soon grew the press. A contest arose round the
    wagons
'Mongst the threatening men, wherein blended the cries of
    the women.
Rapidly then to the spot, and with dignified step, came an
    elder,
Joined the clamoring group, and straightway the uproar
    was silenced,
As he commanded peace, and rebuked with a fatherly
    sternness.
"Has, then, misfortune," he cried, "not yet so bound us
    together,
That we have finally learned to bear and forbear one
    another,
Though each one, it may be, do not measure his share of the
    labor?
He that is happy, forsooth, is contentious! Will sufferings
    never

LUDWIG RICHTER

THE EMIGRANTS IN THE VILLAGE

Teach you to cease from your brawls of old between brother
  and brother?
Grudge not one to another a place on the soil of the
  stranger;
Rather divide what ye have, as yourselves ye would hope to
  find mercy.''

  Thus spoke the man and all became silent: restored to
    good humor,
Peaceably then the people arranged their cattle and
  wagons.
But when the clergyman now had heard what was said by
  the stranger,
And had the steadfast mind of the foreign justice dis-
  covered,
He to the man drew near and with words of meaning ad-
  dressed him:
'' True it is, father, that when in prosperity people are
  living,
Feeding themselves from the earth, which far and wide
  opens her bosom,
And in the years and months renews the coveted bless-
  ings,—
All goes on of itself, and each himself deems the wisest,
Deems the best, and so they continue abiding together,
He of greatest intelligence ranking no higher than others;
All that occurs, as if of itself, going quietly forward.
But let disaster unsettle the usual course of existence,
Tear down the buildings about us, lay waste the crops and
  the garden,
Banish the husband and wife from their old, familiar-grown
  dwelling,
Drive them to wander abroad through nights and days of
  privation,—
Then, ah then! we look round us to see what man is the
  wisest,
And no longer in vain his glorious words will be spoken.

Tell me, art thou not judge among this fugitive people,
Father, who thus in an instant canst bid their passions be
 quiet?
Thou dost appear today as one of those earliest leaders,
Who through deserts and wanderings guided the emigrant
 nations.
Yea, I could even believe I were speaking with Joshua or
 Moses.''

Then with serious look the magistrate answered him,
 saying:
'' Truly our times might well be compared with all others
 in strangeness,
Which are in history mentioned, profane or sacred tra-
 dition;
For who has yesterday lived and today in times like the
 present,
He has already lived years, events are so crowded together.
If I look back but a little, it seems that my head must be
 hoary
Under the burden of years, and yet my strength is still
 active.
Well may we of this day compare ourselves unto that
 people
Who, from the burning bush, beheld in the hour of their
 danger
God the Lord: we also in cloud and in fire have beheld
 Him.''

Seeing the priest was inclined to speak yet more with
 the stranger,
And was desirous of learning his story and that of his
 people,
Privately into his ear his companion hastily whispered:
'' Talk with the magistrate further, and lead him to speak
 of the maiden.
I, however, will wander in search, and as soon as I find her,

Come and report to thee here.'' The minister nodded,
assenting;
And through the gardens, hedges, and barns, went the spy
on his errand.

CLIO

The Age

Now when the foreign judge had been by the minister
questioned
As to his people's distress, and how long their exile had
lasted,
Thus made answer the man: '' Of no recent date are our
sorrows;
Since of the gathering bitter of years our people have
drunken,—
Bitterness all the more dreadful because such fair hope
had been blighted.
Who will pretend to deny that his heart swelled high in his
bosom,
And that his freer breast with purer pulses was beating,
When we beheld the new sun arise in his earliest splendor,
When of the rights of men we heard, which to all should
be common,
Were of a righteous equality told, and inspiriting freedom?
Every one hoped that then he should live his own life, and
the fetters,
Binding the various lands, appeared their hold to be
loosing,—
Fetters that had in the hand of sloth been held and self-
seeking.
Looked not the eyes of all nations, throughout that calam-
itous season,
Toward the world's capital city, for so it had long been
considered,
And of that glorious title was now, more than ever,
deserving?

Were not the names of those men who first delivered the
　　message,
Names to compare with the highest that under the heavens
　　are spoken?
Did not, in every man, grow courage and spirit and lan-
　　guage?
And, as neighbors, we, first of all, were zealously kindled.
Thereupon followed the war, and armèd bodies of French-
　　men
Pressed to us nearer; yet nothing but friendship they
　　seemed to be bringing;
Ay, and they brought it too; for exalted the spirit within
　　them:
They with rejoicing the festive trees of liberty planted,
Promising every man what was his own, and to each his
　　own ruling.
High beat the heart of the youths, and even the aged were
　　joyful;
Gaily the dance began about the newly raised standard.
Thus had they speedily won, these overmastering French-
　　men,
First the spirits of men by the fire and dash of their
　　bearing,
Then the hearts of the women with irresistible graces.
Even the pressure of hungry war seemed to weigh on us
　　lightly,
So before our vision did hope hang over the future,
Luring our eyes abroad into newly opening pathways.
Oh, how joyful the time when with her beloved the maiden
Whirls in the dance, the longed-for day of their union
　　awaiting!
But more glorious that day on which to our vision the
　　highest
Heart of man can conceive seemed near and attainable to
　　us.
Loosened was every tongue, and men — the aged, the strip-
　　ling —

Spoke aloud in words that were full of high feeling and wisdom.

Soon, however, the sky was o'ercast. A corrupt generation
Fought for the right of dominion, unworthy the good to establish;
So that they slew one another, their new-made neighbors and brothers
Held in subjection, and then sent the self-seeking masses against us.
Chiefs committed excesses and wholesale plunder upon us,
While those lower plundered and rioted down to the lowest:
Every one seemed but to care that something be left for the morrow.
Great past endurance the need, and daily grew the oppression:
They were the lords of the day; there was none to hear our complaining.
Then fell trouble and rage upon even the quietest spirit.
One thought only had all, and swore for their wrongs to have vengeance,
And for the bitter loss of their hope thus doubly deluded.
Presently Fortune turned and declared on the side of the German,
And with hurried marches the French retreated before us.
Ah! then as never before did we feel the sad fortunes of warfare:
He that is victor is great and good,— or at least he appears so,—
And he, as one of his own, will spare the man he has conquered,
Him whose service he daily needs, and whose property uses.
But no law the fugitive knows, save of self-preservation,
And, with a reckless greed, consumes all the possessions about him;
Then are his passions also inflamed: the despair that is in him

Out of his heart breaks forth, and takes shape in criminal
    action.
Nothing is further held sacred; but all is for plunder. His
    craving
Turns in fury on woman, and pleasure is changed into
    horror.
Death he sees everywhere round him, and madly enjoys his
    last moments,
Taking delight in blood, in the shriekings of anguish ex-
    ulting.
Thereupon fiercely arose in our men the stern resolution
What had been lost to avenge, and defend what'er was
    remaining.
Every man sprang to his arms, by the flight of the foeman
    encouraged,
And by his blanching cheeks, and his timorous, wavering
    glances.
Ceaselessly now rang out the clanging peal of the tocsin.
Thought of no danger to come restrained their furious
    anger.
Quick into weapons of war the husbandman's peaceful
    utensils
All were converted; dripped with blood the scythe and the
    ploughshare.
Quarter was shown to none: the enemy fell without
    mercy.
Fury everywhere raged and the cowardly cunning of weak-
    ness.
Ne'er may I men so carried away by injurious passion
See again! the sight of the raging wild beast would be
    better.
Let not man prattle of freedom, as if himself he could
    govern!
Soon as the barriers are torn away, then all of the evil
Seems let loose, that by law had been driven deep back into
    corners.''

" Excellent man!'' thereupon with emphasis answered
    the pastor:
" Though thou misjudgest mankind, yet can I not censure
    thee for it.
Evil enough, I confess, thou hast had to endure from man's
    passions.
Yet wouldst thou look behind over this calamitous season,
Thou wouldst acknowledge thyself how much good thou
    also hast witnessed.
How many excellent things that would in the heart have
    lain hidden,
Had not danger aroused them, and did not necessity's
    pressure
Bring forth the angel in man, and make him a god of
    deliv'rance.''

Thereupon answered and said the reverend magistrate,
    smiling:
" There thou remindest me aptly of how we console the
    poor fellow,
After his house has been burned, by recounting the gold
    and the silver
Melted and scattered abroad in the rubbish, that still is
    remaining.
Little enough, it is true; but even that little is precious.
Then will the poor wretch after it dig and rejoice if he
    find it.
Thus I likewise with happier thoughts will gratefully turn
    me
Toward the few beautiful deeds of which I preserve the
    remembrance.
Yes, I will not deny, I have seen old quarrels forgotten,
Ill to avert from the state; I also have witnessed how
    friendship,
Love of parent and child, can impossibilities venture;
Seen how the stripling at once matured into man; how
    the aged

Grew again young; and even the child into youth was
    developed,
Yea, and the weaker sex too, as we are accustomed to call it,
Showed itself brave and strong and ready for every
    emergence.
Foremost among them all, one beautiful deed let me
    mention,
Bravely performed by the hand of a girl, an excellent
    maiden,
Who, with those younger than she, had been left in charge
    of a farmhouse,
Since there, also, the men had marched against the invader.
Suddenly fell on the house a fugitive band of marauders,
Eager for booty, who crowded straightway to the room of
    the women.
There they beheld the beautiful form of the fully grown
    maiden,
Looked on the charming young girls, who rather might still
    be called children.
Savage desire possessed them; at once with merciless
    passion
They that trembling band assailed and the high-hearted
    maiden.
But she had snatched in an instant the sword of one from
    its scabbard,
Felled him with might to the ground, and stretched him
    bleeding before her.
Then with vigorous strokes she bravely delivered the
    maidens,
Smiting yet four of the robbers; who saved themselves only
    by flying.
Then she bolted the gates, and, armed, awaited assistance.''

Now when this praise the minister heard bestowed on
    the maiden,
Rose straightway for his friend a feeling of hope in his
    bosom,

And he had opened his lips to inquire what further befell
    her,
If on this mournful flight she now with her people were
    present;
When with a hasty step the village doctor approached
    them,
Twitched the clergyman's coat, and said in his ear in a
    whisper:
"I have discovered the maiden at last among several
    hundreds;
By the description I knew her, so come, let thine own eyes
    behold her!
Bring too the magistrate with thee, that so we may hear
    him yet further."
But as they turned to go, the justice was summoned to leave
    them,
Sent for by some of his people by whom his counsel was
    needed.
Straightway the preacher, however, the lead of the doctor
    had followed
Up to a gap in the fence where his finger he meaningly
    pointed.
"Seest thou the maiden?" he said: "she has made some
    clothes for the baby
Out of the well-known chintz,—I distinguish it plainly; and
    further
There are the covers of blue that Hermann gave in his
    bundle.
Well and quickly, forsooth, she has turned to advantage the
    presents.
Evident tokens are these, and all else answers well the
    description.
Mark how the stomacher's scarlet sets off the arch of her
    bosom,
Prettily laced, and the bodice of black fits close to her
    figure;
Neatly the edge of her kerchief is plaited into a ruffle,

Which, with a simple grace, her chin's rounded outline
    encircles;
Freely and lightly rises above it the head's dainty oval,
And her luxuriant hair over silver bodkins is braided.
Now she is sitting, yet still we behold her majestical
    stature,
And the blue petticoat's ample plaits, that down from her
    bosom
Hangs in abundant folds about her neatly shaped ankles,
She without question it is; come, therefore, and let us
    discover
Whether she honest and virtuous be, a housewifely maiden.''

    Then, as the seated figure he studied, the pastor made
        answer:
'' Truly, I find it no wonder that she so enchanted the
    stripling,
Since, to a man's experienced eye, she seems lacking in
    nothing.
Happy to whom mother Nature a shape harmonious has
    given!
Such will always commend him, and he can be nowhere a
    stranger.
All approach with delight, and all are delighted to linger,
If to the outward shape correspond but a courteous spirit.
I can assure thee, in her the youth has found him a maiden,
Who, in the days to come, his life shall gloriously brighten,
Standing with womanly strength in every necessity by him.
Surely the soul must be pure that inhabits a body so perfect,
And of a happy old age such vigorous youth is the promise.''

    Thereupon answered and said the doctor in language of
        caution:
'' Often appearances cheat; I like not to trust to externals.
For I have oft seen put to the test the truth of the proverb:
Till thou a bushel of salt with a new acquaintance hast
    eaten,

LUDWIG RICHTER

THE PARSON AND THE APOTHECARY WATCH DOROTHEA

Be not too ready to trust him; for time alone renders thee
    certain
How ye shall fare with each other, and how well your
    friendship shall prosper.
Let us then rather at first make inquiries among the good
    people
By whom the maiden is known, and who can inform us
    about her.''

    '' Much I approve of thy caution,'' the preacher replied
    as he followed.
'' Not for ourselves is the suit, and 'tis delicate wooing for
    others.''

    Toward the good magistrate, then, the men directed
    their footsteps,
Who was again ascending the street in discharge of his
    duties.

    Him the judicious pastor at once addressed and with
    caution.
'' Look! we a maiden have here descried in the neighbor-
    ing garden,
Under an apple-tree sitting, and making up garments for
    children
Out of second-hand stuff that somebody doubtless has
    given;
And we were pleased with her aspect: she seems like a girl
    to be trusted.
Tell us whatever thou knowest: we ask it with honest
    intentions.''

    Soon as the magistrate nearer had come, and looked into
    the garden,
'' Her thou knowest already,'' he said; '' for when I was
    telling
Of the heroic deed performed by the hand of that maiden,

When she snatched the man's sword, and delivered herself
    and her charges,
This was the one! she is vigorous born, as thou seest by her
    stature;
Yet she is good as strong, for her aged kinsman she tended
Until the day of his death, which was finally hastened by
    sorrow
Over his city's distress, and his own endangered pos-
    sessions.
Also, with quiet submission, she bore the death of her lover,
Who a high-spirited youth, in the earliest flush of ex-
    citement,
Kindled by lofty resolve to fight for a glorious freedom,
Hurried to Paris, where early a terrible death he en-
    countered.
For as at home, so there, his foes were deceit and
    oppression.''

Thus the magistrate spoke. The others saluted and
    thanked him,
And from his purse a gold-piece the pastor drew forth;—
    for the silver
He had some hours before already in charity given,
When he in mournful groups had seen the poor fugitives
    passing;—
And to the magistrate handed it, saying: "Apportion the
    money
'Mongst thy destitute people, and God vouchsafe it an
    increase.''
But the stranger declined it, and, answering, said: " We
    have rescued
Many a dollar among us, with clothing and other pos-
    sessions,
And shall return, as I hope, ere yet our stock is exhausted.''

Then the pastor replied, and pressed the money upon
    him:

"None should be backward in giving in days like the present, and no one
Ought to refuse to accept those gifts which in kindness are offered.
None can tell how long he may hold what in peace he possesses,
None how much longer yet he shall roam through the land of the stranger,
And of his farm be deprived, and deprived of the garden that feeds him."

"Ay, to be sure!" in his bustling way interrupted the doctor:
"If I had only some money about me, ye surely should have it,
Little and big; for certainly many among you must need it.
Yet I'll not go without giving thee something to show what my will is,
Even though sadly behind my good-will must lag the performance."
Thus, as he spoke, by its straps his embroidered pocket of leather,
Where his tobacco was kept, he drew forth,—enough was now in it
Several pipes to fill,—and daintily opened, and portioned.
"Small is the gift," he added. The justice, however, made answer:
"Good tobacco can ne'er to the traveller fail to be welcome."
Then did the village doctor begin to praise his canaster.

But the clergyman drew him away, and they quitted the justice.
"Let us make haste," said the thoughtful man: "the youth's waiting in torture;
Come! let him hear, as soon as he may, the jubilant tidings."

So they hastened their steps, and came to where under
    the lindens
Hermann against the carriage was leaning. The horses
    were stamping
Wildly the turf; he held them in check, and, buried in
    musing,
Stood, into vacancy gazing before him; nor saw the two
    envoys,
Till, as they came, they called out and made to him signals
    of triumph.
E'en as far off as they then were, the doctor began to
    address him;
But they were presently nearer come and then the good
    pastor
Grasped his hand and exclaimed, interrupting the word of
    his comrade:
"Hail to thee, O young man! thy true eye and heart have
    well chosen;
Joy be to thee and the wife of thy youth; for of thee she is
    worthy.
Come then and turn us the wagon, and drive straightway
    to the village,
There the good maid to woo, and soon bring her home to
    thy dwelling."

Still, however, the young man stood, without sign of
    rejoicing,
Hearing his messenger's words, though heavenly they were
    and consoling.
Deeply he sighed as he said: "With hurrying wheels we
    came hither,
And shall be forced, perchance, to go mortified homeward
    and slowly.
For disquiet has fallen upon me since here I've been
    waiting,
Doubt and suspicion and all that can torture the heart of
    a lover.

Think ye we have but to come, and that then the maiden
   will follow
Merely because we are rich, while she is poor and an
   exile?
Poverty, too, makes proud, when it comes unmerited!
   Active
Seems she to be, and contented, and so of the world is she
   mistress.
Think ye a maiden like her, with the manners and beauty
   that she has,
Can into woman have grown, and no worthy man's love
   have attracted?
Think ye that love until now can have been shut out from
   her bosom?
Drive not thither too rashly: we might to our mortification
Have to turn softly homewards our horses' heads. For my
   fear is
That to some youth already this heart has been given;
   already
This brave hand has been clasped, has pledged faith to
   some fortunate lover.
Then with my offer, alas! I should stand in confusion before her.''

  Straightway the pastor had opened his lips to speak
   consolation,
When his companion broke in, and said in his voluble
   fashion:
'' Years ago, forsooth, unknown had been such a dilemma.
All such affairs were then conducted in regular fashion.
Soon as a bride for their son had been by the parents
   selected,
First some family friend they into their councils would
   summon,
Whom they afterward sent as a suitor to visit the
   parents
Of the elected bride. Arrayed in his finest apparel,

Soon after dinner on Sunday he sought the respectable
  burgher,
When some friendly words were exchanged upon general
  subjects,
He knowing how to direct the discourse as suited his
  purpose.
After much circumlocution he finally mentioned the
  daughter,
Praising her highly, and praising the man and the house
  that had sent him.
Persons of tact perceived his intent, and the politic envoy
Readily saw how their minds were disposed, and explained
  himself further.
Then were the offer declined, e'en the ' no ' brought not
  mortification;
But did it meet with success, the suitor was ever thereafter
Made the chief guest in the house on every festive occasion.
For, through the rest of their lives, the couple ne'er failed
  to remember
That 'twas by his experienced hand the first knot had been
  gathered.
All that, however, is changed, and, with many another good
  custom,
Quite fallen out of the fashion; for every man woos for
  himself now.
Therefore let every man hear to his face pronounced the
  refusal,
If a refusal there be, and stand shamed in the sight of the
  maiden!''

  '' Let that be as it may!'' made answer the youth, who
  had scarcely
Unto the words paid heed; but in silence had made his
  decision.
'' I will go thither myself, will myself hear my destiny
  spoken
Out of the lips of a maiden in whom I a confidence cherish

Greater than heart of man has e'er before cherished in
    woman.
Say what she will, 'twill be good and wise; of that I am
    certain.
Should I behold her never again, yet this once will I see her;
Yet this once the clear gaze of those dark eyes will
    encounter.
If I must press her ne'er to my heart, yet that neck and that
    bosom
Will I behold once more, that my arm so longs to encircle;
Once more that mouth will see, whose kiss and whose ' yes '
    would for ever
Render me happy, from which a ' no ' will for ever destroy
    me.
But ye must leave me alone. Do not wait for me here;
    but return ye
Back to my father and mother again, and give them the
    knowledge
That their son has not been deceived, that the maiden is
    worthy.
So then leave me alone! I shall follow the footpath that
    crosses
Over the hill by the pear-tree, and thence descends through
    our vineyard,
Taking a shorter way home. And oh, may I bring to our
    dwelling,
Joyful and quick my beloved! but perhaps I alone may
    come creeping
Over that path to the house, and ne'er again tread it with
    gladness.''

    Thus he spoke, and gave up the reins to the hand of the
    pastor,
Who understandingly grasped them, the foaming horses
    controlling,
Speedily mounted the carriage, and sat in the seat of the
    driver.

But thou didst hesitate, provident neighbor, and say in
   remonstrance:
"Heart and soul and spirit, my friend, I willingly trust
   thee;
But as for life and limb, they are not in the safest of
   keeping,
When the temporal reins are usurped by the hand of the
   clergy."

But thou didst laugh at his words, intelligent pastor, and
   answer:
"Sit thee down, and contentedly trust me both body and
   spirit;
For, in holding the reins, my hand grew long ago skilful,
Long has my eye been trained in making the nicest of
   turnings;
For we were practised well in driving the carriage in
   Strasburg,
When I the youthful baron accompanied thither; then
   daily
Rolled the carriage, guided by me, through the echoing
   gateway,
Out over dusty roads till we reached the meadows and
   lindens,
Steering through groups of the town's-folk beguiling the
   day there with walking."

Thereupon, half-reassured, the neighbor ascended the
   wagon,
Sat like one who for a prudent leap is holding him ready,
And the stallions sped rapidly homeward, desiring their
   stable.
Clouds of dust whirled up from under their powerful
   hoof-beats.
Long the youth stood there yet, and saw the dust in its
   rising,
Saw the dust as it settled again: he stood there unheeding.

ERATO

DOROTHEA

Like as the traveller, who, when the sun is approaching its
setting,
Fixes his eyes on it once again ere quickly it vanish,
Then on the sides of the rocks, and on all the darkening
bushes,
Sees its hovering image; whatever direction he look in
That hastes before, and flickers and gleams in radiant
colors,—
So before Hermann's eyes moved the beautiful shape of the
maiden
Softly, and seeming to follow the path that led into the
corn-field.
But he aroused from his wildering dream and turned him-
self slowly
Toward where the village lay and was wildered again; for
again came
Moving to meet him the lofty form of the glorious maiden.
Fixedly gazed he upon her; herself it was and no phantom.
Bearing in either hand a larger jar and a smaller,
Each by the handle, with busy step she came on to the
fountain.
Joyfully then he hastened to meet her; the sight of her gave
him
Courage and strength; and thus the astonished girl he
accosted:
" Do I then find thee, brave-hearted maiden, so soon again
busy,
Rendering aid unto others, and happy in bringing them
comfort?
Say why thou comest alone to this well which lies at such a
distance,
When all the rest are content with the water they find in
the village?

This has peculiar virtues, 'tis true; and the taste is
  delicious.
Thou to that mother wouldst bring it, I trow, whom thy
  faithfulness rescued.''

Straightway with cordial greeting the kindly maiden
  made answer:
'' Here has my walk to the spring already been amply
  rewarded,
Since I have found the good friend who bestowed so
  abundantly on us;
For a pleasure not less than the gifts is the sight of the
  giver.
Come, I pray thee, and see for thyself who has tasted thy
  bounty;
Come, and the quiet thanks receive of all it has solaced.
But that thou straightway the reason may'st know for
  which I am hither
Come to draw, where pure and unfailing the water is
  flowing,
This I must tell thee,— that all the water we have in the
  village
Has by improvident people been troubled with horses and
  oxen
Wading direct through the source which brings the inhabitants water.
And furthermore they have also made foul with their
  washings and rinsings
All the troughs of the village, and all the fountains have
  sullied;
For but one thought is in all, and that how to satisfy
  quickest
Self and the need of the moment, regardless of what may
  come after.''

Thus she spoke, and the broad stone steps meanwhile had
  descended

LUDWIG RICHTER

HERMANN AND DOROTHEA MEET AT THE FOUNTAIN

With her companion beside her, and on the low wall of the
   fountain
Both sat them down. She bent herself over to draw, and he
   also
Took in his hand the jar that remained, and bent himself
   over;
And in the blue of the heavens, they, seeing their image
   reflected,
Friendly greetings and nods exchanged in the quivering
   mirror.

" Give me to drink," the youth thereupon in his gladness
   petitioned,
And she handed the pitcher. Familiarly sat they and rested,
Both leaning over their jars, till she presently asked her
   companion:
" Tell me, why I find thee here, and without thy horses and
   wagon,
Far from the place where I met thee at first?   How camest
   thou hither?"

Thoughtful he bent his eyes on the ground, then quietly
   raised them
Up to her face, and, meeting with frankness the gaze of
   the maiden,
Felt himself solaced and stilled.   But then impossible was it,
That he of love should speak; her eye told not of affection,
Only of clear understanding, requiring intelligent answer.
And he composed himself quickly, and cordially said to
   the maiden:
" Hearken to me, my child, and let me reply to thy question.
'Twas for thy sake that hither I came; why seek to con-
   ceal it?
Know I live happy at home with both my affectionate
   parents,
Faithfully giving my aid their house and estates in
   directing,

Being an only son, and because our affairs are extensive.
Mine is the charge of the farm; my father bears rule in
the household;
While the presiding spirit of all is the diligent mother.
But thine experience doubtless has taught thee how griev-
ously servants,
Now through deceit, and now through their carelessness,
harass the mistress,
Forcing her ever to change and replace one fault with
another.
Long for that reason my mother has wished for a maid in
the household,
Who not with hand alone, but with heart, too, will lend
her assistance,
Taking the daughter's place, whom alas! she was early
deprived of.
Now when today by the wagon I saw thee, so ready and
cheerful,
Witnessed the strength of thine arms, and thy limbs of such
healthful proportion,
When thy intelligent speech I heard, I was smitten with
wonder.
Hastening homeward, I there to my parents and neighbors
the stranger
Praised as she well deserved. But I now am come hither
to tell thee
What is their wish as mine.— Forgive me my stammering
language.''

'' Hesitate not,'' she, answering, said, '' to tell me what
follows.
Thou dost not give me offence; I have listened with gratitude to thee:
Speak it out honestly therefore; the sound of it will not
alarm me.
Thou wouldst engage me as servant to wait on thy father
and mother,

And to look after the well-ordered house of which ye are the
    owners;
And thou thinkest in me to find them a capable servant,
One who is skilled in her work, and not of a rude
    disposition.
Short thy proposal has been, and short shall be also my
    answer.
Yes, I will go with thee home, and the call of fate I will follow.
Here my duty is done: I have brought the newly made
    mother
Back to her kindred again, who are all in her safety
    rejoicing.
Most of our people already are gathered; the others will
    follow.
All think a few days more will certainly see them returning
Unto their homes; for such is the exile's constant delusion.
But by no easy hope do I suffer myself to be cheated
During these sorrowful days which promise yet more days
    of sorrow.
All the bands of the world have been loosed, and what shall
    unite them,
Saving alone the need, the need supreme, that is on us?
If in a good man's house I can earn my living by service,
Under the eye of an excellent mistress, I gladly will do it;
Since of doubtful repute, must be always a wandering
    maiden.
Yes, I will go with thee, soon as I first shall have carried
    the pitchers
Back to my friends, and prayed the good people to give me
    their blessing
Come, thou must see them thyself, and from their hands
    must receive me."

  Joyfully hearkened the youth to the willing maiden's
    decision,
Doubtful whether he ought not at once to make honest
    confession.

Yet it appeared to him best to leave her awhile in her
    error,
Nor for her love to sue, before leading her home to his
    dwelling.
Ah! and the golden ring he perceived on the hand of the
    maiden,
Wherefore he let her speak on, and gave diligent ear to
    her language.

"Come," she presently said, "Let us back to the village;
    for maidens
Always are sure to be blamed if they tarry too long at
    the fountain.
Yet how delightful it is to chat by the murmuring water!"

Then from their seats they rose, and both of them turned
    to the fountain
One more look behind, and a tender longing possessed them.
Both of the water-jars then in silence she took by the
    handle,
Carried them up the steps, while behind her followed her
    lover.
One of the pitchers he begged her to give him to lighten
    the burden.
"Nay, let it be!" she said: "I carry them better so
    balanced.
Nor shall the master, who is to command, be doing me
    service.
Look not so gravely upon me, as thinking my fortune a
    hard one.
Early a woman should learn to serve, for that is her calling;
Since through service alone she finally comes to the head-
    ship,
Comes to the due command that is hers of right in the
    household.
Early the sister must wait on her brother, and wait on her
    parents;

Life must be always with her a perpetual coming and
  going,
Or be a fetching and carrying, making and doing for others.
Happy for her be she wonted to think no way is too
  grievous,
And if the hours of the night be to her as the hours of the
  daytime;
If she find never a needle too fine, nor a labor too trifling;
Wholly forgetful of self, and caring to live but in others!
For she will surely, as mother, have need of every virtue,
When, in the time of her illness, the cries of her infant
  arouse her
Calling for food from her weakness, and cares are to suffer-
  ing added.
Twenty men bound into one were not able to bear such
  a burden;
Nor is it meant that they should, yet should they with
  gratitude view it.''

  Thus she spoke, and was come, meanwhile, with her
  silent companion,
Far as the floor of the barn, at the furthermost end of the
  garden,
Where was the sick woman lying, whom, glad, she had left
  with her daughters,
Those late rescued maidens: fair pictures of innocence
  were they.
Both of them entered the barn; and, e'en as they did so,
  the justice,
Leading a child in each hand, came in from the other
  direction.
These had been lost, hitherto, from the sight of their sor-
  rowing mother;
But in the midst of the crowd the old man now had
  descried them.
Joyfully sprang they forward to meet their dear mother's
  embraces,

And to salute with delight their brother, their unknown
  companion.
Next upon Dorothea they sprang with affectionate greeting,
Asking for bread and fruit, but more than all else for some
  water.
So then she handed the water about; and not only the
  children
Drank, but the sick woman, too, and her daughters, and
  with them the justice.
All were refreshed, and highly commended the glorious
  water;
Acid it was to the taste, and reviving, and wholesome to
  drink of.

Then with a serious face the maiden replied to them,
  saying:
" Friends, for the last time now to your mouth have I lifted
  my pitcher;
And for the last time by me have your lips been moistened
  with water.
But henceforth in the heat of the day when the draught
  shall refresh you,
When in the shade ye enjoy your rest beside a clear fountain,
Think of me then sometimes and of all my affectionate
  service,
Prompted more by my love than the duty I owed you as
  kindred.
I shall acknowledge as long as I live the kindness ye've
  shown me.
'Tis with regret that I leave you; but every one now is a
  burden,
More than a help to his neighbor, and all must be finally
  scattered
Far through a foreign land, if return to our homes be
  denied us.
See, here stands the youth to whom we owe thanks for the
  presents.

He gave the cloak for the baby, and all these welcome
provisions.
Now he is come, and has asked me if I will make one in his
dwelling,
That I may serve therein his wealthy and excellent parents.
And I refuse not the offer; for maidens must always be
serving;
Burdensome were it for them to rest and be served in the
household.
Therefore I follow him gladly. A youth of intelligence
seems he,
And so will also the parents be, as becometh the wealthy.
So then farewell, dear friend; and may'st thou rejoice in
thy nursling,
Living, and into thy face already so healthfully looking!
When thou shalt press him against thy breast in these gay-
colored wrappings,
Oh, then remember the kindly youth who bestowed them
upon us,
And who me also henceforth, thy sister, will shelter and
nourish.
Thou, too, excellent man!'' she said as she turned to the
justice;
'' Take my thanks that in many a need I have found thee
a father.''

Then she knelt down on the floor by the side of the newly
made mother,
Kissing the weeping woman, and taking her low-whispered
blessing.

Thou, meanwhile, worshipful justice, wast speaking to
Hermann and saying:
'' Justly mayst thou, my friend, be counted among the good
masters,
Careful to manage their household affairs with capable
servants.

For I have often observed how in sheep, as in horses and
     oxen,
Men conclude never a bargain without making closest
     inspection,
While with a servant who all things preserves, if honest
     and able,
And who will every thing lose and destroy, if he set to
     work falsely,
Him will a chance or an accident make us admit to our
     dwelling,
And we are left, when too late, to repent an o'er hasty
     decision.
Thou understandest the matter it seems; because thou hast
     chosen,
Thee and thy parents to serve in the house, a maid who is
     honest.
Hold her with care; for as long as thy household is under
     her keeping,
Thou shalt not want for a sister, nor yet for a daughter
     thy parents.''

Many were come, meanwhile, near relatives all of the
     mother,
Bringing her various gifts, and more suitable quarters
     announcing.
All of them, hearing the maiden's decision, gave Hermann
     their blessing,
Coupled with glances of meaning, while each made his
     special reflections.
Hastily one and another would say in the ear of his
     neighbor:
'' If in the master a lover she find, right well were she
     cared for.''
Hermann took her at last by the hand, and said as he did
     so:
'' Let us be going; the day is declining, and distant the
     city.''

Eager and voluble then the women embraced Dorothea.

Hermann drew her away; but other adieus must be spoken:

Lastly the children with cries fell upon her and terrible
weeping,

Clung to her garments, and would not their dear second
mother should leave them.

But in a tone of command the women said, one and another:

"Hush now, children, she's going to the town, and will
presently bring you

Plenty of nice sweet cake that was by your brother be-
spoken

When by the stork just now he was brought past the shop
of the baker.

Soon you will see her come back with sugar-plums
spendidly gilded."

Then did the little ones loose their hold, and Hermann,
though hardly,

Tore her from further embraces away, and far-waving
kerchiefs.

MELPOMENE

Hermann and Dorothea

Toward the setting sun the two thus went on their
journey:

Close he had wrapped himself round with clouds portend-
ing a tempest.

Out from the veil, now here and now there, with fiery
flashes,

Gleaming over the field shot forth the ominous lightning.

"May not these threatening heavens," said Hermann,
"be presently sending

Hailstones upon us and violent rains; for fair is the harvest."

And in the waving luxuriant grain they delighted together:

Almost as high it reached as the lofty shapes that moved
through it.

Thereupon spoke the maiden, and said to her guide and
    companion:
" Friend, unto whom I soon am to owe so kindly a fortune,
Shelter and home, while many an exile's exposed to the
    tempest,
Tell me concerning thy parents, I pray thee, and teach me
    to know them,
Them whom with all my heart I desire to serve in the
    future.
Who understands his master, more easily gives satisfaction,
Having regard to the things which to him seem chief in
    importance,
And on the doing of which his firm-set mind is determined.
Tell me therefore, I pray, how to win thy father and
    mother.''

And to her question made answer the good and intelli-
    gent Hermann:
''Ah, what wisdom thou showest, thou good, thou excellent
    maiden,
Asking thus first of all concerning the tastes of my parents!
Know that in vain hitherto I have labored in serving my
    father,
Taking upon me as were it my own, the charge of the house-
    hold;
Early and late at work in the fields, and o'erseeing the
    vineyard.
But my mother I fully content, who can value my service;
And thou wilt also appear in her eyes the worthiest of
    maidens,
If for the house thou carest, as were it thine own thou wast
    keeping.
Otherwise is it with father, who cares for the outward
    appearance.
Do not regard me, good maiden, as one who is cold and
    unfeeling,
That unto thee a stranger I straightway discover my father.

Nay, I assure thee that never before have words such as
  these are
Freely dropped from my tongue, which is not accustomed
  to prattle;
But from out of my bosom thou lurest its every secret.
Some of the graces of life my good father covets about him,
Outward signs of affection he wishes, as well as of honor;
And an inferior servant might possibly give satisfaction,
Who could turn these to account, while he might be dis-
  pleased with a better.''

  Thereupon said she with joy, the while him hastening
  footsteps
Over the darkening pathway with easy motion she quick-
  ened:
'' Truly I hope to them both I shall equally give satis-
  faction:
For in thy mother's nature I find such an one as mine
  own is,
And to the outward graces I've been from my childhood
  accustomed.
Greatly was courtesy valued among our neighbors the
  Frenchmen,
During their earlier days; it was common to noble and
  burgher,
As to the peasant, and every one made it the rule of his
  household.
So, on the side of us Germans, the children were likewise
  accustomed
Daily to bring to their parents, with kissing of hands and
  with curtseys,
Morning good-wishes, and all through the day to be prettily
  mannered.
Every thing thus that I learned, and to which I've been
  used from my childhood,
All that my heart shall suggest, shall be brought into play
  for thy father.

But who shall tell me of thee, and how thyself shouldst be
treated,
Thou the only son of the house, and henceforth my
master?"

Thus she said, and e'en as she spoke they stood under
the pear-tree.
Down from the heavens the moon at her full was shedding
her splendor.
Night had come on, and wholly obscured was the last gleam
of sunlight,
So that contrasting masses lay side by side with each other,
Clear and bright as the day, and black with the shadows
of midnight;
Gratefully fell upon Hermann's ear the kindly asked
question
Under the shade of the glorious tree, the spot he so
treasured,
Which but this morning had witnessed the tears he had
shed for the exile.
And while they sat themselves down to rest them here for
a little,
Thus spoke the amorous youth, as he grasped the hand of
the maiden:
"Suffer thy heart to make answer, and follow it freely in
all things."
Yet naught further he ventured to say although so pro-
pitious
Seemed the hour; he feared he should only haste on a
refusal.
Ah, and he felt besides the ring on her finger, sad token!
Therefore they sat there, silent and still, beside one another.

First was the maiden to speak: "How sweet is this
glorious moonlight!"
Said she at length: "It is as the light of the day in its
brightness.

LUDWIG RICHTER

HERMANN AND DOROTHEA UNDER THE PEAR TREE

There in the city I plainly can see the houses and court-
yards,
And in the gable — methinks I can number its panes — is
a window.''

" What thou seest,'' the modest youth thereupon made
her answer,—
'' What thou seest is our dwelling, to which I am leading
thee downward,
And that window yonder belongs to my room in the attic,
Which will be thine perhaps, for various changes are
making.
All these fields, too, are ours; they are ripe for the harvest
tomorrow.
Here in the shade we will rest, and partake of our noon-
tide refreshment.
But it is time we began our descent through the vineyard
and garden;
For dost thou mark how yon threatening storm-cloud comes
nearer and nearer,
Charged with lightning, and ready our fair full moon to
extinguish? ''

So they arose from their seats, and over the corn fields
descended,
Through the luxuriant grain, enjoying the brightness of
evening,
Until they came to the vineyard, and so entered into its
shadow.
Then he guided her down o'er the numerous blocks that
were lying,
Rough and unhewn on the pathway, and served as the steps
of the alley.
Slowly the maiden descended, and leaning her hands on
his shoulder,
While with uncertain beams, the moon through the leaves
overlooked them,

Ere she was veiled by the cloud, and so left the couple in
    darkness.
Carefully Hermann's strength supported the maid that
    hung o'er him;
But, not knowing the path and the rough-hewn steps that
    led down it,
Missed she her footing, her ankle turned, and she surely
    had fallen,
Had not the dexterous youth his arm outstretched in an
    instant,
And his beloved upheld.   She gently sank on his shoulder;
Breast was pressed against breast, and cheek against cheek.
    Thus he stood there
Fixed as a marble statue, the force of will keeping him
    steadfast,
Drew her not to him more closely, but braced himself under
    her pressure.
Thus he the glorious burden felt, the warmth of her
    bosom,
And the perfume of her breath, that over his lips was
    exhaling;
Bore with the heart of a man the majestic form of the
    woman.

But she with playfulness said, concealing the pain that
    she suffered:
" That is a sign of misfortune, so timorous persons would
    tell us,
When on approaching a house we stumble not far from the
    threshold;
And for myself, I confess, I could wish for a happier
    omen.
Let us here linger awhile that thy parents may not have to
    blame thee,
Seeing a limping maid, and thou seem an incompetent land-
    lord."

URANIA

Prospect

Muses, O ye who the course of true love so willingly
favor,
Ye who thus far on his way the excellent youth have con-
ducted,
Even before the betrothal have pressed to his bosom the
maiden;
Further your aid vouchsafe this charming pair in uniting,
Straightway dispersing the clouds which over their hap-
piness lower!
Yet first of all declare what is passing meanwhile at the Lion.
Now for the third time again the mother impatient had
entered
Where were assembled the men, whom anxious but now
she had quitted;
Spoke of the gathering storm, and the moonlight's rapid
obscuring;
Then of her son's late tarrying abroad and the dangers
of nightfall;
Sharply upbraided her friends that without having speech
of the maiden,
And without urging his suit, they had parted from Hermann so early.

" Make it not worse than it is," the father replied with
displeasure.
" For, as thou seest, we tarry ourselves and are waiting
the issue."

Calmly, however, from where he was sitting the neighbor
made answer:
" Never in hours of disquiet like this do I fail to be grateful
Unto my late, blessed father, who every root of impatience
Tore from my heart when a child, and left no fibre re-
maining;

So that I learned on the instant to wait as do none of your
    sages.''
  '' Tell us,'' the pastor returned, '' what legerdemain he
    made use of.''
'' That will I gladly relate, for all may draw from it a
    lesson; ''
So made the neighbor reply. '' When a boy I once stood
    of a Sunday
Full of impatience, and looking with eagerness out for the
    carriage
Which was to carry us forth to the spring that lies under
    the lindens.
Still the coach came not. I ran, like a weasel, now hither,
    now thither,
Up stairs and down, and forward and back, 'twixt the door
    and the window;
Even my fingers itched to be moving; I scratched on the
    tables,
Went about pounding and stamping, and hardly could keep
    me from weeping.
All was observed by the calm-tempered man; but at last
    when my folly
Came to be carried too far, by the arm he quietly took me,
Led me away to the window, and spoke in this serious
    language:
' Seest thou yonder the carpenter's shop that is closed for
    the Sunday?
He will re-open tomorrow, when plane and saw will be
    started,
And will keep on through the hours of labor from morning
    till evening.
But consider you this,— a day will be presently coming
When that man shall himself be astir and all of his work-
    men,
Making a coffin for thee to be quickly and skilfully finished.
Then that house of boards they will busily bring over
    hither,

Which must at last receive alike the impatient and patient,
And which is destined soon with close-pressing roof to be
    covered.'
Straightway I saw the whole thing in my mind as if it were
    doing;
Saw the boards fitting together, and saw the black color
    preparing,
Sat me down patiently then, and in quiet awaited the car-
    riage.
Now when others I see, in seasons of anxious expectance,
Running distracted about, I cannot but think of the coffin.''

    Smiling, the pastor replied: '' The affecting picture of
    death stands
Not as a dread to the wise, and not as an end to the pious.
Those it presses again into life, and teaches to use it;
These by affliction it strengthens in hope to future salvation.
Death becomes life unto both. Thy father was greatly
    mistaken
When to a sensitive boy he death in death thus depicted.
Let us the value of nobly ripe age, point out to the young
    man,
And to the aged the youth, that in the eternal progression
Both may rejoice, and life may in life thus find its com-
    pletion.''

    But the door was now opened, and showed the majestical
    couple.
Filled with amaze were the friends, and amazed the affec-
    tionate parents,
Seeing the form of the maid so well matched with that of
    her lover.
Yea, the door seemed too low to allow the tall figures to
    enter,
As they together now appeared coming over the threshold.

    Hermann, with hurried words, presented her thus to his
    parents:

" Here is a maiden," he said; " such a one as ye wish in
the household.
Kindly receive her, dear father: she merits it well; and
thou, mother,
Question her straightway on all that belongs to a house-
keeper's duty,
That ye may see how well she deserves to ye both to be
nearer.''

Quickly he then drew aside the excellent clergyman,
saying:
" Help me, O worthy sir, and speedily out of this trouble;
Loosen, I pray thee, this knot, at whose untying I tremble.
Know that 'tis not as a lover that I have brought hither
the maiden;
But she believes that as servant she comes to the house,
and I tremble
Lest in displeasure she fly as soon as there's mention of
marriage.
But be it straightway decided; for she no longer in error
Thus shall be left, and I this suspense no longer can suffer.
Hasten and show us in this a proof of the wisdom we honor.''

Toward the company then the clergyman instantly
turned him;
But already, alas! had the soul of the maiden been troubled,
Hearing the father's speech; for he, in his sociable fashion,
Had in these playful words, with the kindest intention
addressed her:
"Ay, this is well, my child! with delight I perceive that
my Hermann
Has the good taste of his father, who often showed his in
his young days,
Leading out always the fairest to dance, and bringing the
fairest
Finally home as his wife; our dear little mother here
that was.

For by the bride that a man shall elect we can judge what
    himself is,
Tell what the spirit is in him, and whether he feel his own
    value.
Nor didst thou need for thyself, I'll engage, much time for
    decision;
For, in good sooth, methinks, he's no difficult person to
    follow.''

    Hermann had heard but in part; his limbs were inwardly
    trembling,
And of a sudden a stillness had fallen on all of the circle.

    But by these words of derision, for such she could not
    but deem them,
Wounded, and stung to the depths of her soul, the excellent
    maiden,
Stood, while the fugitive blood o'er her cheeks and e'en to
    her bosom
Poured its flush.   But she governed herself, and her cour-
    age collecting,
Answered the old man thus, her pain not wholly concealing:
'' Truly for such a reception thy son had in no wise pre-
    pared me,
When he the ways of his father described, the excellent
    burgher.
Thou art a man of culture, I know, before whom I am
    standing;
Dealest with every one wisely, according as suits his
    position;
But thou hast scanty compassion, it seems, on one such
    as I am,
Who, a poor girl, am now crossing thy threshold with pur-
    pose to serve thee;
Else, with such bitter derision, thou wouldst not have made
    me remember   [thy son is.
How far removed my fortune from that of thyself and

True, I come poor to thy house, and bring with me naught
    but my bundle
Here where is every abundance to gladden the prosperous
    inmates.
Yet I know well myself; I feel the relations between us.
Say, is it noble, with so much of mockery straightway to
    greet me,
That I am sent from the house while my foot is scarce yet
    on the threshold? ''

    Anxiously Hermann turned and signed to his ally the
    pastor
That he should rush to the rescue and straightway dispel
    the delusion.
Then stepped the wise man hastily forward and looked on
    the maiden's
Tearful eyes, her silent pain and repressed indignation,
And in his heart was impelled not at once to clear up the
    confusion,
Rather to put to the test the girl's disquieted spirit.
Therefore he unto her said in language intended to try her:
'' Surely, thou foreign-born maiden, thou didst not maturely
    consider,
When thou too rashly decidedst to enter the service of
    strangers,
All that is meant by the placing thyself 'neath the rule of
    a master;
For by our hand to a bargain the fate of the year is deter-
    mined,
And but a single ' yea ' compels to much patient endurance.
Not the worst part of the service the wearisome steps to
    be taken,
Neither the bitter sweat of a labor that presses unceasing;
Since the industrious freeman must toil as well as the
    servant.
But 'tis to bear with the master's caprice when he censures
    unjustly,

Or when, at variance with self, he orders now this, now
    the other;
Bear with the petulance, too, of the mistress, easily
    angered,
And with the rude, overbearing ways of unmannerly
    children.
All this is hard to endure, and yet to go on with thy duties
Quickly, without delay, nor thyself grow sullen and stub-
    born.
Yet thou appearest ill fitted for this, since already so deeply
Stung by the father's jests: whereas there is nothing more
    common
Than for a girl to be teased on account of a youth she may
    fancy.''

    Thus he spoke. The maiden had felt the full force of
    his language,
And she restrained her no more; but with passionate out-
    burst her feelings
Made themselves way; a sob broke forth from her now
    heaving bosom,
And, while the scalding tears poured down, she straighway
    made answer:
''Ah, that rational man who thinks to advise us in sorrow,
Knows not how little of power his cold words have in
    relieving
Ever a heart from that woe which a sovereign fate has
    inflicted.
Ye are prosperous and glad; how then should a pleasantry
    wound you?
Yet but the lightest touch is a source of pain to the sick
    man.
Nay, concealment itself, if successful, had profited nothing.
Better show now what had later increased to a bitterer
    anguish,
And to an inward consuming despair might perhaps have
    reduced me.

Let me go back! for here in this house I can tarry no longer.
I will away, and wander in search of my hapless companions,
Whom I forsook in their need; for myself alone choosing the better.
This is my firm resolve, and I therefore may make a confession
Which might for years perhaps have else lain hid in my bosom.
Deeply indeed was I hurt by the father's words of derision;
Not that I'm sensitive, proud beyond what is fitting a servant;
But that my heart in truth had felt itself stirred with affection
Toward the youth who today had appeared to my eyes as a savior.
When he first left me there on the road, he still remained present,
Haunting my every thought; I fancied the fortunate maiden
Whom as a bride, perhaps, his heart had already elected.
When at the fountain I met him again, the sight of him wakened
Pleasure as great as if there had met me an angel from heaven;
And with what gladness I followed, when asked to come as his servant.
True, that I flattered myself in my heart,—I will not deny it,—
While we were hitherward coming, I might peradventure deserve him,
Should I become at last the important stay of the household.
Now I, alas! for the first time see what risk I was running,
When I would make my home so near to the secretly loved one;
Now for the first time feel how far removed a poor maiden

Is from an opulent youth, no matter how great her deserving.

All this I now confess, that my heart ye may not misinterpret,

In that 'twas hurt by a chance to which I owe my awaking.

Hiding my secret desires, this dread had been ever before me,

That at some early day he would bring him a bride to his
dwelling;

And ah, how could I then my inward anguish have suffered!

Happily I have been warned, and happily now has my
bosom

Been of its secret relieved, while yet there is cure for
the evil.

But no more; I have spoken; and now shall nothing
detain me

Longer here in a house where I stay but in shame and
confusion,

Freely confessing my love and that foolish hope that I
cherished.

Not the night which abroad is covered with lowering storm
clouds;

Not the roll of the thunder — I hear its peal — shall deter
me;

Not the pelt of the rain which without is beating in fury;

Neither the blustering tempest; for all these things have I
suffered

During our sorrowful flight, and while the near foe was
pursuing.

Now I again go forth, as I have so long been accustomed,

Carried away by the whirl of the times, and from every
thing parted.

Fare ye well!   I tarry no longer; all now is over."

Thus she spoke and back to the door she hastily turned
her,

Still bearing under her arm, as she with her had brought
it, her bundle.

But with both of her arms the mother seized hold of the
    maiden,
Clasping her round the waist, and exclaiming, amazed and
    bewildered:
"Tell me, what means all this? and these idle tears, say,
    what mean they?
I will not let thee depart: thou art the betrothed of my
    Hermann."

But still the father stood, observing the scene with dis-
    pleasure,
Looked on the weeping girl, and said in a tone of vexation:
"This then must be the return that I get for all my
    indulgence,
That at the close of the day this most irksome of all things
    should happen!
For there is naught I can tolerate less than womanish
    weeping,
Violent outcries, which only involve in disorder and passion,
What with a little of sense had been more smoothly
    adjusted.
Settle the thing for yourselves: I'm going to bed; I've no
    patience
Longer to be a spectator of these your marvelous doings."
Quickly he turned as he spoke, and hastened to go to the
    chamber
Where he was wonted to rest, and his marriage bed was
    kept standing,
But he was held by his son, who said in a tone of entreaty:
"Father, hasten not from us, and be thou not wroth with
    the maiden.
I, only I, am to blame as the cause of all this confusion,
Which by his dissimulation our friend unexpectedly height-
    ened.
Speak, O worthy sir; for to thee my cause I intrusted.
Heap not up sorrow and anger, but rather let all this be
    ended;

For I could hold thee never again in such high estimation,
If thou shouldst show but delight in pain, not superior
  wisdom.''

Thereupon answered and said the excellent clergyman,
  smiling:
'' Tell me, what other device could have drawn this charming confession
Out of the good maiden's lips, and thus have revealed her
  affection?
Has not thy trouble been straightway transformed into
  gladness and rapture?
Therefore speak up for thyself; what need of the tongue
  of another? ''

Thereupon Hermann came forward, and spoke in these
  words of affection:
'' Do not repent of thy tears, nor repent of these passing
  distresses;
For they complete my joy, and — may I not hope it — thine
  also?
Not to engage the stranger, the excellent maid, as a servant,
Unto the fountain I came; but to sue for thy love I came
  thither.
Only, alas! my timorous look could thy heart's inclination
Nowise perceive; I read in thine eyes of nothing but
  kindness,
As from the fountain's tranquil mirror thou gavest me
  greeting.
Might I but bring thee home, the half of my joy was accom-
  plished.
But thou completest it unto me now; oh, blest be thou
  for it! ''
Then with a deep emotion the maiden gazed on the
  stripling;
Neither forbade she embrace and kiss, the summit of
  rapture,

When to a loving pair they come as the longed for assurance,
Pledge of a lifetime of bliss, that appears to them now
never-ending.

Unto the others, meanwhile, the pastor had made ex-
planation.
But with feeling and grace the maid now advanced to the
father,
Bent her before him, and kissing the hand he would fain
have withholden,
Said: "Thou wilt surely be just and forgive one so
startled as I was,
First for my tears of distress, and now for the tears of my
gladness.
That emotion forgive me, and oh! forgive me this also.
For I can scarce comprehend the happiness newly vouch-
safed me.
Yes, let that first vexation of which I, bewildered, was guilty
Be, too, the last. Whatever the maid of affectionate service
Faithfully promised, shall be to thee now performed by the
daughter."

Straightway then, concealing his tears, the father embraced her,
Cordially, too, the mother came forward and kissed her
with fervor,
Pressing her hands in her own: the weeping women were
silent.

Thereupon quickly he seized, the good and intelligent
pastor,
First the father's hand, and the wedding-ring drew from
his finger,—
Not so easily either: the finger was plump and detained it,—
Next took the mother's ring also, and with them betrothed
he the children,

THE BETROTHAL

Ludwig Richter

Saying: " These golden circlets once more their office per-
     forming
Firmly a tie shall unite, which in all things shall equal the
     old one,
Deeply is this young man imbued with love of the maiden,
And, as the maiden confesses, her heart is gone out to
     him also.
Here do I therefore betroth you and bless for the years
     .that are coming,   [a witness."
With the consent of the parents, and having this friend as

     Then the neighbor saluted at once, and expressed his
          good wishes;
But when the clergyman now the golden circlet was drawing
Over the maiden's hand, he observed with amazement the
     other,
Which had already by Hermann been anxiously marked at
     the fountain.
And with a kindly raillery thus thereupon he addressed her:
" So, then thy second betrothal is this?   Let us hope the
     first bridegroom
May not appear at the altar, and so prohibit the marriage."

     But she, answering, said: " Oh, let me to this recollection
Yet one moment devote; for so much is due the good giver,
Him who bestowed it at parting, and never came back to
     his kindred.
All that should come he foresaw, when in haste the passion
     for freedom,
When a desire in the newly changed order of things to be
     working,
Urged him onward to Paris, where chains and death he
     encountered.
' Fare thee well,' were his words; ' I go, for all is in motion
Now for a time on the earth, and every thing seems to be
     parting.
E'en in the firmest states fundamental laws are dissolving;

Property falls away from the hand of the ancient possessor;
Friend is parted from friend; and so parts lover from lover.
Here I leave thee, and where I shall find thee again, or if
    ever,
Who can tell? Perhaps these words are our last ones
    together.
Man's but a stranger here on the earth, we are told and
    with reason;
And we are each of us now become more of strangers than
    ever.
Ours no more is the soil, and our treasures are all of them
    changing:
Silver and gold are melting away from their time-honored
    patterns.
All is in motion as though the already-shaped world into
    chaos
Meant to resolve itself backward into night, and to shape
    itself over.
Mine thou wilt keep thine heart, and should we be ever
    united
Over the ruins of earth, it will be as newly made creatures,
Beings transformed and free, no longer dependent on for-
    tune;
For can aught fetter the man who has lived through days
    such as these are!
But if it is not to be, that, these dangers happily over,
Ever again we be granted the bliss of mutual embraces,
Oh, then before thy thoughts so keep my hovering image
That with unshaken mind thou be ready for good or for
    evil!
Should new ties allure thee again, and a new habitation,
Enter with gratitude into the joys that fate shall prepare
    thee;
Love those purely who love thee; be grateful to them who
    show kindness.
But thine uncertain foot should yet be planted but lightly,
For there is lurking the twofold pain of a new separation.

Blessings attend thy life; but value existence no higher
Than thine other possessions, and all possessions are
    cheating!'
Thus spoke the noble youth, and never again I beheld him.
Meanwhile I lost my all, and a thousand times thought of
    his warning.
Here, too, I think of his words, when love is sweetly pre-
    paring
Happiness for me anew, and glorious hopes are reviving.
Oh, forgive me, excellent friend, that e'en while I hold thee
Close to my side I tremble!   So unto the late-landed sailor
Seem the most solid foundations of firmest earth to be
    rocking."

    Thus she spoke, and placed the two rings on her finger
    together.
But her lover replied with a noble and manly emotion:
" So much the firmer then, amid these universal convul-
    sions,
Be, Dorothea, our union!   We two will hold fast and con-
    tinue,
Firmly maintaining ourselves, and the right to our ample
    possessions.
For that man, who, when times are uncertain, is faltering
    in spirit,
Only increases the evil, and further and further transmits it;
While he refashions the world, who keeps himself stead-
    fastly minded.
Poorly becomes it the German to give to these fearful
    excitements
Aught of continuance, or to be this way and that way
    inclining.
This is our own! let that be our word, and let us maintain it!
For to those resolute peoples respect will be ever accorded,
Who for God and the laws, for parents, women and children,
Fought and died, as together they stood with their front to
    the foeman.

Thou art mine own; and now what is mine, is mine more
    than ever.
Not with anxiety will I preserve it, and trembling enjoy-
    ment;
Rather with courage and strength. Today should the
    enemy threaten,
Or in the future, equip me thyself and hand me my weapons.
Let me but know that under thy care are my house and dear
    parents,
Oh! I can then with assurance expose my breast to the
    foeman.
And were but every man minded like me, there would be
    an upspring
Might against might, and peace should revisit us all with
    its gladness.''

DRAMAS

INTRODUCTION TO IPHIGENIA IN TAURIS

By Arthur H. Palmer, A. M., LL.D.

Professor of German Language and Literature, Yale University

O what literary genus does Goethe's *Iphigenia* belong? Dramatic in form, is it a drama? For A. W. Schlegel "an echo of Greek song," and for many German critics the best modern reproduction of Greek tragedy, it is for others a thoroughly German work in its substitution of profound moral struggles for the older passionate, more external conflicts. Schiller said: "It is, however, so astonishingly modern and un-Greek, that I cannot understand how it was ever thought to resemble a Greek play. It is purely moral; but the sensuous power, the life, the agitation, and everything which specifically belongs to a dramatic work is wanting." He adds, however, that it is a marvelous production which must forever remain the delight and wonderment of mankind. This is the view of G. H. Lewes, whose characterization is so apt also in other respects: "A drama it is not; it is a marvelous dramatic poem. The grand and solemn movement responds to the large and simple ideas which it unfolds. It has the calmness of majesty. In the limpid clearness of its language the involved mental processes of the characters are as transparent as the operations of bees within a crystal hive; while a constant strain of high and lofty music makes the reader feel as if in a holy temple. And above all witcheries of detail there is one capital witchery, belonging to Greek statues more than to other works of human cunning — the perfect unity of impression produced by the whole, so that nothing in it seems *made*, but all to *grow*; nothing is superfluous, but all is in organic dependence; nothing is there for detached effect, but the whole is effect. The poem fills the mind; beautiful as the separate passages are, admirers seldom think of passages, they think of the wondrous whole.''

But may we not deepen and spiritualize our conception of the drama and say that in *Iphigenia*, Goethe created a new dramatic genus, the soul-drama — the first psychological drama of modern literature, the result of ethical and artistic development through two milleniums? Surely a Greek dramatist of the first rank, come to life again in Goethe's age and entering into the heritage of this development, would have modernized both subject and form in the same way.

Most intimate is the relation of *Iphigenia* to Goethe's inner life, and this relation best illumines the spiritual import of the drama. Like his *Torquato Tasso*, it springs entirely from conditions and experiences of the early Weimar years and those just preceding. It was conceived and the first prose version written early in 1779; it received its final metrical form December, 1786 — in Rome indeed, but it owed to Italy only a higher artistic finish.

In his autobiography Goethe has revealed to us that his works are fragments of a great confession. Moods of his pre-Weimar storm and stress vibrate in his *Iphigenia* — feverish unrest, defiance of conventionality, Titanic trust in his individual genius, self-reproach, and remorse for guilt toward those he loved,— Friederike and Lili. Thus feeling his inner conflicts to be like the sufferings of Orestes, he wrote in a letter, August, 1775, shortly after returning to Frankfurt from his first Swiss journey: '' Perhaps the invisible scourge of the Eumenides will soon drive me out again from my fatherland.''

In November, 1775, Goethe went to Weimar, and there he found redemption from his unrest and dejection in the friendship of Frau von Stein. Her beneficent influence effected his new-birth into calm self-control and harmony of spirit. On August 7, 1779, Goethe wrote in his diary: '' May the idea of purity, extending even to the morsel I take into my mouth, become ever more luminous in me! ''

If Orestes is Goethe, Iphigenia is Frau von Stein; and in the personal sense the theme of the drama is the restoration of the poet to spiritual purity by the influence of noble womanhood.

But there is a larger, universally human sense. Such healing of Orestes is typically human; noble womanhood best realizes the ideal of the truly human (*Humanität*). In a way that transcends understanding, one pure, strong human personality may by its influence restore moral vigor and bring peace and hope to other souls rent by remorse and sunk in despair. This Goethe himself expressed as the central thought of this drama in the lines:

> Alle menschlichen Gebrechen
> Sühnet reine Menschlichkeit
>
> (For each human fault and **frailty**
> Pure humanity atones).

The eighteenth century's conception of "humanity," the ideal of the truly human, found two-fold classic, artistic expression in Germany at the same time; in Lessing's *Nathan the Wise* and in Goethe's *Iphigenia in Tauris*, the former rationalistic, the latter broader, more subtle, mystical.

IPHIGENIA IN TAURIS (1787)*

A DRAMA IN FIVE ACTS

TRANSLATED BY ANNA SWANWICK

Like *Torquato Tasso, Iphigenia* was originally written in prose, and in that form was acted at the Weimar Court Theatre about 1779. Goethe himself took the part of Orestes.

DRAMATIS PERSONÆ

IPHIGENIA.   ORESTES.
THOAS, *King of the Taurians.*   PYLADES.
                  ARKAS.

ACT I

SCENE I. *A Grove before the Temple of Diana.*

IPHIGENIA

ENEATH your leafy gloom, ye waving boughs
        Of this old, shady, consecrated grove,
        As in the goddess' silent sanctuary,
        With the same shuddering feeling forth I
                step,
As when I trod it first, nor ever here
Doth my unquiet spirit feel at home.
Long as a higher will, to which I bow,
Hath kept me here conceal'd, still, as at first,
I feel myself a stranger. For the sea
Doth sever me, alas! from those I love,
And day by day upon the shore I stand,
The land of Hellas seeking with my soul;
But to my sighs, the hollow-sounding waves
Bring, save their own hoarse murmurs, no reply.

---

* Permission The Macmillan Co., New York, and G. Bell & Sons, Ltd., London.

Alas for him! who friendless and alone,
Remote from parents and from brethren dwells;
From him grief snatches every coming joy
Ere it doth reach his lip. His yearning thoughts
Throng back for ever to his father's halls,
Where first to him the radiant sun unclosed
The gates of heav'n; where closer, day by day,
Brothers and sisters, leagued in pastime sweet,
Around each other twin'd love's tender bonds.
I will not reckon with the gods; yet truly
Deserving of lament is woman's lot.
Man rules alike at home and in the field,
Nor is in foreign climes without resource;
Him conquest crowneth, him possession gladdens,
And him an honorable death awaits.
How circumscrib'd is woman's destiny!
Obedience to a harsh, imperious lord,
Her duty, and her comfort; sad her fate,
Whom hostile fortune drives to lands remote!
Thus Thoas holds me here, a noble man
Bound with a heavy though a sacred chain.
O how it shames me, goddess, to confess
That with repugnance I perform these rites
For thee, divine protectress! unto whom
I would in freedom dedicate my life.
In thee, Diana, I have always hoped,
And still I hope in thee, who didst infold
Within the holy shelter of thine arm
The outcast daughter of the mighty king.
Daughter of Jove! hast thou from ruin'd Troy
Led back in triumph to his native land
The mighty man, whom thou didst sore afflict,
His daughter's life in sacrifice demanding,—
Hast thou for him, the godlike Agamemnon,
Who to thine altar led his darling child,
Preserv'd his wife, Electra, and his son,
His dearest treasures?— then at length restore

ANSELM FEUERBACH

IPHIGENIA

Thy suppliant also to her friends and home,
And save her, as thou once from death didst save,
So now, from living here, a second death.

SCENE II

IPHIGENIA, ARKAS

ARKAS

The king hath sent me hither, bade me greet
With hail, and fair salute, Diana's priestess.
For new and wondrous conquest, this the day,
When to her goddess Tauris renders thanks.
I hasten on before the king and host,
Himself to herald, and its near approach.

IPHIGENIA

We are prepar'd to give them worthy greeting;
Our goddess doth behold with gracious eye
The welcome sacrifice from Thoas' hand.

ARKAS

Would that I also found the priestess' eye,
Much honor'd, much revered one, found thine eye,
O consecrated maid, more calm, more bright,
To all a happy omen! Still doth grief,
With gloom mysterious, shroud thy inner mind;
Vainly, through many a tedious year we wait
For one confiding utterance from thy breast.
Long as I've known thee in this holy place,
That look of thine hath ever made me shudder;
And, as with iron bands, thy soul remains
Lock'd in the deep recesses of thy breast.

IPHIGENIA

As doth become the exile and the orphan.

ARKAS

Dost thou then here seem exil'd and an orphan?

IPHIGENIA

Can foreign scenes our fatherland replace?

ARKAS

Thy fatherland is foreign now to thee.

IPHIGENIA

Hence is it that my bleeding heart ne'er heals.
In early youth, when first my soul, in love,
Held father, mother, brethren fondly twin'd,
A group of tender germs, in union sweet,
We sprang in beauty from the parent stem,
And heavenward grew; alas, a foreign curse
Then seized and sever'd me from those I loved,
And wrench'd with iron grasp the beauteous bands.
It vanish'd then, the fairest charm of youth,
The simple gladness of life's early dawn;
Though sav'd I was a shadow of myself,
And life's fresh joyance blooms in me no more.

ARKAS

If thou wilt ever call thyself unblest,
I must accuse thee of ingratitude.

IPHIGENIA

Thanks have you ever.

ARKAS

Not the honest thanks
Which prompt the heart to offices of love;
The joyous glance, revealing to the host
A grateful spirit, with its lot content.
When thee a deep mysterious destiny
Brought to this sacred fane, long years ago,
To greet thee, as a treasure sent from heaven,
With reverence and affection, Thoas came.
Benign and friendly was this shore to thee,
To every stranger else with horror fraught,
For, till thy coming, none e'er trod our realm
But fell, according to an ancient rite,
A bloody victim at Diana's shrine.

IPHIGENIA

Freely to breathe alone is not to live.
Say, is it life, within this holy fane,
Like a poor ghost around its sepulchre
To linger out my days? Or call you that
A life of conscious happiness and joy,
When every hour, dream'd listlessly away,
Still leadeth onward to those gloomy days,
Which the sad troop of the departed spend
In self-forgetfulness on Lethe's shore?
A useless life is but an early death;
This woman's destiny hath still been mine.

ARKAS

I can forgive, though I must needs deplore,
The noble pride which underrates itself;
It robs thee of the happiness of life.
But hast thou, since thy coming here, done naught?
Who hath the monarch's gloomy temper cheered?
Who hath with gentle eloquence annull'd,
From year to year, the usage of our sires,
By which, a victim at Diana's shrine,
Each stranger perish'd, thus from certain death
Sending so oft the rescued captive home?
Hath not Diana, harboring no revenge
For this suspension of her bloody rites,
In richest measure heard thy gentle prayer?
On joyous pinions o'er the advancing host,
Doth not triumphant conquest proudly soar?
And feels not every one a happier lot,
Since Thoas, who so long hath guided us
With wisdom and with valor, sway'd by thee.
The joy of mild benignity approves,
Which leads him to relax the rigid claims
Of mute submission? Call thyself useless! Thou,
When from thy being o'er a thousand hearts,
A healing balsam flows? when to a race,

To whom a god consign'd thee, thou dost prove
A fountain of perpetual happiness,
And from this dire inhospitable coast,
Dost to the stranger grant a safe return?

IPHIGENIA

The little done doth vanish to the mind,
Which forward sees how much remains to do.

ARKAS

Him dost thou praise, who underrates his deeds?

IPHIGENIA

Who weigheth his own deeds is justly blam'd.

ARKAS

He too, real worth too proudly who condemns,
As who, too vainly, spurious worth o'er-rateth.
Trust me, and heed the counsel of a man
With honest zeal devoted to thy service:
When Thoas comes today to speak with thee,
Lend to his purposed words a gracious ear.

IPHIGENIA

Thy well-intention'd counsel troubles me:
His offer I have ever sought to shun.

ARKAS

Thy duty and thy interest calmly weigh.
Sithence King Thoas lost his son and heir,
Among his followers he trusts but few,
And trusts those few no more as formerly.
With jealous eye he views each noble's son
As the successor of his realm, he dreads
A solitary, helpless age — perchance
Sudden rebellion and untimely death.
A Scythian studies not the rules of speech,
And least of all the king. He who is used
To act and to command, knows not the art,
From far, with subtle tact, to guide discourse

Through many windings to its destin'd goal.
Thwart not his purpose by a cold refusal,
By an intended misconception. Meet,
With gracious mien, half-way the royal wish.

IPHIGENIA

Shall I then speed the doom that threatens me?

ARKAS

His gracious offer canst thou call a threat?

IPHIGENIA

'Tis the most terrible of all to me.

ARKAS

For his affection grant him confidence.

IPHIGENIA

If he will first redeem my soul from fear.

ARKAS

Why dost thou hide from him thy origin?

IPHIGENIA

A priestess secrecy doth well become.

ARKAS

Naught to a monarch should a secret be;
And, though he doth not seek to fathom thine,
His noble nature feels, ay, deeply feels,
That thou with care dost hide thyself from him.

IPHIGENIA

Ill-will and anger harbors he against me?

ARKAS

Almost it seems so. True, he speaks not of thee,
But casual words have taught me that the wish
Thee to possess hath firmly seiz'd his soul;
O leave him not a prey unto himself,
Lest his displeasure, rip'ning in his breast,
Should work thee woe, so with repentance thou
Too late my faithful counsel shalt recall.

IPHIGENIA

How! doth the monarch purpose what no man
Of noble mind, who loves his honest name,
Whose bosom reverence for the gods restrains,
Would ever think of? Will he force employ
To drag me from the altar to his bed?
Then will I call the gods, and chiefly thee,
Diana, goddess resolute, to aid me;
Thyself a virgin, wilt a virgin shield,
And to thy priestess gladly render aid.

ARKAS

Be tranquil! Passion, and youth's fiery blood
Impel not Thoas rashly to commit
A deed so lawless. In his present mood,
I fear from him another harsh resolve,
Which (for his soul is steadfast and unmov'd)
He then will execute without delay.
Therefore I pray thee, canst thou grant no more;
At least be grateful — give thy confidence.

IPHIGENIA

Oh tell me what is further known to thee.

ARKAS

Learn it from him. I see the king approach:
Him thou dost honor, thine own heart enjoins
To meet him kindly and with confidence.
A man of noble mind may oft be led
By woman's gentle word.

IPHIGENIA (*alone*)

How to observe
His faithful counsel see I not in sooth.
But willingly the duty I perform
Of giving thanks for benefits receiv'd,
And much I wish that to the king my lips
With truth could utter what would please his ear.

Scene III

Iphigenia, Thoas

IPHIGENIA

Her royal gifts the goddess shower on thee
Imparting conquest, wealth, and high renown
Dominion, and the welfare of thy house,
With the fulfilment of each pious wish,
That thou, whose sway for multitudes provides,
Thyself may'st be supreme in happiness!

THOAS

Contented were I with my people's praise;
My conquests others more than I enjoy.
Oh! be he king or subject, he's most blest,
Whose happiness is centred in his home.
My deep affliction thou didst share with me
What time, in war's encounter, the fell sword
Tore from my side my last, my dearest son;
So long as fierce revenge possessed my heart,
I did not feel my dwelling's dreary void;
But now, returning home, my rage appeas'd,
Their kingdom wasted, and my son aveng'd,
I find there nothing left to comfort me.
The glad obedience I was wont to see
Kindling in every eye, is smother'd now
In discontent and gloom; each, pondering, weighs
The changes which a future day may bring,
And serves the childless king, because he must.
Today I come within this sacred fane,
Which I have often enter'd to implore
And thank the gods for conquest. In my breast
I bear an old and fondly-cherish'd wish,
To which methinks thou canst not be a stranger;
I hope, a blessing to myself and realm,
To lead thee to my dwelling as my bride.

IPHIGENIA

Too great thine offer, king, to one unknown;
Abash'd the fugitive before thee stands,
Who on this shore sought only what thou gavest,
Safety and peace.

THOAS

          Thus still to shroud thyself
From me, as from the lowest, in the veil
Of mystery which wrapp'd thy coming here,
Would in no country be deem'd just or right.
Strangers this shore appall'd; 'twas so ordain'd,
Alike by law and stern necessity.
From thee alone — a kindly welcom'd guest,
Who hast enjoy'd each hallow'd privilege,
And spent thy days in freedom unrestrain'd —
From thee I hop'd that confidence to gain
Which every faithful host may justly claim.

IPHIGENIA

If I conceal'd, O king, my name, my race,
It was embarrassment, and not mistrust.
For didst thou know who stands before thee now,
And what accursed head thine arm protects,
Strange horror would possess thy mighty heart;
And, far from wishing me to share thy throne,
Thou, ere the time appointed, from thy realm
Wouldst banish me; wouldst thrust me forth, perchance
Before a glad reunion with my friends
And period to my wand'rings is ordain'd,
To meet that sorrow, which in every clime,
With cold, inhospitable, fearful hand,
Awaits the outcast, exil'd from his home.

THOAS

Whate'er respecting thee the gods decree,
Whate'er their doom for thee and for thy house,
Since thou hast dwelt amongst us, and enjoy'd
The privilege the pious stranger claims,

To me hath fail'd no blessing sent from heaven;
And to persuade me, that protecting thee
I shield a guilty head, were hard indeed.

IPHIGENIA

Thy bounty, not the guest, draws blessings down.

THOAS

The kindness shown the wicked is not blest.
End then thy silence, priestess; not unjust
Is he who doth demand it. In my hands
The goddess placed thee; thou hast been to me
As sacred as to her, and her behest
Shall for the future also be my law:
If thou canst hope in safety to return
Back to thy kindred, I renounce my claims:
But is thy homeward path for ever closed—
Or doth thy race in hopeless exile rove,
Or lie extinguish'd by some mighty woe—
Then may I claim thee by more laws than one.
Speak openly, thou know'st I keep my word.

IPHIGENIA

Its ancient bands reluctantly my tongue
Doth loose, a long hid secret to divulge;
For once imparted, it resumes no more
The safe asylum of the inmost heart,
But thenceforth, as the powers above decree,
Doth work its ministry of weal or woe.
Attend! I issue from the Titan's race.

THOAS

A word momentous calmly hast thou spoken.
Him nam'st thou ancestor whom all the world
Knows as a sometime favorite of the gods?
Is it that Tantalus, whom Jove himself
Drew to his council and his social board?
On whose experienc'd words, with wisdom fraught,
As on the language of an oracle,
E'en gods delighted hung?

IPHIGENIA

'Tis even he;
But the immortal gods with mortal men
Should not, on equal terms, hold intercourse;
For all too feeble is the human race,
Not to grow dizzy on unwonted heights.
Ignoble was he not, and no betrayer;
To be the Thunderer's slave, he was too great;
To be his friend and comrade,— but a man.
His crime was human, and their doom severe;
For poets sing, that treachery and pride
Did from Jove's table hurl him headlong down
To grovel in the depths of Tartarus.
Alas, and his whole race must bear their hate.

THOAS

Bear they their own guilt, or their ancestor's?

IPHIGENIA

The Titan's mighty breast and nervous frame
Was his descendants' certain heritage;
But round their brow Jove forg'd a band of brass.
Wisdom and patience, prudence and restraint,
He from their gloomy, fearful eye conceal'd;
In them each passion grew to savage rage,
And headlong rush'd with violence uncheck'd.
Already Pelops, Tantalus' loved son,
Mighty of will, obtained his beauteous bride,
Hippodamia, child of Œnomaus,
Through treachery and murder; she ere long,
To glad her consort's heart, bare him two sons,
Thyest and Atreus. They with envy marked
The ever-growing love their father bare
To his first-born, sprung from another union.
Hate leagued the pair, and secretly they wrought,
In fratricide, the first dread crime. The sire
Hippodamia held as murderess,
With savage rage he claim'd from her his son,
And she in terror did destroy herself —

THOAS

Thou'rt silent? Pause not in thy narrative;
Repent not of thy confidence — say on!

IPHIGENIA

How blest is he who his progenitors
With pride remembers, to the listener tells
The story of their greatness, of their deeds,
And, silently rejoicing, sees himself
The latest link of this illustrious chain!
For seldom does the selfsame stock produce
The monster and the demigod: a line
Of good or evil ushers in, at last,
The glory or the terror of the world.—
After the death of Pelops, his two sons
Rul'd o'er the city with divided sway.
But such an union could not long endure.
His brother's honor first Thyestes wounds.
In vengeance Atreus drove him from the realm.
Thyestes, planning horrors, long before
Had stealthily procur'd his brother's son,
Whom he in secret nurtur'd as his own.
Revenge and fury in his breast he pour'd,
Then to the royal city sent him forth,
That in his uncle he might slay his sire.
The meditated murder was disclos'd,
And by the king most cruelly aveng'd,
Who slaughter'd as he thought, his brother's son.
Too late he learn'd whose dying tortures met
His drunken gaze; and seeking to assuage
The insatiate vengeance that possess'd his soul,
He plann'd a deed unheard of. He assum'd
A friendly tone, seem'd reconcil'd, appeas'd,
And lur'd his brother, with his children twain,
Back to his kingdom; these he seiz'd and slew;
Then plac'd the loathsome and abhorrent food
At his first meal before the unconscious sire.

And when Thyestes had his hunger still'd
With his own flesh, a sadness seiz'd his soul;
He for his children ask'd,—their steps, their voice
Fancied he heard already at the door;
And Atreus, grinning with malicious joy,
Threw in the members of the slaughter'd boys.—
Shudd'ring, O king, thou dost avert thy face:
So did the sun his radiant visage hide,
And swerve his chariot from the eternal path.
These, monarch, are thy priestess' ancestors,
And many a dreadful fate of mortal doom,
And many a deed of the bewilder'd brain,
Dark night doth cover with her sable wing,
Or shroud in gloomy twilight.

THOAS

Hidden there
Let them abide. A truce to horror now,
And tell me by what miracle thou sprangest
From race so savage.

IPHIGENIA

Atreus' eldest son
Was Agamemnon; he, O king, my sire:
But I may say with truth, that, from a child,
In him the model of a perfect man
I witness'd ever. Clytemnestra bore
To him, myself, the firstling of their love,
Electra then. Peaceful the monarch rul'd,
And to the house of Tantalus was given
A long-withheld repose. A son alone
Was wanting to complete my parents' bliss;
Scarce was this wish fulfill'd, and young Orestes,
The household's darling, with his sisters grew,
When new misfortunes vex'd our ancient house.
To you hath come the rumor of the war,
Which, to avenge the fairest woman's wrongs,
The force united of the Grecian kings

Round Ilion's walls encamp'd. Whether the town
Was humbled, and achieved their great revenge,
I have not heard. My father led the host.
In Aulis vainly for a favoring gale
They waited; for, enrag'd against their chief,
Diana stay'd their progress, and requir'd,
Through Chalcas' voice, the monarch's eldest daughter.
They lured me with my mother to the camp,
They dragged me to the altar, and this head
There to the goddess doomed.—She was appeased;
She did not wish my blood, and shrouded me
In a protecting cloud; within this temple
I first awakened from the dream of death;
Yes, I myself am she, Iphigenia,
Grandchild of Atreus, Agamemnon's child,
Diana's priestess, I who speak with thee.

THOAS

I yield no higher honor or regard
To the king's daughter than the maid unknown;
Once more my first proposal I repeat;
Come follow me, and share what I possess.

IPHIGENIA

How dare I venture such a step, O king?
Hath not the goddess who protected me
Alone a right to my devoted head?
'Twas she who chose for me this sanctuary,
Where she perchance reserves me for my sire,
By my apparent death enough chastis'd,
To be the joy and solace of his age.
Perchance my glad return is near; and how,
If I, unmindful of her purposes,
Had here attach'd myself against her will?
I ask'd a signal, did she wish my stay.

THOAS

The signal is that still thou tarriest here.
Seek not evasively such vain pretexts.

Not many words are needed to refuse,
The *no* alone is heard by the refused.

IPHIGENIA

Mine are not words meant only to deceive;
I have to thee my inmost heart reveal'd.
And doth no inward voice suggest to thee,
How I with yearning soul must pine to see
My father, mother, and my long-lost home?
Oh let thy vessels bear me thither, king?
That in the ancient halls, where sorrow still
In accents low doth fondly breathe my name,
Joy, as in welcome of a new-born child,
May round the columns twine the fairest wreath.
New life thou wouldst to me and mine impart.

THOAS

Then go! Obey the promptings of thy heart;
And to the voice of reason and good counsel,
Close thou thine ear. Be quite the woman, give
To every wish the rein, that brideless
May seize on thee, and whirl thee here and there.
When burns the fire of passion in her breast,
No sacred tie withholds her from the wretch
Who would allure her to forsake for him
A husband's or a father's guardian arms;
Extinct within her heart its fiery glow,
The golden tongue of eloquence in vain
With words of truth and power assails her ear.

IPHIGENIA

Remember now, O king, thy noble words!
My trust and candor wilt thou thus repay?
Thou seem'st, methinks, prepar'd to hear the truth.

THOAS

For this unlook'd-for answer not prepar'd.
Yet 'twas to be expected; knew I not
That with a woman I had now to deal?

IPHIGENIA

Upbraid not thus, O king, our feeble sex!
Though not in dignity to match with yours,
The weapons woman wields are not ignoble.
And trust me, Thoas, in thy happiness
I have a deeper insight than thyself.
Thou thinkest, ignorant alike of both,
A closer union would augment our bliss;
Inspir'd with confidence and honest zeal
Thou strongly urgest me to yield consent;
And here I thank the gods, who give me strength
To shun a doom unratified by them.

THOAS

'Tis not a god, 'tis thine own heart that speaks.

IPHIGENIA

'Tis through the heart alone they speak to us.

THOAS

To hear them have I not an equal right?

IPHIGENIA

The raging tempest drowns the still small voice.

THOAS

This voice no doubt the priestess hears alone.

IPHIGENIA

Before all others should the prince attend it.

THOAS

Thy sacred office, and ancestral right
To Jove's own table, place thee with the gods
In closer union than an earth-born savage.

IPHIGENIA

Thus must I now the confidence atone
Thyself didst wring from me!

THOAS

I am a man.
And better 'tis we end this conference.
Hear then my last resolve. Be priestess still
Of the great goddess who selected thee;
And may she pardon me, that I from her,
Unjustly and with secret self-reproach,
Her ancient sacrifice so long withheld.
From olden time no stranger near'd our shore
But fell a victim at her sacred shrine.
But thou, with kind affection (which at times
Seem'd like a gentle daughter's tender love,
At times assum'd to my enraptur'd heart
The modest inclination of a bride),
Didst so inthral me, as with magic bonds,
That I forgot my duty. Thou didst rock
My senses in a dream: I did not hear
My people's murmurs: now they cry aloud,
Ascribing my poor son's untimely death
To this my guilt. No longer for thy sake
Will I oppose the wishes of the crowd,
Who urgently demand the sacrifice.

IPHIGENIA

For mine own sake I ne'er desired it from thee.
Who to the gods ascribe a thirst for blood
Do misconceive their nature, and impute
To them their own inhuman dark desires.
Did not Diana snatch me from the priest,
Holding my service dearer than my death?

THOAS

'Tis not for us, on reason's shifting grounds,
Lightly to guide and construe rites divine.
Perform thy duty; I'll accomplish mine.
Two strangers, whom in caverns of the shore
We found conceal'd, and whose arrival here
Bodes to my realm no good, are in my power.
With them thy goddess may once more resume
Her ancient, pious, long-suspended rites!
I send them here,— thy duty not unknown.   [*Exit.*]

IPHIGENIA (*alone*)

Gracious protectress! thou hast clouds
To shelter innocence distress'd,
And from the arms of iron fate,
Gently to waft her o'er the sea,
O'er the wide earth's remotest realms,
Where'er it seemeth good to thee.
Wise art thou,— thine all-seeing eye
The future and the past surveys;
Thy glance doth o'er thy children rest,
E'en as thy light, the life of night,
Keeps o'er the earth its silent watch.
O Goddess! keep my hands from blood!
Blessing it never brings, and peace;
And still in evil hours the form
Of the chance-murder'd man appears
To fill the unwilling murderer's soul
With horrible and gloomy fears.
For fondly the Immortals view
Man's widely scatter'd simple race;
And the poor mortal's transient life
Gladly prolong, that he may lift
Awhile to their eternal heavens
His sympathetic joyous gaze.

ACT II

Scene I

Orestes, Pylades

ORESTES

It is the path of death that now we tread:
At every step my soul grows more serene.
When I implor'd Apollo to remove
The grisly band of Furies from my side,
He seem'd, with hope-inspiring, godlike words,
To promise aid and safety in the fane
Of his lov'd sister, who o'er Tauris rules.

Thus the prophetic word fulfils itself,
That with my life shall terminate my woe.
How easy 'tis for me, whose heart is crush'd,
Whose sense is deaden'd by a hand divine,
Thus to renounce the beauteous light of day!
And must the son of Atreus not entwine
The wreath of conquest round his dying brow —
Must I, as my forefathers, as my sire,
Bleed like a victim,— an ignoble death —
So be it! Better at the altar here,
Than in a nook obscure, where kindred hands
Have spread assassination's wily net.
Yield me this brief repose, infernal Powers!
Ye, who, like loosen'd hounds, still scent the blood
Which, trickling from my feet, betrays my path.
Leave me! ere long I come to you below.
Nor you, nor I, should view the light of day.
The soft green carpet of the beauteous earth
Is no arena for unhallow'd fiends.
Below I seek you, where an equal fate
Binds all in murky, never-ending night.
Thee only, thee, my Pylades, my friend,
The guiltless partner of my crime and curse,
Thee am I loath, before thy time, to take
To yonder cheerless shore! Thy life or death
Alone awakens in me hope or fear.

PYLADES

Like thee, Orestes, I am not prepared
Downwards to wander to yon realm of shade.
I purpose still, through the entangled paths,
Which seem as they would lead to blackest night,
Again to wind our upward way to life.
Of death I think not; I observe and mark
Whether the gods may not perchance present
Means and fit moment for a joyful flight.
Dreaded or not, the stroke of death must come;

And though the priestess stood with hand uprais'd,
Prepar'd to cut our consecrated locks,
Our safety still should be my only thought;
Uplift thy soul above this weak despair;
Desponding doubts but hasten on our peril.
Apollo pledg'd to us his sacred word,
That in his sister's holy fane for thee
Were comfort, aid, and glad return prepar'd.
The words of Heaven are not equivocal,
As in despair the poor oppress'd one thinks.

ORESTES

The mystic web of life my mother cast
Around my infant head, and so I grew
An image of my sire; and my mute look
Was aye a bitter and a keen reproof
To her and base Ægisthus. Oh, how oft,
When silently within our gloomy hall
Electra sat, and mus'd beside the fire,
Have I with anguish'd spirit climb'd her knee,
And watch'd her bitter tears with sad amaze!
Then would she tell me of our noble sire:
How much I long'd to see him — be with him!
Myself at Troy one moment fondly wish'd,
My sire's return, the next. The day arrived —

PYLADES

Oh, of that awful hour let fiends of hell
Hold nightly converse! Of a time more fair
May the remembrance animate our hearts
To fresh heroic deeds. The gods require
On this wide earth the service of the good,
To work their pleasure. Still they count on thee;
For in thy father's train they sent thee not,
When he to Orcus went unwilling down.

ORESTES

Would I had seized the border of his robe,
And followed him!

PYLADES

They kindly cared for me
Who held thee here; for hadst thou ceased to live,
I know not what had then become of me;
Since I with thee, and for thy sake alone,
Have from my childhood liv'd, and wish to live.

ORESTES

Remind me not of those delightsome days,
When me thy home a safe asylum gave;
With fond solicitude thy noble sire
The half-nipp'd, tender flow'ret gently rear'd:
While thou, a friend and playmate always gay,
Like to a light and brilliant butterfly
Around a dusky flower, didst day by day
Around me with new life thy gambols urge,
And breathe thy joyous spirit in my soul,
Until, my cares forgetting, I with thee
Was lur'd to snatch the eager joys of youth.

PYLADES

My very life began when thee I lov'd.

ORESTES

Say, then thy woes began, and thou speak'st truly.
This is the sharpest sorrow of my lot,
That, like a plague-infected wretch, I bear
Death and destruction hid within my breast;
That, where I tread, e'en on the healthiest spot,
Ere long the blooming faces round betray
The anguish'd features of a ling'ring death.

PYLADES

Were thy breath venom, I had been the first
To die, that death, Orestes. Am I not,
As ever, full of courage and of joy?
And love and courage are the spirit's wings
Wafting to noble actions.

ORESTES
Noble actions?
Time was, when fancy painted such before us!
When oft, the game pursuing, on we roam'd
O'er hill and valley; hoping that ere long,
Like our great ancestors in heart and hand,
With club and weapon arm'd, we so might track
The robber to his den, or monster huge.
And then at twilight, by the boundless sea,
Peaceful we sat, reclin'd against each other,
The waves came dancing to our very feet,
And all before us lay the wide, wide world;
Then on a sudden one would seize his sword,
And future deeds shone round us like the stars,
Which gemm'd in countless throngs the vault of night.

PYLADES
Endless, my friend, the projects which the soul
Burns to accomplish.   We would every deed
At once perform as grandly as it shows
After long ages, when from land to land
The poet's swelling song hath roll'd it on.
It sounds so lovely what our fathers did,
When, in the silent evening shade reclin'd,
We drink it in with music's melting tones;
And what we do is, as their deeds to them,
Toilsome and incomplete!
Thus we pursue what always flies before;
We disregard the path in which we tread,
Scarce see around the footsteps of our sires,
Or heed the trace of their career on earth.
We ever hasten on to chase their shades,
Which, godlike, at a distance far remote,
On golden clouds, the mountain summits crown.
The man I prize not who esteems himself
Just as the people's breath may chance to raise him.
But thou, Orestes, to the gods give thanks,
That they through thee have early done so much.

ORESTES

When they ordain a man to noble deeds,
To shield from dire calamity his friends,
Extend his empire, or protect its bounds,
Or put to flight its ancient enemies,
Let him be grateful! For to him a god
Imparts the first, the sweetest joy of life.
Me have they doom'd to be a slaughterer,
To be an honor'd mother's murderer,
And shamefully a deed of shame avenging,
Me through their own decree they have o'erwhelm'd.
Trust me, the race of Tantalus is doom'd;
And I, his last descendant, may not perish,
Or crown'd with honor or unstain'd by crime.

PYLADES

The gods avenge not on the son the deeds
Done by the father. Each, or good or bad,
Of his own actions reaps the due reward.
The parents' blessing, not their curse, descends.

ORESTES

Methinks their blessing did not lead us here.

PYLADES

It was at least the mighty gods' decree.

ORESTES

Then is it their decree which doth destroy us.

PYLADES

Perform what they command, and wait the event.
Do thou Apollo's sister bear from hence,
That they at Delphi may united dwell,
There by a noble-thoughted race revered,
Thee, for this deed, the lofty pair will view
With gracious eye, and from the hateful grasp
Of the infernal Powers will rescue thee.
E'en now none dares intrude within this grove.

ORESTES

So shall I die at least a peaceful death.

PYLADES

Far other are my thoughts, and not unskill'd
Have I the future and the past combin'd
In quiet meditation.   Long, perchance,
Hath ripen'd in the counsel of the gods
The great event.   Diana yearns to leave
The savage coast of these barbarians,
Foul with their sacrifice of human blood.
We were selected for the high emprize;
To us it is assign'd, and strangely thus
We are conducted to the threshold here.

ORESTES

My friend, with wondrous skill thou link'st thy wish
With the predestin'd purpose of the gods.

PYLADES

Of what avail is prudence, if it fail
Heedful to mark the purposes of Heaven?
A noble man, who much hath sinn'd, some god
Doth summon to a dangerous enterprize,
Which to achieve appears impossible.
The hero conquers, and atoning serves
Mortals and gods, who thenceforth honor him.

ORESTES

Am I foredoom'd to action and to life,
Would that a god from my distemper'd brain
Might chase this dizzy fever, which impels
My restless steps along a slipp'ry path,
Stain'd with a mother's blood, to direful death;
And pitying, dry the fountain, whence the blood,
For ever spouting from a mother's wounds,
Eternally defiles me!

PYLADES

Wait in peace!
Thou dost increase the evil, and dost take

The office of the Furies on thyself.
Let me contrive,— be still!   And when at length
The time for action claims our powers combin'd,
Then will I summon thee, and on we'll stride,
With cautious boldness to achieve the event.

ORESTES

I hear Ulysses speak.

PYLADES

Nay, mock me not.
Each must select the hero after whom
To climb the steep and difficult ascent
Of high Olympus.   And to me it seems
That him nor stratagem nor art defiles
Who consecrates himself to noble deeds.

ORESTES

I most esteem the brave and upright man.

PYLADES

And therefore have I not desir'd thy counsel.
One step's already taken.   From our guards
E'en now I this intelligence have gained.
A strange and godlike woman holds in check
The execution of that bloody law:
Incense, and prayer, and an unsullied heart,
These are the gifts she offers to the gods.
Rumor extols her highly, it is thought
That from the race of Amazon she springs,
And hither fled some great calamity.

ORESTES

Her gentle sway, it seems, lost all its power
When hither came the culprit, whom the curse,
Like murky night, envelops and pursues.
Our doom to seal, the pious thirst for blood
The ancient cruel rite again unchains:
The monarch's savage will decrees our death;
A woman cannot save when he condemns.

PYLADES

That 'tis a woman, is a ground for hope!
A man, the very best, with cruelty
At length may so familiarize his mind,
His character through custom so transform,
That he shall come to make himself a law
Of what at first his very soul abhorr'd.
But woman doth retain the stamp of mind
She first assum'd.   On her we may depend
In good or evil with more certainty.
She comes; leave us alone.   I dare not tell
At once our names, nor unreserv'd confide
Our fortunes to her.   Now retire awhile,
And ere she speaks with thee we'll meet again.

SCENE II

IPHIGENIA, PYLADES

IPHIGENIA

Whence art thou?   Stranger, speak!   To me thy bearing
Stamps thee of Grecian, not of Scythian race.
                    [*She unbinds his chains.*]
The freedom that I give is dangerous;
The gods avert the doom that threatens you!

PYLADES

Delicious music! dearly welcome tones
Of our own language in a foreign land!
With joy my captive eye once more beholds
The azure mountains of my native coast.
Oh, let this joy that I, too, am a Greek
Convince thee, priestess!   How I need thine aid,
A moment I forget, my spirit rapt
In contemplation of so fair a vision.
If fate's dread mandate doth not seal thy lips,
From which of our illustrious races say,
Dost thou thy godlike origin derive?

IPHIGENIA

The priestess whom the goddess hath herself
Selected and ordained, doth speak with thee.
Let that suffice: but tell me, who art thou,
And what unbless'd o'erruling destiny
Hath hither led thee with thy friend?

PYLADES

The woe,
Whose hateful presence ever dogs our steps,
I can with ease relate.   Oh, would that thou
Couldst with like ease, divine one, shed on us
One ray of cheering hope!   We are from Crete,
Adrastus' sons, and I, the youngest born,
Named Cephalus; my eldest brother, he,
Laodamas.   Between us stood a youth
Savage and wild, who severed e'en in sport
The joy and concord of our early youth.
Long as our father led his powers at Troy,
Passive our mother's mandate we obey'd;
But when, enrich'd with booty, he return'd,
And shortly after died, a contest fierce
Both for the kingdom and their father's wealth,
His children parted.   I the eldest joined;
He slew our brother; and the Furies hence
For kindred murder dog his restless steps.
But to this savage shore the Delphian god
Hath sent us, cheer'd by hope.   He bade us wait
Within his sister's consecrated fane
The blessed hand of aid.   Captives we are,
And, hither brought, before thee now we stand
Ordain'd for sacrifice.   My tale is told.

IPHIGENIA

Fell Troy!   Dear man, assure me of its fall.

PYLADES

Prostrate it lies.   O unto us ensure
Deliverance.   The promised aid of Heaven

More swiftly bring.   Take pity on my brother.
O say to him a kind, a gracious word;
But spare him when thou speakest, earnestly
This I implore: for all too easily
Through joy and sorrow and through memory
Torn and distracted is his inmost being.
A feverish madness oft doth seize on him,
Yielding his spirit, beautiful and free,
A prey to furies.

IPHIGENIA

　　　　　Great as is thy woe,
Forget it, I conjure thee, for a while,
Till I am satisfied.

PYLADES

　　　　　The stately town,
Which ten long years withstood the Grecian host,
Now lies in ruins, ne'er to rise again;
Yet many a hero's grave will oft recall
Our sad remembrance to that barbarous shore.
There lies Achilles and his noble friend.

IPHIGENIA

So are ye godlike forms reduc'd to dust!

PYLADES

Nor Palamede, nor Ajax, ere again
The daylight of their native land beheld.

IPHIGENIA

He speaks not of my father, doth not name
Him with the fallen.   He may yet survive!
I may behold him! still hope on, fond heart!

PYLADES

Yet happy are the thousands who receiv'd
Their bitter death-blow from a hostile hand!
For terror wild, and end most tragical,

Some hostile, angry deity prepar'd,
Instead of triumph, for the home-returning.
Do human voices never reach this shore?
Far as their sound extends, they bear the fame
Of deeds unparallel'd.   And is the woe
Which fills Mycene's halls with ceaseless sighs
To thee a secret still? — And know'st thou not
That Clytemnestra, with Ægisthus' aid,
Her royal consort artfully ensnar'd,
And murder'd on the day of his return? —
The monarch's house thou honorest!   I perceive
Thy breast with tidings vainly doth contend
Fraught with such monstrous and unlook'd for woe.
Art thou the daughter of a friend? art born
Within the circuit of Mycene's walls?
Conceal it not, nor call me to account
That here the horrid crime I first announce.

IPHIGENIA

Proceed, and tell me how the deed was done.

PYLADES

The day of his return, as from the bath
Arose the monarch, tranquil and refresh'd,
His robe demanding from his consort's hand,
A tangled garment, complicate with folds,
She o'er his shoulders flung and noble head;
And when, as from a net, he vainly strove
To extricate himself, the traitor, base
Ægisthus, smote him, and envelop'd thus
Great Agamemnon sought the shades below.

IPHIGENIA

And what reward receiv'd the base accomplice?

PYLADES

A queen and kingdom he possess'd already.

IPHIGENIA

Base passion prompted then the deed of shame?

PYLADES

And feelings, cherish'd long, of deep revenge.

IPHIGENIA

How had the monarch injured Clytemnestra?

PYLADES

By such a dreadful deed, that if on earth
Aught could exculpate murder, it were this.
To Aulis he allur'd her, when the fleet
With unpropitious winds the goddess stay'd;
And there, a victim at Diana's shrine,
The monarch, for the welfare of the Greeks,
Her eldest daughter doomed, Iphigenia.
And this, so rumor saith, within her heart
Planted such deep abhorrence that forthwith
She to Ægisthus hath resigned herself,
And round her husband flung the web of death.

IPHIGENIA (*veiling herself*)

It is enough! Thou wilt again behold me.

PYLADES (*alone*)

The fortune of this royal house, it seems,
Doth move her deeply. Whosoe'er she be,
She must herself have known the monarch well;—
For our good fortune, from a noble house,
She hath been sold to bondage. Peace, my heart!
And let us steer our course with prudent zeal
Toward the star of hope which gleams upon us.

ACT III

Scene I

Iphigenia, Orestes

IPHIGENIA

Unhappy man, I only loose thy bonds
In token of a still severer doom.
The freedom which the sanctuary imparts,
Like the last life-gleam o'er the dying face,
But heralds death. I cannot, dare not, say
Your doom is hopeless; for, with murderous hand,
Could I inflict the fatal blow myself?
And while I here am priestess of Diana,
None, be he who he may, dare touch your heads.
But the incensed king, should I refuse
Compliance with the rites himself enjoin'd,
Will choose another virgin from my train
As my successor. Then, alas! with naught,
Save ardent wishes, can I succor you.
Much honored countrymen! The humblest slave,
Who had but near'd our sacred household hearth,
Is dearly welcome in a foreign land;
How with proportion'd joy and blessing, then,
Shall I receive the man who doth recall
The image of the heroes, whom I learn'd
To honor from my parents, and who cheers
My inmost heart with flatt'ring gleams of hope!

ORESTES

Does prudent forethought prompt thee to conceal
Thy name and race? or may I hope to know
Who, like a heavenly vision, meets me thus?

IPHIGENIA

Yes, thou shalt know me. Now conclude the tale
Of which thy brother only told me half:
Relate their end, who coming home from Troy,
On their own threshold met a doom severe

And most unlook'd for.   Young I was in sooth
When first conducted to this foreign shore,
Yet well I recollect the timid glance
Of wonder and amazement which I cast
On those heroic forms.   When they went forth
It seem'd as though Olympus had sent down
The glorious figures of a bygone world,
To frighten Ilion; and above them all,
Great Agamemnon tower'd preëminent!
Oh, tell me!   Fell the hero in his home,
Through Clytemnestra's and Ægisthus' wiles?

ORESTES

He fell!

IPHIGENIA

Unblest Mycene!   Thus the sons
Of Tantalus, with barbarous hands, have sown
Curse upon curse; and, as the shaken weed
Scatters around a thousand poison-seeds,
So they assassins ceaseless generate,
Their children's children ruthless to destroy.—
Now tell the remnant of thy brother's tale,
Which horror darkly hid from me before.
How did the last descendant of the race,—
The gentle child, to whom the Gods assign'd
The office of avenger,—how did he
Escape that day of blood?   Did equal fate
Around Orestes throw Avernus' net?
Say, was he saved? and is he still alive?
And lives Electra, too?

ORESTES

They both survive.

IPHIGENIA

Golden Apollo, lend thy choicest beams!
Lay them an offering at the throne of Jove!
For I am poor and dumb.

ORESTES

If social bonds
Or ties more close connect thee with this house,
As this thy rapturous joy betrayeth to me,
O then rein in thy heart and hold it fast!
For insupportable the sudden plunge
From happiness to sorrow's gloomy depth.
Thou knowest only Agamemnon's death.

IPHIGENIA

And is not this intelligence enough?

ORESTES

Half of the horror only hast thou heard.

IPHIGENIA

What should I fear? Orestes, Electra lives.

ORESTES

And fearest thou for Clytemnestra naught?

IPHIGENIA

Her, neither hope nor fear have power to save.

ORESTES

She to the land of hope hath bid farewell.

IPHIGENIA

Did her repentant hand shed her own blood?

ORESTES

Not so; yet her own blood inflicted death.

IPHIGENIA

More plainly speak, nor leave me in suspense.
Uncertainty around my anxious head
Her dusky, thousand-folded pinion waves.

ORESTES

Have then the powers above selected me
To be the herald of a dreadful deed,

Which in the drear and soundless realms of night
I fain would hide for ever? 'Gainst my will
Thy gentle voice constrains me; it demands,
And shall receive, a tale of direst woe.
Electra, on the day when fell her sire,
Her brother from impending doom conceal'd;
Him Strophius, his father's relative,
Receiv'd with kindest care, and rear'd him up
With his own son, named Pylades, who soon
Around the stranger twin'd love's fairest bonds.
And as they grew, within their inmost souls
There sprang the burning longing to revenge
The monarch's death. Unlook'd for, and disguis'd,
They reach Mycene, feigning to have brought
The mournful tidings of Orestes' death,
Together with his ashes. Them the queen
Gladly receives. Within the house they enter;
Orestes to Electra shows himself:
She fans the fires of vengeance into flame,
Which in the sacred presence of a mother
Had burn'd more dimly. Silently she leads
Her brother to the spot where fell their sire;
Where lurid blood-marks, on the oft-wash'd floor,
With pallid streaks, anticipate revenge.
With fiery eloquence she pictured forth
Each circumstance of that atrocious deed,—
Her own oppress'd and miserable life,
The prosperous traitor's insolent demeanor,
The perils threat'ning Agamemnon's race
From her who had become their stepmother.—
Then in his hand the ancient dagger thrust,
Which often in the house of Tantalus
With savage fury rag'd,— and by her son
Was Clytemnestra slain.

IPHIGENIA
Immortal powers!
Whose pure and blest existence glides away

'Mid ever shifting clouds, me have ye kept
So many years secluded from the world,
Retain'd me near yourselves, consign'd to me
The childlike task to feed the sacred fire,
And taught my spirit, like the hallow'd flame,
With never-clouded brightness to aspire
To your pure mansions,— but at length to feel
With keener woe the horror of my house?
O tell me of the poor unfortunate!
Speak of Orestes!

ORESTES

O could I speak to tell thee of his death!
Forth from the slain one's spouting blood arose
His mother's ghost;
And to the ancient daughters of the night
Cries,— "Let him not escape,— the matricide!
Pursue the victim, dedicate to you!"
They hear, and glare around with hollow eyes,
Like greedy eagles.   In their murky dens
They stir themselves, and from the corners creep
Their comrades, dire Remorse and pallid Fear;
Before them fumes a mist of Acheron;
Perplexingly around the murderer's brow
The eternal contemplation of the past
Rolls in its cloudy circles.   Once again
The grisly band, commission'd to destroy,
Pollute earth's beautiful and heaven-sown fields,
From which an ancient curse had banish'd them.
Their rapid feet the fugitive pursue;
They only pause to start a wilder fear.

IPHIGENIA

Unhappy one; thy lot resembles his,
Thou feel'st what he, poor fugitive, must suffer.

ORESTES

What say'st thou? why presume my fate like his?

IPHIGENIA

A brother's murder weighs upon thy soul;
Thy younger brother told the mournful tale.

ORESTES

I cannot suffer that thy noble soul
Should by a word of falsehood be deceived.
In cunning rich and practised in deceit
A web ensnaring let the stranger weave
To snare the stranger's feet; between us twain
Be truth!
I am Orestes! and this guilty head
Is stooping to the tomb, and covets death;
It will be welcome now in any shape.
Whoe'er thou art, for thee and for my friend
I wish deliverance — *I* desire it not.
Thou seem'st to linger here against thy will;
Contrive some means of flight, and leave me here:
My lifeless corpse hurl'd headlong from the rock,
My blood shall mingle with the dashing waves,
And bring a curse upon this barbarous shore!
Return together home to lovely Greece,
With joy a new existence to commence.

[ORESTES *retires.*]

IPHIGENIA

At length Fulfilment, fairest child of Jove,
Thou dost descend upon me from on high!
How vast thine image! Scarce my straining eye
Can reach thy hands, which, fill'd with golden fruit
And wreaths of blessing, from Olympus' height
Shower treasures down. As by his bounteous gifts
We recognize the monarch (for what seems
To thousands opulence, is naught to him),
So you, ye heavenly Powers, are also known
By bounty long withheld, and wisely plann'd.
Ye only know what things are good for us;
Ye view the future's wide-extended realm,
While from our eye a dim or starry veil

The prospect shrouds.   Calmly ye hear our prayers,
When we like children sue for greater speed.
Not immature ye pluck heaven's golden fruit;
And woe to him, who with impatient hand,
His date of joy forestalling, gathers death.
Let not this long-awaited happiness,
Which yet my heart hath scarcely realiz'd,
Like to the shadow of departed friends,
Glide vainly by with triple sorrow fraught!

ORESTES (returning)

Dost thou for Pylades and for thyself
Implore the gods, blend not my name with yours;
Thou wilt not save the wretch whom thou wouldst join,
But will participate his curse and woe.

IPHIGENIA

My destiny is firmly bound to thine.

ORESTES

No; say not so: alone and unattended
Let me descend to Hades.   Though thou shouldst
In thine own veil enwrap the guilty one,
Thou couldst not shroud him from his wakeful foes:
And e'en thy sacred presence, heavenly maid,
But driveth them aside and scares them not.
With brazen, impious feet they dare not tread
Within the precincts of this sacred grove:
Yet in the distance, ever and anon,
I hear their horrid laughter, like the howl
Of famish'd wolves, beneath the tree wherein
The traveler hides.   Without, encamp'd they lie,
And should I quit this consecrated grove,
Shaking their serpent locks, they would arise,
And, raising clouds of dust on every side,
Ceaseless pursue their miserable prey.

IPHIGENIA

Orestes, canst thou hear a friendly word?

ORESTES

Reserve it for one favor'd by the gods.

IPHIGENIA

To thee they give anew the light of hope.

ORESTES

Through clouds and smoke I see the feeble gleam
Of the death-stream which lights me down to hell.

IPHIGENIA

Hast thou one sister only, thy Electra?

ORESTES

I knew but one: yet her kind destiny,
Which seemed to us so terrible, betimes
Removed an elder sister from the woe
Which o'er the house of Pelops aye impends.
O cease thy questions, nor thus league thyself
With the Erinnys; still they blow away,
With fiendish joy, the ashes from my soul,
Lest the last embers of the fiery brand
The fatal heritage of Pelops' house,
Should there be quenched. Must then the fire for aye,
Deliberately kindled and supplied
With hellish sulphur, sear my tortured soul?

IPHIGENIA

I scatter fragrant incense in the flame.
O let the pure, the gentle breath of love,
Low murmuring, cool thy bosom's fiery glow.
Orestes, fondly lov'd,— canst thou not hear me?
Hath the terrific Furies' grisly band
Dried up the blood of life within thy veins?
Creeps there, as from the Gorgon's direful head,
A petrifying charm through all thy limbs?
With hollow accents from a mother's blood,
If voices call thee to the shades below,
May not a sister's word with blessing rife
Call from Olympus' height help-rendering gods?

ORESTES

She calls! she calls!—Dost thou desire my doom?
Is there a Fury shrouded in thy form?
Who art thou, that thy voice thus horribly
Can harrow up my bosom's inmost depths?

IPHIGENIA

Thine inmost heart reveals it.   I am she,—
Iphigenia,—look on me, Orestes!

ORESTES

Thou!

IPHIGENIA

My own brother!

ORESTES

Hence, away, begone!
I counsel thee, touch not these fatal locks!
As from Creusa's bridal robe, from me
An inextinguishable fire is kindled.
Leave me!   Like Hercules, a death of shame,
Unworthy wretch, locked in myself, I'll die!

IPHIGENIA

Thou shalt not perish!   Would that I might hear
One quiet word from thee! dispel my doubts,
Make sure the bliss I have implored so long.
A wheel of joy and sorrow in my heart,
Ceaseless revolves.   I from a man unknown
With horror turn; but with resistless might
My inmost heart impels me to my brother.

ORESTES

Is this Lyæus' temple?   Doth the glow
Of holy rage unbridled thus possess
The sacred priestess?

IPHIGENIA

Hear me, oh, look up!
See how my heart, which hath been closed so long

Doth open to the bliss of seeing thee,
The dearest treasure that the world contains,—
Of falling on thy neck, and folding thee
Within my longing arms, which have till now
Met the embraces of the empty wind.
Do not repulse me,—the eternal spring,
Whose crystal waters from Parnassus flow,
Bounds not more gaily on from rock to rock,
Down to the golden vale, than from my heart
The waters of affection freely gush,
And round me form a circling sea of bliss.
Orestes! O my brother!

ORESTES
Lovely nymph!
Nor thy caresses, nor thyself I trust;
Diana claims attendants more severe,
And doth avenge her desecrated fane.
Remove thy circling arm! Wilt thou indeed
Safety and love upon a youth bestow,
And fondly tender him earth's fairest joy?
Unto my friend, more worthy than myself,
Impart thy favors; 'mong yon rocks he roves.
Go, seek him; guide him hence, and heed not me.

IPHIGENIA
Brother, command thyself, and better know
Thy sister, newly found! Misconstrue not
Her pure and heavenly rapture, blaming it
As lustful heat unbridled. O ye gods,
Remove delusion from his rigid gaze,
Lest that this moment, fraught with bliss supreme,
Should make us trebly wretched! She is here,
Thine own, thy long-lost sister! From the altar
The goddess rescued me, and placed me here,
Secure within her consecrated fane —
A captive thou, prepared for sacrifice,
And findest here a sister in the priestess.

ORESTES

Unblessèd one! So may the radiant sun
The final horror of our house behold!
Is not Electra here? That she with us
May also perish, nor her life prolong
For heavier destiny and direr woe.
'Tis well,— I follow, priestess! Fratricide
Is an old custom of our ancient house;
And you, ye gods, I thank, that ye resolve
Childless to root me hence. Thee let me counsel
To view too fondly neither sun nor stars.
Come, follow to the gloomy realms below!
As dragons, gender'd in the sulphur pool,
Swallow each other with voracious rage,
So our accursed race destroys itself.
Childless and guiltless come below with me!
There's pity in thy look! oh, gaze not so,—
'Twas with such looks that Clytemnestra sought
An entrance to her son Orestes' heart,
And yet his uprais'd arm her bosom pierc'd.
His mother fell!—Appear, indignant shade!
Within the circle step, ye fiends of hell,
Be present at the welcome spectacle,
The last, most horrible that ye prepare!
Nor hate, nor vengeance whets the poniard now;
A loving sister is constrain'd to deal
The fatal blow. Weep not! Thou hast no guilt.
From earliest infancy I naught have lov'd,
As thee I could have lov'd, my sister. Come,
The weapon raise, spare not, this bosom rend,
And make an outlet for its boiling streams!
                              [*He sinks exhausted.*]

IPHIGENIA

Alone I cannot bear this bliss and woe.
Where art thou, Pylades? Thine aid I need.
                              [IPHIGENIA *retires.*]

Scene II

ORESTES (*recovering from his swoon and standing up*)

Give yet another! reach from Lethe's stream
The last reviving draught of cool refreshment!
Soon shall its waters in my bosom still
Life's fitful fever; and my spirit then
Adown oblivion's stream shall glide to you,
Ye spirits shrouded in eternal mist.
With tranquil pleasure in your deep repose
A weary son of earth may lave his soul!—
What whisp'ring sounds pervade the dreary grove?
What hollow murmurs haunt its twilight gloom?—
They gather round to view the stranger guest!
Who are yon troop in high communion met,
Like an assembled family of princes?
They mingle peacefully, of every age,
Of either sex: godlike, of kindred mould,
Appear the gliding figures. Yes, 'tis they,
The fathers of my race! With Atreus,
In friendly converse glides Thyestes' shade,
And children playfully around them sport.
Is there no enmity among you now?
And is revenge extinguish'd with the sun?
So am I also welcome, and may hope
To mingle in your solemn company.
Welcome, my sires! Orestes bids you hail!
The seed that ye have sow'd, that hath he reap'd.
Laden with curses he descends to you.
But burdens here are lighter far to bear.
Receive him, oh, receive him in your circle!
Thee, Atreus, I revere, and thee, Thyestes:
Here all are free from enmity and hate.—
Show me my father, whom I only once
In life beheld.—Art thou my father, thou,
My mother leading thus familiarly?
Dares Clytemnestra reach her hand to thee?

Then may Orestes also draw near her,
And say, Behold thy son!—My ancestors,
Behold your son, and bid him welcome here.
Among the sons of ancient Tantalus,
A kind salute on earth was murder's watchword,
And all their joys commence beyond the grave.
Ye welcome me! Ye bid me join your circle!
Oh, lead me to my honor'd ancestor!
Where is our aged sire? Let me behold
The dear, the venerable head of him
Who with the immortal gods in council sat.
Ye seem to shudder and to turn away!
What may this mean? Suffers the godlike man?
Alas! the mighty gods, with ruthless hate,
To his heroic breast, with brazen chains,
Have cruel pangs indissolubly bound.

SCENE III

ORESTES, IPHIGENIA, PYLADES

ORESTES

How! Are ye come already here below?
Welcome, my sister! Still Electra fails;
O that some kindly god, with gentle arrow,
Her too, full speedily, would downward send!
Thee, hapless friend, I must compassionate!
Come with me! Come! To Pluto's gloomy throne,
There to salute our hosts like stranger guests.

IPHIGENIA

Celestial pair, who from the realms above
By night and day shed down the beauteous light
To cheer mankind, but who may not illume
Departed spirits, save a mortal pair!
A brother's and a sister's anguish pity!
For thou, Diana, lov'st thy gentle brother
Beyond what earth and heaven can offer thee;
And dost, with quiet yearning, ever turn
Thy virgin face to his eternal light.

MEETING OF ORESTES, IPHIGENIA AND PYLADES

ANGELICA KAUFFMANN

Let not my only brother, found so late,
Rave in the darkness of insanity!
And is thy will, when thou didst here conceal me,
At length fulfill'd,—wouldst thou to me through him
To him through me, thy gracious aid extend,—
Oh, free him from the fetters of this curse,
Lest vainly pass the precious hours of safety.

PYLADES

Dost thou not know us, and this sacred grove,
And this blest light, which shines not on the dead?
Dost thou not feel thy sister and thy friend,
Who hold thee living in their firm embrace?
Us firmly grasp; we are not empty shades.
Mark well my words! Collect thy scatter'd thoughts!
Attend! Each moment is of priceless worth,
And our return hangs on a slender thread,
Which, as it seems, some gracious fate doth spin.

ORESTES (*to* IPHIGENIA)

My sister, let me for the first time taste,
With open heart; pure joy within thine arms!
Ye gods, who charge the heavy clouds with dread,
And sternly gracious send the long-sought rain
With thunder and the rush of mighty winds,
A horrid deluge on the trembling earth;
Yet dissipate at length man's dread suspense,
Exchanging timid wonder's anxious gaze
For grateful looks and joyous songs of praise,
When in each sparkling drop which gems the leaves,
Apollo, thousand-fold, reflects his beam,
And Iris colors with a magic hand
The dusty texture of the parting clouds;
Oh, let me also in my sister's arms,
And on the bosom of my friend, enjoy
With grateful thanks the bliss ye now bestow;
My heart assures me that your curses cease.
The dread Eumenides at length retire,
The brazen gates of Tartarus I hear

Behind them closing with a thunderous clang.
A quick'ning odor from the earth ascends,
Inviting me to chase, upon its plains,
The joys of life and deeds of high emprize.

PYLADES

Lose not the moments which are limited!
The favoring gale, which swells our parting sail,
Must to Olympus waft our perfect joy.
Quick counsel and resolve the time demands.

ACT IV

Scene I

IPHIGENIA

When the Powers on high decree
For a feeble child of earth
Dire perplexity and woe,
And his spirit doom to pass
With tumult wild from joy to grief,
And back again from grief to joy,
In fearful alternation;
They in mercy then provide,
In the precincts of his home,
Or upon the distant shore,
That to him may never fail
Ready help in hours of need,
A tranquil, faithful friend.
Oh, bless, ye heavenly powers, our Pylades,
And whatsoever he may undertake!
He is in fight the vigorous arm of youth,
And his the thoughtful eye of age in counsel;
For tranquil is his soul; he guardeth there
Of calm a sacred and exhaustless dower,
And from its depths, in rich supply, outpours
Comfort and counsel for the sore distressed.

He tore me from my brother, upon whom,
With fond amaze, I gaz'd and gaz'd again;
I could not realize my happiness,
Nor loose him from my arms, and heeded not
The danger's near approach that threatens us.
To execute their project of escape,
They hasten to the sea, where in a bay
Their comrades in the vessel lie conceal'd
Waiting a signal.   Me they have supplied
With artful answers, should the monarch send
To urge the sacrifice.   Alas! I see
I must consent to follow like a child,
I have not learn'd deception, nor the art
To gain with crafty wiles my purposes.
Detested falsehood! it doth not relieve
The breast like words of truth: it comforts not,
But is a torment in the forger's heart,
And, like an arrow which a god directs,
Flies back and wounds the archer.   Through my heart
One fear doth chase another; perhaps with rage,
Again on the unconsecrated shore,
The Furies' grisly band my brother seize.
Perchance they are surpris'd!   Methinks, I hear
The tread of armèd men.   A messenger
Is coming from the king, with hasty steps.
How throbs my heart, how troubled is my soul,
Now that I gaze upon the face of one,
Whom with a word untrue I must encounter!

SCENE II

IPHIGENIA, ARKAS

ARKAS

Priestess, with speed conclude the sacrifice!
Impatiently the king and people wait.

IPHIGENIA

I had perform'd my duty and thy will,
Had not an unforeseen impediment
The execution of my purpose thwarted.

ARKAS

What is it that obstructs the king's commands?

IPHIGENIA

Chance, which from mortals will not brook control.

ARKAS

Possess me with the reason, that with speed
I may inform the king, who hath decreed
The death of both.

IPHIGENIA

　　　　The gods have not decreed it.
The elder of these men doth bear the guilt
Of kindred murder; on his steps attend
The dread Erinnys. In the inner fane
They seized upon their prey, polluting thus
The holy sanctuary. I hasten now,
Together with my virgin-train, to bathe
The goddess' image in the sea, and there
With solemn rites its purity restore.
Let none presume our silent march to follow!

ARKAS

This hindrance to the monarch I'll announce:
Commence not thou the rite till he permit.

IPHIGENIA

The priestess interferes alone in this.

ARKAS

An incident so strange the king should know.

IPHIGENIA

Here, nor his counsel nor command avails.

ARKAS

Oft are the great consulted out of form.

IPHIGENIA

Do not insist on what I must refuse.

ARKAS

A needful and a just demand refuse not.

IPHIGENIA

I yield, if thou delay not.

ARKAS

I with speed
Will bear these tidings to the camp, and soon
Acquaint thee, priestess, with the king's reply.
There is a message I would gladly bear him;
'Twould quickly banish all perplexity:
Thou didst not heed thy faithful friend's advice.

IPHIGENIA

I willingly have done whate'er I could.

ARKAS

E'en now 'tis not too late to change thy purpose.

IPHIGENIA

To do so is, alas, beyond our power.

ARKAS

What thou wouldst shun, thou deem'st impossible.

IPHIGENIA

Thy wish doth make thee deem it possible.

ARKAS

Wilt thou so calmly venture everything?

IPHIGENIA

My fate I have committed to the gods.

ARKAS

The gods are wont to save by human means.

IPHIGENIA

By their appointment everything is done.

ARKAS

Believe me, all doth now depend on thee.
The irritated temper of the king
Alone condemns these men to bitter death.
The soldiers from the cruel sacrifice
And bloody service long have been disused;
Nay, many, whom their adverse fortunes cast
In foreign regions, there themselves have felt
How godlike to the exil'd wanderer
The friendly countenance of man appears.
Do not deprive us of thy gentle aid!
With ease thou canst thy sacred task fulfil;
For nowhere doth benignity, which comes
In human form from heaven, so quickly gain
An empire o'er the heart, as where a race,
Gloomy and savage, full of life and power,
Without external guidance, and oppress'd
With vague forebodings, bear life's heavy load.

IPHIGENIA

Shake not my spirit, which thou canst not bend
According to thy will.

ARKAS

　　　　　While there is time
Nor labor nor persuasion shall be spar'd.

IPHIGENIA

Thy labor but occasions pain to me;
Both are in vain; therefore, I pray, depart.

ARKAS

I summon pain to aid me, 'tis a friend
Who counsels wisely.

IPHIGENIA

　　　　　Though it shakes my soul,
It doth not banish thence my strong repugnance.

ARKAS

Can then a gentle soul repugnance feel
For benefits bestow'd by one so noble?

IPHIGENIA

From the Painting by Max Zimmebuch

IPHIGENIA

IPHIGENIA

Yes, when the donor, for those benefits,
Instead of gratitude, demands myself.

ARKAS

Who no affection feels doth never want
Excuses. To the king I will relate
What hath befallen. O that in thy soul
Thou wouldst revolve his noble conduct to thee
Since thy arrival to the present day!

SCENE III

IPHIGENIA (*alone*)

These words at an unseasonable hour
Produce a strong revulsion in my breast;
I am alarm'd!— For as the rushing tide
In rapid currents eddies o'er the rocks
Which lie among the sand upon the shore;
E'en so a stream of joy o'erwhelm'd my soul.
I grasp'd what had appear'd impossible.
It was as though another gentle cloud
Around me lay, to raise me from the earth,
And rock my spirit in the same sweet sleep
Which the kind goddess shed around my brow,
What time her circling arm from danger snatched me.
My brother forcibly engross'd my heart;
I listen'd only to his friend's advice;
My soul rush'd eagerly to rescue them,
And as the mariner with joy surveys
The less'ning breakers of a desert isle,
So Tauris lay behind me. But the voice
Of faithful Arkas wakes me from my dream,
Reminding me that those whom I forsake
Are also men. Deceit doth now become
Doubly detested. O my soul, be still!
Beginn'st thou now to tremble and to doubt?
Thy lonely shelter on the firm-set earth

Must thou abandon? and, embark'd once more,
At random drift upon tumultuous waves,
A stranger to thyself and to the world?

Scene IV

Iphigenia, Pylades

PYLADES

Where is she? that my words with speed may tell
The joyful tidings of our near escape!

IPHIGENIA

Oppress'd with gloomy care, I much require
The certain comfort thou dost promise me.

PYLADES

Thy brother is restor'd! The rocky paths
Of this unconsecrated shore we trod
In friendly converse, while behind us lay,
Unmark'd by us, the consecrated grove;
And ever with increasing glory shone
The fire of youth around his noble brow.
Courage and hope his glowing eye inspir'd;
And his exultant heart resigned itself
To the delight, the joy, of rescuing
Thee, his deliverer, also me, his friend.

IPHIGENIA

The gods shower blessings on thee, Pylades!
And from those lips which breathe such welcome news
Be the sad note of anguish never heard!

PYLADES

I bring yet more,—for Fortune, like a prince,
Comes not alone, but well accompanied.
Our friends and comrades we have also found.
Within a bay they had conceal'd the ship,
And mournful sat expectant. They beheld

Thy brother, and a joyous shout uprais'd,
Imploring him to haste the parting hour.
Each hand impatient long'd to grasp the oar,
While from the shore a gently murmuring breeze,
Perceiv'd by all, unfurl'd its wing auspicious.
Let us then hasten; guide me to the fane,
That I may tread the sanctuary, and win
With sacred awe the goal of our desires.
I can unaided on my shoulder bear
The goddess' image: how I long to feel
The precious burden!

> (*While speaking the last words, he approaches the
> Temple, without perceiving that he is not followed
> by* IPHIGENIA: *at length he turns around.*)

Why thus lingering stand?
Why art thou silent? wherefore thus confus'd?
Doth some new obstacle oppose our bliss?
Inform me, hast thou to the king announc'd
The prudent message we agreed upon?

IPHIGENIA

I have, dear Pylades; yet wilt thou chide.
Thy very aspect is a mute reproach.
The royal messenger arriv'd, and I,
According to thy counsel, fram'd my speech.
He seem'd surpris'd, and urgently besought,
That to the monarch I should first announce
The rite unusual, and attend his will.
I now await the messenger's return.

PYLADES

Danger again doth hover o'er our heads!
Alas! Why hast thou failed to shroud thyself
Within the veil of sacerdotal rites?

IPHIGENIA

I never have employ'd them as a veil.

VOL. I — 14

PYLADES

Pure soul! thy scruples will destroy alike
Thyself and us. Why did I not forsee
Such an emergency, and tutor thee
This counsel also wisely to elude?

IPHIGENIA

Chide only me, for mine alone the blame.
Yet other answer could I not return
To him, who strongly and with reason urged
What my own heart acknowledg'd to be right.

PYLADES

The danger thickens; but let us be firm,
Nor with incautious haste betray ourselves;
Calmly await the messenger's return,
And then stand fast, whatever his reply:
For the appointment of such sacred rites
Doth to the priestess, not the king, belong.
Should he demand the stranger to behold,
Who is by madness heavily oppress'd,
Evasively pretend, that in the fane,
Well guarded, thou retainest him and me.
Thus you secure us time to fly with speed,
Bearing the sacred treasure from this race,
Unworthy its possession. Phœbus sends
Auspicious omens, and fulfils his word,
Ere we the first conditions have perform'd.
Free is Orestes, from the curse absolv'd!
Oh, with the freed one, to the rocky isle
Where dwells the god, waft us, propitious gales.
Thence to Mycene, that she may revive;
That from the ashes of the extinguish'd hearth,
The household gods may joyously arise,
And beauteous fire illumine their abode!
Thy hand from golden censers first shall strew
The fragrant incense. O'er that threshold thou
Shalt life and blessing once again dispense,
The curse atone, and all thy kindred grace
With the fresh bloom of renovated life.

IPHIGENIA

As doth the flower revolve to meet the sun,
Once more my spirit to sweet comfort turns,
Struck by thy words' invigorating ray.
How dear the counsel of a present friend,
Lacking whose godlike power, the lonely one
In silence droops! for, lock'd within his breast,
Slowly are ripen'd purpose and resolve,
Which friendship's genial warmth had soon matur'd.

PYLADES

Farewell! I haste to re-assure our friends,
Who anxiously await us: then with speed
I will return, and, hid within the brake,
Attend thy signal.—Wherefore, all at once,
Doth anxious thought o'ercloud thy brow serene?

IPHIGENIA

Forgive me! As light clouds athwart the sun,
So cares and fears float darkling o'er my soul.

PYLADES

Oh, banish fear! With danger it hath form'd
A close alliance,—they are constant friends.

IPHIGENIA

It is an honest scruple, which forbids
That I should cunningly deceive the king,
And plunder him who was my second father.

PYLADES

Him thou dost fly, who would have slain thy brother.

IPHIGENIA

To me, at least, he hath been ever kind.

PYLADES

What Fate commands is not ingratitude.

IPHIGENIA

Alas! it still remains ingratitude;
Necessity alone can justify it.

PYLADES

Thee, before gods and men, it justifies.

IPHIGENIA

But my own heart is still unsatisfied.

PYLADES

Scruples too rigid are a cloak for pride.

IPHIGENIA

I cannot argue, I can only feel.

PYLADES

Conscious of right, thou shouldst respect thyself.

IPHIGENIA

Then only doth the heart know perfect ease,
When not a stain pollutes it.

PYLADES

In this fane
Pure hast thou kept thy heart. Life teaches us
To be less strict with others and ourselves;
Thou'lt learn the lesson too. So wonderful
Is human nature, and its varied ties
Are so involv'd and complicate, that none
May hope to keep his inmost spirit pure,
And walk without perplexity through life.
Nor are we call'd upon to judge ourselves;
With circumspection to pursue his path,
Is the immediate duty of a man;
For seldom can he rightly estimate,
Of his past conduct or his present deeds.

IPHIGENIA

Almost thou dost persuade me to consent.

PYLADES

Needs there persuasion when no choice is granted?
To save thyself, thy brother, and a friend,
One path presents itself, and canst thou ask
If we shall follow it?

IPHIGENIA

Still let me pause,
For such injustice thou couldst not thyself
Calmly return for benefits receiv'd.

PYLADES

If we should perish, bitter self-reproach,
Forerunner of despair, will be thy portion.
It seems thou art not used to suffer much,
When, to escape so great calamity,
Thou canst refuse to utter one false word.

IPHIGENIA

Oh, that I bore within a manly heart!
Which, when it hath conceiv'd a bold resolve,
'Gainst every other voice doth close itself.

PYLADES

In vain thou dost refuse; with iron hand
Necessity commands; her stern decree
Is law supreme, to which the gods themselves
Must yield submission. In dread silence rules
The uncounsell'd sister of eternal fate.
What she appoints thee to endure,— endure;
What to perform,— perform. The rest thou knowest.
Ere long I will return, and then receive
The seal of safety from thy sacred hand.

SCENE V

IPHIGENIA (alone)

I must obey him, for I see my friends
Beset with peril. Yet my own sad fate
Doth with increasing anguish move my heart.
May I no longer feed the silent hope
Which in my solitude I fondly cherish'd?
Shall the dire curse eternally endure?
And shall our fated race ne'er rise again

With blessings crown'd?—All mortal things decay—
The noblest powers, the purest joys of life
At length subside: then wherefore not the curse?
And have I vainly hoped that, guarded here,
Secluded from the fortunes of my race,
I, with pure heart and hands, some future day
Might cleanse the deep defilement of our house?
Scarce was my brother in my circling arms
From raging madness suddenly restor'd,
Scarce had the ship, long pray'd for, near'd the strand
Once more to waft me to my native shores,
When unrelenting Fate, with iron hand,
A double crime enjoins; commanding me
To steal the image, sacred and rever'd,
Confided to my care, and him deceive
To whom I owe my life and destiny.
Let not abhorrence spring within my heart!
Nor the old Titan's hate, toward you, ye gods
Infix its vulture talons in my breast!
Save me and save your image in my soul!

An ancient song comes back upon mine ear—
I had forgotten it, and willingly—
The Parcæ's song, which horribly they sang,
What time, hurl'd headlong from his golden seat,
Fell Tantalus. They with their noble friend
Keen anguish suffer'd; savage was their breast
And horrible their song. In days gone by,
When we were children, oft our ancient nurse
Would sing it to us, and I mark'd it well.

> Oh, fear the immortals,
> Ye children of men!
> Eternal dominion
> They hold in their hands,
> And o'er their wide empire
> Wield absolute sway.

Whom they have exalted
Let him fear them most!
Around golden tables,
On cliffs and clouds resting
The seats are prepar'd.

If contest ariseth,
The guests are hurl'd headlong,
Disgrac'd and dishonor'd,
To gloomy abysses,
And, fetter'd in darkness,
Await the vain longing
A juster decree.

But in feasts everlasting,
Around the gold tables
Still dwell the immortals.
From mountain to mountain
They stride; while ascending
From fathomless chasms
The breath of the Titans,
Half-stifled with anguish,
Like volumes of incense
Fumes up to the skies.

From races ill-fated,
Their aspect joy-bringing,
Oft turn the celestials,
And shun in the children
To gaze on the features
Once lov'd and still speaking
Of their mighty sire.

So chanted the Parcæ;
The banish'd one hearkens
The song, the hoar captive
Immur'd in his dungeon,
His children's doom ponders,
And boweth his head.

ACT V

SCENE I

THOAS, ARKAS

ARKAS

I own I am perplex'd and scarcely know
'Gainst whom to point the shaft of my suspicion,
Whether the priestess aids the captives' flight,
Or they themselves clandestinely contrive it.
'Tis rumor'd that the ship which brought them here
Is lurking somewhere in a bay conceal'd.
This stranger's madness, these new lustral rites,
The specious pretext for delay, excite
Mistrust, and call aloud for vigilance.

THOAS

Summon the priestess to attend me here!
Then go with speed, and strictly search the shore,
From yonder headland to Diana's grove:
Forbear to violate its sacred depths,
A watchful ambush set, attack and seize,
According to your wont, whome'er ye find.

[ARKAS *retires.*]

SCENE II

THOAS (*alone*)

Fierce anger rages in my riven breast,
First against her, whom I esteemed so pure;
Then 'gainst myself, whose foolish lenity
Hath fashion'd her for treason. Man is soon
Inur'd to slavery, and quickly learns
Submission, when of freedom quite depriv'd.
If she had fallen in the savage hands
Of my rude sires, and had their holy rage
Forborne to slay her, grateful for her life,
She would have recogniz'd her destiny,
Have shed before the shrine the stranger's blood,
And duty nam'd what was necessity.

Now my forbearance in her breast allures
Audacious wishes. Vainly I had hoped
To bind her to me; rather she contrives
To shape an independent destiny.
She won my heart through flattery; and now
That I oppose her, seeks to gain her ends
By fraud and cunning, and my kindness deems
A worthless and prescriptive property.

SCENE III

IPHIGENIA, THOAS

IPHIGENIA

Me hast thou summon'd? wherefore art thou here?

THOAS

Wherefore delay the sacrifice? inform me.

IPHIGENIA

I have acquainted Arkas with the reasons.

THOAS

From thee I wish to hear them more at large.

IPHIGENIA

The goddess for reflection grants thee time.

THOAS

To thee this time seems also opportune.

IPHIGENIA

If to this cruel deed thy heart is steel'd,
Thou shouldst not come! A king who meditates
A deed inhuman, may find slaves enow,
Willing for hire to bear one-half the curse,
And leave the monarch's presence undefil'd.
Enrapt in gloomy clouds he forges death,
Flaming destruction then his ministers
Hurl down upon his wretched victim's head,
While he abideth high above the storm,
Calm and untroubled, an impassive god.

THOAS

A wild song, priestess, issued from thy lips.

IPHIGENIA

No priestess, king! but Agamemnon's daughter;
While yet unknown, thou didst respect my words:
A princess now,—and think'st thou to command me?
From youth I have been tutor'd to obey,
My parents first and then the deity;
And thus obeying, ever hath my soul
Known sweetest freedom. But nor then nor now
Have I been taught compliance with the voice
And savage mandates of a man.

THOAS

Not I,

An ancient law doth thy obedience claim.

IPHIGENIA

Our passions eagerly catch hold of laws
Which they can wield as weapons. But to me
Another law, one far more ancient, speaks
And doth command me to withstand thee, king!
That law declaring sacred every stranger.

THOAS

These men, methinks, lie very near thy heart,
When sympathy with them can lead thee thus
To violate discretion's primal law,
That those in power should never be provok'd.

IPHIGENIA

Speaking or silent, thou canst always know
What is, and ever must be, in my heart.
Doth not remembrance of a common doom,
To soft compassion melt the hardest heart?
How much more mine! in them I see myself.
I trembling kneel'd before the altar once,
And solemnly the shade of early death
Environ'd me. Aloft the knife was rais'd
To pierce my bosom, throbbing with warm life;

A dizzy horror overwhelm'd my soul;
My eyes grew dim;—I found myself in safety.
Are we not bound to render the distress'd
The gracious kindness from the gods receiv'd?
Thou know'st we are, and yet wilt thou compel me?

THOAS

Obey thine office, priestess, not the king.

IPHIGENIA

Cease! nor thus seek to cloak the savage force
Which triumphs o'er a woman's feebleness.
Though woman, I am born as free as man.
Did Agamemnon's son before thee stand,
And thou requiredst what became him not,
His arm and trusty weapon would defend
His bosom's freedom. I have only words;
But it becomes a noble-minded man
To treat with due respect the words of woman.

THOAS

I more respect them than a brother's sword.

IPHIGENIA

Uncertain ever is the chance of arms,
No prudent warrior doth despise his foe;
Nor yet defenceless 'gainst severity
Hath nature left the weak; she gives him craft
And, willy, cunning; artful he delays,
Evades, eludes, and finally escapes.
Such arms are justified by violence.

THOAS

But circumspection countervails deceit.

IPHIGENIA

Which a pure spirit doth abhor to use.

THOAS

Do not incautiously condemn thyself.

IPHIGENIA

Oh, couldst thou see the struggle of my soul,
Courageously to ward the first attack
Of an unhappy doom, which threatens me!
Do I then stand before thee weaponless?
Prayer, lovely prayer, fair branch in woman's hand,
More potent far than instruments of war,
Thou dost thrust back. What now remains for me
Wherewith my inborn freedom to defend?
Must I implore a miracle from heaven?
Is there no power within my spirit's depths?

THOAS

Extravagant thy interest in the fate
Of these two strangers. Tell me who they are
For whom thy heart is thus so deeply mov'd.

IPHIGENIA

They are — they seem at least — I think them Greeks.

THOAS

Thy countrymen; no doubt they have renew'd
The pleasing picture of return.

IPHIGENIA (*after a pause*)
Doth man
Lay undisputed claim to noble deeds?
Doth he alone to his heroic breast
Clasp the impossible? What call we great?
What deeds, though oft narrated, still uplift
With shuddering horror the narrator's soul,
But those which, with improbable success,
The valiant have attempted? Shall the man
Who all alone steals on his foes by night,
And raging like an unexpected fire,
Destroys the slumbering host, and press'd at length
By rous'd opponents on his foeman's steeds,
Retreats with booty — be alone extoll'd?

Or he who, scorning safety, boldly roams
Through woods and dreary wilds, to scour the land
Of thieves and robbers? Is naught left for us?
Must gentle woman quite forego her nature,
Force against force employ, like Amazons
Usurp the sword from man, and bloodily
Revenge oppression? In my heart I feel
The stirrings of a noble enterprize;
But if I fail — severe reproach, alas!
And bitter misery will be my doom.
Thus on my knees I supplicate the gods!
Oh, are ye truthful, as men say ye are,
Now prove it by your countenance and aid;
Honor the truth in me! Attend, O king!
A secret plot deceitfully is laid;
Touching the captives thou dost ask in vain;
They have departed hence and seek their friends,
Who, with the ship, await them on the shore.
The eldest, — whom dire madness lately seiz'd,
And hath abandon'd now, — he is Orestes,
My brother, and the other Pylades,
His early friend and faithful confidant.
From Delphi, Phœbus sent them to this shore
With a divine command to steal away
The image of Diana, and to him
Bear back the sister thither, and for this
He promised to the blood-stained matricide,
The Fury-haunted son, deliverance.
I have surrender'd now into thy hands
The remnants of the house of Tantalus.
Destroy us — if thou canst.

THOAS

And dost thou think
That the uncultured Scythian will attend
The voice of truth and of humanity
Which Atreus, the Greek, heard not?

IPHIGENIA

'Tis heard
By every one, born 'neath whatever clime,
Within whose bosom flows the stream of life,
Pure and unhinder'd.— What thy thought? O king,
What silent purpose broods in thy deep soul?
Is it destruction? Let me perish first!
For now, deliv'rance hopeless, I perceive
The dreadful peril into which I have
With rash precipitancy plung'd my friends.
Alas! I soon shall see them bound before me!
How to my brother shall I say farewell?
I, the unhappy author of his death.
Ne'er can I gaze again in his dear eyes!

THOAS

The traitors have contrived a cunning web,
And cast it round thee, who, secluded long,
Giv'st willing credence to thine own desires.

IPHIGENIA

No, no! I'd pledge my life these men are true.
And shouldst thou find them otherwise, O king,
Then let them perish both, and cast me forth,
That on some rock-girt island's dreary shore
I may atone my folly. Are they true,
And is this man indeed my dear Orestes,
My brother, long implor'd,— release us both,
And o'er us stretch the kind protecting arm
Which long hath shelter'd me. My noble sire
Fell through his consort's guilt,— she by her son;
On him alone the hope of Atreus' race
Doth now repose. Oh, with pure heart, pure hand,
Let me depart to purify our house.
Yes, thou wilt keep thy promise; thou didst swear,
That were a safe return provided me,
I should be free to go. The hour is come.

A king doth never grant like common men,
Merely to gain a respite from petition;
Nor promise what he hopes will ne'er be claim'd.
Then first he feels his dignity supreme
When he can make the long-expecting happy.

THOAS

As fire opposes water, and doth seek
With hissing rage to overcome its foe,
So doth my anger strive against thy words.

IPHIGENIA

Let mercy, like the consecrated flame
Of silent sacrifice, encircled round
With songs of gratitude, and joy, and praise,
Above the tumult gently rise to heaven.

THOAS

How often hath this voice assuag'd my soul!

IPHIGENIA

Extend thy hand to me in sign of peace.

THOAS

Large thy demand within so short a time.

IPHIGENIA

Beneficence doth no reflection need.

THOAS

'Tis needed oft, for evil springs from good.

IPHIGENIA

'Tis doubt which good doth oft to evil turn.
Consider not; act as thy feelings prompt thee.

SCENE IV

ORESTES (*armed*), IPHIGENIA, THOAS
ORESTES (*addressing his followers*)

Redouble your exertions! hold them back!
Few moments will suffice; maintain your ground,

And keep a passage open to the ship
For me and for my sister.

(*To* IPHIGENIA, *without perceiving* THOAS.)

Come with speed!
We are betray'd,—brief time remains for flight.

(*He perceives the king.*)

THOAS (*laying his hand on his sword*)
None in my presence with impunity
His naked weapon wears.

IPHIGENIA
Do not profane
Diana's sanctuary with rage and blood.
Command your people to forbear awhile,
And listen to the priestess, to the sister.

ORESTES
Say, who is he that threatens us?

IPHIGENIA
In him
Revere the king, who was my second father.
Forgive me, brother, that my childlike heart
Hath plac'd our fate thus wholly in his hands.
I have betray'd your meditated flight,
And thus from treachery redeem'd my soul.

ORESTES
Will he permit our peaceable return?

IPHIGENIA
Thy gleaming sword forbids me to reply.

ORESTES (*sheathing his sword*)
Then speak! thou seest I listen to thy words.

Scene V

ORESTES, IPHIGENIA, THOAS

Enter PYLADES, *soon after him* ARKAS *both with drawn swords.*

PYLADES

Do not delay! our friends are putting forth
Their final strength, and, yielding step by step,
Are slowly driven backward to the sea.—
A conference of princes find I here?
Is this the sacred person of the king?

ARKAS

Calmly, as doth become thee, thou dost stand,
O king, surrounded by thine enemies.
Soon their temerity shall be chastiz'd;
Their yielding followers fly,— their ship is ours,
Speak but the word and it is wrapt in flames.

THOAS

Go, and command my people to forbear!
Let none annoy the foe while we confer.

[ARKAS *retires.*]

ORESTES

I willingly consent.   Go, Pylades!
Collect the remnant of our friends, and wait
The appointed issue of our enterprize.

[PYLADES *retires.*]

Scene VI

IPHIGENIA, THOAS, ORESTES

IPHIGENIA

Relieve my cares ere ye begin to speak.
I fear contention, if thou wilt not hear
The voice of equity, O king,—if thou
Wilt not, my brother, curb thy headstrong youth.

THOAS

I, as becomes the elder, check my rage.
Now answer me: how dost thou prove thyself
The priestess' brother, Agamemnon's son?

ORESTES

Behold the sword with which the hero slew
The valiant Trojans. From his murderer
I took the weapon, and implor'd the Gods
To grant me Agamemnon's mighty arm,
Success, and valor, with a death more noble.
Select one of the leaders of thy host,
And place the best as my opponent here.
Where'er on earth the sons of heroes dwell,
This boon is to the stranger ne'er refus'd.

THOAS

This privilege hath ancient custom here
To strangers ne'er accorded.

ORESTES

             Then from us
Commence the novel custom! A whole race
In imitation soon will consecrate
Its monarch's noble action into law.
Nor let me only for our liberty,—
Let me, a stranger, for all strangers fight.
If I should fall, my doom be also theirs;
But if kind fortune crown me with success,
Let none e'er tread this shore, and fail to meet
The beaming eye of sympathy and love,
Or unconsoled depart!

THOAS

            Thou dost not seem
Unworthy of thy boasted ancestry.
Great is the number of the valiant men
Who wait upon me; but I will myself,
Although advanc'd in years, oppose the foe,
And am prepar'd to try the chance of arms.

IPHIGENIA

No, no! such bloody proofs are not requir'd.
Unhand thy weapon, king! my lot consider;
Rash combat oft immortalizes man;

If he should fall, he is renown'd in song;
But after ages reckon not the tears
Which ceaseless the forsaken woman sheds;
And poets tell not of the thousand nights
Consum'd in weeping, and the dreary days,
Wherein her anguish'd soul, a prey to grief,
Doth vainly yearn to call her lov'd one back.
Fear warn'd me to beware lest robbers' wiles
Might lure me from this sanctuary, and then
Betray me into bondage.   Anxiously
I question'd them, each circumstance explor'd,
Demanded proofs, now is my heart assur'd.
See here, the mark on his right hand impress'd
As of three stars, which on his natal day
Were by the priest declar'd to indicate
Some dreadful deed therewith to be perform'd.
And then this scar, which doth his eyebrow cleave,
Redoubles my conviction.   When a child,
Electra, rash and inconsiderate,
Such was her nature, loos'd him from her arms,
He fell against a tripos.   Oh, 'tis he!—
Shall I adduce the likeness to his sire,
Or the deep rapture of my inmost heart,
In further token of assurance, king?

THOAS

E'en though thy words had banish'd every doubt,
And I had curb'd the anger in my breast,
Still must our arms decide.   I see no peace.
Their purpose, as thou didst thyself confess,
Was to deprive me of Diana's image.
And think ye I will look contented on?
The Greeks are wont to cast a longing eye
Upon the treasures of barbarians,
A golden fleece, good steeds, or daughters fair;
But force and guile not always have avail'd
To lead them, with their booty, safely home.

ORESTES

The image shall not be a cause of strife!
We now perceive the error which the god,
Our journey here commanding, like a veil,
Threw o'er our minds. His counsel I implor'd,
To free me from the Furies' grisly band.
He answer'd, "Back to Greece the sister bring,
Who in the sanctuary on Tauris' shore
Unwillingly abides; so ends the curse!"
To Phœbus' sister we applied the words,
And he referr'd to thee! The bonds severe,
Which held thee from us, holy one, are rent,
And thou art ours once more. At thy blest touch,
I felt myself restor'd. Within thine arms,
Madness once more around me coil'd its folds,
Crushing the marrow in my frame, and then
Forever, like a serpent, fled to hell.
Through thee, the daylight gladdens me anew,
The counsel of the goddess now shines forth
In all its beauty and beneficence.
Like to a sacred image, unto which
An oracle immutably hath bound
A city's welfare, thee she bore away,
Protectress of our house, and guarded here
Within this holy stillness, to become
A blessing to thy brother and thy race.
Now when each passage to escape seems clos'd,
And safety hopeless, thou dost give us all.
O king, incline thine heart to thoughts of peace!
Let her fulfil her mission, and complete
The consecration of our father's house,
Me to their purified abode restore,
And place upon my brow the ancient crown!
Requite the blessing which her presence brought thee,
And let me now my nearer right enjoy!
Cunning and force, the proudest boast of man,
Fade in the lustre of her perfect truth;

Nor unrequited will a noble mind
Leave confidence, so childlike and so pure.

IPHIGENIA

Think on thy promise; let thy heart be mov'd
By what a true and honest tongue hath spoken!
Look on us, king! an opportunity
For such a noble deed not oft occurs.
Refuse thou canst not,— give thy quick consent.

THOAS

Then go!

IPHIGENIA

Not so, my king! I cannot part
Without thy blessing, or in anger from thee,
Banish us not! the sacred right of guests
Still let us claim: so not eternally
Shall we be sever'd. Honor'd and belov'd
As mine own father was, art thou by me;
And this impression in my soul abides,
Let but the least among thy people bring
Back to mine ear the tones I heard from thee,
Or should I on the humblest see thy garb,
I will with joy receive him as a god,
Prepare his couch myself, beside our hearth
Invite him to a seat, and only ask
Touching thy fate and thee. Oh, may the gods
To thee the merited reward impart
Of all thy kindness and benignity!
Farewell! O turn thou not away, but give
One kindly word of parting in return!
So shall the wind more gently swell our sails,
And from our eyes with soften'd anguish flow,
The tears of separation. Fare thee well!
And graciously extend to me thy hand,
In pledge of ancient friendship.

THOAS (extending his hand)
Fare thee well!

THE FAUST LEGEND FROM MARLOWE TO GOETHE

By Kuno Francke, Ph.D., LL.D., Litt.D.

Professor of the History of German Culture, Harvard University

THE Faust legend is a conglomerate of anonymous popular traditions, largely of medieval origin, which in the latter part of the sixteenth century came to be associated with an actual individual of the name of Faustus whose notorious career during the first four decades of the century, as a pseudo-scientific mountebank, juggler and magician can be traced through various parts of Germany. The Faust Book of 1587, the earliest collection of these tales, is of prevailingly theological character. It represents Faust as a sinner and reprobate, and it holds up his compact with Mephistopheles and his subsequent damnation as an example of human recklessness and as a warning to the faithful.

From this Faust Book, that is from its English translation, which appeared in 1588, Marlowe took his tragedy of *Dr. Faustus* (1589; published 1604). In Marlowe's drama Faust appears as a typical man of the Renaissance, as an explorer and adventurer, as a superman craving for extraordinary power, wealth, enjoyment, and worldly eminence. The finer emotions are hardly touched upon. Mephistopheles is the medieval devil, harsh and grim and fierce, bent on seduction, without any comprehension of human aspirations. Helen of Troy is a she-devil, and becomes the final means of Faust's destruction. Faust's career has hardly an element of true greatness. None of the many tricks, conjurings and miracles, which Faust performs with Mephistopheles' help, has any relation to the deeper meaning of life. From the compact on to the end hardly anything happens which brings Faust inwardly nearer either to heaven or hell. But there is a sturdiness of character and stirring intensity of action, with a happy admixture of buffoonery, through it all. And we feel something of the pathos and paradox of human passions in the fearful agony of Faust's final doom.

The German popular Faust drama of the seventeenth century and its outgrowth the puppet plays, are a reflex both of Marlowe's tragedy and the Faust Book of 1587, although they contain a number of original scenes, notably the Council of the Devils at the beginning. Here again, the underlying sentiment is the abhorrence of human recklessness and extravagance. In some of these plays, the vanity of bold ambition is brought out with particular emphasis through the contrast between the daring and dissatisfied Faust and his farcical counterpart, the jolly and contented Casperle. In the last scene, while Faust in despair and contrition is waiting for the sound of the midnight bell which is to be the signal of his destruction, Casperle, as night watchman, patrols the streets of the town, calling out the hours and singing the traditional verses of admonition to quiet and orderly conduct.

To the sixteenth and seventeenth centuries, then, Faust appeared as a criminal who sins against the eternal laws of life, as a rebel against holiness who ruins his better self and finally earns the merited reward of his misdeeds. He could not appear thus to the eighteenth century. The eighteenth century is the age of Rationalism and of Romanticism. The eighteenth century glorifies human reason and human feeling. The right of man and the dignity of man are its principal watchwords. Such an age was bound to see in Faust a champion of freedom, nature, truth. Such an age was bound to see in Faust a symbol of human striving for completeness of life.

It is Lessing who has given to the Faust legend this turn. His *Faust*, unfortunately consisting only of a few fragmentary sketches, is a defense of Rationalism. The most important of these fragments, preserved to us in copies by some friends of Lessing's, is the prelude, a

council of devils.   Satan is receiving reports from his
subordinates as to what they have done to bring harm to
the realm of God.   The first devil who speaks has set the
hut of some pious poor on fire; the second has buried a
fleet of usurers in the waves.   Both excite Satan's disgust.
"For," he says, "to make the pious poor still poorer
means only to chain him all the more firmly to God"; and
the usurers, if, instead of being buried in the waves, they
had been allowed to reach the goal of their voyage, would
have wrought new evil on distant shores.   Much more
satisfied is Satan with the report of a third devil who has
stolen the first kiss from a young innocent girl and thereby
breathed the flame of desire into her veins; for he has
worked evil in the world of the spirit and that means
much more and is a much greater triumph for hell than to
work evil in the world of bodies.   But it is the fourth devil
to whom Satan gives the prize.   He has not done anything
as yet.   He has only a plan, but a plan which, if carried
out, would put the deeds of all the other devils into the
shade — the plan "to snatch from God his favorite."   This
favorite of God is Faust, "a solitary, brooding youth,
renouncing all passion except the passion for truth, entirely
living in truth, entirely absorbed in it."   To snatch him
from God — that would be a victory, over which the whole
realm of night would rejoice.   Satan is enchanted; the
war against truth is his element.   Yes, Faust must be
seduced, he must be destroyed.   And he shall be destroyed
through his very aspiration.   "Didst thou not say, he has
desire for knowledge?   That is enough for perdition!"
His striving for truth is to lead him into darkness.   Under
such exclamations the devils break up, to set about their
work of seduction; but, as they are breaking up, there is
heard from above a divine voice: "Ye shall not conquer."

It cannot be denied that Goethe's earliest Faust conception, the so-called *Ur-Faust* of 1773 and '74, lacks the
wide sweep of thought that characterizes these fragments
of Lessing's drama.   His Faust of the Storm and Stress

period is essentially a Romanticist. He is a dreamer, craving for a sight of the divine, longing to fathom the inner working of nature, drunk with the mysteries of the universe. But he is also an unruly individualist, a reckless despiser of accepted morality; and it is hard to see how his relation with Gretchen, which forms by far the largest part of the *Ur-Faust*, can lead to anything but a tragic catastrophe. Only Goethe's second Faust conception, which sets in with the end of the nineties of the eighteenth century, opens up a clear view of the heights of life.

Goethe was now in the full maturity of his powers, a man widely separated from the impetuous youth of the seventies whose Promethean emotions had burst forth with volcanic passion. He had meanwhile become a statesman and a philosopher. He had come to know in the court of Weimar a model of paternal government, conservative yet liberally inclined, and friendly to all higher culture. He had found in his truly spiritual relation to Frau von Stein a safe harbor for his tempestuous feelings. He had been brought face to face, during his sojourn in Italy, with the wonders of classic art. The study of Spinoza and his own scientific investigations had confirmed him in a thoroughly monistic view of the world and strengthened his belief in a universal law which makes evil itself an integral part of the good. The example of Schiller as well as his own practical experience had taught him that the untrammelled living out of personality must go hand in hand with incessant work for the common welfare of mankind. All this is reflected in the completed Part First of 1808; it finds its most comprehensive expression in Part Second, the bequest of the dying poet to posterity.

Restless endeavor, incessant striving from lower spheres of life to higher ones, from the sensuous to the spiritual, from enjoyment to work, from creed to deed, from self to humanity — this is the moving thought of Goethe's completed *Faust*. The keynote is struck in the " Prologue in Heaven." Faust, so we hear, the daring idealist, the servant of God, is to be tempted by Mephisto, the despiser of reason, the materialistic scoffer. But we also hear, and we hear it from God's own lips, that the tempter will not succeed. God allows the devil free play, because he knows that he will frustrate his own ends. Faust will be led astray—"man errs while he strives"; but he will not abandon his higher aspirations; through aberration and sin he will find the true way toward which his inner nature instinctively guides him. He will not eat dust. Even in the compact with Mephisto the same ineradicable optimism asserts itself. Faust's wager with the devil is nothing but an act of temporary despair, and the very fact that he does not hope anything from it shows that he will win it. He knows that sensual enjoyment will never give him satisfaction; he knows that, as long as he gives himself up to self-gratification, there will never be a moment to which he would say: "Abide, thou art so fair!" From the outset we feel that by living up to the very terms of the compact, Faust will rise superior to it; that by rushing into the whirlpool of earthly experience and passion, his being will be heightened and expanded.

And thus, everything in the whole drama, all its incidents and all its characters, become episodes in the rounding out of this grand, all-comprehensive personality. Gretchen and Helena, Wagner and Mephisto, Homunculus and Euphorion, the Emperor's court and the shades of the Greek past, the broodings of medieval mysticism and the practical tasks of modern industrialism, the enlightened despotism of the eighteenth century and the ideal democracy of the future—all this and a great deal more enters into Faust's being. He strides on from experience to experience, from task to task, expiating guilt by doing, losing himself and finding himself again. Blinded in old age by Dame Care, he feels a new light kindled within. Dying, he gazes into a far future. And even in the heavenly regions he goes on ever changing into new and higher and finer forms. It is this irrepressible spirit of striving which makes Goethe's *Faust* the Bible of modern humanity.

INTRODUCTION TO FAUST

By Calvin Thomas, LL.D.

Professor of Germanic Languages and Literatures, Columbia University

THE central theme of Goethe's *Faust* may be put in the form of a question thus: Shall a man hate life because it does not match his dreams, or shall he embrace it eagerly and try to make the best of it as a social being? Goethe's answer is at once scientific and religious, which partly explains its vital interest for the modern man. To be sure, his answer is given at the end of a long symbolic poem which contains much that is not exactly relevant to the main issue. It must never be forgotten that *Faust* is not the orderly development of a thesis in ethics, but a long succession of imaginative pictures. Some of them may seem too recondite and fantastic to meet our present-day demand for reality, but on the whole the poem deals with vital issues of the human spirit. At the end of it Faust arrives at a noble view of life, and his last words undoubtedly tell how Goethe himself thought that a good man might wish to end his days—unsated with life to the final moment, and expiring in an ecstasy of altruistic vision.

Goethe was about twenty years old when his imagination began to be haunted by the figure of the sixteenth century magician Doctor Faust. In 1772 or 1773 he commenced writing a play on the subject, little thinking of course that it would occupy him some sixty years. The old legend is a story of sin and damnation. Faust is represented as an eager student impelled by intellectual curiosity to the study of magic. From the point of view of the superstitious folk who created the legend this addiction to magic is itself sinful. But Faust is bad and reckless. By the aid of his black art he calls up a devil named (in the legend) Mephostophiles with whom he makes a contract of service. For twenty-four years Faust is to have all that he desires, and then his soul is to go to perdition. The contract is carried out. With the Devil as comrade and servant he lords it over time and space, feeds on the fat of the land, travels far and wide, and does all sorts of wonderful things. At the end of the stipulated time the Devil gets him.

From the very beginning of his musings on the theme Goethe thought of Faust as a man better than his reputation; as a misunderstood truth-seeker who had dared the terrors with which the popular imagination invested hell, in order that he might exhaust the possibilities of this life. Aside from his desire of transcendental knowledge and wide experience, there was a third trait of the legendary Faust which could hardly seem to Goethe anything but creditable to human nature: his passion for antique beauty. According to the old story Faust at one time wishes to marry; but as marriage is a Christian ordinance and he has forsworn Christianity, the Devil gives him, in place of a lawful wife, a fantom counterfeit of Helena, the ancient Queen of Beauty. The lovely fantom becomes Faust's paramour and bears him a remarkable son called Justus Faustus.

What wonder if the young Goethe, himself disappointed with book-learning, eager for life, and beset by vague yearnings for mystic insight into the nature of things, saw in Faust a symbol of his own experience? But as soon as he began to identify himself with his hero it was all up with Faust's utter damnableness: a young poet does not plan to send his own soul to perdition. At the same time, he could not very well imagine him as an out-and-out good man, since that would have been to turn the legend topsy-turvy. The league with the Devil, who would of course have to be conceived as in some sense or other an embodiment of evil, was the very heart of the old story.

At first Goethe planned his drama on lines that had little

to do with traditional ideas of good and bad, heaven and hell, God and Devil.   Faust is introduced as a youngish professor who has studied everything and been teaching for some ten years, with the result that he feels his knowledge to be vanity and his life a dreary routine of hypocrisy. He resorts to magic in the hope of — what?   It is important for the understanding of the poem in its initial stages to bear in mind that Faust is not at first a votary of the vulgar black art which consists in calling up bad spirits and doing reprehensible things by their assistance.   Further on he shows that he is a master of that art too, but at first he is concerned with " natural magic," which some of the old mystics whom Goethe read conceived as the highest and divinest of sciences.   The fundamental assumption of natural magic is that the universe as a whole and each component part of it is dominated by an indwelling spirit with whom it is possible for the magician to get into communication.   If he succeeds he becomes " like " a spirit — freed from the trammels of the flesh, a partaker of divine knowledge and ecstatic happiness.

Pursuing his wonderful vagaries by means of a magic book that has come into his possession, Faust first experiments with the " sign " of the Macrocosm, but makes no attempt to summon its presiding genius, that is, the World-spirit.   He has a wonderful vision of the harmonious Cosmos, but it is " only a spectacle," whereas he craves food for his soul.   So he turns to the sign of the Earth-spirit, whom he feels to be nearer to him.   By an act of supreme daring he utters the formula which causes the Spirit to appear in fire — grand, awe-inspiring, terrible. A colloquy ensues at the end of which the Spirit rebuffs the presumptuous mortal with the words: " Thou art like the spirit whom thou comprehendest, not like me " — and disappears.   The meaning is that Faust, who knows very little of the Earth, having always led the narrow life of a brooding scholar in one little corner of it, is not fit for intimacy with the mighty being who presides over the

entire planet, with its rush and change, its life and death,
its vast and ceaseless energy. He must have a wider
experience. How shall he get it?

It is a moot question whether Goethe at first conceived
Mephistopheles as the Earth-spirit's envoy, sent for the
express purpose of showing Faust about the world, or
whether the Devil was thought of as coming of his own
accord. Be that as it may, *Faust* is an experience-drama,
and the Devil's function is to provide the experience. And
he is *a* devil, not *the* Devil, conceived as the bitter and
malignant enemy of God, but a subordinate spirit whose
business it is, in the world-economy, to spur man to
activity. This he does partly by cynical criticism and
opposition, but more especially by holding out the lures of
the sensual life. At first Mephistopheles was not thought
of as working solely for a reward in the shape of souls
captured for eternity, but as playing his part for the dia-
bolical pleasure of so doing. In the course of time, however, Goethe invested him more and more with the costume
and traits of the traditionary Devil.

After the Earth-spirit's rebuff Faust is in despair. He
has set all his hope on help from the spirit-world, and the
hope has failed. His famulus Wagner, a type of the
ardent and contented bookworm, comes in to get instruction on the art of public speaking, and Faust lays down
the law to him. After Wagner's exit Faust is hopelessly
despondent. After a mournful arraignment of life he is
about to swallow a cup of poison that he has concocted,
when his hand is staid by the first notes of the Easter
celebration in a neighboring church. It reminds him of
his happy youth when he, too, believed.

The coming day is Easter Sunday. Faust and Wagner
take an afternoon walk together and witness the jollity of
the common people. As they are about to return home at
nightfall they pick up a casual black dog that has been
circling around them. Arrived in his comfortable study,
Faust feels more cheerful. In a mood of religious peace

he sets about translating a passage of the New Testament into German. The dog becomes uneasy and begins to take on the appearance of a horrid monster. Faust sees that he has brought home a spirit and proceeds to conjure the beast. Presently Mephistopheles emerges from his canine disguise in the costume of a wandering scholar. Faust is amused. He enters into conversation with his guest and learns something of his character. A familiar acquaintance ensues, and one day the Devil finds him once more in a mood of bitter despair, advises him to quit the tedious professorial life, and offers to be his comrade and servant on a grand tour of pleasure. After some bickering they enter into a solemn agreement according to which Faust's life is to end whenever he shall " stretch himself on a bed of ease," completely satisfied with the passing moment, and shall say to that moment, " Pray tarry, thou art so fair."

We see that the Devil can win in only one way, namely, by somehow making Faust a contented sensualist. On the other hand, Faust may win in either of two ways. First, he might conceivably go on to his dying day as a bitter pessimist at war with life. In that event he would certainly never be content with the present moment. Secondly, he may outgrow his pessimism, but never come to the point where he is willing to check the flight of Time; when, that is, he shall have no more plans, hopes, dreams, that reach into the future and seem worth living for. The question is, then, whether Mephistopheles, by any lure at his command, can subdue Faust's forward-ranging idealism. The Devil expects to win; Faust wagers his immortal soul that the Devil will not win. In the old story the Devil appears promptly at the end of the twenty-four years, puts his victim to death, and takes possession of his soul. Goethe's Mephistopheles is a gentleman of culture for whom such savagery would be impossible. He will wait until his comrade dies a natural death and then put in his claim in the Devil's fashion; and it will be for the Lord in heaven to decide the case.

Such is the scheme of the drama, but after the compact is made we hear no more of it until just before the end of the Second Part. The action takes the form of a long succession of adventures undertaken for the sake of experience. Duty, obligation, routine, have been left behind. Faust has nothing to do but to go about and try experiments — first in the "little world" of humble folk (the remainder of Part First), and then in the "great world" of court life, government, and war (the Second Part).

By way of beginning Faust is taken to Auerbach's Cellar, where four jolly companions are assembled for a drinking-bout. He is simply disgusted with the grossness and vulgarity of it all. He is too old — so the Devil concludes — for the rôle he is playing and must have his youth renewed. So they repair to an old witch, who gives Faust an elixir that makes him young again. The scene in the witch's kitchen was written in Italy in 1788, by which time Goethe had come to think of his hero as an elderly man. The purpose of the scene was to account for the sudden change of Faust's character from brooding philosopher to rake and seducer. Of course the elixir of youth is at the same time a love-philter.

Then come the matchless scenes that body forth the short romance of Margaret, her quick infatuation, her loss of virgin honor, the death of her mother and brother, her shame and misery, her agonizing death in prison. Here we are in the realm of pure realism, and never again did Goethe's art sound such depths of tragic pathos. The atmosphere of the love-tragedy is entirely different from that of the Faust-legend. Mephistopheles as the abettor of Faust's amorous passion has no need of magic. The rôle of Faust — that of a man pulled irresistibly by sexual passion, yet constantly tormented by his conscience — is repulsive, but very human. As he stands before the prison gate he says that "the whole sorrow of mankind" holds him in its grip. But this is a part of what he wished for. He wished for universal experience — to feel in his own soul all the weal and all the woe of humankind. At the end of the First Part he has drained the cup of sin and suffering.

Imbedded in the love-tragedy is one scene which will seem out of tune with what has just been said — the Walpurgis Night. Here we are back again in the atmosphere of the legend, with its magic, its witchcraft, its gross sensuality. We hardly recognize our friend Faust when we find him dancing with naked witches and singing lewd songs on the Brocken. The scene was written in 1800 when Goethe had become a little cynical with respect to the artistic coherence of *Faust* and looked on it as a " monstrosity." It was a part of the early plan that Faust should add to the burden of his soul by frivolously deserting Margaret in the shame of her approaching motherhood and spending some time in gross pleasures. The visit to the Witches' Sabbath on the Brocken was afterward invented to carry out this idea. In itself the idea was a good one; for if Faust was to drain the cup of sorrow, the ingredient of self-contempt could not be left out of the bitter chalice. A sorrow's crown of sorrow is not so much remembering happier things as remembering that the happy state came to an end by one's own wrongdoing. Still, most modern readers will think that Goethe, in elaborating the Brocken scene as an interesting study of the uncanny and the vile, let his hero sink needlessly far into the mire.

At the beginning of the Second Part Goethe does not reopen the book of crime and remorse with which the First Part closes. He needs a new Faust for whom that is all past — past, not in the sense of being lightly forgotten, but built into his character and remembered, say, as one remembers the ecstasy and the pain of twenty years ago. So he ushers him directly into the new life over a bridge of symbolism. The restoring process which in real life takes many years he concentrates into a single night and represents it as the work of kindly nocturnal fairies and the glorious Alpine sunrise. Faust awakens healed and reinvigorated, and the majesty of Nature inspires in him a resolve to "strive ever onward toward the highest existence."

But these fine words convey a promise which is not at once fulfilled. Like the most of us, Faust does not long continue to abide on the Alpine heights of his own best insight and aspiration. The comrade is at hand who interrupts his lonely communion with the spirit of the mountains and draws him away to the Emperor's court, where the pair soon ingratiate themselves as wonder-workers. They so please his Majesty with their marvelous illusions that they are regularly installed at court as purveyors of amusement. The first demand that is made on them is that they produce, for the entertainment of the court, the shades of the supremely beautiful Paris and Helena. To this end Mephistopheles devises the elaborate hocus-pocus of the Mothers. He sends Faust away to the vasty and viewless realm of the Ideal, instructing him how to bring thence a certain wonderful tripod, from the incense of which the desired forms can be made to appear. The show proceeds successfully, so far as the spectators are concerned, but an accident happens. Faust has been cautioned by his partner not to touch the fantom forms. But the moon-struck idealist falls in love with the beautiful Helena and, disregarding orders, attempts to hold her fast. The consequence is an explosion; the spirits vanish, and Faust receives an electric shock which paralyzes all his bodily functions. He is now in a trance; there is nothing left of him but a motionless body and a mute soul, dreaming of Helena. Mephistopheles pretends to be very much disgusted, but he knows where to go for help.

At the beginning of the second act we return to the old study that was deserted years ago. Faust's former famulus, Dr. Wagner, has now become a world-renowned professor and is engaged in a great experiment, namely, in the production of a chemical man. By the aid of Mephisto's magic the experiment is quickly brought to a successful issue, and Homunculus — one of Goethe's whimsically delightful creations — emerges into being as an incorporeal radiant man in a glass bottle. The wonderful little fellow at once comprehends Faust's malady and prescribes that he be taken to the land of his dreams. So away they go, the three of them, to the Classical Walpurgis Night, which is celebrated annually on the battle-field of Pharsalus in Thessaly. As soon as Faust's feet touch classic soil he recovers his senses and sets out with enthusiasm to find Helena. After some wandering about among the classic fantoms he falls in with Chiron the Centaur, who carries him far away to the foot of Mount Olympus and leaves him with the wise priestess Manto, who escorts him to the Lower World and secures the consent of Queen Persephone to a temporary reappearance of Helena on earth.

Meanwhile Mephistopheles, delighted to find on classic ground creatures no less ugly than those familiar to him in the far Northwest, enters, seemingly by way of a lark, into a curious arrangement with the three daughters of Phorkys. These were imagined by the Greeks as hideous old hags who lived in perpetual darkness and had one eye and one tooth which they used in common. Mephistopheles borrows the form, the eye, and the tooth of a Phorkyad and transforms himself very acceptably into an image of the Supreme Ugliness. In that shape he-she manages the fantasmagory of the third act. As for the third member of the expedition to Thessaly, Homunculus, he is possessed by a consuming desire to "begin existence," that is, to get a body and become a full-fledged member of the genus Homo. His wanderings in search of the best place to begin take him out into the Ægean Sea, where he is entranced by the beauty of the scene. In an ecstasy of prophetic joy he dashes his bottle to pieces against the shell-chariot of the lovely sea-nymph Galatea and dissolves himself with the shining animalculæ of the sea. There he is now — coming up to the full estate of manhood by the various stages of protozoon, amœba, mollusc, fish, reptile, bird, mammal, Man. It will take time, but he has no need to hurry.

Then follows the third act, a classico-romantic fantasmagoria, in which Faust as medieval knight, ruling his multitudinous vassals from his castle in Arcadia, the fabled land of poetry, is wedded to the classic Queen of Beauty. It is all very fantastic, but also very beautiful and marvelously pregnant in its symbolism. But at last the fair illusion comes to an end. Euphorion, the child of Helena and Faust, the ethereal, earth-spurning Genius of Poesy, perishes in an attempt to fly, and his grief-stricken mother follows him back to Hades. Nothing is left to Faust but a majestic, inspiring memory. He gathers the robe of Helena about him, and it bears him aloft and carries him, high up in the air and far above all that is vulgar, back to Germany. His vehicle of cloud lands him on a mountain-summit, where he is soon joined by Mephistopheles, who puts the question, What next? We are now at the beginning of Act IV. Faust proceeds to unfold a grand scheme of conflict with the Sea. On his flight he has observed the tides eternally beating in upon the shore and evermore receding, all to no purpose. This blind waste of energy has excited in him the spirit of opposition. He proposes to fight the sea by building dikes which shall hold the rushing water in check and make dry land of the tide-swept area. Mephistopheles enters readily into his plans. They help the Emperor to win a critical battle, and by way of reward Faust receives a vast tract of swampy sea-shore as his fief.

In Act V the great scheme has all been carried out. What was a watery desolation has been converted into a potential paradise. Faust is a great feudal lord, with a boundless domain and a fleet of ships that bring him the riches of far-away lands. But thus far he has simply been amusing himself on a grand scale. He has thought always mainly of himself. He has courted experience, among other things the experience of putting forth his power in a contest with the sea and performing a great feat of engineering. But it has not brought him a satisfaction in which he can rest. And he has not become a saint. An aged couple, who belong to the old régime and obstinately refuse to part with the little plot of ground on which they have lived for years, anger him to the point of madness. He wants their land so that he may build on it a watch-tower from which to survey and govern his possessions. He sends his servitor to remove them to a better home which he has prepared for them. But Mephistopheles carries out the order with reckless brutality, with the consequence that the old people are killed and their cottage burned to the ground. Thus Faust in his old age — by this time he is a hundred years old — has a fresh burden on his conscience. As he stands on the balcony of his palace at midnight, surveying the havoc he has unintentionally wrought, the smoke of the burning cottage is wafted toward him and takes the form of four gray old women. One of them, Dame Care, slips into the rich man's palace by way of the keyhole and croons in his ear her dismal litany of care. Faust replies in a fine declaration of independence, beginning —

> The circle of the Earth is known to me,
> What's on the other side we can not see.

As Dame Care leaves him she breathes on his eyelids and makes him blind. But the inner light is not quenched. His hunger for life still unabated, he summons up all his energy and orders out an army of workmen to complete a great undertaking on which he has set his heart. On the edge of his domain, running along the distant foothills, is a miasmatic swamp which poisons the air and renders the land uninhabitable. He proposes to drain the swamp and thus create a home for millions yet to come.

His imagination ranges forward, picturing a free, industrious, self-reliant people swarming on the land that he has won from the sea and made fit for human uses. In the ecstasy of altruistic emotion he exclaims: "Such a throng I would fain see, standing with a free people on a free soil; I might say to the passing moment, 'Pray tarry, thou art so fair.' The traces of my earthly life can not pass away in eons." That same instant he sinks back to earth—dying.

Is there in all literature anything finer, grander, more nobly conceived? What follows—the conflict of the angels and devils for the final possession of Faust's soul—need not detain us long. We know how that will turn out. Indeed, the shrewd old Devil, while he goes through the form of making a stiff fight for what he pretends to think his rights, knows from the first that his is a losing battle. While he is watching the body of Faust to see where the soul is going to escape, the angels appear in a glory, bearing roses as their only weapon. With these they put the Devil and his minions to rout and bear away the dead man's soul to the Holy Mountain, singing their triumphal chant—

> Wer immer strebend sich bemüht,
> Den können wir erlösen.

THE TRAGEDY OF FAUST

DRAMATIS PERSONÆ

Characters in the Prologue for the Theatre.

THE MANAGER.
THE DRAMATIC POET.
MERRYMAN.

Characters in the Prologue in Heaven.

THE LORD.
RAPHAEL ⎫
GABRIEL ⎬ The Heavenly Host.
MICHAEL ⎭
MEPHISTOPHELES.

Characters in the Tragedy.

FAUST.
MEPHISTOPHELES.
WAGNER, a Student.
MARGARET.
MARTHA, Margaret's Neighbor.
VALENTINE, Margaret's Brother.
OLD PEASANT.
A STUDENT.
ELIZABETH, an Acquaintance of Margaret's.
FROSCH ⎫
BRANDER ⎬ Guests in Auerbach's Wine Cellar.
SIEBEL ⎟
ALTMAYER ⎭

Witches, old and young; Wizards, Will-o'-the-Wisp, Witch Peddler, Protophantasmist, Servibilis, Monkeys, Spirits, Journeymen, Country-folk, Citizens, Beggar, Old Fortune-teller, Shepherd, Soldier, Students, etc.

In the Intermezzo.

OBERON.   ARIEL.
TITANIA.   PUCK, ETC., ETC.

DEDICATION

Ye wavering shapes, again ye do enfold me,
As erst upon my troubled sight ye stole;
Shall I this time attempt to clasp, to hold ye?
Still for the fond illusion yearns my soul?
Ye press around! Come then, your captive hold me,
As upward from the vapory mist ye roll;
Within my breast youth's throbbing pulse is bounding,
Fann'd by the magic breath your march surrounding.

Shades fondly loved appear, your train attending,
And visions fair of many a blissful day;
First-love and friendship their fond accents blending,
Like to some ancient, half-expiring lay;
Sorrow revives, her wail of anguish sending
Back o'er life's devious labyrinthine way,
And names the dear ones, they whom Fate bereaving
Of life's fair hours, left me behind them grieving.

They hear me not my later cadence singing,
The souls to whom my earlier lays I sang;
Dispersed the throng, their severed flight now winging;
Mute are the voices that responsive rang.
For stranger crowds the Orphean lyre now stringing,
E'en their applause is to my heart a pang;
Of old who listened to my song, glad hearted,
If yet they live, now wander widely parted.

A yearning long unfelt, each impulse swaying,
To yon calm spirit-realm uplifts my soul;
In faltering cadence, as when Zephyr playing,
Fans the Æolian harp, my numbers roll;
Tear follows tear, my steadfast heart obeying
The tender impulse, loses its control;
What I possess as from afar I see;
Those I have lost become realities to me.

[248]

PROLOGUE FOR THE THEATRE

MANAGER. DRAMATIC POET. MERRYMAN

MANAGER

YE twain, in trouble and distress
True friends whom I so oft have found,
Say, for our scheme on German ground,
What prospect have we of success?
Fain would I please the public, win their thanks;
They live and let live, hence it is but meet.
The posts are now erected, and the planks,
And all look forward to a festal treat.
Their places taken, they, with eyebrows rais'd,
Sit patiently, and fain would be amaz'd.
I know the art to hit the public taste,
Yet ne'er of failure felt so keen a dread;
True, they are not accustomed to the best,
But then appalling the amount they've read.
How make our entertainment striking, new,
And yet significant and pleasing too?
For to be plain, I love to see the throng,
As to our booth the living tide progresses;
As wave on wave successive rolls along,
And through heaven's narrow portal forceful presses;
Still in broad daylight, ere the clock strikes four,
With blows their way toward the box they take;
And, as for bread in famine, at the baker's door,
For tickets are content their necks to break.
Such various minds the bard alone can sway,
My friend, oh work this miracle today!

POET

Oh of the motley throng speak not before me,
At whose aspect the Spirit wings its flight!
Conceal the surging concourse, I implore thee,
Whose vortex draws us with resistless might.

[249]

No, to some peaceful heavenly nook restore me,
Where only for the bard blooms pure delight,
Where love and friendship yield their choicest blessing,
Our heart's true bliss, with godlike hand caressing.

What in the spirit's depths was there created,
What shyly there the lip shaped forth in sound;
A failure now, with words now fitly mated,
In the wild tumult of the hour is drown'd;
Full oft the poet's thought for years hath waited
Until at length with perfect form 'tis crowned;
What dazzles, for the moment born, must perish;
What genuine is posterity will cherish.

MERRYMAN

This cant about posterity I hate;
About posterity were I to prate,
Who then the living would amuse? For they
Will have diversion, ay, and 'tis their due.
A sprightly fellow's presence at your play,
Methinks should also count for something too;
Whose genial wit the audience still inspires,
Knows from their changeful mood no angry feeling;
A wider circle he desires,
To their heart's depths more surely thus appealing.
To work, then! Give a master-piece, my friend;
Bring Fancy with her choral trains before us,
Sense, reason, feeling, passion, but attend!
Let folly also swell the tragic chorus.

MANAGER

In chief, of incident enough prepare!
A show they want, they come to gape and stare.
Spin for their eyes abundant occupation,
So that the multitude may wondering gaze,
You by sheer bulk have won your reputation,
The man you are all love to praise.
By mass alone can you subdue the masses,
Each then selects in time what suits his bent.
Bring much, you something bring for various classes,

And from the house goes every one content.
You give a piece, abroad in pieces send it!
'Tis a ragout — success must needs attend it;
'Tis easy to serve up, as easy to invent.
A finish'd whole what boots it to present!
Full soon the public will in pieces rend it.

POET

How mean such handicraft as this you cannot feel!
How it revolts the genuine artist's mind!
The sorry trash in which these coxcombs deal,
Is here approved on principle, I find.

MANAGER

Such a reproof disturbs me not a whit!
Who on efficient work is bent,
Must choose the fittest instrument.
Consider! 'tis soft wood you have to split;
Think too for whom you write, I pray!
One comes to while an hour away;
One from the festive board, a sated guest;
Others, more dreaded than the rest,
From journal-reading hurry to the play.
As to a masquerade, with absent minds, they press,
Sheer curiosity their footsteps winging;
Ladies display their persons and their dress,
Actors unpaid their service bringing.
What dreams beguile you on your poet's height?
What puts a full house in a merry mood?
More closely view your patrons of the night!
The half are cold, the half are rude.
One, the play over, craves a game of cards;
Another a wild night in wanton joy would spend.
Poor fools the muses' fair regards
Why court for such a paltry end?
I tell you, give them more, still more, 'tis all I ask,
Thus you will ne'er stray widely from the goal;
Your audience seek to mystify, cajole; —
To satisfy them — that's a harder task.
What ails thee? art enraptured or distressed?

POET

Depart! elsewhere another servant choose.
What! shall the bard his godlike power abuse?
Man's loftiest right, kind nature's high bequest,
For your mean purpose basely sport away?
Whence comes his mastery o'er the human breast,
Whence o'er the elements his sway,
But from the harmony that, gushing from his soul,
Draws back into his heart the wondrous whole?
With careless hand when round her spindle, Nature
Winds the interminable thread of life;
When 'mid the clash of Being every creature
Mingles in harsh inextricable strife;
Who deals their course unvaried till it falleth,
In rhythmic flow to music's measur'd tone?
Each solitary note whose genius calleth,
To swell the mighty choir in unison?
Who in the raging storm sees passion low'ring?
Or flush of earnest thought in evening's glow?
Who every blossom in sweet spring-time flowering
Along the loved one's path would strow?
Who, Nature's green familiar leaves entwining,
Wreathes glory's garland, won on every field?
Makes sure Olympus, heavenly powers combining?
Man's mighty spirit, in the bard reveal'd!

MERRYMAN

Come then, employ your lofty inspiration,
And carry on the poet's avocation,
Just as we carry on a love affair.
Two meet by chance, are pleased, they linger there,
Insensibly are link'd, they scarce know how;
Fortune seems now propitious, adverse now,
Then come alternate rapture and despair;
And 'tis a true romance ere one's aware.
Just such a drama let us now compose.
Plunge boldly into life — its depths disclose!

Each lives it, not to many is it known,
'Twill interest wheresoever seiz'd and shown;
Bright pictures, but obscure their meaning:
A ray of truth through error gleaming,
Thus you the best elixir brew,
To charm mankind, and edify them too.
Then youth's fair blossoms crowd to view your play,
And wait as on an oracle; while they,
The tender souls, who love the melting mood,
Suck from your work their melancholy food;
Now this one, and now that, you deeply stir,
Each sees the working of his heart laid bare.
Their tears, their laughter, you command with ease,
The lofty still they honor, the illusive love.
Your finish'd gentlemen you ne'er can please;
A growing mind alone will grateful prove.

POET

Then give me back youth's golden prime,
When my own spirit too was growing,
When from my heart th' unbidden rhyme
Gush'd forth, a fount for ever flowing;
Then shadowy mist the world conceal'd,
And every bud sweet promise made,
Of wonders yet to be reveal'd,
As through the vales, with blooms inlaid,
Culling a thousand flowers I stray'd.
Naught had I, yet a rich profusion!
The thirst for truth, joy in each fond illusion.
Give me unquell'd those impulses to prove; —
Rapture so deep, its ecstasy was pain,
The power of hate, the energy of love,
Give me, oh give me back my youth again!

MERRYMAN

Youth, my good friend, you certainly require
When foes in battle round are pressing,
When a fair maid, her heart on fire,

Hangs on your neck with fond caressing,
When from afar, the victor's crown,
To reach the hard-won goal inciteth;
When from the whirling dance, to drown
Your sense, the nights carouse inviteth.
But the familiar chords among
Boldly to sweep, with graceful cunning,
While to its goal, the verse along
Its winding path is sweetly running;
This task is yours, old gentlemen, today;
Nor are you therefore less in reverence held;
Age does not make us childish, as folk say,
It finds us genuine children e'en in eld.

MANAGER

A truce to words, mere empty sound,
Let deeds at length appear, my friends!
While idle compliments you round,
You might achieve some useful ends.
Why talk of the poetic vein?
Who hesitates will never know it;
If bards ye are, as ye maintain,
Now let your inspiration show it.
To you is known what we require,
Strong drink to sip is our desire;
Come, brew me such without delay!
Tomorrow sees undone, what happens not today;
Still forward press, nor ever tire!
The possible, with steadfast trust,
Resolve should by the forelock grasp;
Then she will ne'er let go her clasp,
And labors on, because she must.
On German boards, you're well aware,
The taste of each may have full sway;
Therefore in bringing out your play,
Nor scenes nor mechanism spare!

Heaven's lamps employ, the greatest and the least,
Be lavish of the stellar lights,
Water, and fire, and rocky heights,
Spare not at all, nor birds, nor beast.
Thus let creation's ample sphere
Forthwith in this our narrow booth appear,
And with considerate speed, through fancy's spell,
Journey from heaven, thence through the world, to hell!

PROLOGUE IN HEAVEN

THE LORD. THE HEAVENLY HOSTS. *Afterward* MEPHIS-
TOPHELES

The three Archangels come forward

RAPHAEL

THE Sun, in ancient guise, competing
With brother spheres in rival song,
With thunder-march, his orb completing,
Moves his predestin'd course along;
His aspect to the powers supernal
Gives strength, though fathom him none may;
Transcending thought, the works eternal
Are fair as on the primal day.

GABRIEL

With speed, thought baffling, unabating,
Earth's splendor whirls in circling flight;
Its Eden-brightness alternating
With solemn, awe-inspiring night;
Ocean's broad waves in wild commotion,
Against the rocks' deep base are hurled;
And with the spheres, both rock and ocean
Eternally are swiftly whirled.

MICHAEL

And tempests roar in emulation
From sea to land, from land to sea,
And raging form, without cessation,
A chain of wondrous agency,
Full in the thunder's path careering,
Flaring the swift destructions play;
But, Lord, Thy servants are revering
The mild procession of thy day.

[256]

THE THREE

Thine aspect to the powers supernal
Gives strength, though fathom thee none may;
And all thy works, sublime, eternal,
Are fair as on the primal day.

MEPHISTOPHELES

Since thou, O Lord, approachest us once more,
And how it fares with us, to ask art fain,
Since thou hast kindly welcom'd me of yore,
Thou see'st me also now among thy train.
Excuse me, fine harangues I cannot make,
Though all the circle look on me with scorn;
My pathos soon thy laughter would awake,
Hadst thou the laughing mood not long forsworn.
Of suns and worlds I nothing have to say,
I see alone mankind's self-torturing pains.
The little world-god still the self-same stamp retains,
And is as wondrous now as on the primal day.
Better he might have fared, poor wight,
Hadst thou not given him a gleam of heavenly light;
Reason he names it, and doth so
Use it, than brutes more brutish still to grow.
With deference to your grace, he seems to me
Like any long-legged grasshopper to be,
Which ever flies, and flying springs,
And in the grass its ancient ditty sings.
Would he but always in the grass repose!
In every heap of dung he thrusts his nose.

THE LORD

Hast thou naught else to say? Is blame
In coming here, as ever, thy sole aim?
Does nothing on the earth to thee seem right?

MEPHISTOPHELES

No, Lord! I find things there, as ever, in sad plight.
Men, in their evil days, move my compassion;
Such sorry things to plague is nothing worth.

VOL. I — 17

THE LORD

Know'st thou my servant, Faust?

MEPHISTOPHELES

The doctor?

THE LORD

Right.

MEPHISTOPHELES

He serves thee truly in a wondrous fashion.
Poor fool! His food and drink are not of earth.
An inward impulse hurries him afar,
Himself half conscious of his frenzied mood;
From heaven claimeth he the fairest star,
And from the earth craves every highest good,
And all that's near, and all that's far,
Fails to allay the tumult in his blood.

THE LORD

Though in perplexity he serves me now,
I soon will lead him where more light appears;
When buds the sapling, doth the gardener know
That flowers and fruit will deck the coming years?

MEPHISTOPHELES

What wilt thou wager? Him thou yet shall lose,
If leave to me thou wilt but give,
Gently to lead him as I choose!

THE LORD

So long as he on earth doth live,
So long 'tis not forbidden thee.
Man still must err, while he doth strive.

MEPHISTOPHELES

I thank you; for not willingly
I traffic with the dead, and still aver
That youth's plump blooming cheek I very much prefer.
I'm not at home to corpses; 'tis my way,
Like cats with captive mice to toy and play.

THE LORD

Enough! 'tis granted thee! Divert
This mortal spirit from his primal source;
Him, canst thou seize, thy power exert
And lead him on thy downward course,
Then stand abash'd, when thou perforce must own,
A good man in his darkest aberration,
Of the right path is conscious still.

MEPHISTOPHELES

'Tis done! Full soon thou'lt see my exultation;
As for my bet no fears I entertain.
And if my end I finally should gain,
Excuse my triumphing with all my soul.
Dust he shall eat, ay, and with relish take,
As did my cousin, the renownèd snake.

THE LORD

Here too thou'rt free to act without control;
I ne'er have cherished hate for such as thee.
Of all the spirits who deny,
The scoffer is least wearisome to me.
Ever too prone is man activity to shirk,
In unconditioned rest he fain would live;
Hence this companion purposely I give,
Who stirs, excites, and must, as devil, work.
But ye, the genuine sons of heaven, rejoice!
In the full living beauty still rejoice!
May that which works and lives, the ever-growing,
In bonds of love enfold you, mercy-fraught,
And Seeming's changeful forms, around you flowing,
Do ye arrest, in ever-during thought!

[*Heaven closes, the Archangels disperse.*]

MEPHISTOPHELES (*alone*)

The ancient one I like sometimes to see,
And not to break with him am always civil;
'Tis courteous in so great a lord as he,
To speak so kindly even to the devil.

FAUST—PART I (1808)*

TRANSLATED BY ANNA SWANWICK

NIGHT

A high vaulted narrow Gothic chamber.
FAUST, *restless, seated at his desk.*

FAUST

HAVE, alas! Philosophy,
Medicine, Jurisprudence too,
And to my cost Theology,
With ardent labor, studied through.
And here I stand, with all my lore,
Poor fool, no wiser than before.
Magister, doctor styled, indeed,
Already these ten years I lead,
Up, down, across, and to and fro,
My pupils by the nose,—and learn,
That we in truth can nothing know!
That in my heart like fire doth burn.
'Tis true, I've more cunning than all your dull tribe,
Magister and doctor, priest, parson, and scribe;
Scruple or doubt comes not to enthrall me,
Neither can devil nor hell now appal me—
Hence also my heart must all pleasure forego!
I may not pretend aught rightly to know,
I may not pretend, through teaching, to find
A means to improve or convert mankind.
Then I have neither goods nor treasure,
No worldly honor, rank, or pleasure;
No dog in such fashion would longer live!
Therefore myself to magic I give,
In hope, through spirit-voice and might,
Secrets now veiled to bring to light,
That I no more, with aching brow,
Need speak of what I nothing know;

* Permission The Macmillan Co., New York, and G. Bell and Sons, Ltd., London.

That I the force may recognize
That binds creation's inmost energies;
Her vital powers, her embryo seeds survey,
And fling the trade in empty words away.
O full-orb'd moon, did but thy rays
Their last upon mine anguish gaze!
Beside this desk, at dead of night,
Oft have I watched to hail thy light:
Then, pensive friend! o'er book and scroll,
With soothing power, thy radiance stole!
In thy dear light, ah, might I climb,
Freely, some mountain height sublime,
Round mountain caves with spirits ride,
In thy mild haze o'er meadows glide,
And, purged from knowledge-fumes, renew
My spirit, in thy healing dew!

Woe's me! still prison'd in the gloom
Of this abhorr'd and musty room!
Where heaven's dear light itself doth pass
But dimly through the painted glass!
Hemmed in by book-heaps, piled around,
Worm-eaten, hid 'neath dust and mold,
Which to the high vault's topmast bound,
A smoke-stained paper doth enfold;
With boxes round thee piled, and glass,
And many a useless instrument,
With old ancestral lumber blent —
This is thy world! a world! alas!
And dost thou ask why heaves thy heart,
With tighten'd pressure in thy breast?
Why the dull ache will not depart,
By which thy life-pulse is oppress'd?
Instead of nature's living sphere,
Created for mankind of old,
Brute skeletons surround thee here,
And dead men's bones in smoke and mold.

Up! Forth into the distant land!
Is not this book of mystery
By Nostradamus' proper hand,
An all-sufficient guide? Thou'lt see
The courses of the stars unroll'd;
When nature doth her thoughts unfold
To thee, thy soul shall rise, and seek
Communion high with her to hold,
As spirit doth with spirit speak!
Vain by dull poring to divine
The meaning of each hallow'd sign.
Spirits! I feel you hov'ring near;
Make answer, if my voice ye hear!

> [*He opens the book and perceives the sign of the
> Macrocosmos.*]

Ah! at this spectacle through every sense,
What sudden ecstasy of joy is flowing!
I feel new rapture, hallow'd and intense,
Through every nerve and vein with ardor glowing.
Was it a god who character'd this scroll,
The tumult in my spirit healing,
O'er my sad heart with rapture stealing,
And by a mystic impulse, to my soul,
The powers of nature all around revealing.
Am I a god? What light intense
In these pure symbols do I see
Nature exert her vital energy?
Now of the wise man's words I learn the sense;
  "Unlock'd the spirit-world is lying,
    Thy sense is shut, thy heart is dead!
    Up scholar, lave, with zeal undying,
    Thine earthly breast in the morning-red!"

> [*He contemplates the sign.*]

How all things live and work, and ever blending,
Weave one vast whole from Being's ample range!
How powers celestial, rising and descending,

Their golden buckets ceaseless interchange!
Their flight on rapture-breathing pinions winging,
From heaven to earth their genial influence bringing,
Through the wild sphere their chimes melodious ringing!

A wondrous show! but ah! a show alone!
Where shall I grasp thee, infinite nature, where?
Ye breasts, ye fountains of all life, whereon
Hang heaven and earth, from which the withered heart
For solace yearns, ye still impart
Your sweet and fostering tides — where are ye — where?
Ye gush, and must I languish in despair?

> [*He turns over the leaves of the book impatiently, and
> perceives the sign of the Earth-spirit.*]

How all unlike the influence of this sign!
Earth-spirit, thou to me art nigher,
E'en now my strength is rising higher,
E'en now I glow as with new wine;
Courage I feel, abroad the world to dare,
The woe of earth, the bliss of earth to bear,
With storms to wrestle, brave the lightning's glare,
And mid the crashing shipwreck not despair.

Clouds gather over me —
The moon conceals her light —
The lamp is quench'd —
Vapors are arising — Quiv'ring round my head
Flash the red beams — Down from the vaulted roof
A shuddering horror floats,
And seizes me!
I feel it, spirit, prayer-compell'd, 'tis thou
Art hovering near!
Unveil thyself!
Ha! How my heart is riven now!
Each sense, with eager palpitation,
Is strain'd to catch some new sensation!

I feel my heart surrender'd unto thee!
Thou must! Thou must! Though life should be the fee!
[*He seizes the book, and pronounces mysteriously the
sign of the spirit. A ruddy flame flashes up; the
spirit appears in the flame.*]

SPIRIT

Who calls me?

FAUST (*turning aside*)
Dreadful shape!

SPIRIT
With might,
Thou hast compell'd me to appear,
Long hast been sucking at my sphere,
And now —

FAUST
Woe's me! I cannot bear thy sight!

SPIRIT
To see me thou dost breathe thine invocation,
My voice to hear, to gaze upon my brow;
Me doth thy strong entreaty bow —
Lo! I am here! — What cowering agitation
Grasps thee, the demigod! Where's now the soul's deep
    cry?
Where is the breast, which in its depths a world conceiv'd,
And bore and cherished? which, with ecstasy,
To rank itself with us, the spirits, heaved?
Where art thou, Faust? Whose voice heard I resound
Who toward me press'd with energy profound?
Art thou he? Thou, — who by my breath art blighted,
Who, in his spirit's depths affrighted,
Trembles, a crush'd and writhing worm!

FAUST
Shall I yield, thing of flame, to thee?
Faust, and thine equal, I am he!

SPIRIT

In the currents of life, in action's storm,
    I float and I wave
    With billowy motion!
    Birth and the grave,
    O limitless ocean,
    A constant weaving
    With change still rife,
    A restless heaving,
    A glowing life —
Thus time's whirring loom unceasing I ply,
And weave the life-garment of deity.

FAUST

Thou, restless spirit, dost from end to end
O'ersweep the world; how near I feel to thee!

SPIRIT

Thou'rt like the spirit, thou dost comprehend,
Not me!   *[Vanishes.]*

FAUST (*deeply moved*)

Not thee?
Whom then?
I, God's own image!
And not rank with thee!   *[A knock.]*
Oh death! I know it — 'tis my famulus —
My fairest fortune now escapes!
That all these visionary shapes
A soulless groveller should banish thus!
    [WAGNER *in his dressing gown and night-cap, a lamp*
      in his hand. FAUST *turns round reluctantly.*]

WAGNER

Pardon! I heard you here declaim;
A Grecian tragedy you doubtless read?
Improvement in this art is now my aim,
For now-a-days it much avails. Indeed
An actor, oft I've heard it said, as teacher,
May give instruction to a preacher.

FAUST

Ay, if your priest should be an actor too,
As not improbably may come to pass.

WAGNER

When in his study pent the whole year through,
Man views the world, as through an optic glass,
On a chance holiday, and scarcely then,
How by persuasion can he govern men?

FAUST

If feeling prompt not, if it doth not flow
Fresh from the spirit's depths, with strong control
Swaying to rapture every listener's soul,
Idle your toil; the chase you may forego!
Brood o'er your task! Together glue,
Cook from another's feast your own ragout,
Still prosecute your paltry game,
And fan your ash-heaps into flame!
Thus children's wonder you'll excite,
And apes', if such your appetite;
But that which issues from the heart alone,
Will bend the hearts of others to your own.

WAGNER

The speaker in delivery will find
Success alone; I still am far behind.

FAUST

A worthy object still pursue!
Be not a hollow tinkling fool!
Sound understanding, judgment true,
Find utterance without art or rule;
And when in earnest you are moved to speak,
Then is it needful cunning words to seek?
Your fine harangues, so polish'd in their kind,
Wherein the shreds of human thought ye twist,
Are unrefreshing as the empty wind,
Whistling through wither'd leaves and autumn mist!

WAGNER

Oh God! How long is art,
Our life how short! With earnest zeal
Still as I ply the critic's task, I feel
A strange oppression both of head and heart.
The very means — how hardly are they won,
By which we to the fountains rise!
And, haply, ere one half the course is run,
Check'd in his progress, the poor devil dies.

FAUST

Parchment, is that the sacred fount whence roll
Waters he thirsteth not who once hath quaffed?
Oh, if it gush not from thine inmost soul,
Thou hast not won the life-restoring draught.

WAGNER

Your pardon! 'tis delightful to transport
Oneself into the spirit of the past,
To see in times before us how a wise man thought,
And what a glorious height we have achieved at last.

FAUST

Ay, truly! even to the loftiest star!
To us, my friend, the ages that are pass'd
A book with seven seals, close-fasten'd, are;
And what the spirit of the times men call,
Is merely their own spirit after all,
Wherein, distorted oft, the times are glass'd.
Then truly, 'tis a sight to grieve the soul!
At the first glance we fly it in dismay;
A very lumber-room, a rubbish-hole;
At best a sort of mock-heroic play,
With saws pragmatical, and maxims sage,
To suit the puppets and their mimic stage.

WAGNER

But then the world and man, his heart and brain!
Touching these things all men would something know.

FAUST

Ay! what 'mong men as knowledge doth obtain!
Who on the child its true name dares bestow?
The few who somewhat of these things have known,
Who their full hearts unguardedly reveal'd,
Nor thoughts, nor feelings, from the mob conceal'd,
Have died on crosses, or in flames been thrown.—
Excuse me, friend, far now the night is spent,
For this time we must say adieu.

WAGNER

Still to watch on I had been well content,
Thus to converse so learnedly with you.
But as tomorrow will be Easter-day,
Some further questions grant, I pray;
With diligence to study still I fondly cling;
Already I know much, but would know everything.   [*Exit.*]

FAUST (*alone*)

How him alone all hope abandons never,
To empty trash who clings, with zeal untired,
With greed for treasure gropes, and, joy-inspir'd,
Exults if earth-worms second his endeavor.

And dare a voice of merely human birth,
E'en here, where shapes immortal throng'd, intrude?
Yet ah! thou poorest of the sons of earth,
For once, I e'en to thee feel gratitude.
Despair the power of sense did well-nigh blast,
And thou didst save me ere I sank dismay'd;
So giant-like the vision seem'd, so vast,
I felt myself shrink dwarf'd as I survey'd!

I, God's own image, from this toil of clay
Already freed, with eager joy who hail'd
The mirror of eternal truth unveil'd,
Mid light effulgent and celestial day:—
I, more than cherub, whose unfetter'd soul
With penetrative glance aspir'd to flow
Through nature's veins, and, still creating, know

The life of gods,— how am I punish'd now!
One thunder-word hath hurl'd me from the goal!

 Spirit! I dare not lift me to thy sphere.
 What though my power compell'd thee to appear,
 My art was powerless to detain thee here.
 In that great moment, rapture-fraught,
 I felt myself so small, so great;
 Fiercely didst thrust me from the realm of thought
 Back on humanity's uncertain fate!
 Who'll teach me now?   What ought I to forego?
 Ought I that impulse to obey?
 Alas! our every deed, as well as every woe,
 Impedes the tenor of life's onward way!

E'en to the noblest by the soul conceiv'd,
Some feelings cling of baser quality;
And when the goods of this world are achiev'd,
Each nobler aim is term'd a cheat, a lie.
Our aspirations, our soul's genuine life,
Grow torpid in the din of earthly strife.

 Though youthful phantasy, while hope inspires,
 Stretch o'er the infinite her wing sublime,
 A narrow compass limits her desires,
 When wreck'd our fortunes in the gulf of time.
 In the deep heart of man care builds her nest,
 O'er secret woes she broodeth there,
 Sleepless she rocks herself and scareth joy and rest;
 Still is she wont some new disguise to wear —
 She may as house and court, as wife and child appear,
 As dagger, poison, fire and flood;
 Imagined evils chill thy blood,
 And what thou ne'er shalt lose, o'er that dost shed
  the tear.

 I am not like the gods!   Feel it I must;
 I'm like the earth-worm, writhing in the dust,
 Which, as on dust it feeds, its native fare,
 Crushed 'neath the passer's tread, lies buried there.

Is it not dust, wherewith this lofty wall,
With hundred shelves, confines me round;
Rubbish, in thousand shapes, may I not call
What in this moth-world doth my being bound?
Here, what doth fail me, shall I find?
Read in a thousand tomes that, everywhere,
Self-torture is the lot of human-kind,
With but one mortal happy, here and there?
Thou hollow skull, that grin, what should it say,
But that thy brain, like mine, of old perplexed,
Still yearning for the truth, hath sought the light of day,
And in the twilight wandered, sorely vexed?
Ye instruments, forsooth, ye mock at me,—
With wheel, and cog, and ring, and cylinder;
To nature's portals ye should be the key;
Cunning your wards, and yet the bolts ye fail to stir.
Inscrutable in broadest light,
To be unveil'd by force she doth refuse,
What she reveals not to thy mental sight
Thou wilt not wrest from her with levers and with screws.
Old useless furnitures, yet stand ye here,
Because my sire ye served, now dead and gone.
Old scroll, the smoke of years dost wear,
So long as o'er this desk the sorry lamp hath shone.
Better my little means hath squandered quite away
Than burden'd by that little here to sweat and groan!
Wouldst thou possess thy heritage, essay
By use to render it thine own!
What we employ not but impedes our way;
That which the hour creates, that can it use alone!

But wherefore to yon spot is riveted my gaze?
Is yonder flasket there a magnet to my sight?
Whence this mild radiance that around me plays,
As when, 'mid forest gloom, reigneth the moon's soft light?
Hail, precious phial! Thee, with reverent awe,
Down from thine old receptacle I draw!
Science in thee I hail and human art.

Essence of deadliest powers, refin'd and sure,
Of soothing anodynes abstraction pure,
Now in thy master's need thy grace impart!
I gaze on thee, my pain is lull'd to rest;
I grasp thee, calm'd the tumult in my breast;
The flood-tide of my spirit ebbs away;
Onward I'm summon'd o'er a boundless main,
Calm at my feet expands the glassy plain,
To shores unknown allures a brighter day.

Lo, where a car of fire, on airy pinion,
Comes floating towards me! I'm prepar'd to fly
By a new track through ether's wide dominion,
To distant spheres of pure activity.
This life intense, this godlike ecstasy —
Worm that thou art such rapture canst thou earn?
Only resolve, with courage stern and high,
Thy visage from the radiant sun to turn!
Dare with determin'd will to burst the portals
Past which in terror others fain would steal!
Now is the time, through deeds, to show that mortals
The calm sublimity of gods can feel;
To shudder not at yonder dark abyss
Where phantasy creates her own self-torturing brood;
Right onward to the yawning gulf to press,
Around whose narrow jaws rolleth hell's fiery flood;
With glad resolve to take the fatal leap,
Though danger threaten thee, to sink in endless sleep!

Pure crystal goblet! forth I draw thee now
From out thine antiquated case, where thou
Forgotten hast reposed for many a year!
Oft at my father's revels thou didst shine;
To glad the earnest guests was thine,
As each to other passed the generous cheer.
The gorgeous brede of figures, quaintly wrought,
Which he who quaff'd must first in rhyme expound,
Then drain the goblet at one draught profound,

Hath nights of boyhood to fond memory brought.
I to my neighbor shall not reach thee now,
Nor on thy rich device shall I my cunning show.
Here is a juice, makes drunk without delay;
Its dark brown flood thy crystal round doth fill;
Let this last draught, the product of my skill,
My own free choice, be quaff'd with resolute will,
A solemn festive greeting, to the coming day!

> [*He places the goblet to his mouth.*]
> [*The ringing of bells, and choral voices.*]

CHORUS OF ANGELS

Christ is arisen!
Mortal, all hail to thee,
Thou whom mortality,
Earth's sad reality,
Held as in prison.

FAUST

What hum melodious, what clear silvery chime,
Thus draws the goblet from my lips away?
Ye deep-ton'd bells, do ye, with voice sublime,
Announce the solemn dawn of Easter-day?
Sweet choir! are ye the hymn of comfort singing,
Which once around the darkness of the grave,
From seraph-voices, in glad triumph ringing,
Of a new covenant assurance gave?

CHORUS OF WOMEN

We, his true-hearted,
With spices and myrrh,
Embalmed the departed,
And swathed Him with care;
Here we conveyed Him,
Our Master, so dear;
Alas! Where we laid Him,
The Christ is not here.

CHORUS OF ANGELS

Christ is arisen!
Blessèd the loving one,
Who from earth's trial-throes,
Healing and strengthening woes,
Soars as from prison.

FAUST

Wherefore, ye tones celestial, sweet and strong,
Come ye a dweller in the dust to seek?
Ring out your chimes believing crowds among,
The message well I hear, my faith alone is weak;
From faith her darling, miracle, hath sprung.
Aloft to yonder spheres I dare not soar,
Whence sound the tidings of great joy;
And yet, with this sweet strain familiar when a boy,
Back it recalleth me to life once more.
Then would celestial love, with holy kiss,
Come o'er me in the Sabbath's stilly hour,
While, fraught with solemn meaning and mysterious power,
Chim'd the deep-sounding bell, and prayer was bliss;
A yearning impulse, undefin'd yet dear,
Drove me to wander on through wood and field;
With heaving breast and many a burning tear,
I felt with holy joy a world reveal'd.
Gay sports and festive hours proclaim'd with joyous
    pealing
This Easter hymn in days of old;
And fond remembrance now doth me, with childlike
    feeling,
Back from the last, the solemn step, withhold.
O still sound on, thou sweet celestial strain!
The tear-drop flows — Earth, I am thine again!

CHORUS OF DISCIPLES

He whom we mourned as dead,
Living and glorious,
From the dark grave hath fled,
O'er death victorious;
Almost creative bliss
Waits on His growing powers;
Ah! Him on earth we miss;
Sorrow and grief are ours.
Yearning He left His own,
Mid sore annoy;
Ah! we must needs bemoan,
Master, thy joy!

CHORUS OF ANGELS

Christ is arisen,
Redeem'd from decay.
The bonds which imprison
Your souls, rend away!
Praising the Lord with zeal,
By deeds that love reveal,
Like brethren true and leal
Sharing the daily meal,
To all that sorrow feel
Whisp'ring of heaven's weal,
Still is the Master near,
Still is He here!

BEFORE THE GATE

Promenaders of all sorts pass out.

ARTISANS

Why choose ye that direction, pray?

OTHERS

To the hunting-lodge we're on our way.

THE FIRST

We toward the mill are strolling on.

A MECHANIC

A walk to Wasserhof were best.

A SECOND

The road is not a pleasant one.

THE OTHERS

What will you do?

A THIRD

I'll join the rest.

A FOURTH

Let's up to Burghof, there you'll find good cheer,
The prettiest maidens and the best of beer,
And brawls of a prime sort.

A FIFTH

You scapegrace! How?
Your skin still itching for a row?
Thither I will not go, I loathe the place.

SERVANT GIRL

No, no! I to the town my steps retrace.

ANOTHER

Near yonder poplars he is sure to be.

THE FIRST

And if he is, what matters it to me!
With you he'll walk, he'll dance with none but you,
And with your pleasures what have I to do?

THE SECOND

Today he will not be alone, he said
His friend would be with him, the curly-head.

STUDENT

Why how those buxom girls step on!
Come, brother, we will follow them anon.
Strong beer, a damsel smartly dress'd,
Stinging tobacco — these I love the best.

BURGHER'S DAUGHTER

Look at those handsome fellows there!
'Tis really shameful, I declare;
The very best society they shun,
After those servant-girls forsooth, to run.

SECOND STUDENT (*to the first*)

Not quite so fast! for in our rear,
Two girls, well-dress'd, are drawing near;
Not far from us the one doth dwell,
And, sooth to say, I like her well.
They walk demurely, yet you'll see,
That they will let us join them presently.

THE FIRST

Not I! restraints of all kinds I detest.
Quick! let us catch the wild-game ere it flies;
The hand on Saturday the mop that plies
Will on the Sunday fondle you the best.

BURGHER

No, this new Burgomaster; I like him not, God knows;
No, he's in office; daily more arrogant he grows;
And for the town, what doth he do for it?
Are not things worse from day to day?
To more restraints we must submit;
And taxes more than ever pay.

BEGGAR (*sings*)

Kind gentlemen and ladies fair,
So rosy-cheek'd and trimly dress'd,
Be pleas'd to listen to my prayer;
Relieve and pity the distress'd.
Let me not vainly sing my lay!
His heart's most glad whose hand is free.
Now when all men keep holiday,
Should be a harvest-day to me.

ANOTHER BURGHER

On holidays and Sundays naught know I more inviting
Than chatting about war and war's alarms,
When folk in Turkey, up in arms,
Far off, are 'gainst each other fighting.
We at the window stand, our glasses drain
And watch adown the stream the painted vessels gliding;
Then joyful we at eve come home again,
And peaceful times we bless, peace long-abiding.

THIRD BURGHER

Ay, neighbor! So let matters stand for me!
There they may scatter one another's brains,
And wild confusion round them see —
So here at home in quiet all remains!

OLD WOMAN (*to the* BURGHERS' DAUGHTERS)

Heyday! How smart! The fresh young blood!
Who would not fall in love with you?
Not quite so proud! 'Tis well and good!
And what you wish, that I could help you to.

BURGHER'S DAUGHTER

Come, Agatha! I care not to be seen
Walking in public with these witches. True,
My future lover, last St. Andrew's E'en,
In flesh and blood she brought before my view.

ANOTHER

And mine she show'd me also in the glass.
A soldier's figure, with companions bold;
I look around, I seek him as I pass —
In vain, his form I nowhere can behold.

SOLDIERS

Fortress with turrets
And walls high in air,
Damsel disdainful,
Haughty and fair —

These be my prey!
Bold is the venture,
Costly the pay!

Hark, how the trumpet
Thither doth call us
Where either pleasure
Or death may befall us!
Hail to the tumult!
Life's in the field!
Damsel and fortress
To us must yield.
Bold is the venture,
Costly the pay!
Gaily the soldier
Marches away.

FAUST *and* WAGNER

FAUST

Loosed from their fetters are streams and rills
Through the gracious spring-tide's all-quickening glow;
Hope's budding joy in the vale doth blow;
Old Winter back to the savage hills
Withdraweth his force, decrepid now.
Thence only impotent icy grains
Scatters he as he wings his flight,
Striping with sleet the verdant plains;
But the sun endureth no trace of white;
Everywhere growth and movement are rife,
All things investing with hues of life:
Though flowers are lacking, varied of dye,
Their colors the motley throng supply.
Turn thee around, and, from this height,
Back to the town direct thy sight.
Forth from the hollow, gloomy gate,
Stream forth the masses, in bright array.
Gladly seek they the sun today;

The Lord's Resurrection they celebrate:
For they themselves have risen, with joy,
From tenement sordid, from cheerless room,
From bonds of toil, from care and annoy,
From gable and roof's o'erhanging gloom,
From crowded alley and narrow street,
And from the churches' awe-breathing night
All now have come forth into the light.
Look, only look, on nimble feet,
Through garden and field how spread the throng,
How o'er the river's ample sheet
Many a gay wherry glides along;
And see, deep sinking in the tide,
Pushes the last boat now away.
E'en from yon far hill's path-worn side,
Flash the bright hues of garments gay.
Hark! Sounds of village mirth arise;
This is the people's paradise.
Both great and small send up a cheer;
Here am I man, I feel it here.

WAGNER

Sir Doctor, in a walk with you
There's honor and instruction too;
Yet here alone I care not to resort,
Because I coarseness hate of every sort.
This fiddling, shouting, skittling, I detest;
I hate the tumult of the vulgar throng;
They roar as by the evil one possess'd,
And call it pleasure, call it song.

PEASANTS (*under the linden-tree*)

Dance and Sing.
The shepherd for the dance was dress'd,
With ribbon, wreath, and colored vest,
A gallant show displaying.
And round about the linden-tree,

They footed it right merrily.
    Juchhe! Juchhe!
    Juchheisa! Heisa! He!
So fiddle-bow was braying.
Our swain amidst the circle press'd,
He push'd a maiden trimly dress'd,
And jogg'd her with his elbow;
The buxom damsel turn'd her head,
"Now that's a stupid trick!" she said,
    Juchhe! Juchhe!
    Juchheisa! Heisa! He!
Don't be so rude, good fellow!

Swift in the circle they advanced,
They danced to right, to left they danced,
And all the skirts were swinging.
And they grew red, and they grew warm,
Panting, they rested arm in arm,
    Juchhe! Juchhe!
    Juchheisa! Heisa! He!
To hip their elbow bringing.

Don't make so free! How many a maid
Has been betroth'd and then betray'd;
And has repented after!
Yet still he flatter'd her aside,
And from the linden, far and wide,
    Juchhe! Juchhe!
    Juchheisa! Heisa! He!
Rang fiddle-bow and laughter.

OLD PEASANT

Doctor, 'tis really kind of you,
To condescend to come this way,
A highly learned man like you,
To join our mirthful throng today.
Our fairest cup I offer you,
Which we with sparkling drink have crown'd,

And pledging you, I pray aloud,
That every drop within its round,
While it your present thirst allays,
May swell the number of your days.

FAUST

I take the cup you kindly reach,
Thanks and prosperity to each!

[*The crowd gather round in a circle.*]

OLD PEASANT

Ay, truly! 'tis well done, that you
Our festive meeting thus attend;
You, who in evil days of yore,
So often show'd yourself our friend!
Full many a one stands living here,
Who from the fever's deadly blast
Your father rescu'd, when his skill
The fatal sickness stay'd at last.
A young man then, each house you sought,
Where reign'd the mortal pestilence.
Corpse after corpse was carried forth,
But still unscath'd you issued thence.
Sore then your trials and severe;
The Helper yonder aids the helper here.

ALL

Heaven bless the trusty friend, and long
To help the poor his life prolong!

FAUST

To Him above in homage bend,
Who prompts the helper and Who help doth send.

[*He proceeds with* WAGNER.]

WAGNER

What feelings, great man, must thy breast inspire,
At homage paid thee by this crowd! Thrice blest
Who from the gifts by him possessed
Such benefit can draw! The sire
Thee to his boy with reverence shows;

They press around, inquire, advance,
Hush'd is the fiddle, check'd the dance.
Where thou dost pass they stand in rows,
And each aloft his bonnet throws,
But little fails and they to thee,
As though the Host came by, would bend the knee.

FAUST

A few steps further, up to yonder stone!
Here rest we from our walk. In times long past,
Absorb'd in thought, here oft I sat alone,
And disciplin'd myself with prayer and fast.
Then rich in hope, with faith sincere,
With sighs, and hands in anguish press'd,
The end of that sore plague, with many a tear,
From heaven's dread Lord, I sought to wrest.
The crowd's applause assumes a scornful tone.
Oh, could'st thou in my inner being read
How little either sire or son
Of such renown deserves the meed!
My sire, of good repute, and sombre mood,
O'er nature's powers and every mystic zone,
With honest zeal, but methods of his own,
With toil fantastic loved to brood;
His time in dark alchemic cell,
With brother-adepts he would spend,
And there antagonists compel
Through numberless receipts to blend.
A ruddy lion there, a suitor bold,
In tepid bath was with the lily wed.
Thence both, while open flames around them roll'd,
Were tortur'd to another bridal bed.
Was then the youthful queen descried
With varied colors in the flask —
This was our medicine; the patients died;
"Who were restored?" none cared to ask.
With our infernal mixture thus, ere long,
These hills and peaceful vales among

We rag'd more fiercely than the pest;
Myself the deadly poison did to thousands give;
They pined away, I yet must live
To hear the reckless murderers blest.

WAGNER

Why let this thought your soul o'ercast?
Can man do more than with nice skill,
With firm and conscientious will,
Practise the art transmitted from the past?
If thou thy sire dost honor in thy youth,
His lore thou gladly wilt receive;
In manhood, dost thou spread the bounds of truth,
Then may thy son a higher goal achieve.

FAUST

How blest, in whom the fond desire
From error's sea to rise, hope still renews!
What a man knows not, that he doth require,
And what he knoweth, that he cannot use.
But let not moody thoughts their shadow throw
O'er the calm beauty of this hour serene!
In the rich sunset see how brightly glow
Yon cottage homes, girt round with verdant green!
Slow sinks the orb, the day is now no more;
Yonder he hastens to diffuse new life.
Oh for a pinion from the earth to soar,
And after, ever after him to strive!
Then should I see the world below,
Bathed in the deathless evening-beams,
The vales reposing, every height a-glow,
The silver brooklets meeting golden streams.
The savage mountain, with its cavern'd side,
Bars not my godlike progress. Lo, the ocean,
Its warm bays heaving with a tranquil motion,
To my rapt vision opes its ample tide!
But now at length the god appears to sink;
A new-born impulse wings my flight,

Onward I press, his quenchless light to drink,
The day before me, and behind the night,
The pathless waves beneath, and over me the skies.
Fair dream, it vanish'd with the parting day!
Alas! that when on spirit-wing we rise,
No wing material lifts our mortal clay.
But 'tis our inborn impulse, deep and strong,
Upwards and onwards still to urge our flight,
When far above us pours its thrilling song
The sky-lark, lost in azure light;
When on extended wing amain
O'er pine-crown'd height the eagle soars;
And over moor and lake, the crane
Still striveth toward its native shores.

WAGNER

To strange conceits oft I myself must own,
But impulse such as this I ne'er have known:
Nor woods, nor fields, can long our thoughts engage;
Their wings I envy not the feather'd kind;
Far otherwise the pleasures of the mind
Bear us from book to book, from page to page!
Then winter nights grow cheerful; keen delight
Warms every limb; and ah! when we unroll
Some old and precious parchment, at the sight
All heaven itself descends upon the soul.

FAUST

Thy heart by one sole impulse is possess'd;
Unconscious of the other still remain!
Two souls, alas! are lodg'd within my breast,
Which struggle there for undivided reign:
One to the world, with obstinate desire,
And closely-cleaving organs, still adheres;
Above the mist, the other doth aspire,
With sacred vehemence, to purer spheres.
Oh, are there spirits in the air
Who float 'twixt heaven and earth dominion wielding,
Stoop hither from your golden atmosphere,

Lead me to scenes, new life and fuller yielding!
A magic mantle did I but possess,
Abroad to waft me as on viewless wings,
I'd prize it far beyond the costliest dress,
Nor would I change it for the robe of kings.

WAGNER

Call not the spirits who on mischief wait!
Their troop familiar, streaming through the air,
From every quarter threaten man's estate,
And danger in a thousand forms prepare!
They drive impetuous from the frozen north,
With fangs sharp-piercing, and keen arrowy tongues;
From the ungenial east they issue forth,
And prey, with parching breath, upon thy lungs;
If, waft'd on the desert's flaming wing,
They from the south heap fire upon the brain,
Refreshment from the west at first they bring,
Anon to drown thyself and field and plain.
In wait for mischief, they are prompt to hear;
With guileful purpose our behests obey;
Like ministers of grace they oft appear,
And lisp like angels, to betray.
But let us hence! Gray eve doth all things blend,
The air grows chill, the mists descend!
'Tis in the evening first our home we prize —
Why stand you thus, and gaze with wondering eyes?
What in the gloom thus moves you?

FAUST
Yon black hound
See'st thou, through corn and stubble scampering round?

WAGNER

I've mark'd him long, naught strange in him I see!

FAUST

Note him! What takest thou the brute to be?

WAGNER

But for a poodle, whom his instinct serves
His master's track to find once more.

FAUST

Dost mark how round us, with wide spiral curves,
He wheels, each circle closer than before?
And, if I err not, he appears to me
A line of fire upon his track to leave.

WAGNER

Naught but a poodle black of hue I see;
'Tis some illusion doth your sight deceive.

FAUST

Methinks a magic coil our feet around,
He for a future snare doth lightly spread.

WAGNER

Around us as in doubt I see him shyly bound,
Since he two strangers seeth in his master's stead.

FAUST

The circle narrows, he's already near!

WAGNER

A dog dost see, no spectre have we here;
He growls, doubts, lays him on his belly too,
And wags his tail—as dogs are wont to do.

FAUST

Come hither, Sirrah! join our company!

WAGNER

A very poodle, he appears to be!
Thou standest still, for thee he'll wait;
Thou speak'st to him, he fawns upon thee straight;
Aught thou mayst lose, again he'll bring,
And for thy stick will into water spring.

FAUST

Thou'rt right indeed; no traces now I see
Whatever of a spirit's agency,
'Tis training — nothing more.

WAGNER

A dog well taught
E'en by the wisest of us may be sought.
Ay, to your favor he's entitled too,
Apt scholar of the students, 'tis his due!

[*They enter the gate of the town.*]

STUDY

FAUST (*entering with the poodle*)

Now field and meadow I've forsaken;
O'er them deep night her veil doth draw;
In us the better soul doth waken,
With feelings of foreboding awe.
All lawless promptings, deeds unholy,
Now slumber, and all wild desires;
The love of man doth sway us wholly,
And love to God the soul inspires.

Peace, poodle, peace! Scamper not thus; obey me!
Why at the threshold snuffest thou so?
Behind the stove now quietly lay thee,
My softest cushion to thee I'll throw.
As thou, without, didst please and amuse me,
Running and frisking about on the hill,
So tendance now I will not refuse thee;
A welcome guest, if thou'lt be still.

Ah! when the friendly taper gloweth,
Once more within our narrow cell,
Then in the heart itself that knoweth,
A light the darkness doth dispel.
Reason her voice resumes; returneth
Hope's gracious bloom, with promise rife;
For streams of life the spirit yearneth,
Ah! for the very fount of life.

Poodle, snarl not! with the tone that arises,
Hallow'd and peaceful, my soul within,
Accords not thy growl, thy bestial din.
We find it not strange, that man despises
What he conceives not;
That he the good and fair misprizes —
Finding them often beyond his ken;
Will the dog snarl at them like men?

But ah! Despite my will, it stands confessed;
Contentment welleth up no longer in my breast.
Yet wherefore must the stream, alas, so soon be dry,
That we once more athirst should lie?
Full oft this sad experience hath been mine;
Nathless the want admits of compensation;
For things above the earth we learn to pine,
Our spirits yearn for revelation,
Which nowhere burns with purer beauty blent,
Than here in the New Testament.
To ope the ancient text an impulse strong
Impels me, and its sacred lore,
With honest purpose to explore,
And render into my loved German tongue.
        [*He opens a volume and applies himself to it.*]
'Tis writ, " In the beginning was the Word! "
I pause, perplex'd! Who now will help afford?
I cannot the mere Word so highly prize;
I must translate it otherwise,
If by the spirit guided as I read.
" In the beginning was the Sense! " Take heed,
The import of this primal sentence weigh,
Lest thy too hasty pen be led astray!
Is force creative then of Sense the dower?
" In the beginning was the Power! "
Thus should it stand: yet, while the line I trace,
A something warns me, once more to efface.
The spirit aids! from anxious scruples freed,
I write, " In the beginning was the Deed! "

Am I with thee my room to share,
Poodle, thy barking now forbear,
Forbear thy howling!
Comrade so noisy, ever growling,
I cannot suffer here to dwell.
One or the other, mark me well,
Forthwith must leave the cell.
I'm loath the guest-right to withhold;
The door's ajar, the passage clear;
But what must now mine eyes behold!
Are nature's laws suspended here?
Real is it, or a phantom show?
In length and breadth how doth my poodle **grow**!
He lifts himself with threat'ning mien,
In likeness of a dog no longer seen!
What spectre have I harbor'd thus!
Huge as a hippopotamus,
With fiery eye, terrific tooth!
Ah! now I know thee, sure enough!
For such a base, half-hellish **brood**,
The key of Solomon is good.

SPIRITS (*without*)

Captur'd there within is one!
Stay without and follow none!
Like a fox in iron snare,
Hell's old lynx is quaking **there**,
    But take heed!
Hover round, above, below,
    To and fro,
Then from durance is he freed!
Can ye aid him, spirits all,
Leave him not in mortal thrall!
Many a time and oft hath he
Served us, when at liberty.

The monster to confront, at first,
The spell of Four must be rehears'd;

Salamander shall kindle,
Writhe nymph of the wave,
In air sylph shall dwindle,
And Kobold shall slave.

Who doth ignore
The primal Four,
Nor knows aright
Their use and might,
O'er spirits will he
Ne'er master be!

Vanish in the fiery glow,
Salamander!
Rushingly together flow,
Undine!
Shimmer in the meteor's gleam,
Sylphide!
Hither bring thine homely aid,
Incubus!   Incubus!
Step forth!   I do adjure thee thus!

None of the Four
Lurks in the beast:
He grins at me, untroubled as before;
I have not hurt him in the least.
A spell of fear
Thou now shalt hear.

Art thou, comrade fell,
Fugitive from Hell?
See then this sign,
Before which incline
The murky troops of Hell!
With bristling hair now doth the creature swell.

Canst thou, reprobate,
Read the uncreate,
Unspeakable, diffused
Throughout the heavenly sphere,
Shamefully abused,
Transpierced with nail and spear!

Behind the stove, tam'd by my spells,
Like an elephant he swells;
Wholly now he fills the room,
He into mist will melt away.
Ascend not to the ceiling!   Come,
Thyself at the master's feet now lay!
Thou seest that mine is no idle threat.
With holy fire I will scorch thee yet!
Wait not the might
That lies in the triple-glowing light!
Wait not the might
Of all my arts in fullest measure!

MEPHISTOPHELES (*as the mist sinks, comes forward from behind the stove, in the dress of a traveling scholar*)
Why all this uproar?   What's the master's pleasure?

FAUST
This then the kernel of the brute!
A traveling scholar?   Why I needs must smile.

MEPHISTOPHELES
Your learned reverence humbly I salute!
You've made me swelter in a pretty style.

FAUST
Thy name?

MEPHISTOPHELES
The question trifling seems from one,
Who it appears the Word doth rate so low;
Who, undeluded by mere outward show,
To Being's depths would penetrate alone.

FAUST

With gentlemen like you indeed
The inward essence from the name we read,
As all too plainly it doth appear,
When Beelzebub, Destroyer, Liar, meets the ear.
Who then art thou?

MEPHISTOPHELES

Part of that power which still
Produceth good, whilst ever scheming ill.

FAUST

What hidden mystery in this riddle lies?

MEPHISTOPHELES

The spirit I, which evermore denies!
And justly; for whate'er to light is brought
Deserves again to be reduced to naught;
Then better 'twere that naught should be.
Thus all the elements which ye
Destruction, Sin, or briefly, Evil, name,
As my peculiar element I claim.

FAUST

Thou nam'st thyself a part, and yet a whole I see.

MEPHISTOPHELES

The modest truth I speak to thee.
Though folly's microcosm, man, it seems,
Himself to be a perfect whole esteems:
Part of the part am I, which at the first was all,
A part of darkness, which gave birth to light —
Proud light, who now his mother would enthrall,
Contesting space and ancient rank with night.
Yet he succeedeth not, for struggle as he will,
To forms material he adhereth still;
From them he streameth, them he maketh fair,
And still the progress of his beams they check;
And so, I trust, when comes the final wreck,
Light will, ere long, the doom of matter share.

FAUST

Thy worthy avocation now I guess!
Wholesale annihilation won't prevail,
So thou'rt beginning on a smaller scale.

MEPHISTOPHELES

And, to say truth, as yet with small success.
Oppos'd to naught, this clumsy world,
The something — it subsisteth still;
Not yet is it to ruin hurl'd,
Despite the efforts of my will.
Tempests and earthquakes, fire and flood, I've tried;
Yet land and ocean still unchang'd abide!
And then of humankind and beasts, the accursed brood,—
Neither o'er them can I extend my sway.
What countless myriads have I swept away!
Yet ever circulates the fresh young blood.
It is enough to drive me to despair!
As in the earth, in water, and in air,
A thousand germs burst forth spontaneously;
In moisture, drought, heat, cold, they still appear!
Had I not flame selected as my sphere,
Nothing apart had been reserved for me.

FAUST

So thou with thy cold devil's fist,
Still clench'd in malice impotent,
Dost the creative power resist,
The active, the beneficent!
Henceforth some other task essay,
Of Chaos thou the wondrous son!

MEPHISTOPHELES

We will consider what you say,
And talk about it more anon!
For this time have I leave to go?

FAUST

Why thou shouldst ask, I cannot see.
Since thee I now have learned to know,

At thy good pleasure, visit me.
Here is the window, here the door,
The chimney, too, may serve thy need.

MEPHISTOPHELES

I must confess, my stepping o'er
Thy threshold a slight hindrance doth impede;
The wizard-foot doth me retain.

FAUST

The pentagram thy peace doth mar?
To me, thou son of hell, explain,
How camest thou in, if this thine exit bar?
Could such a spirit aught ensnare?

MEPHISTOPHELES

Observe it well, it is not drawn with care;
One of the angles, that which points without,
Is, as thou seest, not quite closed.

FAUST

Chance hath the matter happily dispos'd!
So thou my captive art? No doubt!
By accident thou thus art caught!

MEPHISTOPHELES

In sprang the dog, indeed, observing naught;
Things now assume another shape,
The devil's in the house and can't escape.

FAUST

Why through the window not withdraw?

MEPHISTOPHELES

For ghosts and for the devil 'tis a law,
Where they stole in, there they must forth. We're free
The first to choose; as to the second, slaves are we.

FAUST

E'en hell hath its peculiar laws, I see!
I'm glad of that! a pact may then be made,
The which you gentlemen will surely keep?

MEPHISTOPHELES

Whate'er therein is promised thou shalt **reap,**
No tittle shall remain unpaid.
But such arrangements time require;
We'll speak of them when next we meet;
Most earnestly I now entreat,
This once permission to retire.

FAUST

Another moment prithee here remain,
Me with some happy word to pleasure.

MEPHISTOPHELES

Now let me go! Ere long I'll come again;
Then thou may'st question at thy leisure.

FAUST

'Twas not my purpose thee to lime;
The snare hast entered of thine own free will:
Let him who holds the devil, hold him still!
So soon he'll catch him not a second time.

MEPHISTOPHELES

If it so please thee, I'm at thy command;
Only on this condition, understand;
That worthily thy leisure to beguile,
I here may exercise my arts awhile.

FAUST

Thou'rt free to do so! Gladly I'll attend;
But be thine art a pleasant one!

MEPHISTOPHELES
                    My friend,
This hour enjoyment more intense
Shall captivate each ravish'd sense,
Than thou could'st compass in the bound
Of the whole year's unvarying round;
And what the dainty spirits sing,
The lovely images they bring,

Are no fantastic sorcery.
Rich odors shall regale your smell,
On choicest sweets your palate dwell,
Your feelings thrill with ecstasy.
No preparation do we need,
Here we together are.   Proceed.

SPIRITS

Hence overshadowing gloom,
Vanish from sight!
O'er us thine azure dome,
Bend, beauteous light!
Dark clouds that o'er us spread,
Melt in thin air!
Stars, your soft radiance shed,
Tender and fair!
Girt with celestial might,
Winging their airy flight,
Spirits are thronging.
Follows their forms of light
Infinite longing!
Flutter their vestures bright
O'er field and grove!
Where in their leafy bower
Lovers the livelong hour
Vow deathless love.
Soft bloometh bud and bower!
Bloometh the grove!
Grapes from the spreading vine
Crown the full measure;
Fountains of foaming wine
Gush from the pressure.
Still where the currents wind,
Gems brightly gleam;
Leaving the hills behind
On rolls the stream;
Now into ample seas,

LIEZEN-MAYER

FAUST AND MEPHISTO

Spreadeth the flood —
Laving the sunny leas,
Mantled with wood.
Rapture the feather'd throng,
Gaily careering,
Sip as they float along;
Sunward they're steering;
On toward the isles of light
Winging their way,
That on the waters bright
Dancingly play.
Hark to the choral strain,
Joyfully ringing!
While on the grassy plain
Dancers are springing;
Climbing the steep hill's side,
Skimming the glassy tide,
Wander they there;
Others on pinions wide
Wing the blue air;
All lifeward tending, upward still wending,
Toward yonder stars that gleam,
Far, far above;
Stars from whose tender beam
Rains blissful love.

MEPHISTOPHELES

Well done, my dainty spirits! now he slumbers!
Ye have entranc'd him fairly with your numbers!
This minstrelsy of yours I must repay.—
Thou art not yet the man to hold the devil fast!—
With fairest shapes your spells around him cast,
And plunge him in a sea of dreams!
But that this charm be rent, the threshold passed,
Tooth of rat the way must clear.
I need not conjure long it seems,
One rustles hitherward, and soon my voice will hear.

The master of the rats and mice,
Of flies and frogs, of bugs and lice,
Commands thy presence; without fear
Come forth and gnaw the threshold here,
Where he with oil has smear'd it.—Thou
Com'st hopping forth already! Now
To work! The point that holds me bound
Is in the outer angle found.
Another bite — so — now 'tis done —
Now, Faustus, till we meet again, dream on.

FAUST (*awaking*)

Am I once more deluded! must I deem
That thus the throng of spirits disappear?
The devil's presence — was it but a dream?
Hath but a poodle scap'd and left me here?

STUDY

FAUST, MEPHISTOPHELES

FAUST

A knock? Come in! Who now would break my rest?

MEPHISTOPHELES

'Tis I!

FAUST

Come in!

MEPHISTOPHELES

Thrice be the words express'd.

FAUST

Then I repeat, Come in!

MEPHISTOPHELES

'Tis well,
I hope that we shall soon agree!
For now your fancies to expel,
Here, as a youth of high degree,
I come in gold-lac'd scarlet vest,

And stiff-silk mantle richly dress'd,
A cock's gay feather for a plume,
A long and pointed rapier, too;
And briefly I would counsel you
To don at once the same costume,
And, free from trammels, speed away,
That what life is you may essay.

FAUST

In every garb I needs must feel oppress'd,
My heart to earth's low cares a prey.
Too old the trifler's part to play,
Too young to live by no desire possess'd.
What can the world to me afford?
Renounce! renounce! is still the word;
This is the everlasting song
In every ear that ceaseless rings,
And which, alas, our whole life long,
Hoarsely each passing moment sings.
But to new horror I awake each morn,
And I could weep hot tears, to see the sun
Dawn on another day, whose round forlorn
Accomplishes no wish of mine — not one.
Which still, with froward captiousness, impains
E'en the presentiment of every joy,
While low realities and paltry cares
The spirit's fond imaginings destroy.
Then must I too, when falls the veil of night,
Stretch'd on my pallet languish in despair.
Appalling dreams my soul affright;
No rest vouchsafed me even there.
The god, who throned within my breast resides,
Deep in my soul can stir the springs;
With sovereign sway my energies he guides,
He cannot move external things;
And so existence is to me a weight,
Death fondly I desire, and life I hate.

MEPHISTOPHELES

And yet, methinks, by most 'twill be confess'd
That Death is never quite a welcome guest.

FAUST

Happy the man around whose brow he binds
The bloodstain'd wreath in conquest's dazzling hour;
Or whom, excited by the dance, he finds
Dissolv'd in bliss, in love's delicious bower!
O that before the lofty spirit's might,
Enraptured, I had rendered up my soul!

MEPHISTOPHELES

Yet did a certain man refrain one night
Of its brown juice to drain the crystal bowl.

FAUST

To play the spy diverts you then?

MEPHISTOPHELES

I own,
Though not omniscient, much to me is known.

FAUST

If o'er my soul the tone familiar, stealing,
Drew me from harrowing thought's bewild'ring maze,
Touching the ling'ring chords of childlike feeling,
With the sweet harmonies of happier days:
So curse I all, around the soul that windeth
Its magic and alluring spell,
And with delusive flattery bindeth
Its victim to this dreary cell!
Curs'd before all things be the high opinion
Wherewith the spirit girds itself around!
Of shows delusive curs'd be the dominion,
Within whose mocking sphere our sense is bound!
Accurs'd of dreams the treacherous wiles,
The cheat of glory, deathless fame!
Accurs'd what each as property beguiles,
Wife, child, slave, plough, whate'er its name!

Accurs'd be mammon, when with treasure
He doth to daring deeds incite:
Or when to steep the soul in pleasure,
He spreads the couch of soft delight!
Curs'd be the grape's balsamic juice!
Accurs'd love's dream, of joys the first!
Accurs'd be hope! accurs'd be faith!
And more than all, be patience curs'd!

CHORUS OF SPIRITS (*invisible*)

Woe! woe!
Thou hast destroy'd
The beautiful world
With violent blow;
'Tis shiver'd! 'tis shatter'd!
The fragments abroad by a demigod scatter'd!
Now we sweep
The wrecks into nothingness!
Fondly we weep
The beauty that's gone!
Thou, 'mongst the sons of earth,
Lofty and mighty one,
Build it once more!
In thine own bosom the lost world restore!
Now with unclouded sense
Enter a new career;
Songs shall salute thine ear,
Ne'er heard before!

MEPHISTOPHELES

My little ones these spirits be.
Hark! with shrewd intelligence,
How they recommend to thee
Action, and the joys of sense!
In the busy world to dwell,
Fain they would allure thee hence:
For within this lonely cell,
Stagnate sap of life and sense.

Forbear to trifle longer with thy grief,
Which, vulture-like, consumes thee in this den.
The worst society is some relief,
Making thee feel thyself a man with men.
Nathless, it is not meant, I trow,
To thrust thee 'mid the vulgar throng.
I to the upper ranks do not belong;
Yet if, by me companion'd, thou
Thy steps through life forthwith wilt take,
Upon the spot myself I'll make
Thy comrade;—
Should it suit thy need,   .
I am thy servant, am thy slave indeed!

FAUST

And how must I thy services repay?

MEPHISTOPHELES

Thereto thou lengthen'd respite hast!

FAUST

No! no!

The devil is an egoist I know:
And, for Heaven's sake, 'tis not his way
Kindness to any one to show.
Let the condition plainly be exprest!
Such a domestic is a dangerous guest.

MEPHISTOPHELES

I'll pledge myself to be thy servant *here*,
Still at thy back alert and prompt to be;
But when together *yonder* we appear,
Then shalt thou do the same for me.

FAUST

But small concern I feel for yonder world;
Hast thou this system into ruin hurl'd,
Another may arise the void to fill.
This earth the fountain whence my pleasures flow,

This sun doth daily shine upon my woe,
And if this world I must forego,
Let happen then,— what can and will.
I to this theme will close mine ears,
If men hereafter hate and love,
And if there be in yonder spheres
A depth below or height above.

MEPHISTOPHELES

In this mood thou mayst venture it.   But make
The compact!   I at once will undertake
To charm thee with mine arts.   I'll give thee more
Than mortal eye hath e'er beheld before.

FAUST

What, sorry Devil, hast thou to bestow?
Was ever mortal spirit, in its high endeavor,
Fathom'd by Being such as thou?
Yet food thou hast which satisfieth never;
Hast ruddy gold, that still doth flow
Like restless quicksilver away;
A game thou hast, at which none win who play —
A girl who would, with amorous eyen,
E'en from my breast a neighbor snare,
Lofty ambition's joy divine,
That, meteor-like, dissolves in air.
Show me the fruit that, ere 'tis pluck'd, doth rot,
And trees, whose verdure daily buds anew!

MEPHISTOPHELES

Such a commission scares me not;
I can provide such treasures, it is true.
But, my good friend, a season will come round
When on what's good we may regale in peace.

FAUST

If e'er upon my couch, stretched at my ease, I'm found,
Then may my life that instant cease!

Me canst thou cheat with glozing wile
Till self-reproach away I cast,—
Me with joy's lure canst thou beguile;—
Let that day be for me the last!
Be this our wager!

MEPHISTOPHELES
Settled!

FAUST
Sure and fast!
When to the moment I shall say,
"Linger awhile! so fair thou art!"
Then mayst thou fetter me straightway,
Then to the abyss will I depart!
Then may the solemn death-bell sound,
Then from thy service thou art free,
The index then may cease its round,
And time be never more for me!

MEPHISTOPHELES
I shall remember: pause, ere 'tis too late.

FAUST
Thereto a perfect right hast thou.
My strength I do not rashly overrate.
Slave am I here, at any rate,
If thine, or whose, it matters not, I trow.

MEPHISTOPHELES
At thine inaugural feast I will this day
Attend, my duties to commence.—
But one thing!—Accidents may happen, hence
A line or two in writing grant, I pray.

FAUST
A writing, Pedant! dost demand from me?
Man, and man's plighted word, are these unknown to thee?
Is't not enough, that by the word I gave,
My doom for evermore is cast?

Doth not the world in all its currents rave,
And must a promise hold me fast?
Yet fixed is this delusion in our heart;
Who, of his own free will, therefrom would part?
How blest within whose breast truth reigneth pure!
No sacrifice will he repent when made!
A formal deed, with seal and signature,
A spectre this from which all shrink afraid.
The word its life resigneth in the pen,
Leather and wax usurp the mastery then.
Spirits of evil! what dost thou require?
Brass, marble, parchment, paper, dost desire?
Shall I with chisel, pen, or graver write?
Thy choice is free; to me 'tis all the same.

MEPHISTOPHELES

Wherefore thy passion so excite,
And thus thine eloquence inflame?
A scrap is for our compact good.
Thou under-signest merely with a drop of blood.

FAUST

If this will satisfy thy mind,
Thy whim I'll gratify, howe'er absurd.

MEPHISTOPHELES

Blood is a juice of very special kind.

FAUST

Be not afraid that I shall break my word!
The scope of all my energy
Is in exact accordance with my vow.
Vainly I have aspired too high;
I'm on a level but with such as thou;
Me the great spirit scorn'd, defied;
Nature from me herself doth hide;
Rent is the web of thought; my mind
Doth knowledge loathe of every kind.

In depths of sensual pleasure drown'd,
Let us our fiery passions still!
Enwrapp'd in magic's veil profound,
Let wondrous charms our senses thrill!
Plunge we in time's tempestuous flow,
Stem we the rolling surge of chance!
There may alternate weal and woe,
Success and failure, as they can,
Mingle and shift in changeful dance!
Excitement is the sphere for man.

MEPHISTOPHELES

Nor goal, nor measure is prescrib'd to you,
If you desire to taste of every thing,
To snatch at joy while on the wing,
May your career amuse and profit too!
Only fall to and don't be over coy!

FAUST

Hearken! The end I aim at is not joy;
I crave excitement, agonizing bliss,
Enamor'd hatred, quickening vexation.
Purg'd from the love of knowledge, my vocation,
The scope of all my powers henceforth be this,
To bare my breast to every pang,— to know
In my heart's core all human weal and woe,
To grasp in thought the lofty and the deep,
Men's various fortunes on my breast to heap,
And thus to theirs dilate my individual mind,
And share at length with them the shipwreck of mankind.

MEPHISTOPHELES

Oh, credit me, who still as ages roll,
Have chew'd this bitter fare from year to year,
No mortal, from the cradle to the bier,
Digests the ancient leaven! Know, this Whole
Doth for the Deity alone subsist!

He in eternal brightness doth exist;
Us unto darkness he hath brought, and here,
Where day and night alternate, is your sphere.

FAUST

But 'tis my will!

MEPHISTOPHELES

Well spoken, I admit!
But one thing puzzles me, my friend;
Time's short, art long; methinks 'twere fit
That you to friendly counsel should attend.
A poet choose as your ally!
Let him thought's wide dominion sweep,
Each good and noble quality
Upon your honored brow to heap;
The lion's magnanimity,
The fleetness of the hind,
The fiery blood of Italy,
The Northern's stedfast mind.
Let him to you the mystery show
To blend high aims and cunning low;
And while youth's passions are aflame
To fall in love by rule and plan!
I fain would meet with such a man;
Would him Sir Microcosmus name.

FAUST

What then am I, if I aspire in vain
The crown of our humanity to gain,
Toward which my every sense doth strain?

MEPHISTOPHELES

Thou'rt after all — just what thou art.
Put on thy head a wig with countless locks,
And to a cubit's height upraise thy socks,
Still thou remainest ever, what thou art.

FAUST

I feel it, I have heap'd upon my brain
The gather'd treasure of man's thought in vain;
And when at length from studious toil I rest,
No power, new-born, springs up within my breast;
A hair's breadth is not added to my height;
I am no nearer to the infinite.

MEPHISTOPHELES

Good sir, these things you view indeed,
Just as by other men they're view'd;
We must more cleverly proceed,
Before life's joys our grasp elude.
The devil! thou hast hands and feet,
And head and heart are also thine;
What I enjoy with relish sweet —
Is it on that account less mine?
If for six stallions I can pay,
Do I not own their strength and speed?
A proper man I dash away,
As their two dozen legs were mine indeed.
Up then, from idle pondering free,
And forth into the world with me!
I tell you what; — your speculative churl
Is like a beast which some ill spirit leads,
On barren wilderness, in ceaseless whirl,
While all around lie fair and verdant meads.

FAUST

But how shall we begin?

MEPHISTOPHELES

We will go hence with speed,
A place of torment this indeed!
A precious life, thyself to bore,
And some few youngsters evermore!
Leave that to neighbor Paunch! Withdraw?
Why wilt thou plague thyself with thrashing straw?

The very best that thou dost know
Thou dar'st not to the striplings show.
One in the passage now doth wait!

FAUST

I'm in no mood to see him now.

MEPHISTOPHELES

Poor lad! He must be tired, I trow;
He must not go disconsolate.
Hand me thy cap and gown; the mask
Is for my purpose quite first rate.

[*He changes his dress.*]

Now leave it to my wit! I ask
But quarter of an hour; meanwhile equip,
And make all ready for our pleasant trip!

[*Exit* FAUST.]

MEPHISTOPHELES (*in* FAUST'S *long gown*)

Mortal! the loftiest attributes of men,
Reason and Knowledge, only thus contemn;
Still let the Prince of lies, without control,
With shows, and mocking charms delude thy soul,
I have thee unconditionally then! —
Fate hath endow'd him with an ardent mind,
Which unrestrain'd still presses on forever,
And whose precipitate endeavor
Earth's joys o'erleaping, leaveth them behind.
Him will I drag through life's wild waste,
Through scenes of vapid dulness, where at last
Bewilder'd, he shall falter, and stick fast;
And, still to mock his greedy haste,
Viands and drink shall float his craving lips beyond —
Vainly he'll seek refreshment, anguish-tost,
And were he not the devil's by his bond,
Yet must his soul infallibly be lost!

A STUDENT *enters.*

STUDENT

But recently I've quitted home,
Full of devotion am I come
A man to know and hear, whose name
With reverence is known to fame.

MEPHISTOPHELES

Your courtesy much flatters me!
A man like other men you see;
Pray have you yet applied elsewhere?

STUDENT

I would entreat your friendly care!
I've youthful blood and courage high;
Of gold I bring a fair supply;
To let me go my mother was not fain;
But here I longed true knowledge to attain.

MEPHISTOPHELES

You've hit upon the very place.

STUDENT

And yet my steps I would retrace.
These walls, this melancholy room,
O'erpower me with a sense of gloom;
The space is narrow, nothing green,
No friendly tree is to be seen:
And in these halls, with benches filled, distraught,
Sight, hearing fail me, and the power of thought.

MEPHISTOPHELES

It all depends on habit. Thus at first
The infant takes not kindly to the breast,
But before long, its eager thirst
Is fain to slake with hearty zest:
Thus at the breasts of wisdom day by day
With keener relish you'll your thirst allay.

STUDENT

Upon her neck I fain would hang with joy;
To reach it, say, what means must I employ?

MEPHISTOPHELES

Explain, ere further time we lose,
What special faculty you choose?

STUDENT

Profoundly learned I would grow,
What heaven contains would comprehend,
O'er earth's wide realm my gaze extend,
Nature and science I desire to know.

MEPHISTOPHELES

You are upon the proper track, I find;
Take heed, let nothing dissipate your mind.

STUDENT

My heart and soul are in the chase!
Though, to be sure, I fain would seize,
On pleasant summer holidays,
A little liberty and careless ease.

MEPHISTOPHELES

Use well your time, so rapidly it flies;
Method will teach you time to win;
Hence, my young friend, I would advise,
With college logic to begin!
Then will your mind be so well braced,
In Spanish boots so tightly laced,
That on 'twill circumspectly creep,
Thought's beaten track securely keep,
Nor will it, ignis-fatuus like,
Into the path of error strike.
Then many a day they'll teach you how
The mind's spontaneous acts, till now
As eating and as drinking free,
Require a process;—one! two! three!
In truth the subtle web of thought

Is like the weaver's fabric wrought:
One treadle moves a thousand lines,
Swift dart the shuttles to and fro,
Unseen the threads together flow,
A thousand knots one stroke combines.
Then forward steps your sage to show,
And prove to you, it must be so;
The first being so, and so the second,
The third and fourth deduc'd we see;
And if there were no first and second,
Nor third nor fourth would ever be.
This, scholars of all countries prize,—
Yet 'mong themselves no weavers rise.
He who would know and treat of aught alive,
Seeks first the living spirit thence to drive:
Then are the lifeless fragments in his hand,
There only fails, alas! the spirit-band.
This process, chemists name, in learned thesis,
Mocking themselves, *Naturæ encheiresis.*

STUDENT

Your words I cannot fully comprehend.

MEPHISTOPHELES

In a short time you will improve, my friend,
When of scholastic forms you learn the use;
And how by method all things to reduce.

STUDENT

So doth all this my brain confound,
As if a mill-wheel there were turning round.

MEPHISTOPHELES

And next, before aught else you learn,
You must with zeal to metaphysics turn!
There see that you profoundly comprehend
What doth the limit of man's brain transcend;
For that which is or is not in the head
A sounding phrase will serve you in good stead.

But before all strive this half year
From one fix'd order ne'er to swerve!
Five lectures daily you must hear;
The hour still punctually observe!
Yourself with studious zeal prepare,
And closely in your manual look,
Hereby may you be quite aware
That all he utters standeth in the book;
Yet write away without cessation,
As at the Holy Ghost's dictation!

STUDENT

This, Sir, a second time you need not say!
Your counsel I appreciate quite;
What we possess in black and white
We can in peace and comfort bear away.

MEPHISTOPHELES

A faculty I pray you name.

STUDENT

For jurisprudence some distaste I own.

MEPHISTOPHELES

To me this branch of science is well known,
And hence I cannot your repugnance blame.
Customs and laws in every place,
Like a disease, and heir-loom dread,
Still trail their curse from race to race,
And furtively abroad they spread.
To nonsense, reason's self they turn;
Beneficence becomes a pest;
Woe unto thee, that thou'rt a grandson born!
As for the law born with us, unexpressed; —
That law, alas, none careth to discern.

STUDENT

You deepen my dislike. The youth
Whom you instruct, is blest in sooth!
To try theology I feel inclined.

MEPHISTOPHELES

I would not lead you willingly astray,
But as regards this science, you will find
So hard it is to shun the erring way,
And so much hidden poison lies therein
Which scarce can you discern from medicine.
Here too it is the best, to listen but to one,
And by the master's words to swear alone.
To sum up all — To words hold fast!
Then the safe gate securely pass'd,
You'll reach the fane of certainty at last.

STUDENT

But then some meaning must the words convey.

MEPHISTOPHELES

Right! But o'er-anxious thought you'll find of no avail;
For there precisely where ideas fail,
A word comes opportunely into play;
Most admirable weapons words are found,
On words a system we securely ground,
In words we can conveniently believe,
Nor of a single jot can we a word bereave.

STUDENT

Your pardon for my importunity;
Yet once more must I trouble you:
On medicine, I'll thank you to supply
A pregnant utterance or two!
Three years! how brief the appointed tide!
The field, heaven knows, is all too wide!
If but a friendly hint be thrown,
'Tis easier than to feel one's way.

MEPHISTOPHELES (*aside*)

I'm weary of the dry pedantic tone,
And must again the genuine devil play.

(*Aloud*)

Of medicine the spirit's caught with ease,

The great and little world you study through,
That things may then their course pursue,
As heaven may please.
In vain abroad you range through science's ample space,
Each man learns only that which learn he can;
Who knows the moment to embrace,
He is your proper man.
In person you are tolerably made,
Nor in assurance will you be deficient:
Self-confidence acquire, be not afraid,
Others will then esteem you a proficient.
Learn chiefly with the sex to deal!
Their thousand ahs and ohs,
These the sage doctor knows,
He only from one point can heal.
Assume a decent tone of courteous ease,
You have them then to humor as you please.
First a diploma must belief infuse,
That you in your profession take the lead:
You then at once those easy freedoms use
For which another many a year must plead;
Learn how to feel with nice address
The dainty wrist;—and how to press,
With ardent, furtive glance, the slender waist,
To feel how tightly it is laced.

STUDENT

There is some sense in that! one sees the how and why.

MEPHISTOPHELES

Gray is, young friend, all theory:
And green of life the golden tree.

STUDENT

I swear it seemeth like a dream to me.
May I some future time repeat my visit,
To hear on what your wisdom grounds your views?

MEPHISTOPHELES

Command my humble service when you choose.

STUDENT

Ere I retire, one boon I must solicit:
Here is my album; do not, Sir, deny
This token of your favor!

MEPHISTOPHELES

Willingly!
[*He writes and returns the book.*]

STUDENT (*reads*)

ERITIS SICUT DEUS, SCIENTES BONUM ET MALUM
[*He reverently closes the book and retires.*]

MEPHISTOPHELES

Let but this ancient proverb be your rule,
My cousin follow still, the wily snake,
And with your likeness to the gods, poor fool,
Ere long be sure your poor sick heart will quake!

FAUST (*enters*)

Whither away?

MEPHISTOPHELES

'Tis thine our course to steer.
The little world, and then the great we'll view.
With what delight, what profit too,
Thou'lt revel through thy gay career!

FAUST

Despite my length of beard I need
The easy manners that insure success;
Th' attempt I fear can ne'er succeed;
To mingle in the world I want address;
I still have an embarrass'd air, and then
I feel myself so small with other men.

MEPHISTOPHELES

Time, my good friend, will all that's needful give;
Be only self-possessed, and thou hast learn'd to live.

FAUST

But how are we to start, I pray?
Steeds, servants, carriage, where are they?

MEPHISTOPHELES

We've but to spread this mantle wide,
'Twill serve whereon through air to ride;
No heavy baggage need you take,
When we our bold excursion make.
A little gas, which I will soon prepare,
Lifts us from earth; aloft through air,
Light-laden, we shall swiftly steer;—
I wish you joy of your new life-career.

AUERBACH'S CELLAR IN LEIPZIG

A Drinking Party

FROSCH

No drinking? Naught a laugh to raise?
None of your gloomy looks, I pray!
You, who so bright were wont to blaze,
Are dull as wetted straw today.

BRANDER

'Tis all your fault; your part you do not bear,
No beastliness, no folly.

FROSCH (*pours a glass of wine over his head*)
There,
You have them both!

BRANDER
You double beast!

FROSCH
'Tis what you ask'd me for, at least!

SIEBEL

Whoever quarrels, turn him out!
With open throat drink, roar, and shout.
Hollo! Hollo! Ho!

ALTMAYER

Zounds, fellow, cease your deaf'ning cheers!
Bring cotton-wool! He splits my ears.

SIEBEL

'Tis when the roof rings back the tone,
Then first the full power of the bass is known.

FROSCH

Right! out with him who takes offence!
A! tara lara da!

ALTMAYER

A! tara lara da!

FROSCH

Our throats are tuned. Come, let's commence!

(*Sings*)

The holy Roman empire now,
How holds it still together?

BRANDER

An ugly song! a song political!
A song offensive! Thank God, every morn,
To rule the Roman empire that you were not born!
I bless my stars at least that mine is not
Either a kaiser's or a chancellor's lot.
Yet, 'among ourselves, should one still lord it o'er the rest;
That we elect a pope I now suggest.
Ye know what quality insures
A man's success, his rise secures.

FROSCH (*sings*)

Bear, lady nightingale above,
Ten thousand greetings to my love.

SIEBEL

No greetings to a sweetheart! No love-songs shall
there be!

FROSCH

Love-greetings and love-kisses! Thou shalt not hinder me!

(*Sings*)

Undo the bolt! in stilly night,
Undo the bolt! the lover wakes.
Shut to the bolt! when morning breaks.

SIEBEL

Ay, sing, sing on, praise her with all thy might!
My turn to laugh will come some day.
Me hath she jilted once, you the same trick she'll play.
Some gnome her lover be! where cross-roads meet,
With her to play the fool; or old he-goat,
From Blocksberg coming in swift gallop, bleat
A good night to her from his hairy throat!
A proper lad of genuine flesh and blood,
Is for the damsel far too good;
The greeting she shall have from me,
To smash her window-panes will be!

BRANDER (*striking on the table*)

Silence! Attend! to me give ear!
Confess, sirs, I know how to live:
Some love-sick folk are sitting here!
Hence, 'tis but fit, their hearts to cheer,
That I a good-night strain to them should give.
Hark! of the newest fashion is my song!
Strike boldly in the chorus, clear and strong!

(*He sings*)

Once in a cellar lived a rat,
He feasted there on butter,
Until his paunch became as fat
As that of Doctor Luther.
The cook laid poison for the guest,
Then was his heart with pangs oppress'd,
As if his frame love wasted.

CHORUS (*shouting*)

As if his frame love wasted.

BRANDER

He ran around, he ran abroad,
Of every puddle drinking.
The house with rage he scratch'd and gnaw'd,
In vain,— he fast was sinking;
Full many an anguish'd bound he gave,
Nothing the hapless brute could save,
As if his frame love wasted.

CHORUS

As if his frame love wasted.

BRANDER

By torture driven, in open day,
The kitchen he invaded,
Convulsed upon the hearth he lay,
With anguish sorely jaded;
The poisoner laugh'd; Ha! ha! quoth she,
His life is ebbing fast, I see,
As if his frame love wasted.

CHORUS

As if his frame love wasted.

SIEBEL

How the dull boors exulting shout!
Poison for the poor rats to strew
A fine exploit it is no doubt.

BRANDER

They, as it seems, stand well with you!

ALTMAYER

Old bald-pate! with the paunch profound!
The rat's mishap hath tamed his nature;
For he his counterpart hath found
Depicted in the swollen creature.

FAUST AND MEPHISTOPHELES

MEPHISTOPHELES

I now must introduce to you
Before aught else, this jovial crew,
To show how lightly life may glide away;
With the folk here each day's a holiday.
With little wit and much content,
Each on his own small round intent,
Like sportive kitten with its tail;
While no sick-headache they bewail,
And while their host will credit give,
Joyous and free from care they live.

BRANDER

They're off a journey, that is clear,—
From their strange manners; they have scarce been here
An hour.

FROSCH

You're right! Leipzig's the place for me!
'Tis quite a little Paris; people there
Acquire a certain easy, finish'd air.

SIEBEL

What take you now these travelers to be?

FROSCH

Let me alone! O'er a full glass you'll see,
As easily I'll worm their secret out
As draw an infant's tooth. I've not a doubt
That my two gentlemen are nobly born;
They look dissatisfied and full of scorn.

BRANDER

They are but mountebanks, I'll lay a bet!

ALTMAYER

Most like.

VOL. I — 21

FROSCH

Mark me, I'll screw it from them yet!

MEPHISTOPHELES (*to* FAUST)

These fellows would not scent the devil out,
E'en though he had them by the very throat!

FAUST

Good-morrow, gentlemen!

SIEBEL

Thanks for your fair salute.
[*Aside, glancing at* MEPHISTOPHELES.]
How! goes the fellow on a halting foot?

MEPHISTOPHELES

Is it permitted here with you to sit?
Then, though good wine is not forthcoming here,
Good company at least our hearts will cheer.

ALTMAYER

A dainty gentleman, no doubt of it!

FROSCH

You're doubtless recently from Rippach? Pray,
Did you with Master Hans there chance to sup?

MEPHISTOPHELES

Today we pass'd him, but we did not stop!
When last we met him he had much to say
Touching his cousins, and to each he sent
Full many a greeting and kind compliment.
[*With an inclination toward* FROSCH.]

ALTMAYER (*aside to* FROSCH)

You have it there!

SIEBEL

Faith! he's a knowing one!

FROSCH

Have patience! I will show him up anon!

MEPHISTOPHELES

We heard erewhile, unless I'm wrong,
Voices well trained in chorus pealing?
Certes, most choicely here must song
Re-echo from this vaulted ceiling!

FROSCH

That you're an amateur one plainly sees!

MEPHISTOPHELES

Oh no, though strong the love, I cannot boast much skill.

ALTMAYER

Give us a song!

MEPHISTOPHELES

As many as you will.

SIEBEL

But be it a brand new one, if you please!

MEPHISTOPHELES

But recently returned from Spain are we,
The pleasant land of wine and minstrelsy.

(*Sings*)

A king there was once reigning,
Who had a goodly flea —

FROSCH

Hark! did you rightly catch the words? a flea!
An odd sort of a guest he needs must be.

MEPHISTOPHELES (*sings*)

A king there was once reigning,
Who had a goodly flea,
Him loved he without feigning,
As his own son were he!
His tailor then he summon'd —
The tailor to him goes:
Now measure me the youngster
For jerkin and for hose!

BRANDER

Take proper heed, the tailor strictly charge,
The nicest measurement to take,
And as he loves his head, to make
The hose quite smooth and not too large!

MEPHISTOPHELES

In satin and in velvet,
Behold the younker dressed;
Bedizen'd o'er with ribbons,
A cross upon his breast.
Prime minister they made him;
He wore a star of state;
And all his poor relations
Were courtiers, rich and great.

The gentlemen and ladies
At court were sore distressed;
The queen and all her maidens
Were bitten by the pest,
And yet they dared not scratch them,
Or chase the fleas away.
If we are bit, we catch them,
And crack without delay.

CHORUS (shouting)

If we are bit, etc.

FROSCH

Bravo! That's the song for me!

SIEBEL

Such be the fate of every flea!

BRANDER

With clever finger catch and kill!

ALTMAYER

Hurrah for wine and freedom still!

MEPHISTOPHELES

Were but your wine a trifle better, friend,
A glass to freedom I would gladly drain.

SIEBEL

You'd better not repeat those words again!

MEPHISTOPHELES

I am afraid the landlord to offend;
Else freely would I treat each worthy guest
From our own cellar to the very best.

SIEBEL

Out with it then! Your doings I'll defend.

FROSCH

Give a good glass, and straight we'll praise you, one and all.
Only let not your samples be too small;
For if my judgment you desire,
Certes, an ample mouthful I require.

ALTMAYER (*aside*)

I guess, they're from the Rhenish land.

MEPHISTOPHELES

Fetch me a gimlet here!

BRANDER

Say, what therewith to bore?
You cannot have the wine-casks at the door?

ALTMAYER

Our landlord's tool-basket behind doth yonder stand.

MEPHISTOPHELES (*takes the gimlet*)
(*To* FROSCH)

Now only say! what liquor will you take?

FROSCH

How mean you that? Have you of every sort?

MEPHISTOPHELES

Each may his own selection make.

ALTMAYER (*to* FROSCH)

Ha! Ha! You lick your lips already at the thought.

FROSCH

Good, if I have my choice, the Rhenish I propose;
For still the fairest gifts the fatherland bestows.

MEPHISTOPHELES (*boring a hole in the edge of the table
opposite to where* FROSCH *is sitting*)

Get me a little wax — and make some stoppers — quick!

ALTMAYER

Why, this is nothing but a juggler's trick!

MEPHISTOPHELES (*to* BRANDER)

And you?

BRANDER

Champagne's the wine for me;
Right brisk, and sparkling let it be!

[MEPHISTOPHELES *bores, one of the party has in the
meantime prepared the wax-stoppers and stopped
the holes.*]

BRANDER

What foreign is one always can't decline,
What's good is often scatter'd far apart.
The French your genuine German hates with all his heart,
Yet has a relish for their wine.

SIEBEL (*as* MEPHISTOPHELES *approaches him*)

I like not acid wine, I must allow,
Give me a glass of genuine sweet!

MEPHISTOPHELES (*bores*)

Tokay

Shall, if you wish it, flow without delay.

ALTMAYER

Come! look me in the face! no fooling now!
You are but making fun of us, I trow.

MEPHISTOPHELES

Ah! ah! that would indeed be making free
With such distinguished guests. Come, no delay;
What liquor can I serve you with, I pray?

ALTMAYER

Only be quick, it matters not to me.

[*After the holes are all bored and stopped.*]

MEPHISTOPHELES (*with strange gestures*)

Grapes the vine-stock bears,
Horns the buck-goat wears!
Wine is sap, the vine is wood,
The wooden board yields wine as good.
With a deeper glance and true
The mysteries of nature view!
Have faith and here's a miracle!
Your stoppers draw and drink your fill!

ALL (*as they draw the stoppers and the wine chosen by
each runs into his glass*)

Oh beauteous spring, which flows so far!

MEPHISTOPHELES

Spill not a single drop, of this beware!

[*They drink repeatedly.*]

ALL (*sing*)

Happy as cannibals are we,
Or as five hundred swine.

MEPHISTOPHELES

They're in their glory, mark their elevation!

FAUST

Let's hence, nor here our stay prolong.

MEPHISTOPHELES

Attend, of brutishness ere long
You'll see a glorious revelation.

SIEBEL (*drinks carelessly; the wine is spilt upon the ground,
and turns to flame*)

Help! fire! help! Hell is burning!

MEPHISTOPHELES (*addressing the flames*)
Stop,
Kind element, be still, I say!
(*To the Company*)
Of purgatorial fire as yet 'tis but a drop.

SIEBEL
What means the knave! For this you'll dearly pay!
Us, it appears, you do not know.

FROSCH
Such tricks a second time he'd better show!

ALTMAYER
Methinks 'twere well we pack'd him quietly away.

SIEBEL
What, sir! with us your hocus-pocus play!

MEPHISTOPHELES
Silence, old wine-cask!

SIEBEL
How! add insult, too!
Vile broomstick!

BRANDER
Hold! or blows shall rain on you!

ALTMAYER (*draws a stopper out of the table; fire springs
out against him*)
I burn! I burn!

SIEBEL
'Tis sorcery, I vow!
Strike home! The fellow is fair game, I trow!
[*They draw their knives and attack* MEPHISTOPHELES.]

MEPHISTOPHELES (*with solemn gestures*)
Visionary scenes appear!
Words delusive cheat the ear!
Be ye there, and be ye here!
[*They stand amazed and gaze at one another.*]

ALTMAYER

Where am I? What a beauteous land!

FROSCH

Vineyards! unless my sight deceives?

SIEBEL

And clust'ring grapes too, close at hand!

BRANDER

And underneath the spreading leaves,
What stems there be! What grapes I see!
   [*He seizes* SIEBEL *by the nose. The others recipro-
      cally do the same, and raise their knives.*]

MEPHISTOPHELES (*as above*)

Delusion, from their eyes the bandage take!
Note how the devil loves a jest to break!
   [*He disappears with* FAUST; *the fellows draw back
      from one another.*]

SIEBEL

What was it?

ALTMAYER

How?

FROSCH

Was that your nose?

BRANDER (*to* SIEBEL)

And look, my hand doth thine inclose!

ALTMAYER

I felt a shock, it went through every limb!
A chair! I'm fainting! All things swim!

FROSCH

Say! What has happened? What's it all about?

SIEBEL

Where is the fellow? Could I scent him out,
His body from his soul I'd soon divide!

ALTMAYER

With my own eyes, upon a cask astride,
Forth through the cellar-door I saw him ride—
Heavy as lead my feet are growing.

[*Turning to the table.*]

I wonder is the wine still flowing!

SIEBEL

'Twas all delusion, cheat and lie.

FROSCH

'Twas wine I drank, most certainly.

BRANDER

But with the grapes how was it, pray?

ALTMAYER

That none may miracles believe, who now will say?

WITCHES' KITCHEN

A large caldron hangs over the fire on a low hearth; various figures appear in the vapor rising from it. A FEMALE MONKEY *sits beside the caldron to skim it, and watch that it does not boil over. The* MALE MONKEY *with the young ones is seated near, warming himself. The walls and ceiling are adorned with the strangest articles of witch-furniture.*

FAUST, MEPHISTOPHELES

FAUST

This senseless, juggling witchcraft I detest!
Dost promise that in this foul nest
Of madness I shall be restored?
Must I seek counsel from an ancient dame?
And can she, by these rites abhorred,
Take thirty winters from my frame?
Woe's me, if thou naught better canst suggest!
Hope has already fled my breast.
Has neither nature nor a noble mind
A balsam yet devis'd of any kind?

MEPHISTOPHELES

My friend, you now speak sensibly. In truth,
Nature a method giveth to renew thy youth:
But in another book the lesson's writ;—
It forms a curious chapter, I admit.

FAUST

I fain would know it.

MEPHISTOPHELES

Good! A remedy
Without physician, gold, or sorcery:
Away forthwith, and to the fields repair;
Begin to delve, to cultivate the ground;
Thy senses and thyself confine
Within the very narrowest round;
Support thyself upon the simplest fare;
Live like a very brute the brutes among;
Neither esteem it robbery
The acre thou dost reap, thyself to dung.
This the best method, credit me,
Again at eighty to grow hale and young.

FAUST

I am not used to it, nor can myself degrade
So far, as in my hand to take the spade.
This narrow life would suit me not at all.

MEPHISTOPHELES

Then we the witch must summon after all.

FAUST

Will none but this old beldame do?
Canst not thyself the potion brew?

MEPHISTOPHELES

A pretty play our leisure to beguile!
A thousand bridges I could build meanwhile.
Not science only and consummate art—
Patience must also bear her part.

A quiet spirit worketh whole years long;
Time only makes the subtle ferment strong.
And all things that belong thereto,
Are wondrous and exceeding rare!
The devil taught her, it is true;
But yet the draught the devil can't prepare.

[Perceiving the beasts.]

Look yonder, what a dainty pair!
Here is the maid! the knave is there!

(To the beasts)

It seems your dame is not at home?

THE MONKEYS

Gone to carouse,
Out of the house,
Thro' the chimney and away!

MEPHISTOPHELES

How long is it her wont to roam?

THE MONKEYS

While we can warm our paws she'll stay.

MEPHISTOPHELES (to FAUST)

What think you of the charming creatures?

FAUST

I loathe alike their form and features!

MEPHISTOPHELES

Nay, such discourse, be it confessed,
Is just the thing that pleases me the best.

(To the MONKEYS)

Tell me, ye whelps, accursed crew!
What stir ye in the broth about?

MONKEYS

Coarse beggar's gruel here we stew.

MEPHISTOPHELES

Of customers you'll have a rout.

THE HE-MONKEY (*approaching and fawning on*
MEPHISTOPHELES)
Quick! quick! throw the dice,
Make me rich in a trice,
Oh give me the prize!
Alas, for myself,
Had I plenty of pelf,
I then should be wise.

MEPHISTOPHELES
How blest the ape would think himself, if he
Could only put into the lottery!
[*In the meantime the young* MONKEYS *have been playing
with a large globe, which they roll forward.*]

THE HE-MONKEY
The world behold;
Unceasingly roll'd,
It riseth and falleth ever;
It ringeth like glass!
How brittle, alas!
'Tis hollow, and resteth never.
How bright the sphere,
Still brighter here!
Now living am I!
Dear son, beware!
Nor venture there!
Thou too must die!
It is of clay;
'Twill crumble away;
There fragments lie.

MEPHISTOPHELES
Of what use is the sieve?

THE HE-MONKEY (*taking it down*)
The sieve would show,
If thou wert a thief or no?

[*He runs to the* She-Monkey, *and makes her look
through it.*]

Look through the sieve!
Dost know him the thief,
And dar'st thou not call him so?

MEPHISTOPHELES (*approaching the fire*)

And then this pot?

THE MONKEYS

The half-witted sot!
He knows not the pot!
He knows not the kettle!

MEPHISTOPHELES

Unmannerly beast!
Be civil at least!

THE HE-MONKEY

Take the whisk and sit down in the settle!
[*He makes* MEPHISTOPHELES *sit down.*]

FAUST (*who all this time has been standing before a looking-
glass, now approaching, and now retiring from it*)

What do I see? what form, whose charms transcend
The loveliness of earth, is mirror'd here!
O Love, to waft me to her sphere,
To me the swiftest of thy pinions lend!
Alas! If I remain not rooted to this place,
If to approach more near I'm fondly lur'd,
Her image fades, in veiling mist obscur'd!—
Model of beauty both in form and face!
Is't possible? Hath woman charms so rare?
In this recumbent form, supremely fair,
The essence must I see of heavenly grace?
Can aught so exquisite on earth be found?

MEPHISTOPHELES

The six days' labor of a god, my friend,
Who doth himself cry bravo, at the end,
By something clever doubtless should be crown'd.
For this time gaze your fill, and when you please
Just such a prize for you I can provide;
How blest is he to whom kind fate decrees,
To take her to his home, a lovely bride!

[FAUST *continues to gaze into the mirror.* MEPHIS-
TOPHELES *stretching himself on the settle and play-
ing with the whisk, continues to speak.*]
Here sit I, like a king upon his throne;
My sceptre this; — the crown I want alone.

THE MONKEYS (*who have hitherto been making all sorts of
strange gestures, bring* MEPHISTOPHELES *a crown, with
loud cries*)

Oh, be so good,
With sweat and with blood
The crown to lime!
[*They handle the crown awkwardly and break it in two
pieces, with which they skip about.*]
'Twas fate's decree!
We speak and see!
We hear and rhyme.

FAUST (*before the mirror*)
Woe's me! well-nigh distraught I feel!

MEPHISTOPHELES (*pointing to the beasts*)
And even my own head almost begins to reel.

THE MONKEYS
If good luck attend,
If fitly things blend,
Our jargon with thought
And with reason is fraught!

FAUST (*as above*)

A flame is kindled in my breast!
Let us begone! nor linger here!

MEPHISTOPHELES (*in the same position*)

It now at least must be confessed,
That poets sometimes are sincere.

[*The caldron which the* SHE-MONKEY *has neglected begins to boil over; a great flame arises, which streams up the chimney. The* WITCH *comes down the chimney with horrible cries.*]

THE WITCH

Ough! ough! ough! ough!
Accursed brute! accursed sow!
The caldron dost neglect, for shame!
Accursed brute to scorch the dame!

(*Perceiving* FAUST *and* MEPHISTOPHELES.)

Whom have we here?
Who's sneaking here?
Whence are ye come?
With what desire?
The plague of fire
Your bones consume!

[*She dips the skimming-ladle into the caldron and throws flames at* FAUST, MEPHISTOPHELES, *and the* MONKEYS. *The* MONKEYS *whimper.*]

MEPHISTOPHELES (*twirling the whisk which he holds in his hand, and striking among the glasses and pots*)

Dash! Smash!
There lies the glass!
There lies the slime!
'Tis but a jest;
I but keep time,
Thou hellish pest,
To thine own chime!

[*While the* WITCH *steps back in rage and astonishment.*]

Dost know me! Skeleton! Vile scarecrow, thou!

Thy lord and master dost thou know?
What holds me, that I deal not now
Thee and thine apes a stunning blow?
No more respect to my red vest dost pay?
Does my cock's feather no allegiance claim?
Have I my visage masked today?
Must I be forced myself to name?

THE WITCH

Master, forgive this rude salute!
But I perceive no cloven foot.
And your two ravens, where are they?

MEPHISTOPHELES

This once I must admit your plea; —
For truly I must own that we
Each other have not seen for many a day.
The culture, too, that shapes the world, at last
Hath e'en the devil in its sphere embraced;
The northern phantom from the scene hath pass'd;
Tail, talons, horns, are nowhere to be traced!
As for the foot, with which I can't dispense,
'Twould injure me in company, and hence,
Like many a youthful cavalier,
False calves I now have worn for many a year.

THE WITCH (*dancing*)

I am beside myself with joy,
To see once more the gallant Satan here!

MEPHISTOPHELES

Woman, no more that name employ!

THE WITCH

But why? what mischief hath it done?

MEPHISTOPHELES

To fable-books it now doth appertain;
But people from the change have nothing won.
Rid of the evil one, the evil ones remain.
Lord Baron call thou me, so is the matter good;
Of other cavaliers the mien I wear.
Dost make no question of my gentle blood;
See here, this is the scutcheon that I bear!

[*He makes an unseemly gesture.*]

THE WITCH (*laughing immoderately*)

Ha! Ha! Just like yourself! You are, I ween,
The same mad wag that you have ever been!

MEPHISTOPHELES (*to* FAUST)

My friend, learn this to understand, I pray!
To deal with witches this is still the way.

THE WITCH

Now tell me, gentlemen, what you desire?

MEPHISTOPHELES

Of your known juice a goblet we require.
But for the very oldest let me ask;
Double its strength with years doth grow.

THE WITCH

Most willingly! And here I have a flask,
From which I've sipp'd myself ere now;
What's more, it doth no longer stink;
To you a glass I joyfully will give.

(*Aside.*)

If unprepar'd, however, this man drink,
He hath not, as you know, an hour to live.

MEPHISTOPHELES

He's my good friend, with whom 'twill prosper well;
I grudge him not the choicest of thy store.
Now draw thy circle, speak thy spell,
And straight a bumper for him pour!

[*The* WITCH, *with extraordinary gestures, describes a circle, and places strange things within it. The glasses meanwhile begin to ring, and the caldron to sound and make music. Lastly, she brings a great book; places the* MONKEYS *in the circle to serve her as a desk, and to hold the torches. She beckons* FAUST *to approach.*]

FAUST (*to* MEPHISTOPHELES)

Tell me, to what doth all this tend?
Where will these frantic gestures end?
This loathsome cheat, this senseless stuff
I've known and hated long enough.

MEPHISTOPHELES

Mere mummery, a laugh to raise!
Pray don't be so fastidious! She
But as a leech, her hocus-pocus plays,
That well with you her potion may agree.

[*He compels* FAUST *to enter the circle.*]

[*The* WITCH, *with great emphasis, begins to declaim from the book.*]

This must thou ken:
Of one make ten,
Pass two, and then
Make square the three,
So rich thou'lt be.
Drop out the four!
From five and six,
Thus says the witch,
Make seven and eight.
So all is straight!
And nine is one,
And ten is none,
This is the witch's one-time-one!

FAUST

The hag doth as in fever rave.

MEPHISTOPHELES

To these will follow many a stave.
I know it well, so rings the book throughout;
Much time I've lost in puzzling o'er its pages,
For downright paradox, no doubt,
A mystery remains alike to fools and sages.
Ancient the art and modern too, my friend.
'Tis still the fashion as it used to be,
Error instead of truth abroad to send
By means of three and one, and one and three.
'Tis ever taught and babbled in the schools.
Who'd take the trouble to dispute with fools?
When words men hear, in sooth, they usually believe,
That there must needs therein be something to conceive.

THE WITCH (*continues*)

The lofty power
Of wisdom's dower,
From all the world conceal'd!
Who thinketh not,
To him I wot,
Unsought it is reveal'd.

FAUST

What nonsense doth the hag propound?
My brain it doth well-nigh confound.
A hundred thousand fools or more,
Methinks I hear in chorus roar.

MEPHISTOPHELES

Incomparable Sibyl cease, I pray!
Hand us thy liquor without more delay.
And to the very brim the goblet crown!
My friend he is, and need not be afraid;
Besides, he is a man of many a grade,
Who hath drunk deep already.

[*The* WITCH, *with many ceremonies, pours the liquor
into a cup; as* FAUST *lifts it to his mouth, a light
flame arises.*]

MEPHISTOPHELES
                    Gulp it down!
No hesitation!   It will prove
A cordial, and your heart inspire!
What! with the devil hand and glove,
And yet shrink back afraid of fire?
[*The* WITCH *dissolves the circle.*   FAUST *steps out.*]

MEPHISTOPHELES
Now forth at once! thou dar'st not rest.

WITCH
And much, sir, may the liquor profit you!

MEPHISTOPHELES (*to the* WITCH)
And if to pleasure thee I aught can do,
Pray on Walpurgis mention thy request.

WITCH
Here is a song, sung o'er, sometimes you'll see,
That 'twill a singular effect produce.

MEPHISTOPHELES (*to* FAUST)
Come, quick, and let thyself be led by me;
Thou must perspire, in order that the juice
Thy frame may penetrate through every part.
Then noble idleness I thee will teach to prize,
And soon with ecstasy thou'lt recognize
How Cupid stirs and gambols in thy heart.

FAUST
Let me but gaze one moment in the glass!
Too lovely was that female form!

MEPHISTOPHELES
                    Nay! nay!
A model which all women shall surpass,
In flesh and blood ere long thou shalt survey.
                    (*Aside.*)
As works the draught, thou presently shalt greet
A Helen in each woman thou dost meet.

A STREET

FAUST (MARGARET *passing by*).

FAUST

Fair lady, may I thus make free
To offer you my arm and company?

MARGARET

I am no lady, am not fair,
Can without escort home repair.

[*She disengages herself and exit.*]

FAUST

By heaven! This girl is fair indeed!
No form like hers can I recall.
Virtue she hath, and modest heed,
Is piquant too, and sharp withal.
Her cheek's soft light, her rosy lips,
No length of time will e'er eclipse!
Her downward glance in passing by,
Deep in my heart is stamp'd for aye;
How curt and sharp her answer too,
To ecstasy the feeling grew!

[MEPHISTOPHELES *enters.*]

FAUST

This girl must win for me! Dost hear?

MEPHISTOPHELES

Which?

FAUST

She who but now passed.

MEPHISTOPHELES

What! She?
She from confession cometh here,
From every sin absolved and free;
I crept near the confessor's chair.
All innocence her virgin soul,
For next to nothing went she there;
O'er such as she I've no control!

MARGARET

From the Painting by Wilhelm von Kaulbach

FAUST

She's past fourteen.

MEPHISTOPHELES

You really talk
Like any gay Lothario,
Who every floweret from its stalk
Would pluck, and deems nor grace, nor truth,
Secure against his arts, forsooth!
This ne'er the less won't always do.

FAUST

Sir Moralizer, prithee, pause;
Nor plague me with your tiresome laws!
To cut the matter short, my friend,
She must this very night be mine,—
And if to help me you decline,
Midnight shall see our compact end.

MEPHISTOPHELES

What may occur just bear in mind!
A fortnight's space, at least, I need,
A fit occasion but to find.

FAUST

With but seven hours I could succeed;
Nor should I want the devil's wile,
So young a creature to beguile.

MEPHISTOPHELES

Like any Frenchman now you speak,
But do not fret, I pray; why seek
To hurry to enjoyment straight?
The pleasure is not half so great,
As when at first, around, above,
With all the fooleries of love,
The puppet you can knead and mold
As in Italian story oft is told.

FAUST

No such incentives do I need.

MEPHISTOPHELES

But now, without offence or jest!
You cannot quickly, I protest,
In winning this sweet child succeed.
By storm we cannot take the fort,
To stratagem we must resort.

FAUST

Conduct me to her place of rest!
Some token of the angel bring!
A kerchief from her snowy breast,
A garter bring me — any thing!

MEPHISTOPHELES

That I my anxious zeal may prove,
Your pangs to soothe and aid your love,
A single moment will we not delay,
Will lead you to her room this very day.

FAUST

And shall I see her? — Have her?

MEPHISTOPHELES

No!
She to a neighbor's house will go;
But in her atmosphere alone
The tedious hours meanwhile you may employ
In blissful dreams of future joy.

FAUST

Can we go now?

MEPHISTOPHELES

'Tis yet too soon.

FAUST

Some present for my love procure!   [*Exit.*]

MEPHISTOPHELES

Presents so soon! 'tis well! success is sure!
Full many a goodly place I know,
And treasures buried long ago;
I must a bit o'erlook them now.   [*Exit.*]

EVENING.   A SMALL AND NEAT ROOM

MARGARET (*braiding and binding up her hair*)

I would give something now to know
Who yonder gentleman could be!
He had a gallant air, I trow,
And doubtless was of high degree:
That written on his brow was seen —
Nor else would he so bold have been.

[*Exit.*]

MEPHISTOPHELES

Come in! tread softly! be discreet!

FAUST (*after a pause*)

Begone and leave me, I entreat!

MEPHISTOPHELES (*looking round*)

Not every maiden is so neat.

[*Exit.*]

FAUST (*gazing round*)

Welcome sweet twilight, calm and blest,
That in this hallow'd precinct reigns!
Fond yearning love, inspire my breast,
Feeding on hope's sweet dew thy blissful pains!
What stillness here environs me!
Content and order brood around.
What fulness in this poverty!
In this small cell what bliss profound!

[*He throws himself on the leather arm-chair beside
the bed.*]

Receive me thou, who hast in thine embrace,
Welcom'd in joy and grief the ages flown!
How oft the children of a by-gone race
Have cluster'd round this patriarchal throne!
Haply she, also, whom I hold so dear,
For Christmas gift, with grateful joy possess'd,
Hath with the full round cheek of childhood, here,
Her grandsire's wither'd hand devoutly press'd.
Maiden! I feel thy spirit haunt the place,

Breathing of order and abounding grace.
As with a mother's voice it prompteth thee
The pure white cover o'er the board to spread,
To stew the crisping sand beneath thy tread.
Dear hand! so godlike in its ministry!
The hut becomes a paradise through thee!
And here —   [*He raises the bed-curtain.*]

How thrills my pulse with strange delight!
Here could I linger hours untold;
Thou, Nature, didst in vision bright,
The embryo angel here unfold.
Here lay the child, her bosom warm
With life; while steeped in slumber's dew,
To perfect grace, her godlike form,
With pure and hallow'd weavings grew!

And thou! ah here what seekest thou?
How quails mine inmost being now!
What wouldst thou here? what makes thy heart so sore?
Unhappy Faust! I know thee now no more.

Do I a magic atmosphere inhale?
Erewhile, my passion would not brook delay!
Now in a pure love-dream I melt away.
Are we the sport of every passing gale?

Should she return and enter now,
How wouldst thou rue thy guilty flame!
Proud vaunter — thou wouldst hide thy brow —
And at her feet sink down with shame.

MEPHISTOPHELES
Quick! quick! below I see her there.

FAUST
Away! I will return no more!

MEPHISTOPHELES
Here is a casket, with a store
Of jewels, which I got elsewhere.

Just lay it in the press; make haste!
I swear to you, 'twill turn her brain;
Therein some trifles I have placed,
Wherewith another to obtain.
But child is child, and play is play.

FAUST

I know not — shall I?

MEPHISTOPHELES
Do you ask?
Perchance you would retain the treasure?
If such your wish, why then, I say,
Henceforth absolve me from my task,
Nor longer waste your hours of leisure.
I trust you're not by avarice led!
I rub my hands, I scratch my head,—
[*He places the casket in the press and closes the lock.*]
Now quick! Away!
That soon the sweet young creature may
The wish and purpose of your heart obey;
Yet stand you there
As would you to the lecture-room repair,
As if before you stood,
Arrayed in flesh and blood,
Physics and metaphysics weird and gray!—
Away!   [*Exeunt.*]

MARGARET (*with a lamp*)
Here 'tis so close, so sultry now,
[*She opens the window.*]
Yet out of doors 'tis not so warm.
I feel so strange, I know not how —
I wish my mother would come home.
Through me there runs a shuddering —
I'm but a foolish timid thing!
[*While undressing herself she begins to sing.*]
There was a king in Thule,
True even to the grave;

To whom his dying mistress
A golden beaker gave.

At every feast he drained it,
Naught was to him so dear,
And often as he drained it,
Gush'd from his eyes the tear.

When death came, unrepining
His cities o'er he told;
All to his heir resigning,
Except his cup of gold.

With many a knightly vassal
At a royal feast sat he,
In yon proud hall ancestral,
In his castle o'er the sea.

Up stood the jovial monarch,
And quaff'd his last life's glow,
Then hurled the hallow'd goblet
Into the flood below.

He saw it splashing, drinking,
And plunging in the sea;
His eyes meanwhile were sinking,
And never again drank he.

[*She opens the press to put away her clothes, and perceives the casket.*]

How comes this lovely casket here? The press
I locked, of that I'm confident.
'Tis very wonderful! What's in it I can't guess;
Perhaps 'twas brought by some one in distress,
And left in pledge for loan my mother lent.
Here by a ribbon hangs a little key!
I have a mind to open it and see!
Heavens! only look! what have we here!
In all my days ne'er saw I such a sight!
Jewels! which any noble dame might wear,
For some high pageant richly dight

This chain — how would it look on me!
These splendid gems, whose may they be?
       [*She puts them on and steps before the glass.*]
Were but the earrings only mine!
Thus one has quite another air.
What boots it to be young and fair?
It doubtless may be very fine;
But then, alas, none cares for you,
And praise sounds half like pity too.

Gold all doth lure,
Gold doth secure
All things.   Alas, we poor!

PROMENADE

FAUST *walking thoughtfully up and down.* To him MEPHISTOPHELES.

MEPHISTOPHELES

By all rejected love! By hellish fire I curse,
Would I knew aught to make my imprecation worse!

FAUST

What aileth thee? what chafes thee now so sore?
A face like that I never saw before!

MEPHISTOPHELES

I'd yield me to the devil instantly,
Did it not happen that myself am he!

FAUST

There must be some disorder in thy wit!
To rave thus like a madman, is it fit?

MEPHISTOPHELES

Think! only think! The gems for Gretchen brought,
Them hath a priest now made his own! —
A glimpse of them the mother caught,
And 'gan with secret fear to groan.
The woman's scent is keen enough;
Doth ever in the prayer-book snuff;

Smells **every** article to ascertain
Whether the thing is holy or profane,
And scented in the jewels rare,
That there was not much blessing there.
" My child," she cries, " ill-gotten good
Ensnares the soul, consumes the blood;
With them we'll deck our Lady shrine,
She'll cheer our souls with bread divine! "
At this poor Gretchen 'gan to pout;
'Tis a gift-horse, at least, she thought,
And sure, he godless cannot be,
Who brought them here so cleverly.
Straight for a priest the mother sent,
Who, when he understood the jest,
With what he saw was well content.
" This shows a pious mind! " Quoth he:
" Self-conquest is true victory.
The Church hath a good stomach, she, with zest,
Whole countries hath swallow'd down,
And never yet a surfeit known.
The Church alone, be it confessed,
Daughters, can ill-got wealth digest."

FAUST

It is a general custom, too,
Practised alike by king and jew.

MEPHISTOPHELES

With that, clasp, chain, and ring, he swept
As they were mushrooms; and the casket,
Without one word of thanks, he kept,
As if of nuts it were a basket.
Promised reward in heaven, then forth he hied—
And greatly they were edified.

FAUST

And Gretchen!

MEPHISTOPHELES

In unquiet mood
Knows neither what she would or should;
The trinkets night and day thinks o'er;
On him who brought them, dwells still more.

FAUST

The darling's sorrow grieves me, bring
Another set without delay!
The first, methinks, was no great thing.

MEPHISTOPHELES

All's to my gentleman child's play!

FAUST

Plan all things to achieve my end!
Engage the attention of her friend!
No milk-and-water devil be,
And bring fresh jewels instantly!

MEPHISTOPHELES

Ay, sir! Most gladly I'll obey.

[FAUST *exit.*]

MEPHISTOPHELES

Your doting love-sick fool, with ease,
Merely his lady-love to please,
Sun, moon, and stars in sport would puff away.

[*Exit.*]

THE NEIGHBOR'S HOUSE

MARTHA (*alone*)

God pardon my dear husband, he
Doth not in truth act well by me!
Forth in the world abroad to roam,
And leave me on the straw at home.
And yet his will I ne'er did thwart,
God knows, I lov'd him from my heart.

[*She weeps.*]

Perchance he's dead! — oh wretched state! —
Had I but a certificate!

(Margaret *comes*.)

MARGARET

Dame Martha!

MARTHA

Gretchen?

MARGARET

Only think!
My knees beneath me well-nigh sink!
Within my press I've found today
Another case, of ebony.
And things — magnificent they are,
More costly than the first, by far.

MARTHA

You must not name it to your mother!
It would to shrift, just like the other.

MARGARET

Nay look at them! now only see!

MARTHA (*dresses her up*)

Thou happy creature!

MARGARET

Woe is me!
Them in the street I cannot wear,
Or in the church, or anywhere.

MARTHA

Come often over here to me,
The gems put on quite privately;
And then before the mirror walk an hour or so,
Thus we shall have our pleasure too.
Then suitable occasions we must seize,
As at a feast, to show them by degrees:
A chain at first, pearl ear-drops then,— your mother
Won't see them, or we'll coin some tale or other.

MARGARET

But, who, I wonder, could the caskets bring?
I fear there's something wrong about the thing!

[*A knock.*]

Good heavens! can that my mother be?

MARTHA (*peering through the blind*)

'Tis a strange gentleman, I see.
Come in!

[MEPHISTOPHELES *enters.*]

MEPHISTOPHELES

I've ventur'd to intrude today.
Ladies, excuse the liberty, I pray.
          [*He steps back respectfully before* MARGARET.]
After dame Martha Schwerdtlein I inquire!

MARTHA

'Tis I.   Pray what have you to say to me?

MEPHISTOPHELES (*aside to her*)

I know you now,— and therefore will retire;
At present you've distinguished company.
Pardon the freedom, Madam, with your leave,
I will make free to call again at eve.

MARTHA (*aloud*)

Why, child, of all strange notions, **he**
For some grand lady taketh thee!

MARGARET

I am, in truth, of humble blood —
The gentleman is far too good —
Nor gems nor trinkets are my own.

MEPHISTOPHELES

Oh 'tis not the mere ornaments alone;
Her glance and mien far more betray.
Rejoiced I am that I may stay.

MARTHA

Your business, Sir?   I long to know —

MEPHISTOPHELES

Would I could happier tidings show!
I trust mine errand you'll not let me **rue**;
Your husband's dead, and greeteth you.

MARTHA

Is dead? True heart! Oh misery!
My husband dead! Oh, I shall die!

MARGARET

Alas! good Martha! don't despair!

MEPHISTOPHELES

Now listen to the sad affair!

MARGARET

I for this cause should fear to love.
The loss my certain death would prove.

MEPHISTOPHELES

Joy still must sorrow, sorrow joy attend.

MARTHA

Proceed, and tell the story of his end!

MEPHISTOPHELES

At Padua, in St. Anthony's,
In holy ground his body lies;
Quiet and cool his place of rest,
With pious ceremonials blest.

MARTHA

And had you naught besides to bring?

MEPHISTOPHELES

Oh yes! one grave and solemn prayer;
Let them for him three hundred masses sing!
But in my pockets, I have nothing there.

MARTHA

No trinket! no love-token did he send!
What every journeyman safe in his pouch will hoard
There for remembrance fondly stored,
And rather hungers, rather begs than spend!

MEPHISTOPHELES

Madam, in truth, it grieves me sore,
But he his gold not lavishly hath spent.

His failings too he deeply did repent,
Ay! and his evil plight bewail'd still **more.**

MARGARET

Alas! That men should thus be doomed **to woe!**
I for his soul will many a requiem pray.

MEPHISTOPHELES

A husband you deserve this very day;
A child so worthy to be loved.

MARGARET

Ah no,
That time hath not yet come for me.

MEPHISTOPHELES

If not a spouse, a gallant let it be.
Among heaven's choicest gifts, I **place,**
So sweet a darling to embrace.

MARGARET

Our land doth no such usage know.

MEPHISTOPHELES

Usage or not, it happens so.

MARTHA

Go on, I pray!

MEPHISTOPHELES

I stood by his bedside.
Something less foul it was than dung;
'Twas straw half rotten; yet, he as a Christian died.
And sorely hath remorse his conscience wrung.
" Wretch that I was," quoth he, with parting **breath,**
" So to forsake my business and my wife!
Ah! the remembrance is my death.
Could I but have her pardon in this life!"—

MARTHA (*weeping*).

Dear soul! I've long forgiven him, indeed!

MEPHISTOPHELES

" Though she, God knows, was more to blame than **I.**"

MARTHA

He lied! What, on the brink of death to lie!

MEPHISTOPHELES

If I am skill'd the countenance to read,
He doubtless fabled as he parted hence.—
"No time had I to gape, or take my ease," he said,
"First to get children, and then get them bread;
And bread, too, in the very widest sense;
Nor could I eat in peace even my proper share."

MARTHA

What, all my truth, my love forgotten quite?
My weary drudgery by day and night!

MEPHISTOPHELES

Not so! He thought of you with tender care.
Quoth he: "Heaven knows how fervently I prayed,
For wife and children when from Malta bound;—
The prayer hath heaven with favor crowned;
We took a Turkish vessel which conveyed
Rich store of treasure for the Sultan's court;
Its own reward our gallant action brought;
The captur'd prize was shared among the crew,
And of the treasure I received my due.'"

MARTHA

How? Where? The treasure hath he buried, pray?

MEPHISTOPHELES

Where the four winds have blown it, who can say?
In Naples as he stroll'd, a stranger there,—
A comely maid took pity on my friend:
And gave such tokens of her love and care,
That he retained them to his blessed end.

MARTHA

Scoundrel! to rob his children of their bread!
And all this misery, this bitter need,
Could not his course of recklessness impede!

MEPHISTOPHELES

Well, he hath paid the forfeit, and is dead.
Now were I in your place, my counsel hear;
My weeds I'd wear for one chaste year,
And for another lover meanwhile would look out.

MARTHA

Alas, I might search far and near,
Not quickly should I find another like my first!
There could not be a fonder fool than mine,
Only he loved too well abroad to roam;
Loved foreign women too, and foreign wine,
And loved besides the dice accurs'd.

MEPHISTOPHELES

All had gone swimmingly, no doubt,
Had he but given you at home,
On his side, just as wide a range.
Upon such terms, to you I swear,
Myself with you would gladly rings exchange!

MARTHA

The gentleman is surely pleas'd to jest!

MEPHISTOPHELES (*aside*)

Now to be off in time, were best!
She'd make the very devil marry her.
(*To* MARGARET)
How fares it with your heart?

MARGARET

How mean you, Sir?

MEPHISTOPHELES (*aside*)

The sweet young innocent!
(*aloud*)
Ladies, farewell!

MARGARET

Farewell!

MARTHA

But ere you leave us, quickly tell!
I from a witness fain had heard,
Where, how, and when my husband died and was interr'd.
To forms I've always been attached indeed,
His death I fain would in the journals read.

MEPHISTOPHELES

Ay, madam, what two witnesses declare
Is held as valid everywhere;
A gallant friend I have, not far from here,
Who will for you before the judge appear.
I'll bring him straight.

MARTHA

I pray you do!

MEPHISTOPHELES

And this young lady, we shall find her too?
A noble youth, far traveled, he
Shows to the sex all courtesy.

MARGARET

I in his presence needs must blush for shame.

MEPHISTOPHELES

Not in the presence of a crownèd king!

MARTHA

The garden, then, behind my house, we'll name,
There we'll await you both this evening.

A STREET

FAUST, MEPHISTOPHELES

FAUST

How is it now? How speeds it? Is't in train?

MEPHISTOPHELES

Bravo! I find you all aflame!
Gretchen full soon your own you'll name.
This eve, at neighbor Martha's, her you'll meet again;
The woman seems expressly made
To drive the pimp and gipsy's trade.

FAUST

}ood!

MEPHISTOPHELES

But from us she something would request.

FAUST

A favor claims return, as this world goes.

MEPHISTOPHELES

Ve have on oath but duly to attest
That her dead husband's limbs, outstretch'd, repose
n holy ground at Padua.

FAUST

Sage indeed!
3o I suppose we straight must journey there!

MEPHISTOPHELES

'ancta simplicitas! For that no need!
Vithout much knowledge we have but to swear.

FAUST

f you have nothing better to suggest,
.gainst your plan I must at once protest.

MEPHISTOPHELES

h, holy man! methinks I have you there!
1 all your life, say, have you ne'er
alse witness borne, until this hour?
ave you of God, the world, and all it doth contain,
f man, and that which worketh in his heart and brain,
ot definitions given, in words of weight and power,
Vith front unblushing, and a dauntless breast?
et, if into the depth of things you go,
ouching these matters, it must be confess'd,
s much as of Herr Schwerdtlein's death you know!

FAUST

hou art and dost remain liar and sophist too.

MEPHISTOPHELES

y, if one did not take a somewhat deeper view!
omorrow, in all honor, thou

Poor Gretchen wilt befool, and vow
Thy soul's deep love, in lover's fashion.

FAUST

And from my heart.

MEPHISTOPHELES

All good and fair!
Then deathless constancy thou'lt swear;
Speak of one all o'ermastering passion —
Will that too issue from the heart?

FAUST

Forbear!
When passion sways me, and I seek to frame
Fit utterance for feeling, deep, intense,
And for my frenzy finding no fit name,
Sweep round the ample world with every sense,
Grasp at the loftiest words to speak my flame,
And call the glow, wherewith I burn,
Quenchless, eternal, yea, eterne —
Is that of sophistry a devilish play?

MEPHISTOPHELES

Yet am I right!

FAUST

Mark this, my friend,
And spare my lungs; who would the right maintain,
And hath a tongue wherewith his point to gain,
Will gain it in the end.
But come, of gossip I am weary quite;
Because I've no resource, thou'rt in the right.

GARDEN

MARGARET *on* FAUST'S *arm*. MARTHA *with* MEPHISTOPHELES *walking up
and down.*

MARGARET

I feel it, you but spare my ignorance,
The gentleman to blame me stoops thus low.

FAUST AND MARGARET

From the Painting by Carl Becker

A traveler from complaisance
Still makes the best of things; I know
Too well, my humble prattle never can
Have power to entertain so wise a man.

FAUST

One glance, one word from thee doth charm me more
Than the world's wisdom or the sage's lore.

[*He kisses her hand.*]

MARGARET

Nay! trouble not yourself!   A hand so coarse,
So rude as mine, how can you kiss!
What constant work at home must I not do perforce!
My mother too exacting is.   [*They pass on.*]

MARTHA

Thus, sir, unceasing travel is your lot?

MEPHISTOPHELES

Traffic and duty urge us!   With what pain
Are we compelled to leave full many a spot,
Where yet we dare not once remain!

MARTHA

In youth's wild years, with vigor crown'd,
'Tis not amiss thus through the world to sweep;
But ah, the evil days come round!
And to a lonely grave as bachelor to creep
A pleasant thing has no one found.

MEPHISTOPHELES

The prospect fills me with dismay.

MARTHA

Therefore in time, dear sir, reflect, I pray.

[*They pass on.*]

MARGARET

Ay, out of sight is out of mind!
Politeness easy is to you;
Friends everywhere, and not a few,
Wiser than I am, you will find.

FAUST

O dearest, trust me, what doth pass for sense
Full oft is self-conceit and blindness!

MARGARET

How?

FAUST

Simplicity and holy innocence —
When will ye learn your hallow'd worth to know!
Ah, when will meekness and humility,
Kind and all-bounteous nature's loftiest dower —

MARGARET

Only one little moment think of me!
To think of you I shall have many an hour.

FAUST

You are perhaps much alone?

MARGARET

Yes, small our household is, I own,
Yet must I see to it. No maid we keep,
And I must cook, sew, knit, and sweep,
Still early on my feet and late;
My mother is in all things, great and small,
So accurate!
Not that for thrift there is such pressing need,
Than others we might make more show indeed;
My father left behind a small estate,
A house and garden near the city-wall.
But fairly quiet now my days, I own;
As soldier is my brother gone;
My little sister's dead; the babe to rear
Occasion'd me some care and fond annoy;
But I would go through all again with joy,
The darling was to me so dear.

FAUST

An angel, sweet, if it resembled thee!

MARGARET

I reared it up, and it grew fond of me.
After my father's death it saw the day;
We gave my mother up for lost, she lay
In such a wretched plight, and then at length
So very slowly she regain'd her strength.
Weak as she was, 'twas vain for her to try
Herself to suckle the poor babe, so I
Reared it on milk and water all alone;
And thus the child became as 'twere my own;
Within my arms it stretched itself and grew,
And smiling, nestled in my bosom too.

FAUST

Doubtless the purest happiness was thine.

MARGARET

But many weary hours, in sooth, were also mine.
At night its little cradle stood
Close to my bed; so was I wide awake
If it but stirred;
One while I was obliged to give it food,
Or to my arms the darling take;
From bed full oft must rise, whene'er its cry I heard,
And, dancing it, must pace the chamber to and fro;
Stand at the wash-tub early; forthwith go
To market, and then mind the cooking too —
Tomorrow like today, the whole year through.
Ah, sir, thus living, it must be confess'd
One's spirits are not always of the best;
Yet it a relish gives to food and rest.   [*They pass on.*]

MARTHA

Poor women! we are badly off, I own;
A bachelor's conversion's hard, indeed!

MEPHISTOPHELES

Madam, with one like you it rests alone,
To tutor me a better course to lead.

MARTHA

Speak frankly, sir, none is there you have met?
Has your heart ne'er attach'd itself as yet?

MEPHISTOPHELES

One's own fire-side and a good wife are gold
And pearls of price, so says the proverb old.

MARTHA

I mean, has passion never stirred your breast?

MEPHISTOPHELES

I've everywhere been well received, I own.

MARTHA

Yet hath your heart no earnest preference known?

MEPHISTOPHELES

With ladies one should ne'er presume to jest.

MARTHA

Ah! you mistake!

MEPHISTOPHELES

I'm sorry I'm so blind!
But this I know — that you are very kind.

[*They pass on.*]

FAUST

Me, little angel, didst thou recognize,
When in the garden first I came?

MARGARET

Did you not see it? I cast down my eyes.

FAUST

Thou dost forgive my boldness, dost not blame
The liberty I took that day,
When thou from church didst lately wend thy way?

MARGARET

I was confused. So had it never been;
No one of me could any evil say.
Alas, thought I, he doubtless in thy mien,
Something unmaidenly or bold hath seen?

FAUST AND MARGARET IN THE GARDEN

It seemed as if it struck him suddenly,
Here's just a girl with whom one may make free!
Yet I must own that then I scarcely knew
What in your favor here began at once to plead;
Yet I was angry with myself indeed
That I more angry could not feel with you.

FAUST

Sweet love!

MARGARET

Just wait awhile!
[*She gathers a star-flower and plucks off the leaves
one after another.*]

FAUST

A nosegay may that be?

MARGARET

No! It is but a game.

FAUST

How?

MARGARET

Go, you'll laugh at me!
[*She plucks off the leaves and murmurs to herself.*]

FAUST

What murmurest thou?

MARGARET (*half aloud*)

He loves me — loves me not.

FAUST

Sweet angel, with thy face of heavenly bliss!

MARGARET (*continues*)

He loves me — not — he loves me — not —
[*plucking off the last leaf with fond joy.*]
He loves me!

FAUST

Yes!

And this flower-language, darling, let it be

A heavenly oracle! He loveth thee!
Know'st thou the meaning of, He loveth thee?

[*He seizes both her hands.*]

MARGARET

I tremble so!

FAUST

Nay! do not tremble, love!
Let this hand-pressure, let this glance reveal
Feelings, all power of speech above;
To give oneself up wholly and to feel
A joy that must eternal prove!
Eternal!—Yes, its end would be despair,
No end!—It cannot end!

[MARGARET *presses his hand, extricates herself, and
runs away. He stands a moment in thought, and
then follows her.*]

MARTHA (*approaching*)

Night's closing.

MEPHISTOPHELES

Yes, we'll presently away.

MARTHA

I would entreat you longer yet to stay;
But 'tis a wicked place, just here about;
It is as if the folk had nothing else to do,
Nothing to think of too,
But gaping watch their neighbors, who goes in and out;
And scandal's busy still, do whatsoe'er one may.
And our young couple?

MEPHISTOPHELES

They have flown up there,
The wanton butterflies!

MARTHA

He seems to take to her.
And she to him. 'Tis of the world the way!

A SUMMER-HOUSE

[MARGARET *runs in, hides behind the door, holds the tip of her finger to her lip, and peeps through the crevice.*]

MARGARET

He comes!

FAUST

Ah, little rogue, so thou
Think'st to provoke me! I have caught thee now!

[*He kisses her.*]

MARGARET (*embracing him, and returning the kiss*)
Dearest of men! I love thee from my heart!

[MEPHISTOPHELES *knocks.*]

FAUST (*stamping*)

Who's there?

MEPHISTOPHELES

A friend!

FAUST

A brute!

MEPHISTOPHELES

'Tis time to part.

MARTHA (*comes*)

Ay, it is late, good sir.

FAUST

Mayn't I attend you, then?

MARGARET

Oh no — my mother would — adieu, adieu!

FAUST

And must I really then take leave of you?
Farewell!

MARTHA

Good-bye!

MARGARET

Ere long to meet again!

[*Exeunt* FAUST *and* MEPHISTOPHELES.]

MARGARET

Good heavens! how all things far and **near**
Must fill his mind—a man like this!
Abash'd before him I appear,
And say to all things only, yes.
Poor simple child, I cannot see
What 'tis that he can find in me.   [*Exit.*]

FOREST AND CAVERN

FAUST (*alone*)

Spirit sublime! Thou gav'st me, gav'st me all
For which I prayed! Not vainly hast thou turn'd
To me thy countenance in flaming fire:
Gavest me glorious nature for my realm,
And also power to feel her and enjoy;
Not merely with a cold and wondering glance,
Thou dost permit me in her depths profound,
As in the bosom of a friend to gaze.
Before me thou dost lead her living tribes,
And dost in silent grove, in air and stream
Teach me to know my kindred. And when roars
The howling storm-blast through the groaning wood,
Wrenching the giant pine, which in its fall
Crashing sweeps down its neighbor trunks and boughs,
While hollow thunder from the hill resounds:
Then thou dost lead me to some shelter'd cave,
Dost there reveal me to myself, and show
Of my own bosom the mysterious depths.
And when with soothing beam, the moon's pale orb
Full in my view climbs up the pathless sky,
From crag and dewy grove, the silvery forms
Of by-gone ages hover, and assuage
The joy austere of contemplative thought.

Oh, that naught perfect is assign'd to man,
I feel, alas! With this exalted joy,
Which lifts me near and nearer to the gods,

Thou gav'st me this companion, unto whom
I needs must cling, though cold and insolent,
He still degrades me to myself, and turns
Thy glorious gifts to nothing, with a breath.
He in my bosom with malicious zeal
For that fair image fans a raging fire;
From craving to enjoyment thus I reel,
And in enjoyment languish for desire.

[MEPHISTOPHELES *enters.*]

MEPHISTOPHELES

Of this lone life have you not had your fill?
How for so long can it have charms for you?
'Tis well enough to try it if you will;
But then away again to something new!

FAUST

Would you could better occupy your leisure,
Than in disturbing thus my hours of joy.

MEPHISTOPHELES

Well! Well! I'll leave you to yourself with pleasure,
A serious tone you hardly dare employ.
To part from one so crazy, harsh, and cross,
Were not in truth a grievous loss.
The live-long day, for you I toil and fret;
Ne'er from his worship's face a hint I get,
What pleases him, or what to let alone.

FAUST

Ay truly! that is just the proper tone!
He wearies me, and would with thanks be paid!

MEPHISTOPHELES

Poor Son of Earth, without my aid,
How would thy weary days have flown?
Thee of thy foolish whims I've cured,
Thy vain imaginations banished.
And but for me, be well assured,
Thou from this sphere must soon have vanished.

VOL. I — 24

In rocky hollows and in caverns drear,
Why like an owl sit moping here?
Wherefore from dripping stones and moss with ooze
   embued,
Dost suck, like any toad, thy food?
A rare, sweet pastime. Verily!
The doctor cleaveth still to thee.

FAUST

Dost comprehend what bliss without alloy
From this wild wand'ring in the desert springs? —
Couldst thou but guess the new life-power it brings,
Thou wouldst be fiend enough to envy me my joy.

MEPHISTOPHELES

What super-earthly ecstasy! at night,
To lie in darkness on the dewy height,
Embracing heaven and earth in rapture high,
The soul dilating to a deity;
With prescient yearnings pierce the core of earth,
Feel in your laboring breast the six-days' birth,
Enjoy, in proud delight what no one knows,
While your love-rapture o'er creation flows —
The earthly lost in beatific vision,
And then the lofty intuition —

(with a gesture.)

I need not tell you how — to close!

FAUST

Fie on you!

MEPHISTOPHELES

    This displeases you? " For shame!"
You are forsooth entitled to exclaim;
We to chaste ears it seems must not pronounce
What, nathless, the chaste heart cannot renounce.
Well, to be brief, the joy as fit occasions rise,
I grudge you not, of specious lies.
But long this mood thou'lt not retain.
Already thou'rt again outworn,

And should this last, thou wilt be torn
By frenzy or remorse and pain.
Enough of this! Thy true love dwells **apart,**
And all to her seems flat and tame;
Alone thine image fills her heart,
She loves thee with an all-devouring **flame.**
First came thy passion with o'erpowering **rush,**
Like mountain torrent, swollen by the melted **snow;**
Full in her heart didst pour the sudden gush,
Now has thy brooklet ceased to flow.
Instead of sitting throned midst forests wild,
It would become so great a lord
To comfort the enamor'd child,
And the young monkey for her love **reward.**
To her the hours seem miserably long;
She from the window sees the clouds float by
As o'er the lofty city-walls they fly.
"If I a birdie were!" so runs her song,
Half through the night and all day long.
Cheerful sometimes, more oft at heart full **sore;**
Fairly outwept seem now her tears,
Anon she tranquil is, or so appears,
And love-sick evermore.

FAUST

Snake! Serpent vile!

MEPHISTOPHELES (*aside*)

Good! If I catch thee with my guile!

FAUST

Vile reprobate! go get thee hence;
Forbear the lovely girl to name!
Nor in my half-distracted sense
Kindle anew the smouldering flame!

MEPHISTOPHELES

What wouldest thou! She thinks you've **taken flight;**
It seems, she's partly in the right.

FAUST

I'm near her still — and should I distant rove,
Her I can ne'er forget, ne'er lose her love;
And all things touch'd by those sweet lips of hers,
Even the very Host, my envy stirs.

MEPHISTOPHELES

'Tis well! I oft have envied you indeed,
The twin-pair that among the roses feed.

FAUST

Pander, avaunt!

MEPHISTOPHELES

Go to! I laugh, the while you rail;
The power which fashion'd youth and maid
Well understood the noble trade;
So neither shall occasion fail.
But hence! — A mighty grief I trow!
Unto thy lov'd one's chamber thou
And not to death shouldst go.

FAUST

What is to me heaven's joy within her arms?
What though my life her bosom warms! —
Do I not ever feel her woe?
The outcast am I not, unhoused, unblest,
Inhuman monster, without aim or rest,
Who, like the greedy surge, from rock to rock,
Sweeps down the dread abyss with desperate shock?
While she, within her lowly cot, which graced
The Alpine slope, beside the waters wild,
Her homely cares in that small world embraced,
Secluded lived, a simple artless child.
Was't not enough, in thy delirious whirl
To blast the stedfast rocks!
Her, and her peace as well,
Must I, God-hated one, to ruin hurl!
Dost claim this holocaust, remorseless Hell!
Fiend, help me to cut short the hours of dread!

Let what must happen, happen speedily!
Her direful doom fall crushing on my head,
And into ruin let her plunge with me!

MEPHISTOPHELES

Why how again it seethes and glows!
Away, thou fool! Her torment ease!
When such a head no issue sees,
It pictures straight the final close.
Long life to him who boldly dares!
A devil's pluck thou'rt wont to show;
As for a devil who despairs—
Nothing I find so mawkish here below.

MARGARET'S ROOM

MARGARET (*alone at her spinning wheel*)

My peace is gone,
   My heart is sore,
I find it never,
   And nevermore!

Where him I have not,
   Is the grave; and all
The world to me
   Is turned to gall.

My wilder'd brain
   Is overwrought;
My feeble senses
   Are distraught.

My peace is gone,
   My heart is sore,
I find it never,
   And nevermore!

For him from the window
   I gaze, at home;
For him and him only
   Abroad I roam.

His lofty step,
  His bearing high,
The smile of his lip,
  The power of his eye,

His witching words,
  Their tones of bliss,
His hand's fond pressure,
  And ah — his kiss!

My peace is gone,
  My heart is sore,
I find it never,
  And nevermore.

My bosom aches
  To feel him near;
Ah, could I clasp
  And fold him here!

Kiss him and kiss him
  Again would I,
And on his kisses
  I fain would die.

MARTHA'S GARDEN
MARGARET *and* FAUST

MARGARET

Promise me, Henry!

FAUST

What I can!

MARGARET

How thy religion fares, I fain would hear.
Thou art a good kind-hearted man,
Only that way not well-disposed, I fear.

FAUST

Forbear, my child! Thou feelest thee I love;
My heart, my blood I'd give, my love to prove,
And none would of their faith or church bereave.

MARGARET

That's not enough, we must ourselves believe!

FAUST

Must we?

MARGARET

Ah, could I but thy soul inspire!
Thou honorest not the sacraments, alas!

FAUST

I honor them.

MARGARET

But yet without desire;
'Tis long since thou hast been either to shrift or mass.
Dost thou believe in God?

FAUST

My darling, who dares say?
Yes, I in God believe.
Question or priest or sage, and they
Seem, in the answer you receive,
To mock the questioner.

MARGARET

Then thou dost not believe?

FAUST

Sweet one! my meaning do not misconceive!
Him who dare name,
And who proclaim —
Him I believe?
Who that can feel,
His heart can steel,
To say: I believe him not?
The All-embracer,
All-sustainer,
Holds and sustains he not
Thee, me, himself?
Lifts not the Heaven its dome above?
Doth not the firm-set earth beneath us lie?
And, beaming tenderly with looks of love,

Climb not the everlasting stars on high?
Do we not gaze into each other's eyes?
Nature's impenetrable agencies,
Are they not thronging on thy heart and brain,
Viewless, or visible to mortal ken,
Around thee weaving their mysterious chain?
Fill thence thy heart, how large soe'er it be;
And in the feeling when thou utterly art blest,
Then call it, what thou wilt —
Call it Bliss! Heart! Love! God!
I have no name for it!
'Tis feeling all;
Name is but sound and smoke
Shrouding the glow of heaven.

MARGARET

All this is doubtless good and fair;
Almost the same the parson says,
Only in slightly different phrase.

FAUST

Beneath Heaven's sunshine, everywhere,
This is the utterance of the human heart;
Each in his language doth the like impart;
Then why not I in mine?

MARGARET

What thus I hear
Sounds plausible, yet I'm not reconciled;
There's something wrong about it; much I fear
That thou art not a Christian.

FAUST

My sweet child!

MARGARET

Alas! it long hath sorely troubled me,
To see thee in such odious company.

FAUST

How so?

MARGARET

The man who comes with thee, I hate,
Yea, in my spirit's inmost depths abhor;
As his loath'd visage, in my life before,
Naught to my heart e'er gave a pang so great.

FAUST

Him fear not, my sweet love!

MARGARET

His presence chills my blood.
Toward all beside I have a kindly mood;
Yet, though I yearn to gaze on thee, I feel
At sight of him strange horror o'er me steal;
That he's a villain my conviction's strong.
May Heaven forgive me, if I do him wrong!

FAUST

Yet such strange fellows in the world must be!

MARGARET

I would not live with such an one as he.
If for a moment he but enter here,
He looks around him with a mocking sneer,
And malice ill-conceal'd;
That he with naught on earth can sympathize is clear;
Upon his brow 'tis legibly revealed
That to his heart no living soul is dear.
So blest I feel, within thine arms,
So warm and happy—free from all alarms;
And still my heart doth close when he comes near.

FAUST

Foreboding angel! check thy fear!

MARGARET

It so o'ermasters me that when,
Or wheresoe'er, his step I hear,
I almost think, no more I love thee then.
Besides, when he is near, I ne'er could pray.

This eats into my heart; with thee
The same, my Henry, it must be.

FAUST

This is antipathy!

MARGARET

I must away.

FAUST

For one brief hour then may I never rest,
And heart to heart, and soul to soul be pressed?

MARGARET

Ah, if I slept alone! Tonight
The bolt I fain would leave undrawn for thee;
But then my mother's sleep is light,
Were we surprised by her, ah me!
Upon the spot I should be dead.

FAUST

Dear angel! there's no cause for dread.
Here is a little phial—if she take
Mixed in her drink three drops, 'twill steep
Her nature in a deep and soothing sleep.

MARGARET

What do I not for thy dear sake!
To her it will not harmful prove?

FAUST

Should I advise it else, sweet love?

MARGARET

I know not, dearest, when thy face I see,
What doth my spirit to thy will constrain;
Already I have done so much for thee,
That scarcely more to do doth now remain.   [*Exit.*]

(MEPHISTOPHELES *enters*)

MEPHISTOPHELES

The monkey! Is she gone?

FAUST

Again hast played the spy?

MEPHISTOPHELES

Of all that pass'd I'm well apprized,
I heard the doctor catechized,
And trust he'll profit much thereby!
Fain would the girls inquire indeed
Touching their lover's faith and creed,
And whether pious in the good old way;
They think, if pliant there, us too he will obey.

FAUST

Thou monster, dost not see that this
Pure soul, possessed by ardent love,
Full of the living faith,
To her of bliss
The only pledge, must holy anguish prove,
Holding the man she loves fore-doomed to endless death!

MEPHISTOPHELES

Most sensual, supersensualist! The while
A damsel leads thee by the nose!

FAUST

Of filth and fire abortion vile!

MEPHISTOPHELES

In physiognomy strange skill she shows;
She in my presence feels she knows not how;
My mask it seems a hidden sense reveals;
That I'm a genius she must needs allow,
That I'm the very devil perhaps she feels.
So then tonight—

FAUST

What's that to you?

MEPHISTOPHELES

I've my amusement in it too!

AT THE WELL

MARGARET *and* BESSY, *with pitchers*

BESSY

Of Barbara hast nothing heard?

MARGARET

I rarely go from home — no, not a word.

BESSY

'Tis true: Sybilla told me so today!
That comes of being proud, methinks;
She played the fool at last.

MARGARET

How so?

BESSY

They say
That two she feedeth when she eats and drinks.

MARGARET

Alas!

BESSY

She's rightly served, in sooth.
How long she hung upon the youth!
What promenades, what jaunts there were
To dancing booth and village fair!
The first she everywhere must shine,
He always treating her to pastry and to wine.
Of her good looks she was so vain,
So shameless too, that to retain
His presents, she did not disdain;
Sweet words and kisses came anon —
And then the virgin flower was gone.

MARGARET

Poor thing!

BESSY

Forsooth dost pity her?
At night, when at our wheels we sat,
Abroad our mothers ne'er would let us stir.
Then with her lover she must chat,
Or on the bench, or in the dusky walk,
Thinking the hours too brief for their sweet talk;
Her proud head she will have to bow,
And in white sheet do penance now!

MARGARET

But he will surely marry her?

BESSY

Not he!

He won't be such a fool! a gallant lad
Like him can roam o'er land and sea;
Besides, he's off.

MARGARET

That is not fair!

BESSY

If she should get him, 'twere almost as bad!
Her myrtle wreath the boys would tear;
And then we girls would plague her too,
For we chopp'd straw before her door would strew!

[*Exit.*]

MARGARET (*walking toward home*)

How stoutly once I could inveigh,
If a poor maiden went astray;
Not words enough my tongue could find,
'Gainst others' sin to speak my mind!
Black as it seemed, I blacken'd it still more,
And strove to make it blacker than before.
And did myself securely bless—
Now my own trespass doth appear!
Yet ah!—what urg'd me to transgress,
God knows, it was so sweet, so dear!

ZWINGER

Inclosure between the City-wall and the Gate. (*In the niche of the wall a
devotional image of the Mater dolorosa, with flower-pots before it.*)

MARGARET (*putting fresh flowers in the pots*)

Ah, rich in sorrow, thou,
Stoop thy maternal brow,
And mark with pitying eye my misery!
The sword in thy pierced heart,

Thou dost with bitter smart
Gaze upwards on thy Son's death agony.
To the dear God on high
Ascends thy piteous sigh,
Pleading for his and thy sore misery.

Ah, who can know
The torturing woe,
The pangs that rack me to the bone?
How my poor heart, without relief,
Trembles and throbs, its yearning grief
Thou knowest, thou alone!

Ah, wheresoe'er I go,
With woe, with woe, with woe,
My anguish'd breast is aching!
When all alone I creep,
I weep, I weep, I weep,
Alas! my heart is breaking!

The flower-pots at my window
Were wet with tears of mine,
The while I pluck'd these blossoms
At dawn to deck thy shrine!

When early in my chamber
Shone bright the rising morn,
I sat there on my pallet,
My heart with anguish torn.

Help! from disgrace and death deliver me!
Ah! rich in sorrow, thou,
Stoop thy maternal brow,
And mark with pitying eye my misery!

NIGHT. STREET BEFORE MARGARET'S DOOR

VALENTINE (*a soldier,* MARGARET'S *brother*)
When seated 'mong the jovial crowd,
Where merry comrades boasting loud
Each named with pride his favorite lass,

And in her honor drain'd his glass;
Upon my elbows I would lean,
With easy quiet view the scene,
Nor give my tongue the rein, until
Each swaggering blade had talked his fill.
Then smiling I my beard would stroke,
The while, with brimming glass, I spoke;
" Each to his taste! — but to my mind,
Where in the country will you find,
A maid, as my dear Gretchen fair,
Who with my sister can compare? "
Cling! clang! so rang the jovial sound!
Shouts of assent went circling round;
Pride of her sex is she! — cried some;
Then were the noisy boasters dumb.

And now! — I could tear out my hair,
Or dash my brains out in despair! —
Me every scurvy knave may twit,
With stinging jest and taunting sneer!
Like skulking debtor I must sit,
And sweat each casual word to hear!
And though I smash'd them one and all, —
Yet them I could not liars call.
 Who comes this way? who's sneaking here?
 If I mistake not, two draw near.
 If he be one, have at him; — well I wot
 Alive he shall not leave this spot!

Faust. Mephistopheles

faust

How far from yon sacristy, athwart the night,
Its beams the ever-burning taper throws,
While ever waning, fades the glimmering light,
As gathering darkness doth around it close!
So night like gloom doth in my bosom reign.

MEPHISTOPHELES

I'm like a tom-cat in a thievish vein
That up fire-ladders tall and steep
And round the walls doth slyly creep;
Virtuous withal I feel, with, I confess,
A touch of thievish joy and wantonness.
Thus through my limbs already burns
The glorious Walpurgis night!
After tomorrow it returns;
Then why one wakes, one knows aright!

FAUST

Meanwhile, the treasure I see glimmering there.
Will it ascend into the open air?

MEPHISTOPHELES

Ere long thou wilt proceed with pleasure
To raise the casket with its treasure;
I took a peep, therein are stored
Of lion-dollars a rich hoard.

FAUST

And not a trinket? not a ring?
Wherewith my lovely girl to deck?

MEPHISTOPHELES

I saw among them some such thing,
A string of pearls to grace her neck.

FAUST

'Tis well! I'm always loath to go,
Without some gift my love to show.

MEPHISTOPHELES

Some pleasures gratis to enjoy
Should surely cause you no annoy.
While bright with stars the heavens appear,
I'll sing a masterpiece of art:
A moral song shall charm her ear,
More surely to beguile her heart.
(*Sings to the guitar.*)

Kathrina, say,
Why lingering stay
At dawn of day
Before your lover's door?
Maiden, beware,
Nor enter there,
Lest forth you fare,
A maiden never more.

Maiden take heed!
Reck well my rede!
Is't done, the deed?
Good night, you poor, poor thing!
The spoiler's lies,
His arts despise,
Nor yield your prize,
Without the marriage ring!

VALENTINE (*steps forward*)

Whom are you luring here?   I'll give it you!
Accursed rat-catchers, your strains I'll end!
First, to the devil the guitar I'll send!
Then to the devil with the singer too!

MEPHISTOPHELES

The poor guitar! 'tis done for now.

VALENTINE

Your skull shall follow next, I trow!

MEPHISTOPHELES (*to* FAUST)

Doctor, stand fast! your strength collect!
Be prompt, and do as I direct.
Out with your whisk! keep close, I pray,
I'll parry! do you thrust away!

VALENTINE

Then parry that!

MEPHISTOPHELES

Why not?

VALENTINE

That too!

MEPHISTOPHELES

With ease!

VALENTINE

The devil fights for you!
Why how is this? my hand's already lamed!

MEPHISTOPHELES (*to* FAUST)

Thrust home!

VALENTINE (*falls*)

Alas!

MEPHISTOPHELES

There!　Now the lubber's tamed!
But quick, away!　We must at once take wing;
A cry of murder strikes upon the ear;
With the police I know my course to steer,
But with the blood-ban 'tis another thing.

MARTHA (*at the window*)

Without! without!

MARGARET (*at the window*)

Quick, bring a light!

MARTHA (*as above*)

They rail and scuffle, scream and fight!

PEOPLE

One lieth here already dead!

MARTHA (*coming out*)

Where are the murderers? are they fled?

MARGARET (*coming out*)

Who lieth here?

PEOPLE

Thy mother's son.

MARGARET

Almighty God!　I am undone!

VALENTINE

I'm dying—'tis a soon-told tale,
And sooner done the deed.
Why, women, do ye howl and wail?
To my last words give heed!

[*All gather round him.*]

My Gretchen, see! still young art thou,
Art not discreet enough, I trow,
Thou dost thy matters ill;
Let this in confidence be said:
Since thou the path of shame dost tread,
Tread it with right good will!

MARGARET

My brother! God! what can this mean?

VALENTINE

                              Abstain,
Nor dare God's holy name profane!
What's done, alas, is done and past!
Matters will take their course at last;
By stealth thou dost begin with one,
Others will follow him anon;
And when a dozen thee have known,
Thou'lt common be to all the town.
When infamy is newly born,
In secret she is brought to light,
And the mysterious veil of night
O'er head and ears is drawn;
The loathsome birth men fain would slay;
But soon, full grown, she waxes bold,
And though not fairer to behold,
With brazen front insults the day:
The more abhorrent to the sight,
The more she courts the day's pure light,

The time already I discern,
When thee all honest folk will spurn,
And shun thy hated form to meet,

As when a corpse infects the street.
Thy heart will sink in blank despair,
When they shall look thee in the face!
A golden chain no more thou'lt wear!
Nor near the altar take in church thy place!
In fair lace collar simply dight
Thou'lt dance no more with spirits light!
In darksome corners thou wilt bide,
Where beggars vile and cripples hide,
And e'en though God thy crime forgive,
On earth, a thing accursed, thou'lt live!

MARTHA

Your parting soul to God commend!
Your dying breath in slander will you spend?

VALENTINE

Could I but reach thy wither'd frame,
Thou wretched beldame, void of shame!
Full measure I might hope to win
Of pardon then for every sin.

MARGARET

Brother! what agonizing pain!

VALENTINE

I tell thee, from vain tears abstain!
'Twas thy dishonor pierced my heart,
Thy fall the fatal death-stab gave.
Through the death-sleep I now depart
To God, a soldier true and brave.

[*Dies.*]

CATHEDRAL

Service, Organ, and Anthem.

MARGARET *amongst a number of people*

EVIL-SPIRIT *behind* MARGARET

EVIL-SPIRIT

How different, Gretchen, was it once with thee,
When thou, still full of innocence,

FRANZ SIMM

VALENTINE'S DEATH

Here to the altar camest,
And from the small and well-con'd book
Didst lisp thy prayer,
Half childish sport,
Half God in thy young heart!
Gretchen!
What thoughts are thine?
What deed of shame
Lurks in thy sinful heart?
Is thy prayer utter'd for thy mother's soul,
Who into long, long torment slept through thee?
Whose blood is on thy threshold? —
And stirs there not already 'neath thy heart
Another quick'ning pulse, that even now
Tortures itself and thee
With its foreboding presence?

MARGARET

Woe! Woe!
Oh, could I free me from the thoughts
That hither, thither, crowd upon my brain,
Against my will!

CHORUS

> *Dies iræ, dies illa,*
> *Solvet sæclum in favilla.*

[The organ sounds.]

EVIL-SPIRIT

Grim horror seizes thee!
The trumpet sounds!
The graves are shaken!
And thy heart
From ashy rest
For torturing flames
Anew created,
Trembles into life!

MARGARET

Would I were hence!
It is as if the organ
Choked my breath,
As if the choir
Melted my inmost heart!

CHORUS

Judex ergo cum sedebit,
Quidquid latet adparebit,
Nil inultum remanebit.

MARGARET

I feel oppressed!
The pillars of the wall
Imprison me!
The vaulted roof
Weighs down upon me! — air!

EVIL-SPIRIT

Wouldst hide thee? sin and shame
Remain not hidden!
Air! light!
Woe's thee!

CHORUS

Quid sum miser tunc dicturus?
Quem patronum rogaturus!
Cum vix justus sit securus.

EVIL-SPIRIT

The glorified their faces turn
Away from thee!
Shudder the pure to reach
Their hands to thee!
Woe!

CHORUS

Quid sum miser tunc dicturus —

MARGARET

Neighbor! your smelling bottle!

[*She swoons away.*]

MARGARET'S DOWNFALL

WALPURGIS-NIGHT
THE HARTZ MOUNTAINS. DISTRICT OF SCHIERKE AND ELEND

FAUST *and* MEPHISTOPHELES

MEPHISTOPHELES

A broomstick dost thou not at least desire?
The roughest he-goat fain would I bestride,
By this road from our goal we're still far wide.

FAUST

While fresh upon my legs, so long I naught require,
Except this knotty staff.   Beside,
What boots it to abridge a pleasant way?
Along the labyrinth of these vales to creep,
Then scale these rocks, whence, in eternal spray,
Adown the cliffs the silvery fountains leap:
Such is the joy that seasons paths like these!
Spring weaves already in the birchen trees;
E'en the late pine-grove feels her quickening powers;
Should she not work within these limbs of ours?

MEPHISTOPHELES

Naught of this genial influence do I know!
Within me all is wintry.   Frost and snow
I should prefer my dismal path to bound.
How sadly, yonder, with belated glow
Rises the ruddy moon's imperfect round,
Shedding so faint a light, at every tread
One's sure to stumble 'gainst a rock or tree!
An Ignis Fatuus I must call instead.
Yonder one burning merrily, I see.
Holla! my friend! may I request your light?
Why should you flare away so uselessly?
Be kind enough to show us up the height!

IGNIS FATUUS

Through reverence, I hope I may subdue
The lightness of my nature; true,
Our course is but a zigzag one.

MEPHISTOPHELES

Ho! ho!
So men, forsooth, he thinks to imitate!
Now, in the devil's name, for once go straight!
Or out at once your flickering life I'll blow.

IGNIS FATUUS

That you are master here is obvious quite;
To do your will, I'll cordially essay;
Only reflect! The hill is magic-mad tonight;
And if to show the path you choose a meteor's light,
You must not wonder should we go astray.

FAUST, MEPHISTOPHELES, IGNIS FATUUS (*in alternate song*)
Through the dream and magic-sphere,
As it seems, we now are speeding;
Honor win, us rightly leading,
That betimes we may appear
In yon wide and desert region!

Trees on trees, a stalwart legion,
Swiftly past us are retreating,
And the cliffs with lowly greeting;
Rocks long-snouted, row on row,
How they snort, and how they blow!

Through the stones and heather springing,
Brook and brooklet haste below;
Hark the rustling! Hark the singing!
Hearken to love's plaintive lays;
Voices of those heavenly days —
What we hope, and what we love!
Like a tale of olden time,
Echo's voice prolongs the chime.

To-whit! To-who! It sounds more near;
Plover, owl, and jay appear,
All awake, around, above?
Paunchy salamanders too
Peer, long-limbed, the bushes through!
And, like snakes, the roots of trees
Coil themselves from rock and sand,
Stretching many a wondrous band,
Us to frighten, us to seize;
From rude knots with life embued,
Polyp-fangs abroad they spread,
To snare the wanderer!   'Neath our tread,
Mice, in myriads, thousand-hued,
Through the heath and through the moss!
And the fire-flies' glittering throng,
Wildering escort, whirls along,
Here and there, our path across.

Tell me, stand we motionless,
Or still forward do we press?
All things round us whirl and fly, .
Rocks and trees make strange grimaces,
Dazzling meteors change their places —
How they puff and multiply!

MEPHISTOPHELES

Now grasp my doublet — we at last
A central peak have reached, which shows,
If round a wondering glance we cast,
How in the mountain Mammon glows.

FAUST

How through the chasms strangely gleams,
A lurid light, like dawn's red glow,
Pervading with its quivering beams,
The gorges of the gulf below!
Here vapors rise, there clouds float by,
Here through the mist the light doth shine;
Now, like a fount, it bursts on high,

Meanders now, a slender line;
Far reaching, with a hundred veins,
Here through the valley see it glide;
Here, where its force the gorge restrains,
At once it scatters, far and wide;
Anear, like showers of golden sand
Strewn broadcast, sputter sparks of light:
And mark yon rocky walls that stand
Ablaze, in all their towering height!

MEPHISTOPHELES

Doth not Sir Mammon for this fête
Grandly illume his palace! Thou
Art lucky to have seen it; now,
The boisterous guests, I feel, are coming straight.

FAUST

How through the air the storm doth whirl!
Upon my neck it strikes with sudden shock.

MEPHISTOPHELES

Cling to these ancient ribs of granite rock,
Else to yon depths profound it you will hurl.
A murky vapor thickens night.
Hark! Through the woods the tempests roar!
The owlets flit in wild affright.
Hark! Splinter'd are the columns that upbore
The leafy palace, green for aye:
The shivered branches whirr and sigh,
Yawn the huge trunks with mighty groan,
The roots, upriven, creak and moan!
In fearful and entangled fall,
One crashing ruin whelms them all,
While through the desolate abyss,
Sweeping the wreck-strewn precipice,
The raging storm-blasts howl and hiss!
Aloft strange voices dost thou hear?
Distant now and now more near?
Hark! the mountain ridge along,
Streameth a raving magic-song!

WITCHES (*in chorus*)

Now to the Brocken the witches hie,
The stubble is yellow, the corn is green;
Thither the gathering legions fly,
And sitting aloft is Sir Urian seen:
O'er stick and o'er stone they go whirling along,
Witches and he-goats, a motley throng.

VOICES

Alone old Baubo's coming now;
She rides upon a farrow sow.

CHORUS

Honor to her, to whom honor is due!
Forward, Dame Baubo! Honor to you!
A goodly sow and mother thereon,
The whole witch chorus follows anon.

VOICE

Which way didst come?

VOICE

O'er Ilsenstein!
There I peep'd in an owlet's nest.
With her broad eye she gazed in mine!

VOICE

Drive to the devil, thou hellish pest!
Why ride so hard?

VOICE

She has graz'd my side,
Look at the wounds, how deep and how wide!

WITCHES (*in chorus*)

The way is broad, the way is long;
What mad pursuit! What tumult wild!
Scratches the besom and sticks the prong;
Crush'd is the mother, and stifled the child.

WIZARDS (*half chorus*)

Like house-encumber'd snail we creep;
While far ahead the women keep,

For when to the devil's house we speed,
By a thousand steps they take the lead.

THE OTHER HALF

Not so, precisely do we view it; —
They with a thousand steps may do it;
But let them hasten as they can,
With one long bound 'tis clear'd by man.

VOICES (*above*)

Come with us, come with us from Felsensee.

VOICES (*from below*)

Aloft to you we would mount with glee!
We wash, and free from all stain are we,
Yet barren evermore must be!

BOTH CHORUSES

The wind is hushed, the stars grow pale,
The pensive moon her light doth veil;
And whirling on, the magic choir
Sputters forth sparks of drizzling fire.

VOICE (*from below*)

Stay! stay!

VOICE (*from above*)

What voice of woe
Calls from the cavern'd depths below?

VOICE (*from below*)

Take me with you! Oh take me too!
Three centuries I climb in vain,
And yet can ne'er the summit gain!
To be with my kindred I am fain.

BOTH CHORUSES

Broom and pitch-fork, goat and prong,
Mounted on these we whirl along;
Who vainly strives to climb tonight,
Is evermore a luckless wight!

DEMI-WITCH (*below*)

I hobble after, many a day;
Already the others are far away!
No rest at home can I obtain —
Here too my efforts are in vain!

CHORUS OF WITCHES

Salve gives the witches strength to rise;
A rag for a sail does well enough;
A goodly ship is every trough;
Tonight who flies not, never flies.

BOTH CHORUSES

And when the topmost peak we round,
Then alight ye on the ground;
The heath's wide regions cover ye
With your mad swarms of witchery!

[*They let themselves down.*]

MEPHISTOPHELES

They crowd and jostle, whirl and flutter!
They whisper, babble, twirl, and splutter!
They glimmer, sparkle, stink and flare —
A true witch-element! Beware!
Stick close! else we shall severed be.
Where art thou?

FAUST (*in the distance*)
Here!

MEPHISTOPHELES
Already, whirl'd so far away!
The master then indeed I needs must play.
Give ground! Squire Voland comes! Sweet folk, give
ground!
Here, doctor, grasp me! With a single bound
Let us escape this ceaseless jar;
Even for me too mad these people are.
Hard by there shineth something with peculiar glare,
Yon brake allureth me; it is not far;
Come, come along with me! we'll slip in there.

FAUST

Spirit of contradiction! Lead! I'll follow straight!
'Twas wisely done, however, to repair
On May-night to the Brocken, and when there,
By our own choice ourselves to isolate!

MEPHISTOPHELES

Mark, of those flames the motley glare!
A merry club assembles there.
In a small circle one is not alone.

FAUST

I'd rather be above, though, I must own!
Already fire and eddying smoke I view;
The impetuous millions to the devil ride;
Full many a riddle will be there untied.

MEPHISTOPHELES

Ay! and full many a riddle tied anew.
But let the great world rave and riot!
Here will we house ourselves in quiet.
A custom 'tis of ancient date,
Our lesser worlds within the great world to create!
Young witches there I see, naked and bare,
And old ones, veil'd more prudently.
For my sake only courteous be!
The trouble small, the sport is rare.
Of instruments I hear the cursed din —
One must get used to it. Come in! come in!
There's now no help for it. I'll step before,
And introducing you as my good friend,
Confer on you one obligation more.
How say you now? 'Tis no such paltry room;
Why only look, you scarce can see the end.
A hundred fires in rows disperse the gloom;
They dance, they talk, they cook, make love, and drink:
Where could we find aught better, do you think?

FAUST

To introduce us, do you purpose here
As devil or as wizard to appear?

MEPHISTOPHELES

Though I am wont indeed to strict incognito,
Yet upon gala-days one must one's orders show.
No garter have I to distinguish me,
Nathless the cloven foot doth here give dignity.
Seest thou yonder snail? Crawling this way she hies;
With searching feelers, she, no doubt,
Hath me already scented out;
Here, even if I would, for me there's no disguise.
From fire to fire, we'll saunter at our leisure,
The gallant you, I'll cater for your pleasure.
    (*To a party seated round some expiring embers*)
Old gentleman, apart, why sit ye moping here?
Ye in the midst should be of all this jovial cheer,
Girt round with noise and youthful riot;
At home one surely has enough of quiet.

GENERAL

In nations put his trust, who may,
Whate'er for them one may have done;
For with the people, as with women, they
Honor your rising stars alone!

MINISTER

Now all too far they wander from the right;
I praise the good old ways, to them I hold,
Then was the genuine age of gold,
When we ourselves were foremost in men's sight.

PARVENU

Ne'er were we 'mong your dullards found,
And what we ought not, that to do were fair;
Yet now are all things turning round and round,
When on firm basis we would them maintain.

AUTHOR

Who, as a rule, a treatise now would care
To read, of even moderate sense?
As for the rising generation, ne'er
Has youth displayed such arrogant pretense.

MEPHISTOPHELES (*suddenly appearing very old*)

Since for the last time I the Brocken scale,
That folk are ripe for doomsday, now one sees;
And just because my cask begins to fail,
So the whole world is also on the lees.

HUCKSTER-WITCH

Stop, gentlemen, nor pass me by,
Of wares I have a choice collection:
Pray honor them with your inspection.
Lose not this opportunity!
Yet nothing in my booth you'll find
Without its counterpart on earth; there's naught,
Which to the world, and to mankind,
Hath not some direful mischief wrought.
No dagger here, which hath not flow'd with blood,
No chalice, whence, into some healthy frame
Hath not been poured hot poison's wasting flood.
No trinket, but hath wrought some woman's shame,
No weapon but hath cut some sacred tie,
Or from behind hath stabb'd an enemy.

MEPHISTOPHELES

Gossip! For wares like these the time's gone by,
What's done is past! what's past is done!
With novelties your booth supply;
Us novelties attract alone.

FAUST

May this wild scene my senses spare!
This, may in truth be called a fair!

MEPHISTOPHELES

Upward the eddying concourse throng;
Thinking to push, thyself art push'd along.

FAUST

Who's that, pray?

MEPHISTOPHELES

Mark her well!   That's Lilith.

FAUST

Who?

MEPHISTOPHELES

Adam's first wife.   Of her rich locks beware!
That charm in which she's parallel'd by few,
When in its toils a youth she doth ensnare
He will not soon escape, I promise you.

FAUST

There sit a pair, the old one with the young;
Already they have bravely danced and sprung!

MEPHISTOPHELES

Here there is no repose today.
Another dance begins; we'll join it, come away!

FAUST (*dancing with the young one*)

Once a fair vision came to me;
Therein I saw an apple-tree,
Two beauteous apples charmed mine eyes;
I climb'd forthwith to reach the prize.

THE FAIR ONE

Apples still fondly ye desire,
From paradise it hath been so.
Feelings of joy my breast inspire
That such too in my garden grow.

MEPHISTOPHELES (*with the old one*)

Once a weird vision came to me;
Therein I saw a rifted tree.
It had a . . . . . ;
But as it was it pleased me too.

THE OLD ONE

I beg most humbly to salute

The gallant with the cloven foot!
Let him . . . have ready here,
If he a . . . does not fear.

PROCTOPHANTASMIST

Accursed mob!   How dare ye thus to meet?
Have I not shown and demonstrated too,
That ghosts stand not on ordinary feet?
Yet here ye dance, as other mortals do!

THE FAIR ONE (*dancing*)

Then at our ball, what doth he here?

FAUST (*dancing*)

Oh!   He must everywhere appear.
He must adjudge, when others dance;
If on each step his say's not said,
So is that step as good as never made.
He's most annoyed, so soon as we advance;
If ye would circle in one narrow round,
As he in his old mill, then doubtless he
Your dancing would approve,— especially
If ye forthwith salute him with respect profound!

PROCTOPHANTASMIST

Still here! what arrogance! unheard of quite!
Vanish; we now have fill'd the world with light!
Laws are unheeded by the devil's host;
Wise as we are, yet Tegel hath its ghost!
How long at this conceit I've swept with all my might,
Lost is the labor: 'tis unheard of quite!

THE FAIR ONE

Cease here to teaze us any more, I pray.

PROCTOPHANTASMIST

Spirits, I plainly to your face declare:
No spiritual control myself will bear,
Since my own spirit can exert no sway.

[*The dancing continues.*]

Tonight, I see, I shall in naught succeed;
But I'm prepar'd my travels to pursue,
And hope, before my final step indeed,
To triumph over bards and devils too.

MEPHISTOPHELES

Now in some puddle will he take his station,
Such is his mode of seeking consolation;
Where leeches, feasting on his rump, will drain
Spirits alike and spirit from his brain.
(*To* FAUST, *who has left the dance*)
But why the charming damsel leave, I pray,
Who to you in the dance so sweetly sang?

FAUST

Ah! in the very middle of her lay,
Out of her mouth a small red mouse there sprang.

MEPHISTOPHELES

Suppose there did! One must not be too nice.
'Twas well it was not gray, let that suffice.
Who 'mid his pleasures for a trifle cares?

FAUST

Then saw I —

MEPHISTOPHELES

What?

FAUST

Mephisto, seest thou there
Standing far off, a lone child, pale and fair?
Slow from the spot her drooping form she tears,
And seems with shackled feet to move along;
I own, within me the delusion's strong,
That she the likeness of my Gretchen wears.

MEPHISTOPHELES

Gaze not upon her! 'Tis not good! Forbear!
'Tis lifeless, magical, a shape of air,
An idol. Such to meet with, bodes no good;
That rigid look of hers doth freeze man's blood,

And well-nigh petrifies his heart to stone:—
The story of Medusa thou hast known.

FAUST

Ay, verily! a corpse's eyes are those,
Which there was no fond loving hand to close.
That is the bosom I so fondly press'd,
That my sweet Gretchen's form, so oft caress'd!

MEPHISTOPHELES

Deluded fool! 'Tis magic, I declare!
To each she doth his lov'd one's image wear.

FAUST

What bliss! what torture! vainly I essay
To turn me from that piteous look away.
How strangely doth a single crimson line
Around that lovely neck its coil entwine,
It shows no broader than a knife's blunt edge!

MEPHISTOPHELES

Quite right. I see it also, and allege
That she beneath her arm her head can bear,
Since Perseus cut it off.—But you I swear
Are craving for illusions still!
Come then, ascend yon little hill!
As on the Prater all is gay,
And if my senses are not gone,
I see a theatre,—what's going on?

SERVIBILIS

They are about to recommence;—the play
Will be the last of seven, and spick-span new—
'Tis usual here that number to present.
A dilettante did the piece invent,
And dilettanti will enact it too.
Excuse me, gentlemen; to me's assign'd,
As dilettante to uplift the curtain.

MEPHISTOPHELES

You on the Blocksberg I'm rejoiced to find,
That 'tis your most appropriate sphere is certain.

WALPURGIS-NIGHT'S DREAM; OR, OBERON AND TITANIA'S GOLDEN WEDDING-FEAST

INTERMEZZO

THEATRE

MANAGER

Vales, where mists still shift and play,
  To ancient hill succeeding,—
These our scenes;— so we, today,
  May rest, brave sons of Mieding.

HERALD

That the marriage golden be,
  Must fifty years be ended;
More dear this feast of gold to me,
  Contention now suspended.

OBERON

Spirits, if present, grace the scene,
  And if with me united,
Then gratulate the king and queen,
  Their troth thus newly plighted!

PUCK

Puck draws near and wheels about,
  In mazy circles dancing!
Hundreds swell his joyous shout,
  Behind him still advancing.

ARIEL

Ariel wakes his dainty air,
  His lyre celestial stringing.—
Fools he lureth, and the fair,
  With his celestial singing.

OBERON

Wedded ones, would ye agree,
  We court your imitation:
Would ye fondly love as we,
  We counsel separation.

TITANIA

If husband scold and wife retort,
  Then bear them far asunder;
Her to the burning south transport,
  And him the North Pole under.

THE WHOLE ORCHESTRA (*fortissimo*)

Flies and midges all unite
  With frog and chirping cricket,
Our orchestra throughout the night,
  Resounding in the thicket!

(*Solo*)

Yonder doth the bagpipe come!
  Its sack an airy bubble.
Schnick, schnick, schnack, with nasal hum,
  Its notes it doth redouble.

EMBRYO SPIRIT

Spider's foot and midge's wing,
  A toad in form and feature;
Together verses it can string,
  Though scarce a living creature.

A LITTLE PAIR

Tiny step and lofty bound,
  Through dew and exhalation;
Ye trip it deftly on the ground,
  But gain no elevation.

INQUISITIVE TRAVELLER

Can I indeed believe my eyes?
  Is't not mere masquerading?
What! Oberon in beauteous guise,
  Among the groups parading!

ORTHODOX

No claws, no tail to whisk about,
  To fright us at our revel;—
Yet like the gods of Greece, no doubt,
  He too's a genuine devil.

NORTHERN ARTIST

These that I'm hitting off today
   Are sketches unpretending;
Toward Italy without delay,
   My steps I think of bending.

PURIST

Alas! ill-fortune leads me here,
   Where riot still grows louder;
And 'mong the witches gather'd here,
   But two alone wear powder!

YOUNG WITCH

Your powder and your petticoat,
   Suit hags, there's no gainsaying;
Hence I sit fearless on my goat,
   My naked charms displaying.

MATRON

We're too well-bred to squabble here,
   Or insult back to render;
But may you wither soon, my dear,
   Although so young and tender.

LEADER OF THE BAND

Nose of fly and gnat's proboscis,
   Throng not the naked beauty!
Frogs and crickets in the mosses,
   Keep time and do your duty!

WEATHERCOCK (*toward one side*)

What charming company I view
   Together here collected!
Gay bachelors, a hopeful crew,
   And brides so unaffected!

WEATHERCOCK (*toward the other side*)

Unless indeed the yawning ground
   Should open to receive them,
From this vile crew, with sudden bound,
   To Hell I'd jump and leave them.

XENIEN

With small sharp shears, in insect guise,
  Behold us at your revel!
That we may tender, filial-wise,
  Our homage to the devil.

HENNINGS

Look now at yonder eager crew,
  How naïvely they're jesting!
That they have tender hearts and true,
  They stoutly keep protesting!

MUSAGET

Oneself amid this witchery
  How pleasantly one loses;
For witches easier are to me
  To govern than the Muses!

CI-DEVANT GENIUS OF THE AGE

With proper folks when we appear,
  No one can then surpass us!
Keep close, wide is the Blocksberg here
  As Germany's Parnassus.

INQUISITIVE TRAVELLER

How name ye that stiff formal man,
  Who strides with lofty paces?
He tracks the game where'er he can,
  " He scents the Jesuits' traces."

CRANE

Where waters troubled are or clear,
  To fish I am delighted;
Thus pious gentlemen appear
  With devils here united.

WORLDLING

By pious people, it is true,
  No medium is rejected;
Conventicles, and not a few,
  On Blocksberg are erected.

DANCER

Another chorus now succeeds,
   Far off the drums are beating.
Be still! The bitterns 'mong the reeds
   Their one note are repeating.

DANCING MASTER

Each twirls about and never stops,
   And as he can he fareth.
The crooked leaps, the clumsy hops,
   Nor for appearance careth.

FIDDLER

To take each other's life, I trow,
   Would cordially delight them!
As Orpheus' lyre the beasts, so now
   The bagpipe doth unite them.

DOGMATIST

My views, in spite of doubt and sneer,
   I hold with stout persistence,
Inferring from the devils here,
   The evil one's existence.

IDEALIST

My every sense rules Phantasy
   With sway quite too potential;
Sure I'm demented if the *I*
   Alone is the essential.

REALIST

This entity's a dreadful bore,
   And cannot choose but vex me;
The ground beneath me ne'er before
   Thus totter'd to perplex me.

SUPERNATURALIST

Well pleased assembled here I view
   Of spirits this profusion;
From devils, touching angels too,
   I gather some conclusion.

SCEPTIC

The ignis fatuus they track out,
    And think they're near the treasure.
Devil alliterates with doubt,
    Here I abide with pleasure.

LEADER OF THE BAND

Frog and cricket in the mosses,—
    Confound your gasconading!
Nose of fly and gnat's proboscis;—
    Most tuneful serenading!

THE KNOWING ONES

Sans souci, so this host we greet,
    Their jovial humor showing;
There's now no walking on our feet,
    So on our heads we're going.

THE AWKWARD ONES

In seasons past we snatch'd, 'tis true,
    Some tit-bits by our cunning;
Our shoes, alas, are now danced through,
    On our bare soles we're running.

WILL-O'-THE-WISPS

From marshy bogs we sprang to light,
    Yet here behold us dancing;
The gayest gallants of the night,
    In glitt'ring rows advancing.

SHOOTING STAR

With rapid motion from on high,
    I shot in starry splendor;
Now prostrate on the grass I lie;—
    Who aid will kindly render?

THE MASSIVE ONES

Room! wheel round! They're coming! lo!
    Down sink the bending grasses.
Though spirits, yet their limbs, we know,
    Are huge substantial masses.

PUCK

Don't stamp so heavily, I pray;
Like elephants you're treading!
And 'mong the elves be Puck today,
The stoutest at the wedding!

ARIEL

If nature boon, or subtle sprite,
Endow your soul with pinions; —
Then follow to yon rosy height,
Through ether's calm dominions!

ORCHESTRA (*pianissimo*)

Drifting cloud and misty wreathes
Are fill'd with light elysian;
O'er reed and leaf the zephyr breathes —
So fades the fairy vision!

A GLOOMY DAY. A PLAIN

FAUST *and* MEPHISTOPHELES

FAUST

In misery! despairing! long wandering pitifully on the face of the earth and now imprisoned! This gentle hapless creature, immured in the dungeon as a malefactor and reserved for horrid tortures! That it should come to this! To this! — Perfidious, worthless spirit, and this thou hast concealed from me! — Stand! ay, stand! roll in malicious rage thy fiendish eyes! Stand and brave me with thine insupportable presence! Imprisoned! In hopeless misery! Delivered over to the power of evil spirits and the judgment of unpitying humanity! — And me, the while, thou wert lulling with tasteless dissipations, concealing from me her growing anguish, and leaving her to perish without help!

MEPHISTOPHELES

She is not the first.

FAUST

Hound! Execrable monster! — Back with him, oh thou

infinite spirit! back with the reptile into his dog's shape, in which it was his wont to scamper before me at eventide, to roll before the feet of the harmless wanderer, and to fasten on his shoulders when he fell! Change him again into his favorite shape, that he may crouch on his belly before me in the dust, whilst I spurn him with my foot, the reprobate!—Not the first!—Woe! Woe! By no human soul is it conceivable, that more than one human creature has ever sunk into a depth of wretchedness like this, or that the first in her writhing death-agony should not have atoned in the sight of all-pardoning Heaven for the guilt of all the rest! The misery of this one pierces me to the very marrow, and harrows up my soul; thou art grinning calmly over the doom of thousands!

MEPHISTOPHELES

Now we are once again at our wit's end, just where the reason of you mortals snaps! Why dost thou seek our fellowship, if thou canst not go through with it? Wilt fly, and art not proof against dizziness? Did we force ourselves on thee, or thou on us?

FAUST

Cease thus to gnash thy ravenous fangs at me! I loathe thee!—Great and glorious spirit, thou who didst vouchsafe to reveal thyself unto me, thou who dost know my very heart and soul, why hast thou linked me with this base associate, who feeds on mischief and revels in destruction?

MEPHISTOPHELES

Hast done?

FAUST

Save her!—or woe to thee! The direst of curses on thee for thousands of years!

MEPHISTOPHELES

I cannot loose the bands of the avenger, nor withdraw his bolts.—Save her!—Who was it plunged her into perdition? I or thou?

FAUST (*looks wildly around*)

MEPHISTOPHELES

Would'st grasp the thunder? Well for you, poor mortals, that 'tis not yours to wield! To smite to atoms the being, however innocent, who obstructs his path, such is the tyrant's fashion of relieving himself in difficulties!

FAUST

Convey me thither! She shall be free!

MEPHISTOPHELES

And the danger to which thou dost expose thyself? Know, the guilt of blood, shed by thy hand, lies yet upon the town. Over the place where fell the murdered one, avenging spirits hover and watch for the returning murderer.

FAUST

This too from thee? The death and downfall of a world be on thee, monster! Conduct me thither, I say and set her free!

MEPHISTOPHELES

I will conduct thee. And what I can do,—hear! Have I all power in heaven and upon earth? I'll cloud the senses of the warder,— do thou possess thyself of the keys and lead her forth with human hand! I will keep watch! The magic steeds are waiting, I bear thee off. Thus much is in my power.

FAUST

Up and away!

NIGHT. OPEN COUNTRY

FAUST. MEPHISTOPHELES

(*Rushing along on black horses*)

FAUST

What weave they yonder round the Ravenstone?

MEPHISTOPHELES

I know not what they shape and brew.

FAUST

They're soaring, swooping, bending, stooping.

MEPHISTOPHELES

A witches' pack.

FAUST

They charm, they strew.

MEPHISTOPHELES

On! On!

DUNGEON

FAUST (*with a bunch of keys and a lamp before a small iron door*)

A fear unwonted o'er my spirit falls;
Man's concentrated woe o'erwhelms me here!
She dwells immur'd within these dripping walls;
Her only trespass a delusion dear!
Thou lingerest at the fatal door?
Thou dread'st to see her face once more?
On! While thou dalliest, draws her death-hour near.

[*He seizes the lock. Singing within.*]

My mother, the harlot,
She took me and slew!
My father, the scoundrel,
Hath eaten me too!
My sweet little sister
Hath all my bones laid,
Where soft breezes whisper
All in the cool shade!
Then became I a wood-bird, and sang on the spray,
Fly away! little bird, fly away! fly away!

FAUST (*opening the lock*)

Ah! she forebodes not that her lover's near,
The clanking chains, the rustling straw, to hear.

[*He enters.*]

MARGARET (*hiding her face in the bed of straw*)

Woe! woe! they come! oh bitter 'tis to die!

FAUST (*softly*)

Hush! hush! be still! I come to set thee free.

MARGARET (*throwing herself at his feet*)

If thou art human, feel my misery!

FAUST

Thou wilt awake the jailer with thy cry!

[*He grasps the chains to unlock them.*]

MARGARET (*on her knees*)

Who, headsman, unto thee this power
O'er me could give?
Thou com'st for me at midnight-hour.
Be merciful, and let me live!
Is morrow's dawn not time enough?

[*She stands up.*]

I'm still so young, so young —
And must so early die!
Fair was I too, and that was my undoing.
My love is now afar, he then was nigh;
Torn lies the garland, the fair blossoms strew'd.
Nay, seize me not with hand so rude!
Spare me! What harm have I e'er done to thee?
Oh let me not in vain implore!
I ne'er have seen thee in my life before!

FAUST

Can I endure this bitter agony?

MARGARET

I now am at thy mercy quite.
Let me my babe but suckle once again!
I fondled it the live-long night;
They took it from me but to give me pain,
And now, they say that I my child have slain.
Gladness I ne'er again shall know.
Then they sing songs about me, — 'tis wicked of the
 throng —
An ancient ballad endeth so;
Who bade them thus apply the song?

FAUST (*throwing himself on the ground*)
A lover at thy feet bends low,
To loose the bonds of wretchedness and woe.

MARGARET (*throws herself beside him*)
Oh, let us kneel and move the saints by prayer!
Look! look! yon stairs below,
Under the threshold there,
Hell's flames are all aglow!
Beneath the floor,
With hideous noise,
The devils roar!

FAUST (*aloud*)
Gretchen! Gretchen!

MARGARET (*listening*)
That was my lov'd one's voice!

[*She springs up, the chains fall off.*]
Where is he? I heard him calling me.
Free am I! There's none shall hinder me.
To his neck will I fly,
On his bosom will lie!
Gretchen, he called!—On yon threshold he stood;
Amidst all the howling of hell's fiery flood,
The scoff and the scorn of its devilish crew,
The tones of his voice, sweet and loving, I knew.

FAUST
'Tis I!

MARGARET
'Tis thou! O say so once again!

[*embracing him.*]
'Tis he! 'Tis he! where's now the torturing pain?
Where are the fetters? where the dungeon's gloom?
'Tis thou! To save me thou art come!
And I am sav'd!—
Already now the street I see
Where the first time I caught a glimpse of thee.
There to the pleasant garden shade,
Where I and Martha for thy coming stay'd.

FAUST (*endeavoring to lead her away*)
Come! come away!

MARGARET
Oh do not haste!
I love to linger where thou stayest.   [*caressing him.*]

FAUST
Ah haste! For if thou still delayest,
Our lingering we shall both deplore.

MARGARET
How, dearest? canst thou kiss no more!
So short a time away from me, and yet,
To kiss thou couldst so soon forget!
Why on thy neck so anxious do I feel —
When formerly a perfect heaven of bliss
From thy dear looks and words would o'er me steal?
As thou wouldst stifle me thou then didst kiss! —
Kiss me!
Or I'll kiss thee!   [*She embraces him.*]
Woe! woe! Thy lips are cold, —
Are dumb!
Thy love where hast thou left?
Who hath me of thy love bereft?

[*She turns away from him.*]

FAUST
Come! Follow me, my dearest love, be bold!
I'll cherish thee with ardor thousand-fold;
I but entreat thee now to follow me!

MARGARET (*turning toward him*)
And art thou he? and art thou really he?

FAUST
'Tis I! Oh come!

MARGARET
Thou wilt strike off my chain,
And thou wilt take me to thine arms again.
How comes it that thou dost not shrink from me? —
And dost thou know, love, whom thou wouldst set free?

FAUST

Come! come! already night begins to wane.

MARGARET

I sent my mother to her grave,
I drown'd my child beneath the wave.
Was it not given to thee and me — thee too?
'Tis thou thyself! I scarce believe it yet.
Give me thy hand! It is no dream! 'Tis true!
Thine own dear hand! — But how is this? 'Tis wet!
Quick, wipe it off! Meseems that yet
There's blood thereon.
Ah God! what hast thou done?
Put up thy sword,
I beg of thee!

FAUST

Oh, dearest, let the past forgotten be!
Death is in every word.

MARGARET

No, thou must linger here in sorrow!
The graves I will describe to thee,
And thou to them must see
Tomorrow:
The best place give to my mother,
Close at her side my brother,
Me at some distance lay —
But not too far away!
And the little one place on my right breast.
Nobody else will near me lie!
To nestle beside thee so lovingly,
That was a rapture, gracious and sweet!
A rapture I never again shall prove;
Methinks I would force myself on thee, love,
And thou dost spurn me, and back retreat —
Yet 'tis thyself, thy fond kind looks I see.

FAUST

If thou dost feel 'tis I, then come with me!

MARGARET

What, there? without?

FAUST

Yes, forth in the free air.

MARGARET

Ay, if the grave's without,— If death lurk there!
Hence to the everlasting resting-place,
And not one step beyond!— Thou'rt leaving me?
Oh Henry! would that I could go with thee!

FAUST

Thou canst! But will it! Open stands the door.

MARGARET

I dare not go! I've naught to hope for more.
What boots it to escape? They lurk for me!
'Tis wretched to beg, as I must do,
And with an evil conscience thereto!
'Tis wretched, in foreign lands to stray;
And me they will catch, do what I may!

FAUST

With thee will I abide.

MARGARET

Quick! Quick!
Save thy poor child!
Keep to the path
The brook along,
Over the bridge
To the wood beyond,
To the left, where the plank is,
In the pond.
Seize it at once!
It fain would rise,
It struggles still!
Save it. Oh save!

FAUST

Dear Gretchen, more collected be!
One little step, and thou art free!

MARGARET

Were we but only past the hill!
There sits my mother upon a stone —
My brain, alas, is cold with dread! —
There sits my mother upon a stone,
And to and fro she shakes her head;
She winks not, she nods not, her head it **droops sore**;
She slept so long, she waked no more;
She slept, that we might taste of bliss:
Ah! those were happy times, I wis!

FAUST

Since here avails nor argument nor **prayer**,
Thee hence by force I needs must bear.

MARGARET

Loose me! I will not suffer violence!
With murderous hand hold not so fast!
I have done all to please thee in the past!

FAUST

Day dawns! My love! My love!

MARGARET

Yes! day draws near,
The day of judgment too will soon appear!
It should have been my bridal! No one tell,
That thy poor Gretchen thou hast known too well.
Woe to my garland!
Its bloom is o'er!
Though not at the dance —
We shall meet once more.
The crowd doth gather, in silence it **rolls**;
The squares, the streets,
Scarce hold the throng.
The staff is broken, — the death-bell tolls, —
They bind and seize me! I'm hurried along,
To the seat of blood already I'm bound!
Quivers each neck as the naked steel
Quivers on mine the blow to deal —
The silence of the grave now broods around!

FAUST

Would I had ne'er been born!

MEPHISTOPHELES (*appears without*)

Up! or you're lost.
Vain hesitation! Babbling, quaking!
My steeds are shivering,
Morn is breaking.

MARGARET

What from the floor ascendeth like a ghost?
'Tis he! 'Tis he! Him from my presence chase!
What would he in this holy place?
It is for me he cometh!

FAUST

Thou shalt live!

MARGARET

Judgment of God! To thee my soul I give!

MEPHISTOPHELES (*to* FAUST)

Come, come! With her I'll else abandon thee!

MARGARET

Father, I'm thine! Do thou deliver me!
Ye angels! Ye angelic hosts! descend,
Encamp around to guard me and defend!—
Henry! I shudder now to look on thee!

MEPHISTOPHELES

She now is judged!

VOICES (*from above*)

Is saved!

MEPHISTOPHELES (*to* FAUST)

Come thou with me!

[*vanishes with* FAUST.]

VOICE (*from within, dying away*)

Henry! Henry!

END OF PART I.

FAUST — SELECTIONS FROM PART II (1832)

ACT THE FIRST

A PLEASING LANDSCAPE

FAUST, *reclining upon flowery turf, restless, seeking sleep*

TWILIGHT
Circle of spirits, hovering, flit around; —
Graceful, tiny forms.

ARIEL
Song, accompanied by Æolian harps

WHEN, in vernal showers descending,
Blossoms gently veil the earth,
When the fields' green wealth, up-tending,
Gleams on all of mortal birth;
Tiny elves, where help availeth,
Large of heart, there fly apace;
Pity they whom grief assaileth,
Be he holy, be he base.

Ye round this head on airy wing careering,
Attend, in noble Elfin guise appearing;
Assuage the cruel strife that rends his heart,
The burning shaft remove of keen remorse,
From rankling horror cleanse his inmost part:
Four are the pauses of the nightly course;
Them, without rest, fill up with kindly art.
And first his head upon cool pillow lay,
Then bathe ye him in dew from Lethe's stream;
His limbs, cramp-stiffen'd, will more freely play,
If sleep-refreshed he wait morn's wakening beam.

Perform the noblest Elfin-rite,
Restore ye him to the holy light!

CHORUS (*singly, two or more, alternately and together*)
Softly when warm gales are stealing
O'er the green-environed ground,
Twilight sheddeth all-concealing
Mists and balmy odors round:
Whispers low sweet peace to mortals,
Rocks the heart to childlike rest,
And of day-light shuts the portals
To these eyes, with care oppressed.

Night hath now descended darkling,
Holy star is linked to star;
Sovereign fires, or faintly sparkling,
Glitter near and shine afar;
Glitter here lake-mirror'd, yonder
Shine adown the clear night sky;
Sealing bliss of perfect slumber,
Reigns the moon's full majesty.

Now the hours are cancelled; sorrow,
Happiness, have passed away:
Whole thou shalt be on the morrow!
Feel it! Trust the new-born day!
Swell the hills, green grow the valleys,
In the dusk ere breaks the morn;
And in silvery wavelets dallies,
With the wind, the ripening corn.

Cherish hope, let naught appall thee!
Mark the East, with splendor dyed!
Slight the fetters that enthrall thee;
Fling the shell of sleep aside!
Gird thee for the high endeavor;
Shun the crowd's ignoble ease!
Fails the noble spirit never,
Wise to think, and prompt to seize.

[*A tremendous tumult announces the uprising of the Sun.*]

ARIEL
Hark, the horal tempest nears,

Sounding but for spirit ears,
Lo! the new-born day appears;
Clang the rocky portals, climb
Phœbus' wheels with thund'rous chime:
Breaks with tuneful noise the light!
Blare of trumpet, clarion sounding,
Eye-sight dazing, ear astounding!
Hear not the unheard; take flight!
Into petaled blossoms glide
Deeper, deeper, still to bide,
In the clefts, 'neath thickets! ye,
If it strike you, deaf will be.

FAUST

Life's pulses reawakened freshly bound,
The mild ethereal twilight fain to greet.
Thou, Earth, this night wast also constant found,
And, newly-quickened, breathing at my feet,
Beginnest now to gird me with delight;
A strong resolve dost rouse, with noble heat
Aye to press on to being's sovereign height.
The world in glimmering dawn still folded lies;
With thousand-voicèd life the woods resound;
Mist-wreaths the valley shroud; yet from the skies
Sinks heaven's clear radiance to the depths profound;
And bough and branch from dewy chasms rise,
Where they had drooped erewhile in slumber furled;
Earth is enamelled with unnumber'd dyes,
Leaflet and flower with dew-drops are impearled;
Around me everywhere is paradise.

Gaze now aloft! Each mountain's giant height
The solemn hour announces, herald-wise;
They early may enjoy the eternal light,
To us below which later finds its way.
Now are the Alpine slopes and valleys dight
With the clear radiance of the new-born day,
Which, downward, step by step, steals on apace.—

It blazes forth,— and, blinded by the ray,
With aching eyes, alas! I veil my face.
So when a hope, the heart hath long held fast,
Trustful, still striving toward its highest goal,
Fulfilment's portals open finds at last;—
Sudden from those eternal depths doth roll
An over-powering flame;— we stand aghast!
The torch of life to kindle we were fain;—
A fire-sea,— what a fire!— doth round us close;
Love is it? Is it hate? with joy and pain,
In alternation vast, that round us glows?
So that to earth we turn our wistful gaze,
In childhood's veil to shroud us once again!

So let the sun behind me pour its rays!
The cataract, through rocky cleft that roars,
I view, with growing rapture and amaze.
From fall to fall, with eddying shock, it pours,
In thousand torrents to the depths below,
Aloft in air up-tossing showers of spray.
But see, in splendor bursting from the storm,
Arches itself the many-colored bow,
And ever-changeful, yet continuous form,
Now drawn distinctly, melting now away,
Diffusing dewy coolness all around!
Man's efforts there are glassed, his toil and strife;
Reflect, more true the emblem will be found:
This bright reflected glory pictures life!

IMPERIAL PALACE.   THRONE-ROOM
Council of State, in expectation of the EMPEROR

TRUMPETS
Enter courtiers of every grade, splendidly attired. The
Emperor ascends the throne; to the right the
ASTROLOGER.

EMPEROR
I greet you, trusty friends and dear,
Assembled thus from far and wide!—

I see the wise man at my side,
But wherefore is the fool not here?

PAGE

Entangled in thy mantle's flow.
He tripped upon the stair below;
The mass of fat they bare away,
If dead or drunken—who can say?

SECOND PAGE

Forthwith another comes apace,
With wondrous speed to take his place;
Costly, yet so grotesque his gear,
All start amazed as he draws near.
Crosswise the guards before his face,
Entrance to bar, their halberds hold—
Yet there he is, the fool so bold.

MEPHISTOPHELES (*kneeling before the throne*)

What is accursed and gladly hailed?
What is desired and chased away?
What is upbraided and assailed?
What wins protection every day?
Whom darest thou not summon here?
Whose name doth plaudits still command?
What to thy throne now draweth near?
What from this place itself hath banned?

EMPEROR

For this time thou thy words may'st spare!
This is no place for riddles, friend;
They are these gentlemen's affair.—
Solve them! an ear I'll gladly lend.
My old fool's gone, far, far away, I fear;
Take thou his place, come, stand beside me here!

[MEPHISTOPHELES *ascends and places himself at the*
EMPEROR'S *left.*]

Murmur of the Crowd

Here's a new fool—for plague anew!
Whence cometh he?—How passed he through?

The old one fell — he squander'd hath.—
He was a tub — now 'tis a lath.—

EMPEROR

So now, my friends, beloved and leal,
Be welcome all, from near and far!
Ye meet 'neath an auspicious star;
For us above are written joy and weal.
But tell me wherefore, on this day,
When we all care would cast away,
And don the masker's quaint array,
And naught desire but to enjoy,
Should we with state affairs ourselves annoy?
But if ye think it so must be indeed,
Why, well and good, let us forthwith proceed!

CHANCELLOR

The highest virtue circles halo-wise
Our Cæsar's brow; virtue, which from the throne,
He validly can exercise alone:
Justice! — What all men love and prize,
What all demand, desire, and sorely want,
It lies with him, this to the folk to grant.
But ah! what help can intellect command,
Goodness of heart, or willingness of hand,
When fever saps the state with deadly power,
And mischief breedeth mischief, hour by hour?
To him who downward from this height supreme
Views the wide realm, 'tis like a troubled dream,
Where the deformed deformity o'ersways,
Where lawlessness, through law, the tyrant plays,
And error's ample world itself displays.

One steals a woman, one a steer,
Lights from the altar, chalice, cross,
Boasts of his deed full many a year,
Unscathed in body, without harm or loss.
Now to the hall accusers throng;
On cushioned throne the judge presides;

Surging meanwhile in eddying tides,
Confusion waxes fierce and strong.

He may exalt in crime and shame,
Who on accomplices depends;
Guilty! the verdict they proclaim,
When Innocence her cause defends.
So will the world succumb to ill,
And what is worthy perish quite;
How then may grow the sense which still
Instructs us to discern the right?
E'en the right-minded man, in time,
To briber and to flatterer yields;
The judge, who cannot punish crime,
Joins with the culprit whom he shields.—
I've painted black, yet fain had been
A veil to draw before the scene.

Pause

Measures must needs be taken; when
All injure or are injured, then
E'en Majesty becomes a prey.

FIELD MARSHAL

In these wild days what tumults reign!
Each smitten is and smites again,
Deaf to command, will none obey.
The burgher, safe behind his wall,
Within his rocky nest, the knight,
Against us have conspired, and all
Firmly to hold their own unite.
Impatient is the hireling now,
With vehemence he claims his due;
And did we owe him naught, I trow,
Off he would run, nor bid adieu.
Who thwarts what fondly all expect,
He hath disturbed a hornet's nest;
The empire which they should protect,
It lieth plundered and oppress'd.

Their furious rage may none restrain;
Already half the world's undone;
Abroad there still are kings who reign —
None thinks 'tis his concern, not one.

TREASURER

Who will depend upon allies!
For us their promised subsidies
Like conduit-water, will not flow.
Say, Sire, through your dominions vast
To whom hath now possession passed!
Some upstart, wheresoe'er we go,
Keeps house, and independent reigns.
We must look on, he holds his own;
So many rights away we've thrown,
That for ourselves no right remains.
On so-called parties in the state
There's no reliance, now-a-days;
They may deal out or blame or praise,
Indifferent are love and hate.
The Ghibelline as well as Guelph
Retire, that they may live at ease!
Who helps his neighbor now?   Himself
Each hath enough to do to please.
Barred are the golden gates; while each
Scrapes, snatches, gathers all within his reach —
Empty, meanwhile, our chest remains.

STEWARD

What worry must I, also, bear!
Our aim each day is still to spare —
And more each day we need; my pains,
Daily renewed, are never o'er.
The cooks lack nothing; — deer, wild-boar,
Stags, hares, fowls, turkeys, ducks and geese, —
Tribute in kind, sure payment, these
Come fairly in, and none complains.
But now at last wine fails; and if of yore
Up-piled upon the cellar-floor,

Cask rose on cask, a goodly store,
From the best slopes and vintage; now
The swilling of our lords, I trow,
Unceasing, drains the very lees.
E'en the Town-council must give out
Its liquor;—bowls and cups they seize,
And 'neath the table lies the drunken rout.
Now must I pay, whate'er betides;
Me the Jew spares not; he provides
Anticipation-bonds which feed
Each year on that which must succeed;
The swine are never fattened now;
Pawned is the pillow or the bed,
And to the table comes fore-eaten bread.

EMPEROR (*after some reflection, to* MEPHISTOPHELES)
Say, fool, another grievance knowest thou?

MEPHISTOPHELES

I, nowise.   On this circling pomp to gaze,
On thee and thine!   There can reliance fail
Where majesty resistless sways,
And ready power makes foemen quail?
Where loyal will, through reason strong,
And prowess, manifold, unite,
What could together join for wrong,
For darkness, where such stars give light?

Murmur of the Crowd
He is a knave — he comprehends —
He lies — while lying serves his ends —
Full well I know — what lurks behind —
What next? — Some scheme is in the wind! —

MEPHISTOPHELES

Where is not something wanting here on earth?
Here this,— there that: of gold is here the dearth.
It cannot from the floor be scrap'd, 'tis true;
But what lies deepest wisdom brings to view.

In mountain-veins, walls underground,
Is gold, both coined and uncoined, to be found.
And if ye ask me,— bring it forth who can?
Spirit- and nature-power of gifted man.

CHANCELLOR

Nature and spirit — christians ne'er should hear
Such words, with peril fraught and fear.
These words doom atheists to the fire.
Nature is sin, spirit is devil; they,
Between them, doubt beget, their progeny,
Hermaphrodite, mis-shapen, dire.
Not so with us! Within our Cæsar's land
Two orders have arisen, two alone,
Who worthily support his ancient throne:
Clergy and knights, who fearless stand,
Bulwarks 'gainst every storm, and they
Take church and state as their appropriate pay.
Through lawless men, the vulgar herd
To opposition have of late been stirred;
The heretics these are, the wizards, who
The city ruin and the country too.
With thy bold jests, to this high sphere,
Such miscreants wilt smuggle in;
Hearts reprobate to you are dear;
They to the fool are near of kin.

MEPHISTOPHELES

Herein your learned men I recognize!
What you touch not, miles distant from you lies;
What you grasp not, is naught in sooth to you;
What you count not, cannot, you deem, be true;
What you weigh not, that hath for you no weight;
What you coin not, you're sure is counterfeit.

EMPEROR

Therewith our needs are not one whit the less.
What meanest thou with this thy Lent-address?
I'm tired of this eternal If and How.
'Tis gold we lack; so good, procure it thou!

MEPHISTOPHELES

I'll furnish more, ay, more than all you ask.
Though light it seems, not easy is the task.
There lies the gold, but to procure it thence,
That is the art: who knoweth to commence?
Only consider, in those days of terror,
When human floods swamped land and folk together,
How every one, how great soe'er his fear,
All that he treasured most, hid there or here;
So was it 'neath the mighty Roman's sway,
So on till yesterday, ay, till today:
That all beneath the soil still buried lies —
The soil is Cæsar's, his shall be the prize.

TREASURER

Now for a fool he speaketh not amiss;
Our Cæsar's ancient right, in sooth, was this.

CHANCELLOR

Satan for you spreads golden snares; 'tis clear,
Something not right or pious worketh here.

STEWARD

To us at court if welcome gifts he bring,
A little wrong is no such serious thing.

FIELD MARSHAL

Shrewd is the fool, he bids what all desire;
The soldier, whence it comes, will not inquire.

MEPHISTOPHELES

You think yourselves, perchance, deceived by me;
Ask the Astrologer! This man is he!
Circle round circle, hour and house, he knows.—
Then tell us, how the heavenly aspect shows.

Murmur of the Crowd

Two rascals — each to other known —
Phantast and fool — so near the throne —
The old, old song,— now trite with age —
The fool still prompts — while speaks the sage.—

ASTROLOGER (*speaks*, MEPHISTOPHELES *prompts*)
The sun himself is purest gold; for pay
And favor serves the herald, Mercury;
Dame Venus hath bewitched you from above,
Early and late, she looks on you with love;
Chaste Luna's humor varies hour by hour;
Mars, though he strike not, threats you with his power,
And Jupiter is still the fairest star;
Saturn is great, small to the eye and far;
As metal him we slightly venerate,
Little in worth, though ponderous in weight.
Now when with Sol fair Luna doth unite.
Silver with gold, cheerful the world and bright!
Then easy 'tis to gain whate'er one seeks;
Parks, gardens, palaces, and rosy cheeks;
These things procures this highly learned man.
He can accomplish what none other can.

EMPEROR
Double, methinks, his accents ring,
And yet they no conviction bring.

Murmur
    Of what avail! — a worn-out tale —
    Calendery — and chemistry —
    I the false word — full oft have heard —
    And as of yore — we're hoax'd once more.

MEPHISTOPHELES
The grand discovery they misprize,
As, in amaze, they stand around;
One prates of gnomes and sorceries,
Another of the sable hound.
What matters it, though witlings rail,
Though one his suit 'gainst witchcraft press,
If his sole tingle none the less,
If his sure footing also fail?
Ye of all swaying Nature feel
The secret working, never-ending,

VOL. I — 28

And, from her lowest depths up-tending,
E'en now her living trace doth steal.
If sudden cramps your limbs surprise,
If all uncanny seem the spot —
There dig and delve, but dally not!
There lies the fiddler, there the treasure lies!

Murmur

Like lead it lies my foot about —
Cramp'd is my arm — 'tis only gout —
Twitchings I have in my great toe —
Down all my back strange pains I know —
Such indications make it clear
That sumless treasuries are here.

EMPEROR

To work — the time for flight is past. —
Put to the test your frothy lies!
These treasures bring before our eyes!
Sceptre and sword aside I'll cast,
And with these royal hands, indeed,
If thou lie not, to work proceed.
Thee, if thou lie, I'll send to hell!

MEPHISTOPHELES

Thither to find the way I know full well! —
Yet can I not enough declare,
What wealth unown'd lies waiting everywhere:
The countryman, who ploughs the land,
Gold-crocks upturneth with the mould;
Nitre he seeks in lime-walls old,
And findeth, in his meagre hand,
Scared, yet rejoiced, rouleaus of gold.
How many a vault upblown must be,
Into what clefts, what shafts, must he
Who doth of hidden treasure know,
Descend, to reach the world below!
In cellars vast, impervious made,
Goblets of gold he sees displayed,
Dishes and plates, row after row;

There beakers, rich with rubies, stand;
And would he use them, close at hand
Well stored the ancient moisture lies;
Yet — would ye him who knoweth, trust? —
The staves long since have turned to dust,
A tartar cask their place supplies!
Not gold alone and jewels rare,
Essence of noblest wines are there,
In night and horror veiled.   The wise,
Unwearied here pursues his quest.
To search by day, that were a jest;
'Tis darkness that doth harbor mysteries.

EMPEROR

What can the dark avail?   Look thou to that!
If aught have worth, it cometh to the light.
Who can detect the rogue at dead of night?
Black are the cows, and gray is every cat.
These pots of heavy gold, if they be there —
Come, drive thy plough, upturn them with thy share!

MEPHISTOPHELES

Take spade and hoe thyself; — dig on —
Great shalt thou be through peasant toil —
A herd of golden calves anon
Themselves shall tear from out the soil;
Then straight, with rapture newly born,
Thyself thou canst, thy sweet-heart wilt adorn.
A sparkling gem, lustrous, of varied dye,
Beauty exalts as well as majesty.

EMPEROR

To work, to work!   How long wilt linger?

MEPHISTOPHELES

                              Sire,
Relax, I pray, such vehement desire!
First let us see the motley, joyous show!
A mind distraught conducts not to the goal.
First must we calmness win through self-control,

Through things above deserve what lies below.
Who seeks for goodness, must himself be good;
Who seeks for joy, must moderate his blood;
Who wine desires, the luscious grape must press;
Who craveth miracles, more faith possess.

EMPEROR

So be the interval in gladness spent!
Ash-Wednesday cometh, to our heart's content.
Meanwhile we'll solemnize, whate'er befall,
More merrily the joyous Carnival.

[Trumpets. Exeunt.]

MEPHISTOPHELES

That merit and success are link'd together,
This to your fools occurreth never;
Could they appropriate the wise man's stone,
That, not the wise man, they would prize alone.

* * * * * * * * * *

ACT THE SECOND

HIGH-VAULTED, NARROW GOTHIC CHAMBER, FORMERLY FAUST'S, UNALTERED

MEPHISTOPHELES (*stepping from behind a curtain. While he raises it and looks back,* FAUST *is seen, stretched upon an old-fashioned bed*)

Lie there, ill-starred one! In love's chain,
Full hard to loose, he captive lies!
Not soon his senses will regain
Whom Helena doth paralyze.

(Looking round)

Above, around, on every side
I gaze, uninjured all remains:
Dimmer, methinks, appear the color'd panes,
The spiders' webs are multiplied,
Yellow the paper, and the ink is dry;
Yet in its place each thing I find;

And here the very pen doth lie,
Wherewith himself Faust to the Devil signed,
Yea, quite dried up, and deeper in the bore,
The drop of blood, I lured from him of yore—
O'erjoyed to own such specimen unique
Were he who objects rare is fain to seek—;
Here on its hook hangs still the old fur cloak,
Me it remindeth of that merry joke,
When to the boy I precepts gave, for truth,
Whereon, perchance, he's feeding now, as youth.
The wish comes over me, with thee allied,
Enveloped in thy worn and rugged folds,
Once more to swell with the professor's pride!
How quite infallible himself he holds;
This feeling to obtain your savants know;
The devil parted with it long ago.

*[He shakes the fur cloak which he has taken down;
crickets, moths, and chafers fly out.]*

CHORUS OF INSECTS

We welcome thy coming,
Our patron of yore!
We're dancing and humming,
And know thee once more.
Us singly, in silence,
Hast planted, and lo!
By thousands, oh Father,
We dance to and fro.
The rogue hides discreetly
The bosom within;
We looseskins fly rather
Forth from the fur skin.

MEPHISTOPHELES

O'erjoyed I am my progeny to know!
We're sure to reap in time, if we but sow.
I shake the old fur-mantle as before,
And here and there out flutters one or more.—
Above, around, hasten, belovèd elves,

In hundred thousand nooks to hide yourselves!
'Mid boxes there of by-gone time,
Here in these age-embrownèd scrolls,
In broken potsherds, foul with grime,
In yonder skulls' now eyeless holes!
Amid such rotten, mouldering life,
Must foolish whims for aye be rife.

                  [*Slips into the fur mantle.*]

Come shroud my shoulders as of yore!
Today I'm principal once more;
But useless 'tis, to bear the name:
Where are the folk to recognize my claim?

    [*He pulls the bell, which emits a shrill penetrating
        sound, at which the halls shake and the doors
        spring open.*]

FAMULUS (*tottering up the long dark passage*)
    What a clamor!   What a quaking!
    Stairs are rocking, walls are shaking:
    Through the windows' quivering sheen,
    Are the stormful lightnings seen;
    Springs the ceiling,— thence, below,
    Lime and mortar rattling flow:
    And, though bolted fast, the door
    Is undone by magic power!
    There, in Faust's old fleece bedight,
    Stands a giant,— dreadful sight!
    At his glance, his beck, at me!
    I could sink upon my knee.
    Shall I fly, or shall I stay?
    What will be my fate today!

MEPHISTOPHELES
Come hither, friend!— Your name is Nicodemus?

FAMULUS
Most honor'd Sir, such is my name.— Oremus!

MEPHISTOPHELES
That we'll omit!

FAMULUS

O joy, me you do not forget.

MEPHISTOPHELES

I know it well: old, and a student yet;
My mossy friend, even a learned man
Still studies on, because naught else he can:
Thus a card-house each builds of medium height;
The greatest spirit fails to build it quite.
Your master, though, that title well may claim —
The noble Doctor Wagner, known to fame,
First in the learned world!   'Tis he, they say,
Who holds that world together; every day
Of wisdom he augments the store!
Who crave omniscience, evermore
In crowds upon his teaching wait;
He from the rostrum shines alone;
The keys doth like Saint Peter own,
And doth of Hell and Heaven ope the gate;
As before all he glows and sparkles,
No fame, no glory but grows dim,
Even the name of Faustus darkles!
Inventor there is none like him.

FAMULUS

Pardon, most honor'd Sir, excuse me, pray —
If I presume your utterance to gainsay —
This bears not on the question any way;
A modest mind is his allotted share.
The disappearance, unexplained as yet,
Of the great man, his mind doth sorely fret;
Comfort from his return and health are still his prayer.
The chamber, as in Doctor Faustus' day,
Maintains, untouched, its former state,
And for its ancient lord doth wait.
Venture therein I scarcely may.
What now the aspect of the stars? —
Awe-struck the very walls appear;
The door-posts quivered, sprang the bars —
Else you yourself could not have entered here.

MEPHISTOPHELES

Where then bestowed himself hath he?
Lead me to him! bring him to me!

FAMULUS

Alas! Too strict his prohibition,
Scarce dare I, without his permission.
Months, on his mighty work intent,
Hath he, in strict seclusion spent.
Most dainty 'mong your men of books,
Like charcoal-burner now he looks,
With face begrimed from ear to nose;
His eyes are blear'd while fire he blows;
Thus for the crisis still he longs;
His music is the clang of tongs.

MEPHISTOPHELES

Admittance unto me deny?
To hasten his success, the man am I.

[*Exit* FAMULUS. MEPHISTOPHELES *seats himself
with a solemn air.*]

Scarce have I ta'en my post, when lo!
Stirs from behind a guest, whom well I know;
Of the most recent school, this time, is he,
And quite unbounded will his daring be.

BACCALAUREUS (*storming along the passage*)
Open find I door and gate!
Hope at last springs up elate,
That the living shall no more
Corpse-like rot, as heretofore,
And, while breathing living breath,
Waste and moulder as in death.

Here partition, screen, and wall
Are sinking, bowing to their fall,
And, unless we soon retreat,
Wreck and ruin us will greet.
Me, though bold, nor soon afraid,
To advance shall none persuade.

What shall I experience next?
Years ago, when sore perplexed,
Came I not a freshman here,
Full of anxious doubt and fear,
On these gray-beards then relied,
By their talk was edified?

What from musty tomes they drew,
They lied to me; the things they knew
Believed they not; with falsehood rife,
Themselves and me they robbed of life.
How? — Yonder is the murky glare,
There's one still sitting in the Chair —

Drawing near I wonder more —
Just as him I left of yore,
There he sits, in furry gown,
Wrapped in shaggy fleece, the brown!
Then he clever seemed, indeed,
Him as yet I could not read;
Naught will it avail today;
So have at him, straight-away!

If Lethe's murky flood not yet hath passed,
Old Sir, through your bald pate, that sideways bends,
The scholar recognize, who hither wends,
Outgrown your academic rods at last.
The same I find you, as of yore;
But I am now the same no more.

MEPHISTOPHELES

Glad am I that I've rung you here.
I prized you then not slightingly;
In grub and chrysalis appear
The future brilliant butterfly.
A childish pleasure then you drew
From collar, lace, and curls.— A queue
You probably have never worn? —
Now to a crop I see you shorn.
All resolute and bold your air —
But from the *absolute* forbear!

BACCALAUREUS

We're in the ancient place, mine ancient Sir,
But think upon time's onward flow,
And words of double-meaning spare!
Quite otherwise we hearken now.
You fooled the simple, honest youth;
It cost but little art in sooth,
To do what none today will dare.

MEPHISTOPHELES

If to the young the naked truth one speaks,
It pleases in no wise the yellow beaks;
But afterward, when in their turn
On their own skin the painful truth they learn,
They think, forsooth, from their own head it came;
"The master was a fool," they straight proclaim.

BACCALAUREUS

A rogue perchance!—For where's the teacher found
Who to our face, direct, will Truth expound?
Children to edify, each knows the way,
To add or to subtract, now grave, now gay.

MEPHISTOPHELES

For learning there's in very truth a time;
For teaching, I perceive, you now are prime.
While a few suns and many moons have waned,
A rich experience you have doubtless gained!

BACCALAUREUS

Experience! Froth and scum alone,
Not with the mind of equal birth!
Confess! what men have always known,
As knowledge now is nothing worth.

MEPHISTOPHELES (*after a pause*)

I long have thought myself a fool;
Now shallow to myself I seem, and dull.

BACCALAUREUS

That pleases me! Like reason that doth sound;
The first old man of sense I yet have found!

MEPHISTOPHELES

I sought for hidden treasures, genuine gold —
And naught but hideous ashes forth I bore!

BACCALAUREUS

Confess that pate of yours, though bare and old,
Than yonder hollow skull is worth no more!

MEPHISTOPHELES (*good-naturedly*)

Thou know'st not, friend, how rude is thy reply.

BACCALAUREUS

In German to be courteous is to lie.

MEPHISTOPHELES (*still moving his wheel-chair ever nearer
to the proscenium, to the pit*)

Up here I am bereft of light and air;
I perhaps shall find a refuge with you there?

BACCALAUREUS

When at their worst, that men would something be,
When they are naught, presumptuous seems to me.
Man's life is in the blood, and where, in sooth,
Pulses the blood so strongly as in youth?
That's living blood, which with fresh vigor rife,
The newer life createth out of life.
There all is movement, something there is done;
Falleth the weak, the able presses on!
While half the world we 'neath our sway have brought,
What have ye done? Slept, nodded, dream'd, and thought,
Plan after plan rejected; — nothing won.
Age is, in sooth, a fever cold,
With frost of whims and peevish need:
When more than thirty years are told,
As good as dead one is indeed:
You it were best, methinks, betimes to slay.

MEPHISTOPHELES

The devil here has nothing more to say.

BACCALAUREUS

Save through my will, no devil dares to be.

MEPHISTOPHELES (*aside*)

The devil now prepares a fall for thee!

BACCALAUREUS

The noblest mission this of youth's estate.
The world was not, till it I did create;
The radiant Sun I led from out the sea;
Her changeful course the Moon began with me;
The Day arrayed herself my steps to meet,
The Earth grew green, and blossom'd me to greet:
At my command, upon yon primal Night,
The starry hosts unveiled their glorious light.
Who, beside me, the galling chains unbound,
Which cramping thought had cast your spirits round?
But I am free, as speaks my spirit-voice,
My inward light I follow, and rejoice;
Swift I advance, enraptur'd, void of fear,
Brightness before me, darkness in the rear.   [*Exit.*]

MEPHISTOPHELES

Go, in thy pride, Original, thy way!—
True insight would, in truth, thy spirit grieve!
What wise or stupid thoughts can man conceive,
Unponder'd in the ages passed away?—
Yet we for him need no misgiving have;
Changed will he be, when a few years are past;
Howe'er absurdly may the must behave,
Nathless it yields a wine at last.—
(*To the younger part of the audience, who do not applaud.*)
Though to my words you're somewhat cold,
Good children, me you don't offend;
Reflect! The devil, he is old;
Grow old then, him to comprehend!

LABORATORY

(After the fashion of the middle ages; cumbrous, useless
apparatus, for fantastic purposes)

WAGNER (*at the furnace*)

Soundeth the bell, the fearful clang
Thrills through these sooty walls; no more
Upon fulfilment waits the pang
Of hope or fear;—suspense is o'er;
The darknesses begin to clear,
Within the inmost phial glows
Radiance, like living coal, that throws,
As from a splendid carbuncle, its rays;
Athwart the gloom its lightning plays.
A pure white lustre doth appear;
O may I never lose it more!—
My God! what rattles at the door?

MEPHISTOPHELES (*entering*)

Welcome! As friend I enter here.

WAGNER

Hail to the star that rules the hour!
(*Softly*)
On breath and utterance let a ban be laid!
Soon will be consummate a work of power.

MEPHISTOPHELES (*in a whisper*)

What is it, then?

WAGNER

A man is being made.

MEPHISTOPHELES

A man? and pray what loving pair
Have in your smoke-hole their abode?

WAGNER

Nay! Heaven forbid! As nonsense we declare
The ancient procreative mode;

The tender point, life's spring, the gentle strength
That took and gave, that from within hath pressed,
And seized, intent itself to manifest,
The nearest first, the more remote at length,—
This from its dignity is now dethron'd!
The brute indeed may take delight therein,
But man, by whom such mighty gifts are own'd,
Must have a purer, higher origin.

(*He turns to the furnace*)

It flashes, see!—Now may we trustful hold,
That if, of substances a hundred-fold,
Through mixture,—for on mixture it depends—
The human substance duly we compose,
And then in a retort enclose,
And cohobate; in still repose
The work is perfected, our labor ends.

(*Again turning to the furnace*)

It forms! More clear the substance shows!
Stronger, more strong, conviction grows!
What Nature's mystery we once did style,
That now to test, our reason tries,
And what she organized erewhile,
We now are fain to crystallize.

MEPHISTOPHELES

Who lives, doth much experience glean;
By naught in this world will he be surprised;
Already in my travel-years I've seen
Full many a race of mortals crystallized.

WAGNER (*still gazing intently on the phial*)

It mounts, it glows, and doth together run,
One moment, and the work is done!
As mad, a grand design at first is view'd;
But we henceforth may laugh at fate,
And so a brain, with thinking-power embued,
Henceforth your living thinker will create.

(*Surveying the phial with rapture*)
The glass resounds, with gracious power possessed;
It dims, grows clear; living it needs must be!
And now in form of beauty dressed,
A dainty mannikin I see.
What more can we desire, what more mankind?
Unveiled is now what hidden was of late;
Give ear unto this sound, and you will find,
A voice it will become, articulate.—

HOMUNCULUS (*in the phial, to* WAGNER)
Now, Fatherkin, how goes it? 'Twas no jest!
Come, let me to thy heart be fondly pressed —
Lest the glass break, less tight be thine embrace
This is the property of things: the All
Scarcely suffices for the natural;
The artificial needs a bounded space.
(*To* MEPHISTOPHELES)
But thou, Sir Cousin, Rogue, art thou too here?
At the right moment! Thee I thank. 'Tis clear
To us a happy fortune leadeth thee;
While I exist, still must I active be,
And to the work forthwith myself would gird;
Thou'rt skill'd the way to shorten.

WAGNER
　　　　　Just one word!
I oft have been ashamed that knowledge failed,
When old and young with problems me assailed.
For instance: no one yet could comprehend,
How soul and body so completely blend,
Together hold, as ne'er to part, while they
Torment each other through the live-long day.
So then —

MEPHISTOPHELES
　　Forbear! The problem solve for me,
Why man and wife so wretchedly agree?

Upon this point, my friend, thou 'lt ne 'er be clear;
The mannikin wants work, he 'll find it here.

HOMUNCULUS

What's to be done?

MEPHISTOPHELES (*pointing to a side door*)
Yonder thy gifts display!

WAGNER (*still gazing into the phial*)
A very lovely boy, I needs must say!
(*The side door opens;* FAUST *is seen stretched upon a couch*)

HOMUNCULUS (*amazed*)

Momentous!
(*The phial slips from* WAGNER's *hands, hovers over* FAUST, *and sheds a light upon him*)
Girt with beauty! — Water clear
In the thick grove; fair women, who undress;
Most lovely creatures! — grows their loveliness:
But o 'er the rest one shines without a peer,
As if from heroes, nay from gods she came;
In the transparent sheen her foot she laves;
The tender life-fire of her noble frame
She cools in yielding crystal of the waves.—
Of swiftly moving wings what sudden noise?
What plash, what plunge the liquid glass destroys?
The maidens fly, alarmed; alone, the queen,
With calm composure gazes on the scene;
With womanly and proud delight, she sees
The prince of swans press fondly to her knees,
Persistent, tame; familiar now he grows.—
But suddenly up-floats a misty shroud,
And with thick-woven veil doth over-cloud
The loveliest of all lovely shows.

MEPHISTOPHELES

Why thou in sooth canst everything relate!
Small as thou art, as phantast thou art great.
I can see nothing —

HOMUNCULUS

I believe it. Thou,
Bred in the north, in the dark ages, how,
In whirl of priesthood and knight-errantry,
Have for such sights thy vision free!
In darkness only thou'rt at home.

(*Looking round*)

Ye brown, repulsive blocks of stone,
Arch-pointed, low, with mould o'ergrown!
Should he awake, new care were bred,
He on the spot would straight be dead.
Wood-fountains, swans, fair nymphs undressed,
Such was his dream, presageful, rare;
In place like this how could he rest,
Which I, of easy mood, scarce bear!
Away with him!

MEPHISTOPHELES

I like your plan, proceed!

HOMUNCULUS

Command the warrior to the fight,
The maiden to the dancers lead!
They're satisfied, and all is right.
E'en now a thought occurs, most bright;
'Tis classical Walpurgis-night —
Most fortunate! It suits his bent,
So bring him straightway to his element!

MEPHISTOPHELES

Of such I ne'er have heard, I frankly own.

HOMUNCULUS

Upon your ear indeed how should it fall?
Only romantic ghosts to you are known;
Your genuine ghost is also classical.

MEPHISTOPHELES

But whitherward to travel are we fain?
Your antique colleagues are against my grain.

HOMUNCULUS

North-westward, Satan, lies thy pleasure-ground;
But, this time, we to the south-east are bound.—
An ample vale Peneios floweth through,
'Mid bush and tree its curving shores it laves;
The plain extendeth to the mountain caves,
Above it lies Pharsalus, old and new.

MEPHISTOPHELES

Alas! Forbear! For ever be eschewed
Those wars of tyranny and servitude!
I'm bored with them: for they, as soon as done,
Straight recommence; and no one calls to mind
That he in sooth is only played upon
By Asmodeus, who still lurks behind.
They battle, so 'tis said, for freedom's rights—
More clearly seen, 'tis slave 'gainst slave who fights.

HOMUNCULUS

Leave we to men their nature, quarrel-prone!
Each must defend himself, as best he can,
From boyhood up; so he becomes a man.
The question here is, how to cure this one?
              (*Pointing to* FAUST)
Hast thou a means, here let it tested be;
Canst thou do naught, then leave the task to me.

MEPHISTOPHELES

Full many a Brocken-piece I might essay,
But bolts of heathendom foreclose the way.
The Grecian folk were ne'er worth much, 'tis true,
Yet with the senses' play they dazzle you;
To cheerful sins the human heart they lure,
While ours are reckoned gloomy and obscure.
And now what next?

HOMUNCULUS

                  Of old thou wert not shy;
And if I name Thessalian witches,—why,
I something shall have said,—of that I'm sure.

MEPHISTOPHELES (*lustfully*)

Thessalian witches — well! the people they
Concerning whom I often have inquired.
Night after night, indeed, with them to stay,
That were an ordeal not to be desired;
But for a trial trip —

HOMUNCULUS

The mantle there
Reach hither, wrap it round the knight!
As heretofore, the rag will bear
Both him and thee; the way I'll light.

WAGNER (*alarmed*)

And I?

HOMUNCULUS

At home thou wilt remain,
Thee most important work doth there detain;
The ancient scrolls unfolding cull
Life's elements, as taught by rule,
And each with other then combine with care;
Upon the *What,* more on the *How,* reflect!
Meanwhile as through a piece of world I fare,
I may the dot upon the " I " detect.
Then will the mighty aim accomplish'd be;
Such high reward deserves such striving; — wealth,
Honor and glory, lengthen'd life, sound health,
Knowledge withal and virtue — possibly.
Farewell!

WAGNER

Farewell! That grieves my heart full sore!
I fear indeed I ne'er shall see thee more.

MEPHISTOPHELES

Now to Peneios forth we wend!
We must not slight our cousin's aid.
(*To the spectators*)
At last, in sooth, we all depend
On creatures we ourselves have made.

*   *   *   *   *   *   *   *   *   *

ACT THE THIRD

BEFORE THE PALACE OF MENELAUS IN SPARTA

Enter HELENA, *with a chorus of captive Trojan women*
PENTHALIS, *leader of the chorus*

HELENA

The much admired and much upbraided, Helena,
From yonder strand I come, where erst we disembark'd,
Still giddy from the roll of ocean's billowy surge,
Which, through Poseidon's favor and through Euros'
  might,
On lofty crested backs hither hath wafted us,
From Phrygia's open field, to our ancestral bays.
Yonder King Menelaus, glad of his return,
With his brave men of war, rejoices on the beach.
But oh, thou lofty mansion, bid me welcome home,
Thou, near the steep decline, which Tyndareus, my sire,
From Pallas' hill returning, here hath builded up;
Which also was adorned beyond all Sparta's homes,
What time with Clytemnestra, sister-like, I grew,
With Castor, Pollux, too, playing in joyous sport.
Wings of yon brazen portals, you I also hail!
Through you, ye guest-inviting, hospitable gates,
Hath Menelaus once, from many princes chosen,
Shone radiant on my sight, in nuptial sort arrayed.
Expand to me once more, that I the king's behest
May faithfully discharge, as doth the spouse beseem.
Let me within, and all henceforth behind remain,
That, charged with doom, till now darkly hath round me
  stormed!
For since, by care untroubled, I these sites forsook,
Seeking Cythera's fane, as sacred wont enjoined,
And by the spoiler there was seized, the Phrygian,
Happened have many things, whereof men far and wide
Are fain to tell, but which not fain to hear is he
Of whom the tale, expanding, hath to fable grown.

Disparage not, oh glorious dame,
Honor'd possession of highest estate!
For sole unto thee is the greatest boon given;
The fame of beauty that all over-towers!
The hero's name before him resounds,
So strides he with pride;
Nathless at once the stubbornest yields
To beauty, the presence which all things subdues.

HELENA

Enough! I with my spouse, ship-borne, have hither sped,
And to his city now by him before am sent.
But what the thought he harbors, that I cannot guess.
Come I as consort hither? Come I as a queen?
Come I as victim for the prince's bitter pangs,
And for the evils dire, long suffered by the Greeks?
Conquered I am; but whether captive, know I not:
For the Immortal Powers fortune and fame for me
Have doomed ambiguous; direful ministers that wait
On beauty's form, who even on this threshold here,
With dark and threat'ning mien, stand bodeful at my side!
Already, ere we left the hollow ship, my spouse
Looked seldom on me, spake no comfortable word;
As though he mischief brooded, facing me he sat.
But now, when to Eurotas' deeply curving shores
Steering our course, scarce had our foremost vessel's beak
The land saluted, spake he, as by God inspired:
" Here let my men of war, in ordered ranks, disbark;
I marshal them, drawn up upon the ocean strand;
But thou, pursue thy way, not swerving from the banks,
Laden with fruit, that bound Eurotas' sacred stream,
Thy coursers guiding o'er the moist enamelled meads,
Until thou may'st arrive at that delightful plain,
Where Lacedæmon, once a broad fruit-bearing field,
By mountains stern surrounded lifteth now its walls.
Set thou thy foot within the tower-crown'd princely house,
Assemble thou the maids, whom I at parting left,

And with them summon too the wise old stewardess.
Bid her display to thee the treasures' ample store,
As by thy sire bequeathed, and which, in peace and war,
Increasing evermore, I have myself up-piled.
All standing shalt thou find in ancient order; for,
This is the prince's privilege, that to his home,
When he returns at last, safe everything he finds,
Each in its proper place, as he hath left it there.
For nothing of himself the slave hath power to change.''

CHORUS

Oh gladden now, with glorious wealth,
Ever increasing, thine eye and heart!
For beautiful chains, the adornment of crowns,
Are priding themselves, in haughty repose;
But step thou in, and challenge them all,
They arm themselves straight;
I joy to see beauty contend for the prize,
With gold, and with pearls, and with jewels of price.

HELENA

Forthwith hath followed next this mandate of my lord:
''Now when in order thou all things hast duly seen,
As many tripods take, as needful thou may'st deem,
And vessels manifold, which he at hand requires,
Who duly would perform the sacrificial rite,
The caldrons, and the bowls, and shallow altar-plates;
Let purest water, too, from sacred fount be there,
In lofty pitchers; further, store of season'd wood,
Quick to accept the flame, hold thou in readiness;
A knife, of sharpest edge, let it not fail at last.
But I all other things to thy sole care resign.''
So spake he, urging me at once to part; but naught,
Breathing the breath of life, the orderer appoints,
That, to the Olympians' honor, he to slaughter doom'd:
Suspicious seems it! yet, dismiss I further care;
To the high Gods' decree be everything referred,
Who evermore fulfil, what they in thought conceive;
It may, in sooth, by men, as evil or as good

Be counted, it by us, poor mortals, must be borne.
Full oft the ponderous axe on high the priest hath raised,
In consecration o'er the earth-bowed victim's neck.
Nor could achieve the rite, for he was hinderèd,
Or by approaching foe, or intervening God.

CHORUS

What now will happen, canst thou not guess;
Enter, queen, enter thou in,
Strong of heart!
Evil cometh and good
Unexpected to mortals;
Though foretold, we credit it not.
Troya was burning, have we not seen
Death before us, terrible death!
And are we not here,
Bound to thee, serving with joy,
Seeing the dazzling sunshine of heaven,
And of earth too the fairest,
Kind one — thyself — happy are we!

HELENA

Come what come may!   Whate'er impends, me it behoves
To ascend, without delay, into the royal house,
Long missed, oft yearned-for, well-nigh forfeited;
Before mine eyes once more it stands, I know not how.
My feet now bear me not so lightly as of yore,
When up the lofty steps I, as a child, have sprung.

CHORUS

Fling now, O sisters, ye
Captives who mourn your lot,
All your sorrows far from you.
Share ye your mistress' joy!
Share ye Helena's joy,
Who to the dear paternal hearth,
Though returning full late in sooth,
Nathless with surer, firmer tread
Joyfully now approaches!

Praise ye the holy ones,
Happy restoring ones,
God's, the home-leaders, praise ye!
Soars the enfranchised one,
As upon out-spread wings,
Over the roughest fate, while in vain
Pines the captured one, yearning-fraught
Over the prison-battlements
Arms out-stretching, in anguish.

Nathless her a god hath seized,
The exiled one,
And from Ilion's wreck
Bare her hitherward back once more,
To the ancient, the newly-adornèd
Father-house,
After unspeakable
Pleasure and anguish,
Earlier youthful time,
Newly quicken'd, to ponder.

PENTHALIS (*as leader of the chorus*)

Forsake ye now of song the joy-surrounded path,
As toward the portal-wings turn ye forthwith your gaze!
What see I, sisters? Here, returneth not the queen?
With step of eager haste, comes she not back to us? —
What is it, mighty queen, that in the palace-halls,
Instead of friendly hail, could there encounter thee,
And shatter thus thy being? Thou conceal'st it not;
For I abhorrence see, impressed upon thy brow,
And noble anger, that contendeth with surprise.

HELENA (*who has left the folded doors open, excited*)

No vulgar fear beseems the daughter of high Zeus,
And her no lightly-fleeting terror-hand may touch;
But that dire horror which, from womb of ancient Night,
In time primeval rising, still in divers shapes,
Like lurid clouds, from out the mountain's fiery gorge,
Whirls itself forth, may shake even the hero's breast.

Thus have the Stygian Gods, with horror fraught, today
Mine entrance to the house so marked, that fain I am,
Back from the oft-time trod, long-yearned-for threshold
    now,
Like to a guest dismissed, departing, to retire.
Yet no, retreated have I hither to the light;
No further shall ye drive me, Powers, who'er ye be!
Some expiation, I'll devise, then purified,
The hearth-flame welcome may the consort as the lord.

LEADER OF THE CHORUS

Discover, noble queen, to us thy handmaidens,
Devotedly who serve thee, what hath come to pass!

HELENA

What I have seen ye, too, with your own eyes, shall see,
If ancient Night, within her wonder-teeming womb,
Hath not forthwith engulfed, once more, her ghastly birth;
But yet, that ye may know, with words I'll tell it you:—
What time the royal mansion's gloomy inner court,
Upon my task intent, with solemn step I trod,
I wondered at the drear and silent corridors.
Fell on mine ear no sound of busy servitors,
No stir of rapid haste, officious, met my gaze;
Before me there appeared no maid, no stewardess,
Who every stranger erst, with friendly greeting, hailed.
But when I neared at length the bosom of the hearth,
There saw I, by the light of dimly smouldering fire,
Crouched on the ground, a crone, close-veiled, of stature
    huge,
Not like to one asleep, but as absorbed in thought!
With accent of command I summon her to work,
The stewardess in her surmising, who perchance
My spouse, departing hence, with foresight there had
    placed;
Yet, closely muffled up, still sits she, motionless;
At length, upon my threat, up-lifts she her right arm,
As though from hearth and hall she motioned me away.
Wrathful from her I turn, and forthwith hasten out,

Toward the steps, whereon aloft the Thalamos
Rises adorned, thereto the treasure-house hard by;
When, on a sudden, starts the wonder from the floor;
Barring with lordly mien my passage, she herself
In haggard height displays, with hollow eyes, blood-grimed,
An aspect weird and strange, confounding eye and thought.
Yet speak I to the winds; for language all in vain
Creatively essays to body forth such shapes.
There see herself! The light she ventures to confront!
Here are we master, till the lord and monarch comes;
The ghastly brood of Night doth Phœbus, beauty's friend,
Back to their caverns drive, or them he subjugates.

[PHORKYAS *stepping on the threshold, between the
door-posts.*]

CHORUS

Much have I lived through, although my tresses
Youthfully waver still round my temples;
Manifold horrors have mine eyes witnessed;
Warfare's dire anguish, Ilion's night,
When it fell;

Through the o'erclouded, dust over-shadow'd
Tumult of war, to gods have I hearken'd,
Fearfully shouting; hearken'd while discord's
Brazen voices clang through the field
Rampart-wards.

Ah, yet standing were Ilion's
Ramparts; nathless the glowing flames
Shot from neighbor to neighbor roof,
Ever spreading from here and there,
With their tempest's fiery blast,
Over the night-darkened city.—

Flying, saw I through smoke and glare,
And the flash of the tonguèd flames,
Dreadful, threatening gods draw near;
Wondrous figures, of giant mould,
Onward striding through the weird
Gloom of fire-luminous vapor.

Saw I them, or did my mind,
Anguish-torn, itself body forth
Phantoms so terrible — never more
Can I tell; but that I this
Horrible shape with eyes behold,
This of a surety know I!
Yea, with my hands could clutch it even,
Did not fear, from the perilous
Venture, ever withhold me.

Tell me, of Phorkyas'
Daughters which art thou?
For to that family
Thee must I liken.
Art thou, may be, one of the gray-born?
One eye only, and but one tooth
Using still alternately?
One of the Graiæ art thou?
Darest thou, Horror,
Thus beside beauty,
Or to the searching glance
Phœbus' unveil thee?
Nathless step thou forward undaunted;
For the horrible sees he not,
As his hallowed glances yet
Never gazed upon shadows.

But a tragical fate, alas,
Us, poor mortals, constrains to bear
Anguish of vision, unspeakable,
Which the contemptible, ever-detestable,
Doth in lovers of beauty wake!

Yea, so hearken then, if thou dar'st
Us to encounter, hear our curse,
Hark to each imprecation's threat,
Out of the curse-breathing lips of the happy ones,
Who by the gods created are!

PHORKYAS

Trite is the word, yet high and true remains the sense:
That Shame and Beauty ne'er together, hand in hand,
Their onward way pursue, earth's verdant path along.
Deep-rooted in these twain dwelleth an ancient grudge,
So that, where'er they happen on their way to meet,
Upon her hated rival turneth each her back;
Then onward speeds her course with greater vehemence,
Shame filled with sorrow, Beauty insolent of mood,
Till her at length embraces Orcus' hollow night,
Unless old age erewhile her haughtiness hath tamed.
You find I now, ye wantons, from a foreign shore,
With insolence o'erflowing, like the clamorous flight
Of cranes, with shrilly scream that high above our heads,
A long and moving cloud, croaking send down their noise,
Which the lone pilgrim lures wending his silent way,
Aloft to turn his gaze; yet on their course they fare,
He also upon his: so will it be with us.

Who are ye then, that thus around the monarch's house,
With Mænad rage, ye dare like drunken ones to rave?
Who are ye then that ye the house's stewardess
Thus bay, like pack of hounds hoarsely that bay the moon?
Think ye, 'tis hid from me, the race whereof ye are?
Thou youthful, war-begotten, battle-nurtured brood,
Lewd and lascivious thou, seducers and seduced,
Unnerving both, the soldier's and the burgher's strength!
Seeing your throng, to me a locust-swarm ye seem,
Which, settling down, conceals the young green harvest-
field.
Wasters of others' toil! ye dainty revellers,
Destroyers in its bloom of all prosperity!
Thou conquer'd merchandise, exchanged and marketed!

HELENA

Who in the mistress' presence chides her handmaidens,
Audacious, doth o'erstep her household privilege;
For her alone beseems, the praise-worthy to praise,

As also that to punish which doth merit blame.
Moreover with the service am I well-content,
Which these have rendered me, what time proud Ilion's
    strength
Beleaguer'd stood, and fell and sank; nor less indeed
When we, of our sea-voyage the dreary changeful woe
Endured, where commonly each thinks but of himself.
Here also I expect the like from this blithe train;
Not what the servant is, we ask, but how he serves.
Therefore be silent thou, and snarl at them no more!
If thou the monarch's house till now hast guarded well,
Filling the mistress' place, that for thy praise shall count;
But now herself is come, therefore do thou retire,
Lest chastisement be thine, instead of well-earn'd meed!

PHORKYAS

The menial train to threat, a sacred right remains,
Which the illustrious spouse of heaven-favor'd lord
Through many a year doth earn of prudent governance.
Since that, now recognized, thy ancient place as queen,
And mistress of the house, once more thou dost resume,
The long-time loosen'd reins grasp thou; be ruler here,
And in possession take the treasures, us with them!
Me before all protect, who am the elder-born,
From this young brood, who seem, thy swan-like beauty
    near,
But as a basely wingèd flock of cackling geese!

LEADER OF THE CHORUS
How hideous beside beauty showeth hideousness!

PHORKYAS
How foolish by discretion's side shows foolishness!
  [*Henceforth the choristers respond in turn, stepping
      forth singly from the chorus.*]

FIRST CHORISTER
Tell us of Father Erebus, tell us of Mother Night!

PHORKYAS
Speak thou of Scylla, speak of her, thy sister-born!

SECOND CHORISTER

From thy ancestral tree springs many a monster forth.

PHORKYAS

To Orcus hence, away!   Seek thou thy kindred there!

THIRD CHORISTER

Who yonder dwell, in sooth, for thee are far too young.

PHORKYAS

Tiresias, the hoary, go, make love to him!

FOURTH CHORISTER

Orion's nurse of old, was thy great-grand-daughter.

PHORKYAS

Harpies, so I suspect, did rear thee up in filth.

FIFTH CHORISTER

Thy cherished meagreness, whereon dost nourish that?

PHORKYAS

'Tis not with blood, for which so keenly thou dost thirst.

SIXTH CHORISTER

For corpses dost thou hunger, loathsome corpse thyself!

PHORKYAS

Within thy shameless jaw the teeth of vampires gleam.

SEVENTH CHORISTER

Thine I should stop were I to tell thee who thou art.

PHORKYAS

First do thou name thyself; the riddle then is solved.

HELENA

Not wrathful, but in grief, step I between you now,
Forbidding such alternate quarrel's angry noise;
For to the ruler naught more hurtful can befall,
Than, 'mong his trusty servants, sworn and secret strife;
The echo of his mandate then to him no more
In swift accomplished deed responsively returns;
No, stormful and self-will'd, it rages him around,
The self-bewilder'd one, and chiding still in vain.

Nor this alone; ye have in rude unmanner'd wrath
Unblessèd images of dreadful shapes evoked,
Which so encompass me, that whirl'd I feel myself
To Orcus down, despite these my ancestral fields.
Is it remembrance?   Was it frenzy seized on me?
Was I all that? and am I? shall I henceforth be
The dread and phantom-shape of those town-wasting ones?
The maidens quail: but thou, the eldest, thou dost stand,
Calm and unmoved; speak, then, to me some word of sense!

PHORKYAS

Who of long years recalls the fortune manifold,
To him heaven's highest favor seems at last a dream.
But thou, so highly favored, past all bound or goal,
Saw'st, in thy life-course, none but love-inflamèd men,
Kindled by impulse rash to boldest enterprise.
Theseus by passion stirred full early seized on thee,
A man of glorious form, and strong as Heracles.

HELENA

Forceful he bore me off, a ten-year slender roe,
And in Aphidnus' keep shut me, in Attica.

PHORKYAS

But thence full soon set free, by Castor, Pollux too,
In marriage wast thou sought by chosen hero-band.

HELENA

Yet hath Patroclus, he, Pelides' other self,
My secret favor won, as willingly I own.

PHORKYAS

But thee thy father hath to Menelaus wed,
Bold rover of the sea, and house-sustainer too.

HELENA

His daughter gave he, gave to him the kingdom's sway;
And from our wedded union sprang Hermione.

PHORKYAS

But while he strove afar, for Crete, his heritage,
To thee, all lonely, came an all too beauteous guest.

HELENA

Wherefore the time recall of that half-widowhood,
And what destruction dire to me therefrom hath grown!

PHORKYAS

That voyage unto me, a free-born dame of Crete,
Hath also capture brought, and weary servitude.

HELENA

As stewardess forthwith, he did appoint thee here,
With much intrusted,— fort and treasure boldly won.

PHORKYAS

All which thou didst forsake, by Ilion's tower-girt town
Allured, and by the joys, the exhaustless joys of love.

HELENA

Remind me not of joys: No, an infinitude
Of all too bitter woe o'erwhelm'd my heart and brain.

PHORKYAS

Nathless 'tis said thou didst in two-fold shape appear;
Seen within Ilion's walls, and seen in Egypt too.

HELENA

Confuse thou not my brain, distraught and desolate!
Here even, who I am in sooth I cannot tell.

PHORKYAS

'Tis also said, from out the hollow shadow-dream,
Achilles, passion-fired, hath joined himself to thee,
Whom he hath loved of old, 'gainst all resolves of Fate.

HELENA

As phantom I myself, to him a phantom bound;
A dream it was — thus e'en the very words declare.
I faint, and to myself a phantom I become.

[*She sinks into the arms of the semi-chorus.*]

CHORUS

Silence! Silence!
False seeing one, false speaking one, thou!
Through thy horrible, single-tooth'd lips,

Ghastly, what exhaleth
From such terrible loathsome gulf!
For the malignant one, kindliness feigning,
Rage of wolf 'neath the sheep's woolly fleece,
Far more terrible is unto me than
Jaws of the hound three-headed.
Anxiously watching stand we here:
When? How? Where of such malice
Bursteth the tempest
From this deep-lurking brood of Hell?
Now, 'stead of friendly words, freighted with comfort,
Lethe-bestowing, gracious and mild,
Thou art summoning from times departed,
Thoughts of the past most hateful,
Overshadowing not alone
All sheen gilding the present,
Also the future's
Mildly glimmering light of hope.

Silence! Silence!
That fair Helena's soul,
Ready e'en now to take flight,
Still may keep, yea firmly keep
The form of all forms, the loveliest,
Ever illumined of old by the sun.

[HELENA *has revived, and again stands in the midst.*]

*   *   *   *   *   *   *   *   *   *

(*The scene is entirely changed.   Close arbors recline against
a series of rocky caverns.   A shady grove extends to
the base of the encircling rocks.* FAUST *and* HELENA
are not seen.   The CHORUS *lies sleeping, scattered here
and there.*)

PHORKYAS

How long these maids have slept, in sooth I cannot tell;
Or whether they have dreamed what I before mine eyes
Saw bright and clear, to me is equally unknown.
So wake I them.   Amazed the younger folks shall be,
Ye too, ye bearded ones, who sit below and wait,

Hoping to see at length these miracles resolved.
Arise! Arise! And shake quickly your crisped locks!
Shake slumber from your eyes! Blink not, and list to me!

CHORUS

Only speak, relate, and tell us, what of wonderful hath
    chanced!
We more willingly shall hearken that which we cannot
    believe;
For we are aweary, weary, gazing on these rocks around.

PHORKYAS

Children, how, already weary, though you scarce have
    rubbed your eyes?
Hearken then! Within these caverns, in these grottoes,
    in these bowers,
Shield and shelter have been given, as to lover-twain idyllic,
To our lord and to our lady —

CHORUS
How, within there?

PHORKYAS
Yea, secluded
From the world; and me, me only, they to secret service
    called.
Highly honored stood I near them, yet, as one in trust
    beseemeth,
Round I gazed on other objects, turning hither, turning
    thither,
Sought for roots, for barks and mosses, with their prop-
    erties acquainted;
And they thus remained alone.

CHORUS

Thou would'st make believe that yonder, world-wide spaces
    lie within,
Wood and meadow, lake and brooklet; what strange fable
    spinnest thou!

PHORKYAS

Yea, in sooth, ye inexperienced, there lie regions undis-
covered:

Hall on hall, and court on court; in my musings these I
track.

Suddenly a peal of laughter echoes through the cavern'd
spaces;

In I gaze, a boy is springing from the bosom of the woman

To the man, from sire to mother: the caressing and the
fondling,

All love's foolish playfulnesses, mirthful cry and shout of
rapture,

Alternating, deafen me.

Naked, without wings, a genius, like a faun, with nothing
bestial,

On the solid ground he springeth; but the ground, with
counter-action,

Up to ether sends him flying; with the second, third
rebounding

Touches he the vaulted roof.

Anxiously the mother calleth: Spring amain, and at thy
pleasure;

But beware, think not of flying, unto thee is flight denied.

And so warns the faithful father: In the earth the force
elastic

Lies, aloft that sends thee bounding; let thy toe but touch
the surface,

Like the son of earth, Antæus, straightway is thy strength
renewed.

And so o'er these rocky masses, on from dizzy ledge to
ledge,

Leaps he ever, hither, thither, springing like a stricken ball.

But in cleft of rugged cavern suddenly from sight he
vanished;

And now lost to us he seemeth, mother waileth, sire con-
soleth,

Anxiously I shrug my shoulders. But again, behold, what
  vision!
Lie there treasures hidden yonder? Raiment broidered
  o'er with flowers
He becomingly hath donned;
Tassels from his arms are waving, ribbons flutter on his
  bosom,
In his hand the lyre all-golden, wholly like a tiny Phœbus,
Boldly to the edge he steppeth, to the precipice; we wonder,
And the parents, full of rapture, cast them on each other's
  heart;
For around his brow what splendor! Who can tell what
  there is shining?
Gold-work is it, or the flaming of surpassing spirit-power?
Thus he moveth, with such gesture, e'en as boy himself
  announcing
Future master of all beauty, through whose limbs, whose
  every member,
Flow the melodies eternal: and so shall ye hearken to him,
And so shall ye gaze upon him, to your special wonderment.

CHORUS

This call'st thou marvelous,
Daughter of Creta?
Unto the bard's pregnant word
Hast thou perchance never listened?
Hast thou not heard of Ionia's,
Ne'er been instructed in Hellas'
Legends, from ages primeval,
Godlike, heroical treasure?
All, that still happeneth
Now in the present,
Sorrowful echo 'tis,
Of days ancestral, more noble;
Equals not in sooth thy story
That which beautiful fiction,
Than truth more worthy of credence,
Chanted hath of Maia's offspring!

This so shapely and potent, yet
Scarcely-born delicate nursling,
Straight have his gossiping nurses
Folded in purest swaddling fleece,
Fastened in costly swathings,
With their irrational notions.
Potent and shapely, ne'ertheless,
Draws the rogue his flexible limbs,
Body firm yet elastic,
Craftily forth; the purple shell,
Him so grievously binding,
Leaving quietly in its place;
As the perfected butterfly,
From the rigid chrysalid,
Pinion unfolding, rapidly glides,
Boldly and wantonly sailing through
Sun-impregnated ether.

So he, too, the most dextrous,
That to robbers and scoundrels,
Yea, and to all profit-seekers,
He a favoring god might be,
This he straightway made manifest,
Using arts the most cunning.
Swift from the ruler of ocean he
Steals the trident, yea, e'en from Arès
Steals the sword from the scabbard;
Arrow and bow from Phœbus too,
Also his tongs from Hephæstos:
Even Zeus', the father's, bolt,
Him had fire not scared, he had ta'en.
Eros also worsted he,
In limb-grappling, wrestling match;
Stole from Cypria as she caressed him,
From her bosom, the girdle.

(An exquisite, purely melodious lyre-music resounds from the cave. All become attentive, and appear soon to be inwardly moved; henceforth, to the pause indicated, there is a full musical accompaniment.)

PHORKYAS

Hark those notes so sweetly sounding;
Cast aside your fabled lore:
Gods, in olden time abounding,—
Let them go! their day is o'er.

None will comprehend your singing;
Nobler theme the age requires:
From the heart must flow, up-springing,
What to touch the heart aspires.

[She retires behind the rock.]

CHORUS

To these tones, so sweetly flowing,
Dire one! dost incline thine ears,
They in us, new health bestowing,
Waken now the joy of tears.

Vanish may the sun's clear shining,
In our soul if day arise,
In our heart we, unrepining,
Find what the whole world denies.

(HELENA, FAUST, EUPHORION in the costume indicated above)

EUPHORION

Songs of childhood hear ye ringing,
Your own mirth it seems; on me
Gazing, thus in measure springing,
Leap your parent-hearts with glee.

HELENA

Love, terrestrial bliss to capture,
Two in noble union mates;
But to wake celestial rapture,
He a precious three creates.

FAUST

All hath been achieved.   For ever
I am thine, and mine thou art,
Blent our beings are — oh never
May our present joy depart!

CHORUS

Many a year of purest pleasure,
In the mild light of their boy,
Crowns this pair in richest measure.
Me their union thrills with joy!

EUPHORION

Now let me gambol,
Joyfully springing!
Upward to hasten
Through ether winging,
This wakes my yearning,
This prompts me now!

FAUST

Gently! son, gently!
Be not so daring!
Lest ruin seize thee
Past all repairing,
And our own darling
Whelm us in woe!

EUPHORION

From earth my spirit
Still upward presses;
Let go my hands now,
Let go my tresses,
Let go my garments,
Mine every one!

HELENA

To whom, bethink thee,
Now thou pertainest!
Think how it grieves us

When thou disdainest
Mine, thine, and his,—the all
That hath been won.

CHORUS

Soon shall, I fear me,
The bond be undone!

HELENA *and* FAUST

Curb for thy parents' sake,
To us returning,
Curb thy importunate
Passionate yearning!
Make thou the rural plain
Tranquil and bright.

EUPHORION

But to content you
Stay I my flight.
(*Winding among the* CHORUS *and drawing them forth to
dance*)
Round this gay troop I flee
With impulse light.
Say is the melody,
Say is the movement right?

HELENA

Yea, 'tis well done; advance,
Lead to the graceful dance
These maidens coy!

FAUST

Could I the end but see!
Me this mad revelry
Fills with annoy.

EUPHORION *and the* CHORUS
(*Dancing and singing, they move about in interweaving
lines*)
Moving thine arms so fair
With graceful motion,
Tossing thy curling hair

In bright commotion;
When thou with foot so light
Over the earth doth skim,
Thither and back in flight,
Moving each graceful limb;
Thou hast attained thy goal,
Beautiful child,
All hearts thou hast beguiled,
Won every soul.   [*Pause.*]

EUPHORION

Gracefully sporting,
Light-footed roes,
New frolic courting
Scorn ye repose:
I am the hunter,
Ye are the game.

CHORUS

Us wilt thou capture,
Urge not thy pace;
For it were rapture
Thee to embrace,
Beautiful creature,
This our sole aim!

EUPHORION

Through trees and heather,
Bound all together,
O'er stock and stone!
Whate'er is lightly won,
That I disdain;
What I by force obtain,
Prize I alone.

HELENA *and* FAUST

What vagaries, sense confounding!
Naught of measure to be hoped for!
Like the blare of trumpet sounding,
Over vale and forest ringing.
What a riot!   What a cry!

CHORUS (*entering quickly one by one*)
Us he passed with glance scorn-laden;
Hastily still onward springing,
Bearing now the wildest maiden
Of our troop, he draweth nigh.

EUPHORION (*bearing a young maiden*)
I this wilful maid and coy
Carry to enforced caress;
For my pleasure, for my joy
Her resisting bosom press,
Kiss her rebel lips, that so
She my power and will may know.

MAIDEN
Loose me! in this frame residing,
Burns a spirit's strength and might;
Strong as thine, our will presiding
Swerveth not with purpose light.
Thinkest, on thy strength relying,
That thou hast me in a strait?
Hold me, fool! thy strength defying,
For my sport, I'll scorch thee yet!
[*She flames up and flashes into the air.*]
Follow where light breezes wander,
Follow to rude caverns yonder,
Strive thy vanish'd prey to net!

EUPHORION (*shaking off the last flames*)
Rocks all around I see,
Thickets and woods among!
Why should they prison me?
Still am I fresh and young.
Tempests, they loudly roar,
Billows, they lash the shore;
Both far away I hear;
Would I were near!
[*He springs higher up the rock.*]

HELENA, FAUST, *and* CHORUS

Wouldst thou chamois-like aspire?
Us thy threaten'd fall dismays!

EUPHORION

Higher must I climb, yet higher,
Wider still must be my gaze.
Know I now, where I stand:
'Midst of the sea-girt land,
'Midst of great Pelops' reign,
Kin both to earth and main.

CHORUS

Canst not near copse and wold
Tarry, then yonder,
Ripe figs and apple-gold
Seeking, we'll wander;
Grapes too shall woo our hand,
Grapes from the mantling vine.
Ah, let this dearest land,
Dear one, be thine!

EUPHORION

Dream ye of peaceful day?
Dream on, while dream ye may!
War! is the signal cry,
Hark! cries of victory!

CHORUS

War who desireth
While peace doth reign,
To joy aspireth
Henceforth in vain.

EUPHORION

All whom this land hath bred,
Through peril onward led,
Free, of undaunted mood,
Still lavish of their blood,
With soul untaught to yield,
Rending each chain!

To such the bloody field,
Brings glorious gain.

CHORUS

High he soars,—mark, upward gazing,—
And to us not small doth seem:
Victor-like, in harness blazing,
As of steel and brass the gleam!

EUPHORION

Not on moat or wall relying,
On himself let each one rest!
Firmest stronghold, all defying,
Ever is man's iron breast!

Dwell for aye unconquered would ye?
Arm, by no vain dreams beguiled!
Amazons your women should be,
And a hero every child!

CHORUS

O hallowed Poesie,
Heavenward still soareth she!
Shine on, thou brightest star,
Farther and still more far!
Yet us she still doth cheer;
Even her voice to hear,
Joyful we are.

EUPHORION

Child no more; a stripling bearing
Arms appears, with valor fraught:
Leagued with the strong, the free, the daring,
In soul already who hath wrought.
Hence away!
No delay!
There where glory may be sought.

HELENA *and* FAUST

Scarcely summoned to life's gladness,
Scarcely given to day's bright gleam,
Downward now to pain and sadness

Wouldst thou rush, from heights supreme!
Are then we
Naught to thee?
Is our gracious bond a dream?

EUPHORION
Hark!   What thunders seaward rattle,
Echoing from vale to vale!
'Mid dust and foam, in shock of battle,
Throng on throng, to grief and bale!
And the command
Is, firm to stand;
Death to face, nor ever quail.

HELENA, FAUST, *and* CHORUS
Oh what horror!   Hast thou told it!
Is then death for thee decreed?

EUPHORION
From afar shall I behold it?
No!   I'll share the care and need!

HELENA, FAUST *and* CHORUS
Rashness to peril brings,
And deadly fate!

EUPHORION
Yet — see a pair of wings
Unfoldeth straight!
Thither — I must, I must —
Grudge not my flight!

[*He casts himself into the air; his garments support him
for a moment; his head flames, a trail of light follows
him.*]

CHORUS
Icarus!   Icarus!
Oh woeful sight!

(*A beautiful youth falls at the parents' feet; we imagine
that in the dead we recognize a well-known form; yet
suddenly the corporeal part vanishes; the aureole rises
like a comet to heaven; dress, mantle, and lyre remain
lying on the ground.*)

HELENA *and* FAUST
Follows on joy new-born
Anguishful moan!

EUPHORION'S VOICE (*from the depths*)
Leave me in realms forlorn,
Mother, not all alone!　　　　　　　　　　　[*Pause.*]

CHORUS (*dirge*)
Not alone — for hope we cherish,
Where thou bidest thee to know!
Ah, from daylight though thou perish,
Ne'er a heart will let thee go!
Scarce we venture to bewail thee,
Envying we sing thy fate:
Did sunshine cheer, or storm assail thee,
Song and heart were fair and great.

Earthly fortune was thy dower,
Lofty lineage, ample might,
Ah, too early lost, thy flower
Withered by untimely blight!
Glance was thine the world discerning,
Sympathy with every wrong,
Woman's love for thee still yearning,
And thine own enchanting song.

Yet the beaten path forsaking,
Thou didst run into the snare;
So with law and usage breaking,
On thy wilful course didst fare;
Yet at last high thought has given
To thy noble courage weight,
For the loftiest thou has striven —
It to win was not thy fate.

Who does win it? Unreplying,
Destiny the question hears,
When the bleeding people lying,
Dumb with grief, no cry uprears! —

Now new songs chant forth, in sorrow
Deeply bowed lament no more;
Them the earth brings forth tomorrow,
As she brought them forth of yore!

[*Full pause. The music ceases.*]

*   *   *   *   *   *   *   *   *   *

ACT THE FIFTH

OPEN COUNTRY

WANDERER

Yes, 'tis they, their branches rearing,
Hoary lindens, strong in age; —
There I find them, reappearing,
After my long pilgrimage!
'Tis the very spot; — how gladly
Yonder hut once more I see,
By the billows raging madly,
Cast ashore, which sheltered me!
My old hosts, I fain would greet them,
Helpful they, an honest pair;
May I hope today to meet them?
Even then they aged were.
Worthy folk, in God believing!
Shall I knock? or raise my voice?
Hail to you if, guest receiving,
In good deeds ye still rejoice!

BAUCIS (*a very aged woman*)

Stranger dear, beware of breaking
My dear husband's sweet repose!
Strength for brief and feeble waking
Lengthened sleep on age bestows.

WANDERER

Mother, say then, do I find thee,
To receive my thanks once more,
In my youth who didst so kindly,
With thy spouse, my life restore?

Baucis, to my lips half-dying,
Art thou, who refreshment gave?

> [*The husband steps forth.*]

Thou Philemon, strength who plying,
Snatched my treasure from the wave?
By your flames, so promptly kindled,
By your bell's clear silver sound—
That adventure, horror-mingled,
Hath a happy issue found.
Forward let me step, and gazing
Forth upon the boundless main,
Kneel, and thankful prayers upraising,
Ease of my full heart the strain!

> [*He walks forward upon the downs.*]

PHILEMON (*to* BAUCIS)

Haste to spread the table, under
The green leafage of our trees.
Let him run, struck dumb with wonder,
Scarce he'll credit what he sees.

[*He follows the wanderer. Standing beside him.*]

Where the billows did maltreat you,
Wave on wave in fury rolled,
There a garden now doth greet you,
Fair as Paradise of old.
Grown more aged, as when stronger,
I could render aid no more;
And, as waned my strength, no longer
Rolled the sea upon the shore;
Prudent lords, bold serfs directing,
It with trench and dyke restrained;
Ocean's rights no more respecting,
Lords they were, where he had reigned.
See, green meadows far extending;—
Garden, village, woodland, plain.
But return we, homeward wending,
For the sun begins to wane.
In the distance sails are gliding,

Nightly they to port repair;
Bird-like, in their nests confiding,
For a haven waits them there.
Far away mine eye discerneth
First the blue fringe of the main;
Right and left, where'er it turneth,
Spreads the thickly-peopled plain.

IN THE GARDEN
The three at table

BAUCIS (*to the stranger*)

Art thou dumb? No morsel raising
To thy famished lips?

PHILEMON

I trow,
He of wonders so amazing
Fain would hear; inform him thou.

BAUCIS

There was wrought a wonder truly,
Yet no rest it leaves to me;
Naught in the affair was duly
Done, as honest things should be!

PHILEMON

Who as sinful can pronounce it?
'Twas the emperor gave the shore; —
Did the trumpet not announce it
As the herald passed our door?
Footing firm they first have planted
Near these downs. Tents, huts, appeared;
O'er the green, the eye, enchanted,
Saw ere long a palace reared.

BAUCIS

Shovel, axe, no labor sparing,
Vainly plied the men by day;
Where the fires at night shone flaring,
Stood a dam, in morning's ray.

Still from human victims bleeding,
Wailing sounds were nightly borne;
Seaward sped the flames, receding;
A canal appeared at morn!
Godless is he, naught respecting;
Covets he our grove, our cot;
Though our neighbor, us subjecting,
Him to serve will be our lot.

PHILEMON

Yet he bids, our claims adjusting,
Homestead fair in his new land.

BAUCIS

Earth, from water saved, mistrusting,
On thine own height take thy stand.

PHILEMON

Let us, to the chapel wending,
Watch the sun's last rays subside;
Let us ring, and prayerful bending,
In our father's God confide!

PALACE

Spacious ornamental garden; broad, straight canal. FAUST
in extreme old age, walking about, meditating.

LYNCEUS, THE WARDER (*through a speaking trumpet*)
The sun sinks down, the ships belated
Rejoicing to the haven steer.
A stately galley, deeply freighted,
On the canal, now draweth near;
Her chequer'd flag the breeze caresses
The masts unbending bear the sails:
Thee now the grateful seaman blesses,
Thee at this moment Fortune hails.

[*The bell rings on the downs.*]

FAUST (*starting*)
Accursed bell! Its clamor sending,
Like spiteful shot it wounds mine ear!

Before me lies my realm unending;
Vexation dogs me in the rear;
For I, these envious chimes still hearing,
Must at my narrow bounds repine;
The linden grove, brown hut thence peering,
The moldering church, these are not mine.
Refreshment seek I, there repairing?
Another's shadow chills my heart,
A thorn, nor foot nor vision sparing,—
O far from hence could I depart!

WARDER (*as above*)

How, wafted by the evening gales,
Blithely the painted galley sails;
On its swift course, how richly stored!
Chest, coffer, sack, are heaped aboard.

*A splendid galley, richly and brilliantly laden with the
produce of foreign climes.*

MEPHISTOPHELES. THE THREE MIGHTY COMRADES

CHORUS

Here do we land,
Here are we now.
Hail to our lord;
Our patron, thou!

(*They disembark. The goods are brought ashore.*)

MEPHISTOPHELES

So have we proved our worth — content
If we our patron's praises earn:
With but two ships abroad we went,
With twenty we to port return.
By our rich lading all may see
The great successes we have wrought.
Free ocean makes the spirit free:
There claims compunction ne'er a thought!
A rapid grip there needs alone;
A fish, a ship, on both we seize.
Of three if we the lordship own,

Straightway we hook a fourth with ease,
Then is the fifth in sorry plight—
Who hath the power, has still the right;
The *What* is asked for, not the *How*.
Else know I not the seaman's art:
War, commerce, piracy, I trow,
A trinity, we may not part.

THE THREE MIGHTY COMRADES

No thank and hail;
No hail and thank!
As were our cargo
Vile and rank!
Disgust upon
His face one sees:
The kingly wealth
Doth him displease!

MEPHISTOPHELES

Expect ye now
No further pay;
For ye your share
Have ta'en away.

THE THREE MIGHTY COMRADES

To pass the time,
As was but fair;
We all expect
An equal share.

MEPHISTOPHELES

First range in order,
Hall on hall,
These wares so costly,
One and all!
And when he steps
The prize to view,
And reckons all
With judgment true,
He'll be no niggard;

As is meet,
Feast after feast
He 'll give the fleet,
The gay birds come with morning tide;
Myself for them can best provide.

[*The cargo is removed.*]

MEPHISTOPHELES (*to* FAUST)

With gloomy look, with earnest brow
Thy fortune high receivest thou.
Thy lofty wisdom has been crowned;
Their limits shore and sea have bound;
Forth from the shore, in swift career,
O 'er the glad waves, thy vessels steer;
Speak only from thy pride of place,
Thine arm the whole world doth embrace.
Here it began; on this spot stood
The first rude cabin formed of wood;
A little ditch was sunk of yore
Where plashes now the busy oar.
Thy lofty thought, thy people 's hand,
Have won the prize from sea and land.
From here too —

FAUST

That accursed here!

It weighs upon me! Lend thine ear; —
To thine experience I must tell,
With thrust on thrust, what wounds my heart;
To bear it is impossible —
Nor can I, without shame, impart:
The old folk there above must yield;
Would that my seat those lindens were;
Those few trees not mine own, that field,
Possession of the world impair.
There I, wide view o 'er all to take,
From bough to bough would scaffolds raise;
Would, for the prospect, vistas make
On all that I have done to gaze;

To see at once before me brought
The master-work of human thought,
Where wisdom hath achieved the plan,
And won broad dwelling-place for man.—
Thus are we tortured;—in our weal,
That which we lack, we sorely feel!
The chime, the scent of linden-bloom,
Surround me like a vaulted tomb.
The will that nothing could withstand,
Is broken here upon the sand:
How from the vexing thought be safe?
The bell is pealing, and I chafe!

MEPHISTOPHELES

Such spiteful chance, 'tis natural,
Must thy existence fill with gall.
Who doubts it! To each noble ear,
This clanging odious must appear;
This cursed ding-dong, booming loud,
The cheerful evening-sky doth shroud,
With each event of life it blends,
From birth to burial it attends,
Until this mortal life doth seem,
Twixt ding and dong, a vanished dream!

FAUST

Resistance, stubborn selfishness,
Can trouble lordliest success,
Till, in deep angry pain one must
Grow tired at last of being first!

MEPHISTOPHELES

Why let thyself be troubled here?
Is colonizing not thy sphere?

FAUST

Then go, to move them be thy care!
Thou knowest well the homestead fair,
I've chosen for the aged pair —

MEPHISTOPHELES

We'll bear them off, and on new ground
Set them, ere one can look around.
The violence outlived and past,
Shall a fair home atone at last.

[*He whistles shrilly.*]

The Three *enter*

MEPHISTOPHELES

Come! straight fulfil the lord's behest;
The fleet tomorrow he will feast.

THE THREE

The old lord us did ill requite;
A sumptuous feast is ours by right.

MEPHISTOPHELES (*to the spectators*)

What happ'd of old, here happens too:
Still Naboth's vineyard meets the view.

(I *Kings*, XVI.)

DEEP NIGHT

LYNCEUS THE WARDER (*on the watch-tower singing*)

Keen vision my birth-dower,
I'm placed on this height,
Still sworn to the watch-tower,
The world's my delight.
I gaze on the distant,
I look on the near,
On moon and on planet,
On wood and the deer:
The beauty eternal
In all things I see;
And pleased with myself
All bring pleasure to me.
Glad eyes, look around ye
And gaze, for whate'er
The sight they encounter,
It still hath been fair!

(*Pause*)

Not alone for pleasure-taking
Am I planted thus on high;
What dire vision, horror-waking,
From yon dark world scares mine eye!
Fiery sparkles see I gleaming
Through the lindens' two-fold night;
By the breezes fanned, their beaming
Gloweth now with fiercer light!
Ah! the peaceful hut is burning;
Stood its moss-grown walls for years;
They for speedy help are yearning—
And no rescue, none appears!
Ah the aged folk, so kindly,
Once so careful of the fire,
Now, to smoke a prey, they blindly
Perish, oh misfortune dire!
'Mid red flames, the vision dazing,
Stands the moss-hut, black and bare;
From the hell, so fiercely blazing,
Could we save the honest pair!
Lightning-like the fire advances,
'Mid the foliage, 'mid the branches;
Withered boughs,— they flicker, burning,
Swiftly glow, then fall;— ah me!
Must mine eyes, this woe discerning,
Must they so far-sighted be!
Down the lowly chapel crashes
'Neath the branches' fall and weight;
Winding now, the pointed flashes
To the summit climb elate.
Roots and trunks the flames have blighted,
Hollow, purple-red, they glow!

(*Long pause. Song*)

Gone, what once the eye delighted,
With the ages long ago!

FAUST (*on the balcony, toward the downs*)
  From above what plaintive whimper?
  Word and tone are here too late!
  Wails my warder; me, in spirit
  Grieves this deed precipitate!
  Though in ruin unexpected
  Charred now lie the lindens old,
  Soon a height will be erected,
  Whence the boundless to behold.
  I the home shall see, enfolding
  In its walls, that ancient pair,
  Who, my gracious care beholding,
  Shall their lives end joyful there.

MEPHISTOPHELES *and* THE THREE (*below*)
  Hither we come full speed. We crave
  Your pardon! Things have not gone right!
  Full many a knock and kick we gave,
  They opened not, in our despite;
  Then rattled we and kick'd the more,
  And prostrate lay the rotten door;
  We called aloud with threat severe,
  Yet sooth we found no listening ear.
  And as in such case still befalls,
  They heard not, would not hear our calls;
  Forthwith thy mandate we obeyed,
  And straight for thee a clearance made.
  The pair — their sufferings were light,
  Fainting they sank, and died of fright.
  A stranger, harbor'd there, made show
  Of force, full soon was he laid low;
  In the brief space of this wild fray,
  From coals, that strewn around us lay,
  The straw caught fire; 'tis blazing free,
  As funeral death-pyre for the three.

FAUST
To my commandments deaf were ye!
Exchange I wished, not robbery.

For this your wild and ruthless part; —
I curse it! Share it and depart!

CHORUS

The ancient saw still rings today:
Force with a willing mind obey;
If boldly thou canst stand the test,
Stake house, court, life, and all the rest!

[*Exeunt.*]

FAUST

The stars their glance and radiance veil;
Smoulders the sinking fire, a gale
Fans it with moisture-laden wings,
Vapor to me and smoke it brings.
Rash mandate — rashly, too, obeyed! —
What hither sweeps like spectral shade?

MIDNIGHT

Four gray women enter

FIRST

My name, it is Want.

SECOND

And mine, it is Blame.

THIRD

My name, it is Care.

FOURTH

Need, that is my name.

THREE (*together*)

The door is fast-bolted, we cannot get in;
The owner is wealthy, we may not within.

WANT

There fade I to shadow.

BLAME

There cease I to be.

NEED

His visage the pampered still turneth from me.

CARE

Ye sisters, ye cannot, ye dare not go in;
But Care through the key-hole an entrance may win.

[CARE *disappears*.]

WANT

Sisters, gray sisters, away let us glide!

BLAME

I bind myself to thee, quite close to thy side.

NEED

And Need at your heels doth with yours blend her breath.*

THE THREE

Fast gather the clouds, they eclipse star on star.
Behind there, behind, from afar, from afar,
There comes he, our brother, there cometh he — Death.

FAUST (*in the palace*)

Four saw I come, but only three went hence.
Of their discourse I could not catch the sense;
There fell upon mine ear a sound like breath,
Thereon a gloomy rhyme-word followed — Death;
Hollow the sound, with spectral horror fraught!
Not yet have I, in sooth, my freedom wrought;
Could I my pathway but from magic free,
And quite unlearn the spells of sorcery,
Stood I, oh nature, man alone 'fore thee,
Then were it worth the trouble man to be!
Such was I once, ere I in darkness sought,
And curses dire, through words with error fraught,
Upon myself and on the world have brought;
So teems the air with falsehood's juggling brood,
That no one knows how them he may elude!
If but one day shines clear, in reason's light —
In spectral dream envelopes us the night;

* Not and Tod, the German equivalents for Need and Death, form a rhyme.
As this cannot be rendered in English, I have introduced a slight alteration
into my translation.

From the fresh fields, as homeward we advance —
There croaks a bird: what croaks he? some mischance!
Ensnared by superstition, soon and late;
As sign and portent, it on us doth wait —
By fear unmanned, we take our stand alone;
The portal creaks, and no one enters,— none.

(*Agitated*)

Is some one here?

CARE

The question prompteth, yes!

FAUST

What art thou then?

CARE

Here, once for all, am I.

FAUST

Withdraw thyself!

CARE

My proper place is this.

FAUST (*first angry, then appeased. Aside*)
Take heed, and speak no word of sorcery.

CARE

Though by outward ear unheard,
By my moan the heart is stirred;
And in ever-changeful guise,
Cruel force I exercise;
On the shore and on the sea,
Comrade dire hath man in me
Ever found, though never sought,
Flattered, cursed, so have I wrought.
Hast thou as yet Care never known?

FAUST

I have but hurried through the world, I own.
I by the hair each pleasure seized;
Relinquished what no longer pleased,
That which escaped me I let go,

I've craved, accomplished, and then craved again;
Thus through my life I've storm'd — with might and main,
Grandly, with power, at first; but now indeed,
It goes more cautiously, with wiser heed.
I know enough of earth, enough of men;
The view beyond is barred from mortal ken;
Fool, who would yonder peer with blinking eyes,
And of his fellows dreams above the skies!
Firm let him stand, the prospect round him scan,
Not mute the world to the true-hearted man.
Why need he wander through eternity?
What he can grasp, that only knoweth he.
So let him roam adown earth's fleeting day;
If spirits haunt, let him pursue his way;
In joy or torment ever onward stride,
Though every moment still unsatisfied!

CARE

To him whom I have made mine own
All profitless the world hath grown:
Eternal gloom around him lies;
For him suns neither set nor rise;
With outward senses perfect, whole,
Dwell darknesses within his soul;
Though wealth he owneth, ne'ertheless
He nothing truly can possess.
Weal, woe, become mere phantasy;
He hungers 'mid satiety;
Be it joy, or be it sorrow,
He postpones it till the morrow;
Of the future thinking ever,
Prompt for present action never.

FAUST

Forbear! Thou shalt not come near me!
I will not hear such folly. Hence!
Avaunt! This evil litany
The wisest even might bereave of sense.

CARE

Shall he come or go? He ponders;—
All resolve from him is taken;
On the beaten path he wanders,
Groping on, as if forsaken.
Deeper still himself he loses,
Everything his sight abuses,
Both himself and others hating,
Taking breath—and suffocating,
Without life—yet scarcely dying,
Not despairing—not relying.
Rolling on without remission:
Loathsome ought, and sad permission,
Now deliverance, now vexation,
Semi-sleep,—poor recreation,
Nail him to his place and wear him,
And at last for hell prepare him.

FAUST

Unblessèd spectres! Ye mankind have so
Treated a thousand times, their thoughts deranging;
E'en uneventful days to mar ye know,
Into a tangled web of torment changing!
'Tis hard, I know, from demons to get free,
The mighty spirit-bond by force untying;
Yet Care, I never will acknowledge thee,
Thy strong in-creeping, potency defying.

CARE

Feel it then now; as thou shalt find
When with a curse from thee I've wended:
Through their whole lives are mortals blind—
So be thou, Faust, ere life be ended!

[*She breathes on him.*]

FAUST (*blind*)

Deeper and deeper night is round me sinking;
Only within me shines a radiant light.
I haste to realize, in act, my thinking;

The master's word, that only giveth might.
Up, vassals, from your couch! my project bold,
Grandly completed, now let all behold!
Seize ye your tools; your spades, your shovels ply;
The work laid down, accomplish instantly!
Strict rule, swift diligence,— these twain
The richest recompense obtain.
Completion of the greatest work demands
One guiding spirit for a thousand hands.

GREAT FORE–COURT OF THE PALACE

Torches

MEPHISTOPHELES (*as overseer leading the way*)
This way! this way! Come on! come on!
Le Lemures, loose of tether,
Of tendon, sinew, and of bone,
Half natures, patched together!

LEMURES (*in chorus*)
At thy behest we're here at hand;
Thy destined aim half guessing —
It is that we a spacious land
May win for our possessing.
Sharp-pointed stakes we bring with speed,
Long chains wherewith to measure.
But we've forgotten why indeed
To call us was thy pleasure.

MEPHISTOPHELES
No artist-toil we need today:
Sufficeth your own measure here:
At his full length the tallest let him lay!
Ye others round him straight the turf uprear;
As for our sires was done of yore,
An oblong square delve ye once more.
Out of the palace to the narrow home —
So at the last the sorry end must come!

LEMURES (*digging, with mocking gestures*)

In youth when I did live and love,
Methought, it was very sweet!
Where frolic rang and mirth was rife,
Thither still sped my feet.

Now with his crutch hath spiteful age
Dealt me a blow full sore:
I stumbled o'er a yawning grave,
Why open stood the door!

FAUST (*comes forth from the palace, groping his way by
the door posts*)

How doth the clang of spades delight my soul!
For me my vassals toil, the while
Earth with itself they reconcile,
The waves within their bounds control,
And gird the sea with stedfast zone —

MEPHISTOPHELES (*aside*)

And yet for us dost work alone,
While thou for dam and bulwark carest;
Since thus for Neptune thou preparest,
The water-fiend, a mighty fête;
Before thee naught but ruin lies;
The elements are our allies;
Onward destruction strides elate.

FAUST

Inspector!

MEPHISTOPHELES

Here.

FAUST

As many as you may,
Bring crowds on crowds to labor here;
Them by reward and rigor cheer;
Persuade, entice, give ample pay!
Each day be tidings brought me at what rate
The moat extends which here we excavate.

MEPHISTOPHELES (*half aloud*)

They speak, as if to me they gave
Report, not of a moat — but of a grave.*

FAUST

A marsh along the mountain chain
Infecteth what's already won;
Also the noisome pool to drain —
My last, best triumph then were won:
To many millions space I thus should give,
Though not secure, yet free to toil and live;
Green fields and fertile; men, with cattle blent,
Upon the newest earth would dwell content,
Settled forthwith upon the firm-based hill,
Up-lifted by a valiant people's skill;
Within, a land like Paradise; outside,
E'en to the brink, roars the impetuous tide,
And as it gnaws, striving to enter there,
All haste, combined, the damage to repair.
Yea, to this thought I cling, with virtue rife,
Wisdom's last fruit, profoundly true:
Freedom alone he earns as well as life,
Who day by day must conquer them anew.
So girt by danger, childhood bravely here,
Youth, manhood, age, shall dwell from year to year;
Such busy crowds I fain would see,
Upon free soil stand with a people free;
Then to the moment might I say:
Linger awhile, so fair thou art!
Nor can the traces of my earthly day
Through ages from the world depart!
In the presentiment of such high bliss,
The highest moment I enjoy — 'tis this.

(FAUST *sinks back, the* LEMURES *lay hold of him and lay him upon the ground.*)

*   *   *   *   *   *   *   *   *   *

---

* The play of words contained in the original cannot be reproduced in translation, the German for Moat being Graben, and for grave Grab.